# Augustine and Time

# Augustine in Conversation: Tradition and Innovation

## *Series Editors:* John Doody and Kim Paffenroth

This series produces edited volumes that explore Augustine's relationship to a particular discipline or field of study. This "relationship" is considered in several different ways: some contributors consider Augustine's practice of the particular discipline in question; some consider his subsequent influence on the field of study; and others consider how Augustine himself has become an object of study by their discipline. Such variety adds breadth and new perspectives—*innovation*—to our ongoing conversation with Augustine on topics of lasting import to him and us, while using Augustine as our conversation partner lends focus and a common thread—*tradition*—to our disparate fields and interests.

## Titles in Series

*Augustine and Time*
Edited by John Doody, Sean Hannan, and Kim Paffenroth
*Augustine and Politics*
Edited by John Doody, Kevin L. Hughes, and Kim Paffenroth
*Augustine and Literature*
Edited by Robert P. Kennedy, Kim Paffenroth, and John Doody
*Augustine and History*
Edited by Christopher T. Daly, John Doody, and Kim Paffenroth
*Augustine and Liberal Education*
Edited by Kim Paffenroth and Kevin L. Hughes
*Augustine and World Religions*
Edited by Brian Brown, John A. Doody, and Kim Paffenroth
*Augustine and Philosophy*
Edited by Phillip Cary, John Doody, and Kim Paffenroth
*Augustine and Apocalyptic*
Edited by John Doody, Kari Kloos, and Kim Paffenroth
*Augustine and Social Justice*
Edited by Teresa Delgado, John Doody, and Kim Paffenroth
*Augustine and Kierkegaard*
Edited by Kim Paffenroth, John Doody, and Helen Tallon Russell
*Augustine and Wittgenstein*
Edited by Kim Paffenroth, John Doody, and Alexander Eodice

# Augustine and Time

Edited by
John Doody, Sean Hannan, and
Kim Paffenroth

LEXINGTON BOOKS
*Lanham • Boulder • New York • London*

Published by Lexington Books
An imprint of The Rowman & Littlefield Publishing Group, Inc.
4501 Forbes Boulevard, Suite 200, Lanham, Maryland 20706
www.rowman.com

6 Tinworth Street, London SE11 5AL, United Kingdom

Copyright © 2021 The Rowman & Littlefield Publishing Group, Inc.

*All rights reserved.* No part of this book may be reproduced in any form or by any electronic or mechanical means, including information storage and retrieval systems, without written permission from the publisher, except by a reviewer who may quote passages in a review.

"Keeping Time in Mind: St. Augustine's Proposed Solution to a Perplexing Problem" by Alexander R. Eodice reprinted with the permission of Rowman & Littlefield Publishing Group, all rights reserved.

"Time After Augustine" by James Wetzel is reprinted with the permission of Cambridge University Press.

"Time, Mirror of the Soul" by Cristiane Negreiros Abbud Ayoub was originally printed in Portuguese by *Dissertatio*.

British Library Cataloguing in Publication Information Available

**Library of Congress Cataloging-in-Publication Data**

Library of Congress Control Number: 2021932659

ISBN: 978-1-7936-3775-8 (cloth)
ISBN: 978-1-7936-3776-5 (electronic)

# Contents

| | |
|---|---|
| Introduction | vii |
| **PART I: INTERPRETING AUGUSTINE ON TIME** | **1** |
| 1 Time, Eternity, and History in Augustine's Early Works<br>*Thomas Clemmons* | 3 |
| 2 Keeping Time in Mind: Saint Augustine's Proposed Solution to a Perplexing Problem<br>*Alexander R. Eodice* | 21 |
| 3 Time after Augustine<br>*James Wetzel* | 37 |
| **PART II: TIME, LANGUAGE, AND SONG** | **55** |
| 4 Living as Singing: Augustine's Understanding of the Voice of Creatures in the *Confessiones*<br>*Makiko Sato* | 57 |
| 5 Time, Mirror of the Soul<br>*Cristiane Negreiros Abbud Ayoub* | 73 |
| 6 The Inner Word and the Outer World: Time, Temporality, and Language in Augustine and Gadamer<br>*Matthew W. Knotts* | 89 |
| **PART III: TIME, EMBODIMENT, AND GENDER** | **107** |
| 7 Augustinian Temporality and Resurrected Bodies<br>*Paul Ulishney* | 109 |

| | | |
|---|---|---|
| **8** | Love in the Time of Augustine: Rape, Suicide, and Resurrection in *City of God*<br>Patricia Grosse | 127 |
| **9** | Augustine and the Gendered Self in Time<br>Megan Loumagne Ulishney | 141 |

**PART IV: AUGUSTINIAN TEMPORALITY IN THE MIDDLE AGES** — **159**

| | | |
|---|---|---|
| **10** | Augustine and Avicenna on the Puzzle of Time without Time<br>Celia Hatherly | 161 |
| **11** | The Timing of Creation: Aquinas's Reception of Augustine<br>Daniel W. Houck | 179 |
| **12** | Augustine's Dilemma: Divine Eternity and the Reality of Temporal Passage<br>Brendan Case | 191 |
| **13** | Thomas Bradwardine: A Fourteenth-Century Augustinian View of Time<br>Sarah Hogarth Rossiter | 209 |
| **14** | Time after Time: Gregory of Rimini, Contingents Past and Future, and Augustinian Critique<br>Matthew Vanderpoel | 227 |

**PART V: AUGUSTINIAN AND BUDDHIST TEMPORALITIES** — **243**

| | | |
|---|---|---|
| **15** | Non-Presentism in Antiquity: South Asian Buddhist Perspectives<br>Sonam Kachru | 245 |
| **16** | Breaking the Stream of Consciousness: Momentariness and the Eternal Present<br>Davey K. Tomlinson | 271 |
| **17** | Out of the Abyss: On Pedagogical Relationality and Time in the *Confessions* and the *Lotus Sutra*<br>Joy Brennan | 291 |

Bibliography — 309

Index — 333

About the Editors and Contributors — 339

# Introduction

In 2007, the musicologist Karol Berger released a study aimed at locating the precise boundary-marker between premodern and modern experiences of time. To do so, he turned not to the complex theories of time laid out by ancient thinkers in (for example) the Christian or Buddhist traditions, but to two luminaries of eighteenth-century music. Bach, according to Berger, wrote music that drew his listeners away from their quotidian lives and toward an eternal beauty lying outside of time entirely. The compositions of Mozart, on the contrary, reveled in linear temporality, transforming it from everyday dreariness into an inspiring march toward a future filled with progress. Tellingly, Berger explains this shift from Bach to Mozart as a movement not just from the premodern to the modern, but from "Christian" temporality into modernity.[1]

As Jeremy S. Begbie has argued, Berger's characterization of "Christian" temporality leaves much to be desired. This is to be expected, since it would be impossible to responsibly summarize and synthesize every possible Christian account of time (or every possible modern account of time, for that matter). Aside from the crudeness of Berger's dichotomy, Begbie offers a more particular criticism: Berger has relied too much on Augustine of Hippo. On this reading, it was Augustine who poisoned the Christian well by overemphasizing the desirability of the "otherworldly goal" of "escaping time."[2]

Pushing back against Berger, Begbie offers a spirited defense of the dexterity and maneuverability of Christian approaches to time. Curiously, however, he does so not by defending Augustine, but instead by appealing almost exclusively to a certain "scriptural" doctrine of temporality, grounded in his reading of the works of the theologians Richard Bauckham and Jürgen Moltmann.[3] Along the way, Augustine falls by the wayside. Indeed, Begbie is happy to join Berger in blaming Augustine, whom he relegates to a footnote, for derailing the otherwise noble trajectory of the history of philosophical and theological speculation about time. Regarding Augustine's "treatment of the nature and character of time and eternity," writes Begbie, "for all his astonishing perception and insight, questions still need to be asked about whether his reflections are sufficiently rooted in the Christologically shaped ontology mandated by the Biblical texts."[4] While modern theologians and their readings of the Bible stand here for an open-ended, world-embracing, life-affirming temporality, Augustine is left to play the role of the stern Church Father who strayed a bit too far from the idyllic view of early Christianity up through the Council of Nicaea. Worse yet, he might even have been too much of a Platonist.

But if Augustine is accused by these two scholars—who represent quite different corners of the twenty-first-century academy—of having implanted incorrect or unhealthy or simply retrograde ideas in the heart of the way we think about time, then we might want to pause and ask: What exactly were Augustine's views on temporality? Can we sum up even this one Christian author's account of time is such a breezy and almost dismissive manner? Regardless of whether the goal is to criticize or defend Augustinian temporality, we first need to get clear on what exactly Augustinian temporality could turn out to be.

The greater difficulty, of course, arises from the fact that Augustine himself was always honest about his confusion concerning the topic of time. Nowhere is this clearer than in Book XI of his *Confessions*, which is where most attempts to interpret Augustinian temporality begin (although they need not end there, since the problem of time is a recurring theme across Augustine's corpus). Such a sentiment of confusion can be felt in what is perhaps the most frequently cited passage from *Confessions* 11, in which Augustine ponders the very definition of time, which somehow becomes all the more puzzling due to the fact that our ways of speaking about time strike us as so obviously familiar. It is only when we are interrogated about temporality that we begin to uncover the depths of our own ignorance.[5]

Augustine's befuddlement speaks not just to the abstract aporias of the philosophy of time but also to the concrete realities of the psychology of temporal experience and the hermeneutical challenges involved in making sense of our own times. Before we rush to accuse Augustine of foreclosing possibilities in the human experience of time, then, it would be wise to linger alongside Augustine in this spirit of creative confusion, at least for a little while. Only by doing so can we allow ourselves to listen to what Augustine has to say about matters as weighty as the relation between temporality and eternity, the stability or instability of the self in time, and the relative reality of the past, the present, and the future.

These questions Augustine raises about time doubtless bear upon other aspects of his thought. We cannot understand his idea of God, for instance, without making sense of his timeless notion of God's eternity. We cannot attribute to him the invention of selfhood before we set the *quaestio* of the self alongside the *quaestiones* of temporality both subjective and objective. We cannot make claims about the future of Augustinian temporality if we fail to confront his challenge to conventional practices of defining the future over against both the past and the present. These questions also remain, in many ways, open, ready to be answered anew from any number of distinct disciplinary and interdisciplinary viewpoints.

The goal of this volume, then, is to explore a wide range of the possible paths left open for us by Augustine. Some of these paths are rooted in the historical question of what modes of temporality might have been thinkable for a fourth- and fifth-century Latin Christian bishop in North Africa. Other paths lead us onward to Augustine's legacy in later Christian thought, especially in the high and late Middle Ages, when his philosophy of time was received by figures like Thomas Aquinas, John Wyclif, and Gregory of Rimini. Still others guide us into more theologically and philosophically adventurous clearings, where Augustine can be found conversing with thinkers as diverse as Elizabeth Grosz and Hans-Georg Gadamer.

Perhaps the most fruitful paths are those that spirit the reader outside of the Christian tradition entirely, putting Augustine into conversation with accounts of time articulated in the contexts of Islam or Buddhism. Here Begbie's insinuation that Augustinian temporality is insufficiently Christocentric becomes more help than hindrance.[6] What Begbie sees as something lacking in *Confessions* 11, we might instead frame as an open-ended invitation to interreligious dialogue across traditions. Rather than being driven back to the Bible as if it were the end of the conversation, Augustine's theorization of time on the basis of his reading of Scripture (especially Genesis 1) enables him to say something about time that is of interest not just to a certain subset of modern theologians, but to anyone fascinated by the fact that we cannot seem to answer our own questions about what it is like to live in time.

Given the breadth of approaches represented here, this volume has been divided both historically and thematically. In part I, we lay down the foundations for our discussion of Augustine by asking ourselves how best to interpret his writings on time in their proper contexts, which are again both historical and thematic. Thomas Clemmons gets things started by reminding us that Augustine's comments on time were not restricted to *Confessions* 11 alone. In his Cassiciacum dialogues, for example, he toyed with various approaches to the question of how the human soul should orient itself within the finite span of mortal life. Yet it is in Augustine's early anti-Manichaean diatribes that the true depths of the relationship between time and creation begin to surface, as Augustine defends his reading of Genesis against the followers of Mani. *Confessions* 11, too, announces itself as an exegesis of

Genesis before focusing in on time proper. Clemmons's expert analysis demonstrates convincingly that this later approach was rooted in Augustine's initial forays against Manichaeism in the years immediately following upon his conversion and ordination.

Turning our attention more directly to the account of time in *Confessions* 11 itself, Alexander R. Eodice's chapter offers a straightforwardly philosophical reading of the work. While Clemmons contextualized Augustine's argument in light of his earlier writings, Eodice brings to light its thematic connections with modern theories of time from Ludwig Wittgenstein to A. N. Prior and beyond. In so doing, Eodice produces an interpretation of Augustine as a subjectivist about time, happy to reduce temporality to the mind's temporal experience. More strikingly, Eodice further suggests that an appeal to Wittgenstein's philosophy of language can help us understand the way that Augustine's use of terms might have gotten in his own way.

Whereas Eodice found in Wittgenstein hope for the dissolution of Augustine's aporias about time, James Wetzel's chapter frames Wittgenstein as a foil for Augustine. Such a maneuver allows Wetzel to push back against the tendency to take Augustinian temporality as irreducibly subjective or psychologizing. Instead, Wetzel finds in Augustine a subtle, textured reflection on the knotty entanglements that make it so hard for us to discern time from sin, intention from distention, or even subjectivity from objectivity.

Having laid the interpretive groundwork for further interrogation of Augustine on temporality, part II of the volume pivots in the direction of the more specific problem of how time relates to language and song, both of which serve as exemplars for Augustine. As Makiko Sato suggests, the bond between time and music should be appreciated as a leitmotif recurring again and again throughout Augustine's oeuvre. In *Confessions* 11, he makes singing a song the privileged example of how memory, awareness, and expectation work together to make human time-consciousness possible. In Book X, somewhat more darkly, he makes listening to a hymn exemplary of the seductive distractions that lead us astray (even in church). If we wish to master the full range of notes, both high and low, hit by Augustine in his engagement with time, Sato argues that we must simultaneously attune ourselves to his theory of music.

On a more philosophically adventurous note, Cristiane Negreiros Abbud Ayoub offers an exploration of the theme of dilation in Augustine's approach to time. Emphasizing Augustine's use of Joshua 10:12–13, in which God makes the sun stand still so that Joshua can emerge victorious in battle, she argues that there is an indelible link between virtue, justice, and temporality in *Confessions* 11. The extension of time may itself be related to the moral character of what is achieved in time. Picking up on Sato's musicological themes, she also finds resonances of war-chants (like the *jubilus*) in Augustine's metrical analysis of the Ambrosian hymn *Deus Creator Omnium*.

As the quotation from *Confessions* 11 above makes clear, thinking about time always means thinking about how we talk about time. For Augustine, time posed hermeneutical problems touching upon the exegesis of Genesis and the interpretation of human practices of signification in general. Accordingly, Matthew W. Knotts's essay centers language in its reading of Augustine. And there could be no better interlocutor for Augustine on language and interpretation than Hans-Georg Gadamer. Placing Augustine into conversation with Gadamer, Knotts argues that temporality is the vector through which human speakers strive to make the inner words found in their own minds intelligible to one another as outer words, which arise and pass away in time.

Keeping to our focus on specific problems in Augustinian temporality, part III of the volume emphasizes the relationship between time and the body. Paul Ulishney makes the case that this relationship comes into view most fully when we attend to what Augustine has to say about the status of resurrection bodies after the eschaton. Only by doing so, suggests Ulishney, can we settle a quandary that has long plagued readers of Augustine: How are we to synchronize the physical time of bodies with the psychological time of souls? In addition, by foregrounding Augustine's sermons, Ulishney reminds us that the Bishop of Hippo never intended for his statements on time to apply only to secluded philosophers. These were ideas meant to provoke every member of his community.

Taking up the torch of resurrection, Patricia Grosse argues that how we picture post-eschatological bodies informs how we relate to our own living bodies in time. While the former would seem to have to exist outside of time or perhaps in some sort of quasi-temporal condition, the latter find themselves ravaged by the vicissitudes of temporality, not yet having been brought to enjoy the rest of the very end. This is what makes one and the same factor, such as sexuality, a source of anxiety for the temporal body but a font of joy for the paradisiacal body. And while we cannot know perfectly the shape of the perfection to come, we do, according to Grosse's take on Augustine, have reason to hope for a redeemed eschatological sexuality.

These themes of sexuality and embodiment carry over to Megan Loumagne Ulishney's essay on gender and selfhood in Augustine's approach to time. Loumagne Ulishney takes us in a bold new direction, rereading Augustine in light of New Feminist Materialists like Elizabeth Grosz and Anne Fausto-Sterling. Likewise, New Feminist Materialism is reimagined in light of Augustine, revealing that matter has a prominent role to play in his incarnational theology, despite his earlier proximity to the Manichaeans and Neoplatonists. As a result, Loumagne Ulishney is able to demonstrate that body-affirming theologians need not ground their views in process theology, but can instead find sufficient resources in Augustine's juxtaposition of time and eternity.

Part IV is somewhat longer than the other parts of the volume, owing to the fact that it tills the fertile fields of the reception of Augustinian temporality in the Middle Ages. To set the stage, we begin with Celia Hatherly's philosophical assessment of the difference between the accounts of time found in Augustine and Avicenna. While Avicenna himself surely never read Augustine, his importance as a conduit of Aristotelianism into the high and late Middle Ages means that there is much to gain from tracking how these two thinkers diverge on the issue of temporality. Ultimately, Hatherly establishes by way of rigorous logic that Avicenna would never have been able to accept Augustine's cosmological claim that it is possible for time to "begin."

Daniel W. Houck's chapter brings us from Arabic-language philosophy to thirteenth-century scholasticism at the University of Paris. Touching upon the now-familiar themes of Scriptural hermeneutics and the exegesis of Genesis, Houck argues that Aquinas's account of God's creative activity is consonant with Augustine's comments about a simultaneous creation at the beginning of time. In so doing, the piece forges constructive connections at the intersection of theology and evolutionary biology, showing that the development of new species over vast time-scales is by no means incompatible with Augustinian and Thomistic cosmologies.

Taking us into the fourteenth century, Brendan Case underlines the fact that Augustine's attitude toward time resonated still more strongly in the later Middle Ages. By shedding new light upon John Wyclif's reception of Augustine, Case proposes that it was the precise scope of divine immutability that was becoming most hotly contested in this era. Given Augustine's insistence on the timelessness of God's eternity, Wyclif and his contemporaries felt moved to redescribe the relationship between the past, present, and future. As Case argues, this attempt at redescription led to multiple interpretations of Augustinian temporality, which can be categorized according to John McTaggart's modern distinction between the A-Series and B-Series, which governs much of the discourse about time in analytic philosophy.

Staying in the fourteenth century, the next chapter sees Sarah Hogarth Rossiter patiently walking us through the revival of Augustinian temporality in Thomas Bradwardine, who was all too briefly Archbishop of Canterbury. Before being consecrated Archbishop and dying of the plague, Bradwardine was a member of the Oxford Calculators and the confessor to Edward III during the outbreak of the Hundred Years' War. His appreciation of the finer points of the philosophy of time shines through most brilliantly, however, in his apology for Augustine's doctrine of grace, which he defends on the basis of his own theory of future contingents.

Like Bradwardine, Gregory of Rimini sought to revive Augustinian temporality in the face of perceived Pelagian opponents in the fourteenth century. Matthew Vanderpoel's chapter adeptly frames Gregory's intervention not just in light of the aforementioned problem of future contingents but more provocatively in light of the possibility (raised by Gregory himself) of "past contingents." By leading us down this path, Vanderpoel invites us to reorient the way we conceive of late medieval thought altogether. As the example of the nominalist Augustinian Gregory shows, any interpretation of the fourteenth century that reduces to a simplistic contrast between radical and conservative can only be impoverished. Taken together, the chapters by Case, Hogarth Rossiter, and Vanderpoel construct a fresh framework for future studies of the afterlife of Augustinian temporality in the Reformation and its wake.

Part V of our volume, however, brings us toward our conclusion by putting Augustine into conversation with approaches to time drawn from another tradition entirely. By positioning Augustinian temporality alongside a broad selection of Buddhist temporalities, we get a better sense of the fact that Augustine has something of value to say even to those operating outside of any particular Christian paradigm. For Begbie, as mentioned earlier, that makes Augustinian temporality into a liability for Christianity. And yet, as our final three contributions illustrate, Augustine's ability to spur on interreligious dialogue should not be dismissed too hastily.

Sonam Kachru grounds our cross-cultural discussion by establishing the parameters of a problem posed by thinkers in both South Asian and Mediterranean antiquity: Is the present moment the realest or most important phase of temporality? According to modern advocates of the mindfulness movement, some kind of therapeutic presentism is indeed the order of the day. While said advocates would like to find in both Buddhism and Stoicism some warrant for their belief, Kachru elegantly demonstrates that Buddhist philosophers were just as likely to argue against presentism as for it. Augustine, too, is often found to be occupying the ambiguous middle ground between presentism and non-presentism.

Davey K. Tomlinson's chapter builds on Kachru's erudite survey by zeroing in on the question of whether or not Augustinian temporality is well suited to the Buddhist method of breaking time down into discrete moments. Three of Augustine's chief interlocutors here are Prajñākaragupta, Jñānaśrīmitra, and Ratnakīrti, all of whom engage with the problem of momentariness and its connection to the possibility of self-awareness in light of the passing away of all temporal things. While Augustine and these Buddhist thinkers are equally attentive to the paradoxes of time, Tomlinson suggests that they differ on the fundamental issue of whether it makes any sense to hope for some eschatological escape from time, rather than sinking into the presence of instantaneous self-awareness.

Finally, Joy Brennan concludes our volume by inviting us to consider the relationship between Augustine and Buddhism on an even more precise scale. Inventively reinterpreting one key Buddhist text, the *Lotus Sutra*, Brennan argues that there is a kind of doubling of selfhood that occurs both in that sutra and in Augustine's self-critical autobiography. Perhaps even more than a doubling, these texts suggest a multiplication that approaches infinity, not unlike the figure of *mise en abyme*. But whereas Augustine's collapse into the infinite abyss at the core of his own self is experienced as a fateful fall, the *Lotus Sutra* frames its own abyssal multiplication as the emergence of something like eternity within time itself.

It is our hope that this volume, too, will serve as a hall of mirrors, each chapter reflecting a different facet of Augustinian temporality. Such an interdisciplinary *mise en abyme* should have the effect of helping to multiply the possible interpretations of Augustine on time. While we may not be able to reach infinity, we should at least try to go as far as our finitude allows.

## NOTES

1. Karol Berger, *Bach's Cycle, Mozart's Arrow: an Essay on the Origins of Musical Modernity* (Berkeley: University of California Press, 2007), 158. See also the summary of Berger's argument in Jeremy S. Begbie, "Time and Eternity: Richard Bauckham and the Fifth Evangelist," in *In the Fullness of Time: Essays on Christology, Creation, and Eschatology in Honor of Richard Bauckham*, ed. Daniel M. Gurtner, Grant Macaskill, and Jonathan T. Pennington (Grand Rapids: Eerdmans, 2016), 29–48, here 30–34.

2. Berger, 169.

3. Begbie, "Time and Eternity," 35, emphasizes texts like Bauckham's own "Time and Eternity," in *God Will Be All in All: the Eschatology of Jürgen Moltmann*, ed. Bauckham (Edinburgh: T&T Clark, 1999), 155–226.

4. Begbie, "Time and Eternity," 35. Here Begbie cites his own *Theology, Music, and Time* (Cambridge: Cambridge University Press, 2000), 75–85, which features a more sustained and careful discussion of Augustine.

5. Augustine, *Confessions*, tr. Henry Chadwick (Oxford: Oxford University Press, 1991), 11.14.17, 230–231.

6. Recall Begbie, "Time and Eternity," 35.

*Part I*

# INTERPRETING AUGUSTINE ON TIME

*Chapter 1*

# Time, Eternity, and History in Augustine's Early Works

Thomas Clemmons

Augustine's most famous discussion of time is found in Book XI of the *Confessions* (*Conf.*). Through his examination of present, past, and future time, he arrives at his well-known articulation of a "triple present."[1] In Book XI, he also treats time in relation to *distentio*, including the *distentio*, *extentio*, and *intentio* of the soul.[2] In Book XII, Augustine turns to eternity and the *caelum caeli* of Psalm 115.[3] These passages from the *Conf.* have been taken by scholars to indicate Augustine's "subjective" conception of time.[4] In contrast, others have rightly, I judge, argued for his objective view of time.[5]

The former claim of Augustine's "subjective" view of time is often predicated on his early writings in which, it is argued, Augustine like Plotinus binds time with the descent of Soul or even World-Soul.[6] Augustine's early works, such as *De immortalitate animae* (*imm. an.*), *De musica* (*mus.*), *De Genesi contra Manichaeos* (*Gn. adu. Man.*), and *De uera religione* (*uera rel.*), are undoubtedly important precursors to the more expansive discussion of the *Conf.* Many of the points raised in the *Conf.* have parallel treatments in these early writings. The concerns of this chapter are these less famous, and less focused, early discussions of time, eternity, and history.

I have divided Augustine's early writings before 391 into two sections, the dialogues produced in Italy and the works composed in North Africa. This division seems to reflect a shift or increased focus in his articulation of time, eternity, and history. Before turning to his early writings, I briefly outline the contours of the understanding of time, eternity, and history in Plotinus and Manichaeism. While Augustine's reliance on Plotinus is fraught with complexity, it provides an important backdrop.[7] In addition, the Manichaean articulation of time and Augustine's response is less frequently treated by those who argue for his "subjective" conception of time. However, it is precisely the Manichaean framework that involves Augustine and drives his concern with time, eternity, and especially history.

## PLOTINUS AND MANICHAEISM ON TIME, ETERNITY, AND HISTORY

Of the *Enneads*, "On Time and Eternity" (3.7) treats time most extensively and thoroughly.[8] While it is unlikely that Augustine read this *Ennead*, it provides us with the most complete depiction of Plotinus's understanding of time.[9] In *Enn.* 3.7, Plotinus describes time as an image of eternity.[10] This is an analogy between Nous and Psyche, through which eternity is described as the life of Nous and time the life of Psyche (Soul).[11] Eternity in this image is an aspect of the intelligible realm similar to beauty or truth.[12] Central to Plotinus's understanding of time is the distinction between what A. Smith calls "manifested time" and "real time."[13] Time in this world is a "manifestation" of "real time." "Real time" however is "the life of the soul."[14] Time, then, is analogous to Soul in that just as Soul is between the Nous and the cosmos, so is "real time" between eternity and "manifested time."

Advancing from this image, Plotinus explains time as an aspect or dimension of Soul at the level of the hypostasis Soul, World-Soul, and in a different way for individual souls.[15] However, *Enn.* 4.4 describes time as being generated by Soul.[16] In this account, time is framed as Soul in its fallen form seeking to imitate the eternity and stability of the upper hypostases.[17] In other places, Plotinus describes the procession of Soul as a consequence arising "naturally" from the fullness of the higher hypostases.[18]

Plotinus's ambiguity over the causes of the descent of Soul—either because of its nature or *tolma* (audacity)—potentially makes time itself ambiguously moral.[19] If time itself is made by the tolmic descent of Soul, then time may be perceived as a condition caused by the rebellious audacity of Soul seeking to imitate the higher hypostases.[20] While the more straightforward reading of Plotinus's account is that time is a "natural" consequence of the fullness of the higher hypostases, scholars who hold that Augustine held to a "subjective" view of time incline to the tolmic account. When this account is transferred through Augustine's appropriation of Plotinus, time becomes the negative result of sin.[21]

The evidence for this reading is limited. It requires the amplification of certain passages to indicate the fall of World-Soul or even more confusingly the fall of the human hypostasis Soul.[22] While the particularities of this argument have been treated elsewhere, it may suffice simply to assert the paucity and inconsistencies of the evidence.[23] More explicitly present in Augustine's early writings is Plotinus's conception of eternity and the link between the λογισμοί (*rationes*) in the soul and Nous (*Ratio*) itself. The link between the *rationes* and *Ratio* permits the ascent of the soul to Nous, even perhaps in this life. Hence, the soul is able to share in eternity amid the flux of time. Beyond the fact that Augustine does not explain time as a consequence of the generation or descent of Soul, what is lacking in Plotinus, which is present increasingly in Augustine, is the significance of history.

In comparison with Plotinus and the broader Platonic tradition, Manichaeism's conception of time is radically different. Because of Manichaeism's materialism, the two Kingdoms, the Light and the Darkness, are understood substantially.[24] Because the two substances are everlasting, the conflict between the Light and Darkness frames the Manichaean conception of time through the Three Times: the Former, Present, and Future.[25]

The Former Time is the period prior to the invasion of the Kingdom of Darkness. In this time prior to the created cosmos, there is only utterly separate Light and Darkness. The Light has the enduring qualities, or even substantial predicates, of wisdom, rest, and splendor.[26] In contrast, the Darkness has the eternal characteristics of folly, restlessness, jealousy, and lust. The Former Time, which lasted for unknown aeons, provides the backdrop for the struggle and mixture that is the condition of the Present Time.

The Present Time begins with the attack of the Kingdom of Darkness on the Light. The ensuing struggle results in the entrapment of some of the Light within the Darkness. The admixture of Light and Darkness yields the making of the universe, which is often depicted as the providential action of the Kingdom of Light. The universe functions as a mechanism for extracting the entrapped Light, most notably through the sun and moon.[27] In response, the Darkness makes its own vehicles to inhibit the retrieval of the Light, namely, humanity.[28] Humans are made by the Darkness in the image of the Light, which makes humanity the perverse image of the Light.[29]

The human is, to some degree, the microcosm of the cosmic struggle, for within the human, Light is trapped in the prison of the body. Yet, unlike the cosmos, which is formed and governed by the Light, the human is formed, and to some degree governed by the Darkness. There is an asymmetry between the cosmos and the human, which highlights the uniqueness of the human in the conflict between Light and Darkness. The human, who may hinder and thwart the cosmic designs of the forces of Light, is the primary battlefield and requires the direct action of the Light through messengers and prophets. Therefore, it is this locus, the human, especially the human body, which is to a large degree the center of the Manichaean myth.

The uniqueness of the human in the Manichaean narrative bends the focus to the Present Time. The cosmos and all in it point to the heightened struggle of the individual in whom the cosmic struggle is most poignantly enacted.

It is this immediate Present Time (the now) that for Augustine provides the primary interpretive focus of Manichaeism.[30]

Augustine's understanding of Manichaeism does not wholly ignore cosmological dimensions of the Manichaean narrative.[31] He acknowledges the place of the sun, the slow removal of Light in the Present Time, and even notes the Manichaean belief in the weakening of humanity through every generation following Adam.[32] In addition, Augustine observes that the Manichaean framework does not have a conception of eternity, but simply everlasting temporality. Augustine thus sees Manichaeism as "time-bound," with the focus easily collapsed onto the singular point of the human struggle against Darkness within the Present Time.

## TIME, ETERNITY, AND HISTORY IN AUGUSTINE'S ITALIAN WRITINGS

In his earliest writings, the Cassiciacum Dialogues, Augustine's considerations of time are dispersed and positioned within his larger discussions of the pursuit of Wisdom. To this end, he comments on the flux of human existence as well as the ordering of divine providence.[33] The human is lost amid the waves of time, caught in the confusion of desires.[34] True stability is only found in the eternal God.[35]

In response to the perceived chaos of temporality, Augustine devotes a significant portion of Book II of *De ordine* (*ord.*) to the ascent of the mind to intelligible or divine things. The study of the liberal arts aids in the advance of the mind from sensible toward intelligible realities.[36] These branches of learning may with qualification provide some understanding of the soul, place, time, eternity, and the two worlds, sensible and intelligible.[37] In particular, the arts assist in understanding the flux of time and perpetual change in the sensible world. Time is an inevitable aspect of the sensible world. However, in the intelligible world, time and change do not cloud one's vision of the beautiful and perfect whole.[38]

In *Contra Academicos* (*Acad.*) Augustine returns to Plato's philosophy of the two worlds. The one is the intelligible world, in which truth itself dwells, and the other the sensible, which is manifest to the human in the senses. In that intelligible realm, there is the truth, whereas in the sensible world, there is the verisimilitude of truth. Hence, the sensible world is made in the image of the intelligible world.[39]

While Augustine's discussion in both works is certainly Platonic, it is hardly Plotinian *simpliciter*. He emphasizes the Incarnation in both works and notes that only true philosophy, disclosed in the mysteries of Christianity, leads to God.[40] In *Acad.* he states that not even the most subtle *Ratio* would lead souls, who are blinded by error and the passions of the body, to the intelligible world, save by an act of God. Hence, the highest God by a clemency for the whole of humanity sent down the authority of the divine Intellect (*diuini intellectus auctoritatem*) all the way to a human body. This God, the Son incarnate, not only by his precepts but also by his very deeds arouses souls to recover their homeland without the contest of arguments.[41]

Augustine has perhaps borrowed the Plotinian term of *Intellectus* (or Nous) and moved it into *time* from the stability of timelessness, which is a central quality of Nous for Plotinus. Augustine has even permitted the *Intellectus* to take up a human body. This incarnate *Intellectus* not only instructs but also acts to assist souls to return to God. All this happens *in time*, not as an extension of the dynamic movement of Soul, but as the activity of the highest God. Hence, it is *in time* (which he will later link more specifically with *historia* or the divine dispensation) that Augustine finds certainty in Christ, his life, teachings, and the church and scriptures founded on Christ's authority.[42] The temporal activity of God may lead the soul to the God that dwells in eternity.

The opening prayer of the *Soliloquia* (*sol.*) treats time and eternity more explicitly than the scattered references of the dialogues. God, who is one true and eternal substance, orders the temporal by his laws established in eternity.[43] To the end of perceiving God, Augustine treats number or mathematical symbols. Number is known in time but is not altered in time or reduced through the flow of time. However useful number may be, Augustine is careful to observe that God is very different from other intelligible things, such as mathematical symbols. To illustrate God's difference, *Ratio*, Augustine's interlocutor in the *sol.*, outlines a limited analogy so that Augustine may learn something of God from sensible things. The sun, which is, shines, and illuminates, provides an analogy to God, who also is, shines, and causes other things to be known.[44]

As elsewhere, the analogy of the sun is used by Augustine to criticize the Manichaean understanding of the sun as worthy of adoration. The sun is a created reality, which is not the same as the divine Light, nor does the sun actively liberate the Light from this world. The sun merely points to the intelligible (as do all created things). *Ratio*, therefore, advises Augustine to flee the sensible world so that he may perceive God, who is outside of all time.[45]

Just as in the other dialogues, however, Augustine does not conclude with certainty of reason's ascent. Indeed, Augustine doubts that he will be able to flee from all sensible things. In response, *Ratio* observes how illustrious beauty (*illa pulchritudo*) functions as a physician (*medicus*) healing souls so that they might see and love this beauty.[46] Once again Augustine expresses that the God who dwells in *aeternitas* and *stabilitas* acts *in time*.[47]

In *De immortalitate animae* (*imm. an.*), an incomplete companion to *sol.*, Augustine outlines his argument about the eternality of the arts. Because the arts are discovered, not made, by the mind, Augustine argues that the human mind is immortal and all true *rationes* are deep within it.[48] The soul is affected by the eternal *rationes* in ascent to God.[49] Augustine's explanation here may be drawn from Plotinus where the λογισμοί (*logismoi*), while different from the *logos* itself, may aid the soul in its ascent.[50] These *logismoi* are useful for the fallen or individuated soul *in time*. In a similar manner, Augustine appears to be discussing the therapeutic value of the *logismoi* (or *rationes*) in the ascent of the mind to the eternal. Yet, unlike Plotinus, Augustine also claims that the very *Logos* or *Ratio*, the unchangeable Truth and Wisdom, through clemency became flesh.[51]

In addition to the therapeutic function of the *rationes*, Augustine observes that time and movement are not the same things.[52] There are things that cause movement in another in time and yet are not themselves changed or moved. The soul, in fact, is such a thing, which "moves" things such as the body *in time*. Time is thus a condition not excluded from the soul, but also not "generated" by the soul.

In a manner similar to the *Conf.*, Augustine states that time is divisible such that even the shortest syllable, for example, depends on expectation and memory.[53] Just as in the *Conf.*, Augustine explains that expectation has to do with future things, memory with the past.[54] The intention to act is in the present through which the future becomes the past.[55] Augustine even suggests something like his "triple present" in the mind that intends, expects, and remembers. Therefore, in this early work composed before his baptism, Augustine outlines the place of memory and expectation in attempting to understand time.

In the last work composed in Italy, *De quantitate animae* (*an. quant.*), Augustine again discusses the eternal arts and immortal soul.[56] The treatise closes with seven grades for the soul's ascent and a discussion of how the arts (in relation to the *rationes*) assist in this ascent. Augustine calls the seventh grade of the soul's ascent a kind of dwelling (*quaedam mansio*) where one enjoys the highest good, God. He says that this grade is a breath of serenity (*cuius serenitatis atque aeternitatis afflatus*). This highest ascent to the "dwelling" with the "breath of serenity and eternity" is not merely abstract. Rather, other great souls have spoken and *are* speaking about such lofty things. This mediation by others points to Augustine's understanding of the "how" of this ascent, which depends upon the very Power and Wisdom of God to dwell in enjoyment of the highest cause or *principium* of all things.[57]

The link between temporality and eternity, where God dwells, is much more pronounced in *an. quan.* than in earlier writings. The marvelous and beautiful things of this world do not compare to what is taught in the church. The church nourishes souls as a mother so that even the resurrection of the body may be held as certain. The church trains *in time* and offers the confession of Christ against those who believe that such an in-breaking into time is absurd. Human nature, Augustine writes, was assumed by the almighty, eternal, changeless Son of God to be both an exemplar and the beginnings (*primitias*) of human salvation. This in-breaking of the eternal is found in the very history (*historia*) of Christ, such as his birth from a virgin and the other miraculous things of his life.[58]

In the last chapters of *an. quant.*, Augustine has advanced to an articulation of one's "dwelling" with God through the incarnation of the eternal Son. The church nourishes one in faith wherein the *historia* of Christ and the anticipation of what is to come in the resurrection lead to the contemplation of Truth. To say this differently, Augustine acknowledges that *in time* the human comes to know the eternal through the *historia* of the eternal Son incarnate. Thus, one comes to this highest end, to see all things in God, only through true religion (*uera religio*).[59]

## TIME, ETERNITY, AND HISTORY IN AUGUSTINE'S THAGASTE WRITINGS

Upon returning to North Africa, Augustine completed the sixth, and final, book of his lengthy treatise on music. In Book VI of *De musica* (*mus.*), many of the topics discussed in the previous section are taken up again, though with greater clarity. For example, Augustine provides a more lengthy exposition on *aeternitas*. He outlines how the human should pursue higher things in which the highest unchangeable, undisturbed, and eternal equality remains. It is in *aeternitas* that there is no time, since there is no change. From eternity, times are made, ordered, and controlled in imitation of eternity. In part, this imitation is the order and measure of both the movements and times the created order follows. Hence, the course of heaven returns to the same state and recalls the heavenly bodies to their same position. All the revolutions, whether days, months, years, centuries, or other movements of the stars, obey the laws of equality, unity, and order. So it is that terrestrial things are subject to celestial things: every temporal circuit joins together in harmonious succession as if a poem of the universe.[60]

Augustine, therefore, returns to the theme outlined in *ord*. Divine Providence has ordered things beautifully, though the individual human is blinded to it. In aversion from God, the human has lost the whole (*uniuersum*) and is now ordered in part (*in parte*).[61] The habit (*consuetudo*) of the flesh (*carnis*) (citing Romans 7:25) wholly frames human perception. Time is not the problem, but rather the limit of possessing merely a temporally bound, partial view through a partial existence.

Because of this *consuetudo*, the human's understanding of time and all temporal things has become skewed. By following the variety of time (*uarietas temporis*), the human is not able to perceive the highest and unchangeable equality (*aequalitas*), which is not found in temporal and changeable things.[62] This falling or turning away is caused by pride, by which the soul has preferred imitating God to serving God.[63] Yet, the attempt to imitate God, Augustine notes, results in the difficulty of loving God, who is not divisible and does not change in time (*nihil uariatum tempore*).[64]

Augustine's comments are consistent with the Plotinian description of the descent of individual souls in the fragmentation of time. However, he is also criticizing the Manichaean conception of God as being identical to the soul of Light trapped in mixture. For Augustine, this view prohibits any understanding of eternity as distinct from temporality since God is expressly confined to dwelling amid the agony of the Present Time. Hence the Manichaeans are trapped off from what the soul should seek in its love: constancy and eternity, which can only be found in God.[65]

At first, Augustine's advice is again to turn to numbers (*in rationis numeros*). Because numbers are not changeable, but eternal and unchangeable, it shows that they are given to the soul by the eternal and unchangeable God.[66] However, numbers only aid in the ascent from a vision bound by fleeting time. Augustine, instead, relies on the unsurpassable authority of the Scriptures to show that the Lord is the sweetness for the soul. In the "light" of God, the human is able to see light. Augustine takes "in the light" (from Psalm 35:10–11) as a reference to Christ. The human sees God through the light that is Christ.[67] In Christ, one is able to perceive the unity of things, which were all made through one *principium*, Christ. Hence, Augustine concludes his reflection on the ascent to God, as he had in *De beata uita* (*beata u.*) and will in the *Conf.*, with the Ambrosian hymn *Deus Creator omnium*.[68] The hymn provides an image of the eternal God as witnessed through time, in memory, intention, and expectation.

In *Gn. adu. Man.*, as well as in *De moribus ecclesiae catholicae et manichaeorum* (*mor.*), Augustine directly engages Manichaeism. Augustine frames transformation through Christ who in the mystery (*sacramentum*) of the Incarnation liberated humanity (*ad nos liberandos*) to the "*nouus homo*."[69] Because one is conformed to the object of love, transformation is from love of sensible, temporal things to eternal things to God.[70] This love of God is framed specifically as Christological: to love God is to cling to God and Jesus Christ. Indeed, knowledge of this very Truth is eternal life.[71]

Even more than in the conclusion of *an. quant.*, here Augustine locates this transformation in the church. It is through the church, its teaching and profession of Christ and the unity of the bible, that one comes to love truly God and neighbor.[72] About the church Augustine writes:

You [the church] do not confuse what eternity, what truth, and what in the end peace itself distinguishes. Nor do you separate what the one majesty joins together. But you also include love and charity toward neighbor, so that there is an abundance of every medicine in you for the various diseases with which souls are sick on account of their sins.[73]

The love that the church nurtures through its *disciplina*, Augustine argues, unites humans at a deeper level. It even unites humans across nations and through time.[74] The stress in *mor.* is on the transformation that occurs *in time* through the profession and teaching of the church.[75]

In contrast, Augustine criticizes the Manichaean way of life that expresses the tension and corruption constitutive of life and the created world.[76] He claims that Manichaeans hold that evil, the Darkness, subjects to corruption *in time* the eternal and highest Good, the Light.[77] As noted earlier, in Manichaeism, time functions as a constant, but does so, as Augustine observes, mythologically. Hence, the Manichaean belief that the divine substance of Light is slowly released throughout the ongoing Present Time is overshadowed by the liberation of Light through the Elect.[78] In contrast, most human actions, like eating and even human generation, further trap the Light in the world. The framework is "mythological" not because it is false or simply unreal, but rather because it collapses time into a repetitive present. The perpetual struggle to liberate the Light resets repeatedly the total hermeneutical focus of the Present Time.

In *De Genesi contra Manichaeos* (*Gn. adu. Man.*), Augustine returns to his Christological reading of *mus.* When commenting on Genesis 1:1, "In the beginning God made heaven and earth," Augustine discusses how this beginning (*principium*) is Christ. Just as he took "in the light" to mean "in Christ," Augustine takes "*in principio*" to mean "*in Christo*," in *Gn. adu. Man.* He even weds this reading to Christ's proclamation in John 8:25, "The beginning, which I am, is also speaking to you."[79] Through this Christological exegesis, Augustine makes evident his stark divergence from Plotinus: God both created time and also spoke among humanity.

Augustine presents his interpretation in response to the Manichaean criticism that the God of Genesis acts capriciously when making what did not exist through all the eternal times (*aeterna tempora*). Though this criticism may be made in jest by Manichaeans, it again reveals their conception of time. There are eternal times before the making of this world, which for the Manichaeans was only made in response to the invasion of the Darkness. The invasion ended the eternal ages of the Former Time and initiated the enduring struggle of the Present Time.

Augustine's criticism of Manichaeism is not simply found in his Christological reading, but also in his claim that before the beginning of time there was not time (*ante principium temporis non erat tempus*). Time was made by God so that before God made time(s), there was no time(s).[80] One cannot say that there was any time when God had not yet made something. Indeed, there is no time that God has not made, for God is the maker of all times.[81]

It is very clear here, as it has been in his earlier writings, that Augustine does not hold a "subjective" theory of time. Time, all temporality, is made by God either as such or along with the heavens and the earth. As Augustine notes Book II of *Gn. adu. Man.*, the single "day" of Genesis 2 refers to all of time. This time is experienced by both the visible and invisible creations.[82] The soul is included in this, for all visible and invisible creatures belong to time and are mutable. God, who is before all times, alone is immutable.[83]

In contrast to God's eternity and stability, the Manichaeans, Augustine contends, do not understand that God is the maker of all times. There were not eternal times in which God dwelled before the making of the earth. If this were the case, then this Present Time is a different kind of time. It is a time of conflict and agony in intermixture, for God no longer dwells in eternal peace. While the Former Time would be an eternal time of peace and separation, the Present Time is defined by corruption and hard-fought liberation.

For Augustine, because God made all things *de nihilo*, not from the very substance of God (*de seipso*), created things are not the same as or equal to God.[84] The distinction between God and all created things, especially humanity, permits Augustine to assert that God is outside of time and also to liberate time from being bound with a singular quality, such as conflict, corruptive mixture, or even movement. Hence, as Augustine has noted in his other writings, God is able to draw the human to share in eternity, just as God is also able to enter into time.

As he has observed in earlier writings, sin has amplified the difficulty of perceiving and loving God. Hence, Augustine reads the results of sin in relation to God's corrective actions *in time*. The flaming sword of the cherubim of Genesis 3:24 is interpreted as the temporal punishments and pains sent in the whirling flux of time. The tribulations faced in time press upon the human. Time is the occasion for mercy and regeneration. Indeed, renewal and restoration, including resurrection unto eternal life, are brought about in time and in history through Christ.[85]

Augustine develops the place of history when he summarizes the seven days of creation. He notes how the events are presented as the *historia* of things done in order to observe especially the pronouncement of things to come (*prophetia*).[86] In Book II of *Gn. adu. Man.*, Augustine expands his exegetical use of history and prophecy to specific figures and images such as Adam or the "coats of skin."[87] That is, Augustine's use of *historia* and *prophetia* is not simply allegorical; it is drawn into his hermeneutic of history in regard to God's activity in time.[88] When expanded beyond the mere text, the bible offers a way of interpreting time by way of God's activity in Christ, both in creation and in the Incarnation and its effects.[89] This it seems is the ground for Augustine's later observation that the wood of the Cross is the station of stability amid the flows of time.

Augustine's increased understanding of the place of history is most clearly demonstrated in *De uera religione* (*uera rel.*), the last work written before he was ordained.[90] He begins by discussing the *tempora Christiana*, the Christian times, in which the Christian religion is above all the best way to truth and beatitude.[91] The soul needs the Christian religion if it is to gaze at the unchanging form of things and the beauty that is neither stretched out over space, nor varied in time.

Augustine is not merely observing that the Christian religion aids in living a moral life. He contends that rational beings alone are able to enjoy contemplation of the eternity of God, to be influenced by God's eternity, and to earn eternal life. Instead of God's eternity, the human loves passing things and limits oneself to the senses of the body and empty images. The human is not simply *in time* but seeks stability in those things that fade in time. Augustine asserts that what humanity needs, indeed what a Platonist would expect, is a divine human, the Power and Wisdom of God, to teach humanity in his love and authority to convert them to saving faith.[92]

Augustine has set Christ as a remedy restoring the whole of humanity to the worship of the God who dwells in eternity. This religion spread from one region of the world (*Israel*) that worshipped God, up to today where all the nations praise God, professing John 1:1–3, "*In principio erat Uerbam.*"[93] For in perceiving, enjoying, and loving this Word, the mind is healed and made strong enough to drink in such a brilliant Light.[94]

Augustine's assertion is not simply directed against the Manichaeans, who draw their myth from their aesthetic of the Light and Darkness. It is also aimed at followers of Plato who follow the rites of the oracles, while giving private reverence to Plato.[95] Yet, these Christian times have engendered the conversion of the populace and the pious love of many, such as the clerics and ascetics, who devote their whole lives to God. In contrast to the fractured view of the Platonists, the Christian religion demonstrates that there is no difference between philosophy, the love of wisdom, and religion.[96]

The source of the Christian religion, Augustine avers, is the history and prophecy of the temporal dispensation of divine providence. This temporal dispensation was for the transformation and renewal of the whole of humanity unto eternal life.[97] The belief in this dispensation, which Augustine describes in a creedal-like statement, yields a way of life in concord with divine precepts. This faith and resulting form of life will purify the mind so that it will perceive the eternity of the Trinity, existing with no future or past, never changing but always remaining in the same manner. The eternity of God is perceived in part through the *historia* or dispensation of God's temporal activity. It is through this dispensation that the human may perceive the mercy of the highest God for the whole of humanity.[98]

From this confession of the significance of history, Augustine turns directly to Manichaeism. The Manichaean profession of the two natures confused throughout the world tethers the human in this mixture, placing two souls at war in one body.[99] This war infects the whole of the Present Time and effectively traps the human in a perpetual Present Time of agonistic struggle for liberation. The Manichaean system, thereby, allows for no conception of time, save struggle, and no function for history.

Augustine identifies the errors of Manichaeans in their love of the soul, body, or imagination above God. More specifically, he militates against collapsing the human's vision to simply the creaturely and the temporal. The Manichaeans have no conceptual space for eternity. For Augustine eternity has implications *in time*; if the human clings to the eternal Creator, the human will be affected by eternity.[100] Yet, the human in sin is not able to ascend to eternity without the aid of God. This aid was given in "our times" (*nostris temporibus*) in the Christian religion founded on the temporal activity of God in the Incarnation.[101] Through the Incarnation, *in time* and as a human, God liberated human nature to partake in eternity.[102]

The reason for God's action in time is in part because humanity in Paradise was expelled into this age (*saeculum*), that is, from eternal things toward temporal things. This is not a transfer to evil things or evil times. Temporal, fleeting things are good, though lesser goods. Indeed, it is in this temporal world that the human learns to love the highest good all the more.[103] Time itself is not the problem. Time, of course, has its own beauty in its order and successions.[104] Yet, it is the focus on time, the attempt to find stability in things that fade with time's movement that scatters the human.[105] The human seeks more in time, more in the present, than it can possibly bear.

Thus, Augustine presents a tension between temporality, which confuses, misleads, and stretches out the human, and the temporal medicine (*temporalis medicina*), which heals the human.[106] Through Christ, the church and Scriptures present publicly what God is doing in time for the whole of humanity. Other individuals, like the patriarchs, prophets, and apostles, also present in history divine things for the benefit of humanity.[107] In the *historia* of Christ, eternity is witnessed as present in time. Hence, everlasting Truth, who orders all things, both enters into time and stands motionless in eternity above all times.[108]

This is an important insight for Augustine. Eternity is not competitive with time. Indeed, eternity seems to be a different modality than time. Eternal life, Augustine states, surpasses temporal life by its vivacity.[109] Eternity is only perceived through understanding because it does not change or possess intervals of time such as past or future movements. The past ceases, as the future is not yet; eternity, in contrast, simply is. Thus, eternity consists of a kind of presence. To speak more properly: eternity "is" presence.

In contrast to the Manichaean conception of the Present Time, Augustine argues for the centrality of faith in *historia* for perceiving eternal things.[110] Indeed, he emphatically concludes his discussion of reason and ascent with a defense of the necessity of the Scriptures. In his citation of Romans 1:20, a verse calling for the ascent from the temporal to the spiritual to the divinity of God, Augustine realizes the fullness of the integration of eternity *into time* through the *historia* of Christ.[111]

## CONCLUSION

From the preceding survey of Augustine's early understanding of time, eternity, and history, I want to emphasize a few points. Augustine seems to draw from Plotinus his understanding of eternity and the *rationes* that enable the soul to ascend. The insight into eternity, which may have come through Ambrose, is at the center of Augustine's criticism of Manichaeism.

However, Augustine does not explicitly link time with the "descent" of "Soul" or World-Soul. Moreover, in the most suggestive passage in his early corpus, Augustine speaks simply of a *uitalis motus*, which has the potency for ordering and ministering times. He immediately turns to discuss blessed souls (angels) who are above this *uitalis motus*. The angels, who are not made or governed by the *uitalis motus*, are part of the spiritual creation and interact directly with humanity.[112] Thus, the theory of the descent of World-Soul or the hypostasis Soul lacks evidence that Soul "makes" time, an act which Augustine always credits to God. Even in his early writings, Augustine holds to the objectivity of time.

The broader Neoplatonic framing of time and eternity is consistently fractured by Augustine's belief in the Incarnation. He does not even preserve the divine Intellect (Plotinus's Nous) from entering time. Time and eternity increasingly do not seem to be oppositional or competitive as such. Indeed, in his early optimism concerning the possibility of the blessed life, Augustine even suggests the possibility of participating in eternity in this life *in time*.

Augustine's insights concerning eternity also inform his criticism of Manichaeism. Manichaeans are trapped in the struggle to liberate the Light from Darkness in the Present Time. The modality of time is constricted as it is ever more narrowly applied to the conflict of the Present Time. Hence, Augustine's early examination of *memoria*, *intentio*, and *expectatio* indicates the difficulty of locating or securing time. Yet it is from this foundation that

Augustine begins to turn to *historia* in his Thagastan works. Far from offering a kind of historicism, Augustine comes to understand the interpretive importance of the temporal dispensation of God's action in time (specifically the *historia* of Christ). *Historia* of this kind expands the notion of the present and provides an enduring significance to time (or at least to a specific time). In this way, the present time or the "now" always includes the *memoria* of God's activity, its continued presence, and the expectation of its culmination. This full present then provides an image of eternity, which, at least in *uera rel.*, Augustine construes as "presence." It also explains why Augustine can both argue for the resurrection of the body unto eternal life, which suggests "time," and at the same time explain how the resurrected "dwell" unendingly in God's eternity.

Augustine's understanding of time, eternity, and history certainly advances over the course of his life. However, many of the images and descriptions of time, eternity, and history discussed in his early writings are also found in his later works, especially the *Conf.* While the later writings treat these topics in a more integrated and complete manner, much of the groundwork can already be found in Augustine's earliest forays into temporality.

## NOTES

1. *Conf.* 11.20.26 (CCL 27: 206–7). All translations are my own.
2. *Conf.* 11.26.33–11.29.39 (CCL 27: 211–5).
3. *Conf.* 12.2.2 (CCL 27: 217); 12.9.9 (CCL 27: 221).
4. See Roland Teske, *Paradoxes of Time in Saint Augustine* (Milwaukee: Marquette University, 1996): 2–50, esp. 40–50. See also Bertrand Russell, *Human Knowledge: Its Scope and Limits* (New York: Simon and Schuster, 1948).
5. John Cavadini, "Time and Ascent in *Confessiones* XI," in J. Lienhard, E. Muller, and R. Teske, eds., *Augustine*: Presbyter Factus Sum (New York: Peter Lang, 1994): 171–185; Sean Hannan, *On Time, Change, History, and Conversion* (New York: Bloomsbury Academic, 2020).
6. See Roland Teske, "The World-Soul and Time in St. Augustine," *Augustinian Studies* 14 (1983): 75–92.
7. For Origen's possible influence through his adaptation of extension (διάστημα) and dimension (διάστασις), see P. Tzamalikos, "Origen: The Source of Augustine's Theory of Time," *Filosofia* 17 (1987): 396–418, esp. 400–404. For biblical influences see O'Daly, "Time as *Distentio* and St. Augustine's Exegesis of Philippians 3, 12–14," *Revue des Études Augustiniennes* 23 (1977): 265–271.
8. *Enn.* 4.4 is also important for Plotinus's conception of time.
9. Augustine likely read *Enn.* 1.6; 3.2; 4.3; 5.1. See Paul Henry, *Plotin et L'Occident* (Louvain: Spicilegium Sacrum Lovaniense, 1934): 110–116; 121–133. Robert O'Connell, "*Ennead* VI 4–5 in the Works of Saint Augustine," *Revue des Études Augustiniennes* 9 (1963): 1–39, adds *Enn.* 1.4; 1.8; 3.2–3; 4.7–8; 5.2–3; 5.6; 6.4–6; 6.9.

10. Gerard O'Daly, *Augustine's Philosophy of Mind* (Berkeley: University of California, 1987), 152, observes that the approach of proceeding from image (time) to model (eternity) or model to image is not used by Augustine.

11. *Enn.* 3.7.11 (*Plotini Opera Tomus I*, Museum Lessianum Series Philosophica [MLSP] 33: 386–9); 4.4.15.

12. *Enn.* 3.7.4 (MLSP 33: 372–4). Concerning eternity, see Andrew Smith, "Eternity and Time," in Lloyd Gerson, ed., *The Cambridge Companion to Plotinus* (Cambridge: Cambridge University, 1996), 202: "Plotinus has narrowly negotiated the thin line between giving eternity a precise and distinct ontological status and seeing it as a quality."

13. Andrew Smith, "Soul and Time in Plotinus," in J. Holzhausen ed., *Psyche – Seele – Anima: Festschrift für Karin Alt* (Stuttgart: B.G. Teubner, 1998): 335.

14. Smith, "Soul," 335.

15. *Enn.* 3.7.13 (MLSP 33: 391–4).

16. *Enn.* 4.4.15 (MLSP 34: 92); 3.7.11 (MLSP 33: 386–9).

17. The hypostasis Soul does not descend; however, Soul descends in various forms as individuated souls and World-Soul. Whether Soul seeks to imitate Nous or the utter transcendence of the One is unclear.

18. *Enn.* 4.8.6 (MLSP 34: 242–4); 6.7.8 (MLSP 35: 221–2).

19. *Enn.* 5.1.1 (MLSP 34: 260–1).

20. N. Joseph Torchia, *Plotinus, Tolma, and the Descent of Being: An Exposition and Analysis* (New York: Peter Lang, 1993).

21. A. Smith claims that Augustine holds a "subjectivist view of time," while Plotinus holds that time is generated by Soul. At the lower level of individual souls, the time of "this world" is not a subjective, individual generation, but rather communicated to the world through the World-Soul. Smith, "Eternity," 209–210.

22. Teske, "The World-Soul," and Robert J. O'Connell, "The *De Genesi contra Manichaeos* and the Origin of the Soul," *Revue des Études Augustiniennes* 39 (1993): 129–141.

23. See Thomas Clemmons, "*De Genesi aduersus Manichaeos*: Augustine's Anthropology and the Fall of the Soul," *Augustinian Studies* 51, no. 1 (2020): 47–78.

24. Because "matter" is at times equated with the Darkness, the Light may be imaged differently. For the Darkness as matter (*hyle*), see Alexander of Lycopolis, *Of the Manichaeans* 2, trans. James B. H. Hawkins, in *Ante-Nicene Fathers*, Vol. 6. *Gregory Thaumaturgus, Dionysius the Great, Julius Africanus, Anatolius and Minor Writers, Methodius, Arnobius* (Peabody, MA: Hendrickson Publishers, 2004): 241–2.

25. For an overview, see Samuel Lieu, *Manichaeism in the Later Roman Empire and Medieval China* (Manchester: Manchester University Press, 1985).

26. See G. Haloun and W.B. Henning, "The Compendium of the Doctrines and Styles of the Teaching of Mani, the Buddha of Light," in *Asia Major* 3, no. 2 (1952): 184–212.

27. *Kephalaia* 57.145–146, in Iain Gardner, *The Kephalaia of the Teacher* (Leiden: Brill, 1995): 151–153.

28. *Kephalaia* 55.133.4–133.30 in Gardner, 141–142.

29. *Kephalaia* 64.157.32–158.23 in Gardner, 166–167.

30. The Future Time is the resolution of the agony of the Present and of the struggle of the particular individual. For the Future Time, see François Decret, *Aspects du Manichéisme dans l'Afrique Romaine: Les controverses de Fortunatus, Faustus, et Felix avec saint Augustin* (Paris: Études Augustiniennes, 1970): 311–322.

31. Mani was certainly concerned with the cosmos. See *Conf.* 5.3.6 and Alexander, *Of the Manichaeans* 22.

32. *mor.* 2.19.73 (CSEL 90: 153–4); also, *Kephalaia* 57.146–147 in Gardner, 153–154.

33. *Acad.* 1.1.1 (CCL 29: 3–4).

34. *beata u.* 1.2 (CCL 29: 65–6).

35. *beata u.* 2.11 (CCL 29: 71–2).

36. *ord.* 2.12.35–2.15.43 (CCL 29: 127–31).

37. *ord.* 2.16.44 (CCL 29: 131); 2.18.47 (CCL 29: 132–3).

38. *ord.* 2.19.50–2.19.51 (CCL 29: 134–5).

39. *Acad.* 3.17.37 (CCL 29: 57).

40. *ord.* 2.5.16 (CCL 29: 115–6).

41. *Acad.* 3.19.42 (CCL 29: 60).

42. Augustine concludes that it is in the authority of Christ that he is certain (*certus*) that he will find truth and true wisdom. He is confident (*confido*), not certain, that he will find the same in the teachings of Plato. *Acad.* 3.20.44 (CCL 29: 61).

43. *sol.* 1.1.4 (CSEL 89: 7–9): *Deus cuius legibus in aeuo stantibus*. See also *lib. arb.* 1.6.14-1.6.15 (CCL 29: 219–20); 1.8.18 (CCL 29: 222–3); 1.14.30 (CCL 29: 231–2).

44. *sol.* 1.8.15 (CSEL 89: 23–4).

45. *sol.* 1.14.24 (CSEL 89: 36–7). *Penitus esse ista sensibilia fugienda cauendumque magnopere dum hoc corpus agimus.* See also *lib. arb.* 1.15.32 (CCL 29: 233); 1.16.34 (CCL 29: 234–5).

46. *sol.* 1.14.25 (CSEL 89: 37–9).

47. These terms are from *an. quant.* 33.76 (CSEL 89: 224–5). See also *lib. arb.* 1.15.31 (CCL 29: 232–3). *stabile ac sempiternum* in contrast to *mutabile* and *temporale*. Also, *ineffabilis* at *ord.* 2.4.11 (CCL 29: 113).

48. *imm. an.* 4.6 (CSEL 89: 107).

49. ibid., 15.24 (CSEL 89: 125–7).

50. *Enn.* 4.4.12 (MLSP 34: 86–8). See also Smith, "Soul," 339–342.

51. *imm. an.* 15.24 (CSEL 89: 125–7).

52. ibid., 3.3 (CSEL 89: 103–5). This is a rejection of time as the movement of the heavens. See also *Gn. adu. Man.* 1.14.21 (CSEL 91: 88).

53. ibid. (CSEL 89: 104): *Porro quod sic agitur et exspectatione opus est ut peragi et memoria ut comprehendi queat quantum potest.*

54. ibid. (CSEL 89: 104): *Et exspectatio futurarum rerum est, praeteritarum uero memoria.*

55. ibid. (CSEL 89: 104): *At intentio ad agendum praesentis est temporis per quod futurum in praeteritum transit [. . .].*

56. *an. quant.* 20.34 (CSEL 89: 173–4).

57. ibid., 33.76 (CSEL 89: 223–5).

58. ibid.
59. ibid., 36.80 (CSEL 89: 229–30).
60. *mus.* 6.11.29 (CSEL 102: 215): *Ubi nullum est tempus, quia mutabilitas nulla est et unde tempora fabricantur et ordinantur et modificantur aeternitatem imitantia dum caeli conuersio ad idem redit et caelestia corpora ad idem reuocat [. . .].*
61. ibid., 6.11.30 (CSEL 102: 215).
62. ibid., 6.12.37 (CSEL 102: 220).
63. ibid., 6.12.40 (CSEL 102: 222).
64. ibid., 6.14.44 (CSEL 102: 224).
65. ibid.
66. ibid., 6.12.36 (CSEL 102: 219–20).
67. ibid., 6.16.52 (CSEL 102: 229): In lumine *scilicet in Christo accipiendum qui sapientia dei est* et lumen toties appellatur (Ps 35 :10–11).
68. ibid., 6.17.56–57 (CSEL 102: 231–2).
69. *mor.* 1.19.36 (CSEL 90: 40–1).
70. ibid., 1.20.37–21.39 (CSEL 90: 41–5).
71. ibid., 1.25.47 (CSEL 90: 52): *Aeterna igitur uita est ipsa cognitio ueritatis.*
72. ibid., 1.25.50–51 (CSEL 90: 54–55).
73. ibid., 1.30.62 (CSEL 90: 65–66). Translation is my own.
74. ibid., 1.30.63 (CSEL 90: 66–7).
75. ibid., 1.34.76–80 (CSEL 90: 79–87); 1.18.33 (CSEL 90: 37–8).
76. ibid., 2.15.36 (CSEL 90: 121); 2.17.62–18.65 (CSEL 90: 143–7); see also *Gn. adu. Man.* 1.3.6 (CSEL 91: 72–3).
77. ibid., 2.1.1–2.3 (CSEL 90: 88–90).
78. ibid., 2.11.22 (CSEL 90: 107–8); 2.16.43–46 (CSEL 90: 127–131).
79. *Gn. adu. Man.* 1.2.3 (CSEL 91: 68–70). Translation is my own.
80. ibid., 1.2.3 (CSEL 91: 69): *Deus enim fecit et tempora: et ideo antequam faceret tempora non erant tempora.*
81. ibid. (CSEL 91: 69): *Quomodo enim erat tempus quod Deus non fecerat cum omnium temporum ipse sit fabricator?*
82. ibid., 2.6.7 (CSEL 91: 126): *Dies autem iste cuius nomine uniuersum tempus significari diximus insinuat nobis non solum uisibilem sed etiam inuisibilem creaturam tempus posse sentire.*
83. ibid., 2.6.7 (CSEL 91: 127): *ut sic intellegeremus non solum uisibilem sed etiam inuisibilem creaturam pertinere ad tempus propter mutabilitatem; quia solus Deus incommutabilis qui est ante tempora.*
84. ibid., 1.2.4 (CSEL 91: 70).
85. ibid., 2.22.34–23.35 (CSEL 91: 156–9); 2.27.41 (CSEL 91: 166–8).
86. ibid., 1.23.41 (CSEL 91: 110–1).
87. ibid., 2.2.3 (CSEL 91: 120–1).
88. Consider, for example, ibid., 2.27.41 (CSEL 91: 167–8).
89. ibid., 2.24.37 (CSEL 91: 160–2).
90. For a treatment of these themes, see Thomas Clemmons, "The Common, History, and the Whole: Guiding Themes in *De uera religione*," *Augustinianum* 58 (2018): 125–154.

91. *uera rel.* 3.3 (CCL 32: 188–9).
92. ibid.
93. ibid., 3.4 (CCL 32: 190).
94. ibid., 30.56–31.58 (CCL 32: 223–6); 39.72–73 (CCL 32: 234–5).
95. ibid., 3.5 (CCL 32: 191–2).
96. ibid., 5.8 (CCL 32: 193).
97. ibid., 7.13 (CCL 32: 196): *Huius religionis sectandae caput est historia et prophetia dispensationis temporalis diuinae prouidentiae, pro salute generis humani in aeternam uitam reformandi atque reparandi.*
98. ibid., 7.13–8.14 (CCL 32: 196–7): Augustine lists the Virgin birth, Incarnation, death and resurrection of Christ, resurrection of the dead, as well as the understanding of the eternity of the Trinity and the mutability of all creation.
99. ibid., 9.16 (CCL 32: 198). For the two souls, see Thomas Clemmons, "On the Two Wills: Augustine against Agonism toward Peace," in A. Dupont, E. Eguiarte Bendimez, C. A. Villabona Vargas, eds., *Agustin de Hipona como Doctor Pacis*, Vol. 2 (Bogota: Editorial Uniagustiniana, 2019): 269–288.
100. ibid., 10.18–19 (CCL 32: 199): *Aeterno enim creatori adhaerentes et nos aeternitate afficiamur necesse est.*
101. ibid., 10.19 (CCL 32: 200).
102. ibid., 16.30 (CCL 32: 205–6).
103. ibid., 18.37 (CCL 32: 209–10).
104. ibid., 43.80 (CCL 32: 240–1).
105. ibid., 21.41 (CCL 32: 212–3).
106. ibid., 24.45 (CCL 32: 215–6). Augustine also discusses the temporal dispensation and medicine of divine providence in relation to the aging and growth of the old and new "man" of St. Paul; see ibid., 26.48–49 (CCL 32: 217–9).
107. ibid., 25.46 (CCL 32: 216); 28.51 (CCL 32: 220–1).
108. ibid., 43.81 (CCL 32: 241).
109. ibid., 49.97 (CCL 32: 250): *Aeterna enim uita uitam temporalem uiuacitate ipsa superat.*
110. ibid., 50.98–50.99 (CCL 32: 250–1).
111. ibid., 51.100–52.101 (CCL 32: 252–3).
112. *mus.* 6.17.58 (CSEL 102: 232–3).

*Chapter 2*

# Keeping Time in Mind

## *Saint Augustine's Proposed Solution to a Perplexing Problem*

Alexander R. Eodice

It is a commonplace to think of human consciousness as temporally ordered; the past, as Proust might say, is "incarnate in the present" through recollection and the future is, in some sense, felt as real through conscious acts of expectation.[1] Moreover, the temporality of consciousness is manifest in a manifold of ways through the ordinary metaphors used in association with certain states of experience. It is not uncommon, for instance, to describe joyful experiences in terms of "time flying" or painful ones in terms of "time standing still"; we sense the appropriate by thinking "it is just the right time" or feel hope in thinking that "time heals all wounds." In many respects, what it means to be conscious is to feel time in certain ways—as fleeting, as passing slowly, as an instant, as extensive, and so on. Through such metaphors, we come to see that the very conception of ourselves is largely a function of such a temporal consciousness, in so far as a unified life is presented, or represented, through memory and anticipation.

While such a metaphorical understanding of time in consciousness provides the ground for the kind of autobiographical narrative that constitutes much of his *Confessions*, Saint Augustine takes a decidedly different turn in Book 11 of that work.[2] There he shifts from the rhetoric of autobiography to a more discursive and properly philosophical treatment of the nature of time; he endeavors to understand time as distinct from eternity and as a feature of the created universe. In raising certain puzzles about the measurability and divisibility of time as a kind of physical phenomenon, he is seemingly left with the prospect of having to assert the unreality of time. Discontent with this conclusion, he asserts that time is real but only as a function of consciousness; in this instance, however, the claim is put forward as a conclusion to a lengthy philosophical argument and is not simply the rhetorical underpinning of an autobiographical and confessional narrative.

In this chapter, I review the major strands in Augustine's line of reasoning about time as expounded in Book XI of the *Confessions*. The argument prefigures many more modern philosophical concerns about the nature of time, its movement, measurability, and objectivity, and poses problems that have yet to be determinately resolved. Wittgenstein, in *The Blue and Brown Books*, offers a particularly potent criticism of Augustine's argument by focusing on the kinds of puzzles and perplexities that emerge from a "mystifying use of our language" about time.[3] Following the exposition of Augustine's argument, I then consider several critical responses, paying particular attention to Wittgenstein's approach as a way of understanding the source of Augustine's puzzlement and as a possible resolution of it. In all, it should be readily apparent that the discussion of time constitutes one of Augustine's most enduring contributions to philosophy.[4]

## AUGUSTINE ON TIME

Augustine strikingly opens his discussion with a question to God that embraces the distinction between eternity and time.[5] With this distinction in mind and with the knowledge that all things that are mutable must be made, Augustine wonders about the beginning of the universe, about how all created things come to be at all. Eternity and temporality are in strict opposition to each other, and it is precisely this opposition that poses a particularly perplexing problem when trying to define the nature of time. Eternity is tenseless, unchanging, and indivisible; in it, there is no past, present, or future, no before or after. Time, as it seems to be a changing feature of the physical world correlated with successive mental states (remembering the past, attending to the present, anticipating the future), must, like all objects subject to change, have been created. Eternity is not infinitely extended time; it is timelessness. Augustine occasionally speaks as if we could understand the eternal as a sort of constant present, but even this would not suffice as a definition of eternity; at best, given the limitations of human imagination and language, experience of the present would provide a "metaphorical base for the leap that carries the contemplative mind towards the eternal" but only to have the mind retract "before the impossible abyss is vaulted."[6] It is within the overarching framework of this notion of eternity that Augustine provides his argument concerning the nature of time.[7]

With this distinction in place, Augustine begins his argument by noting that it would be self-contradictory to suppose that time was created in time. It is senseless, he argues, to ask what God was doing before he created anything.

"Before" itself is a tensed term and as such makes sense only in a temporal context; in eternity, there is no before or after. God created all things, including time, from the perspective of a tenseless and changeless eternity, so it is impossible for there to have been a time when God created time as that would imply the contradiction that there was a time before time.[8] For Augustine, there could be no time "when there was no time."

"What then is time?" Augustine wonders. While recognizing that the word "time" is common in ordinary language and that we seemingly understand the term when we or others use it, he is nonetheless perplexed by the question. His perplexity results from the attempt to wrest the term from its place in common discourse and view the question as one about the definition or nature of time. And so he famously remarks: "What is time? If no one asks me, I know; if I want to explain it to a questioner, I do not know."[9] With this, he is asking what kind of object or thing is time. The question seems to spring naturally from his commitment to the idea that time is created, like all things, by God. What, then, are the defining marks of this kind of created thing?

Augustine begins with the affirmation that time moves; its movement is the very indication of its changeability. Time passes from the present to the past and from the present approaches the future; if this were not the case, there would be no past or future time, but only an "eternal" present, which would not be time but eternity. Leaving aside the idea that eternity can be understood as an everlasting present, the salient point here is that time exists only to the extent that it "tends not to be." Neither the past nor the future can properly be said to exist, since the past is no longer and the future is not yet; it is difficult, as well, to determine the existence of the present since it flows immediately into the past.[10]

The perplexity compounds for Augustine. Despite the difficulty we encounter in attempting to assert the existence of the past, present, and future, we are inclined to apply durational terms to the past and the future. We speak of the past or future, respectively, as a long/short time ago or a long/short time ahead. But if the past is no longer and the future not yet, in what sense can we attribute to them any durational length? In so far as neither the past nor the future exist in the present, neither can be said to have any duration, for only that which currently exists could be said to have such length. Thus, it would seem we should be able to determine the duration of the present. But how long could the present be? By considering varying "lengths of time"—a hundred years, a year, a month, a day, an hour, a minute, and so on—he infers that only an indivisible "moment" can be considered the present, but it would be so fleeting as to have no durational extent whatsoever. If the present, then, is anything, it is a temporally dimensionless point and so is not divisible; if it were a complex of moments, the present would be divisible into the past and future, in which case it could not be simply the present.[11]

So far, the Augustinian puzzle takes the following shape: since neither the past nor the future exist, they cannot be measured, and since the present, though it exists, is an irreducible atom of time, it cannot be measured, and since time is composed of the past, present, and future, time itself cannot, seemingly, be measured. "Yet," Augustine says, "we are aware of periods of time," and "we measure how much one is longer than another."[12] How is it possible to measure time given the ontological problem associated with the existence or duration of the parts of time? Augustine's initial and rather enigmatic response is that we can measure time passing but not time that has passed. I take it that the significance of this remark has to do again with the notion of time as a created thing that moves; time's passing is, like all motion, perceptible and thus measureable, but as Augustine eventually determines, the movement of time is not a kind of motion in the physical world.

Perhaps in a final attempt to validate ordinary intuitions about time, Augustine considers the prospect that the future and the past may exist in "secret" places; it may be that "time comes forth from some secret place when future becomes present, and departs into some secret place when form present it becomes past."[13] For it seems that unless the future and past truly existed, neither prophecy nor historical description could be true.[14] Augustine argues, however, that if the future and the past actually exist, then it should be possible to know them where they are, precisely as future and past, but he does not know them where they are. Yet, wherever and whatever they are, they are manifest in the present—through memory and anticipation. When we remember past events, it is not as if those events still exist; instead the past is recollected through mental images, which exist in the present. It is likewise with respect to the future; we anticipate that certain events will occur, that is, the sun will rise tomorrow, but such events do not exist now. What do exist now are the signs and causes of future as presented to a conscious mind.

On the basis of his argument up to this point, Augustine arrives at the skeptical conclusion that it is impossible to assert the existence of the past and future. It is thus technically incorrect to say that time consists of three distinctly existing components, the past, present, and future; however, he adds:

> Perhaps it would be more correct to say there are three times, a present of things past, a present of things present, a present of things future. For these three exist in the mind, and I find them nowhere else: the present of things past is memory, the present of things present is sight, the present of things future is expectation. If we are allowed to speak thus, I see and admit that there are three times, that three times truly are.[15]

In this respect, the skeptical conclusion regarding the ontological status of the future and the past gives way to a kind of linguistic idealism. The past and future, metaphysically understood, could not conceivably be the present, but they could be understood, grammatically, as the past present and the future present. In an idealized language, it is possible to construct, as A. N. Prior notes, complex sentences expressing these times by prefixing to a sentence in the present tense the phrase "It was the case that" or "It will be the case that" to form the past present and future present, respectively.[16] We can say, for example:

It was the case that I am reading the *Confessions*.
or
It will be the case that I am reading the *Confessions*.

While these are not ordinary locutions, the constructions may reveal, as Prior observes, "the truth behind Augustine's suggestion of the 'secret place' where past and future times 'are,' and his insistence that wherever they are, they are not there as past or future but as present."[17] We may then, according to Augustine, "continue to say that there are three times, past, present and future; for, though it is incorrect, custom allows it."[18] Custom allows it in the sense that grammar allows it. That said, Augustine recognizes that in making this claim, we bump up against the limits of language. "There are few things that we phrase properly," he writes; "most things we phrase badly." Despite this, "what we are trying to say is understood."[19]

Having asserted that it is impossible to measure past and future time, but that it is possible to measure time passing, Augustine proceeds to analyze the concept of measurement as it pertains to time. He recognizes that we do, in fact, measure time in its passing; it is empirically possible to compare durational lengths and determine proportions among them. The oddity in this, however, is that "no time has yet been discovered which has any duration."[20] Augustine, once again, appeals to ordinary language and recognizes the fact that we use temporal expressions extensively in common discourse.[21] The meaningfulness of such expressions must be grounded in an intelligible sense of how we measure intervals of time.

In an initial attempt to discover how we measure time and what exactly is measured by the measuring process, Augustine considers the possibility that time is simply the movement of celestial bodies. He rejects this idea for several reasons. First, why should we limit the measurement of time to the motion of the heavenly bodies rather than consider the movement of all bodies? So, for instance, if the light of heaven were to cease but the potter's wheel kept turning, we should still have to say that the wheel turned faster or slower or at equal intervals, and though the turning of the potter's wheel would clearly not signal the seasons or days or years, it is not that it involves no time at all. Second, what if the sun moved at different rates of speed, completing a circuit from east to west, for example, in half the time it usually takes. Augustine wonders whether a day would be defined as that movement itself or simply the time it takes for the sun to make its circuit. Third, even if the sun stood still, other occurrent events would have a measureable duration. Such logical possibilities lead Augustine to the specific conclusion that time is not the movement of heavenly bodies.[22]

But could time be the movement of bodies at all? While it is the case that no body moves except in time, such movement could not be identified as time, for the simple reason that we can measure how long any particular body happens to be in motion or how long it takes to traverse the distance between two points in space. Moreover, we can measure the time a body is at rest and determine proportions relative to its resting and moving states. From this, Augustine arrives at the more general conclusion that time is not the movement of bodies at all.[23] It is evident that in making such claims, Augustine ultimately rejects any idea that time is a dimension of the physical universe.[24]

In saying that time is not physical motion, Augustine does not yet say what time is. Holding firm to the idea that time is measureable, he proceeds with his analysis by asking what it is he uses to measure time. Do we measure a longer time by a shorter time, analogous to how we measure a beam in terms of cubits?[25] What follows is a remarkable series of passages in which Augustine introduces "with the beguiling innocence of the accomplished orator," as James McEvoy describes, "one of those sudden lunges of his that prove determinant of the entire sequence of his thought."[26] Augustine specifically suggests that we do not measure the length of a poem in terms of pages, for this would be to measure space; instead, we measure the poem metrically in terms of lines, feet, and syllables in the context of its being spoken.[27] Augustine cautions that this is not an exact measurement of time, for a poem and its constituent lines, feet, and syllables can be recited at varying speeds so that shorter lines may take longer to utter than longer lines spoken swiftly.

The description almost perfectly conveys why time cannot be measured in any way approximating the measurement of physical objects in space; instead time is measured more along the lines of poetic or even musical rhythm, cadence, and tempo; that is, it is not simply the sound that matters, but the "way the sound moves." Moreover, the aural imagery points to the radical separation of time from space, in that it demonstrates the aesthetic (primarily in the sense of immediate) quality of sound.

The conclusion Augustine initially draws from such observations is that time is extendedness, but at this point, he is still unsure as to what it is a distention of. He tentatively suggests that time is *probably* extendedness of the mind. He gives a final example in an effort to arrive at a more secure stopping place. Here he considers the line *Deus creator omnium* from a hymn by Ambrose, which contains eight syllables that alternate between short and long:

> Each long syllable has double the time of each short syllable. I pronounce them and I say that it is so, and so it is, as quite obvious to the ear. As my ear distinguishes I measure a long syllable by a short and see that it contains it twice. But since I hear a syllable only before the one before it has ceased—the one before being short and the one following long—how am I to keep hold of the short syllable, and how shall I set it against the long one to measure it and find the long one is twice its length—given that the long syllable does not begin to sound until the short one has ceased? And again can I measure the long one while it is present, since I cannot measure it until it has completed? And its completion is its passing out of existence.[28]

In order to determine proportions and intervals, it is necessary, as per this example, for the sound to be punctuated by gaps of momentary silence. A sound cannot be measured while it lasts, but only in terms of what precedes or follows it. Each discrete sound or syllable, upon its completion, is impressed upon the mind and stored in memory.

The past no longer exists and so cannot be measured; the future does not yet exist and so cannot be measured; the present while passing cannot be compared to other moments and so cannot be measured, but still, Augustine argues, we measure time. Time is extendedness, but must be an extendedness of the mind. Moments once completed are stored in memory and relations among them only then determined. If time were a continuum of instants with no punctuated gaps, it would, like an unending sound, be immeasurable.

By means of the acts of remembrance, attention, and expectation, the mind imposes temporal order on experience. In so far as time is extendedness of the mind, it is the mind itself that is measured when we measure time. It is not the present, a dimensionless point, but our attention that endures and through it the future is diminished on its way to becoming part of an increasingly larger past, and since neither the future nor the past exists independent of the mind, a long past is simply a long memory and a long future is simply a long expectation.[29] Thus, time flows or has directionality but only for creatures with minds.[30] While it is impossible to measure the past, present, and future as external things, it is possible to measure time in the sense of employing mental operations in the determination of relations among the impressions given through experience. Augustine concludes that "either that is what time is, or I am not measuring time at all."[31]

In rejecting the more ancient understanding of time as a dimension of or movement in the physical world and in acknowledging that time is of the essence of mind itself, Augustine's theory marks a pivotal turn in the history of the philosophy of time. In many respects, Augustine anticipates Kant's notion that time is the form of inner sensibility, not itself a property of objects but an "intuition of ourselves" and a condition for the possibility of ordering phenomenal experiences successively in consciousness. For Augustine, time is subjective, not in the sense of being a private experience but in the sense that the mind—any human mind—contributes temporal order to the vast manifold of impressions it receives, and it is by means of this that we both perceive the world and conceive of ourselves as moving through time.[32]

## CRITICAL RESPONSES TO AUGUSTINE ON TIME

Augustine's argument on time is open to several lines of attack. In this section, I consider three such approaches: the first is directed against the argument's opening idea that, given the distinction between time and eternity, time cannot be created in time; the second questions the argument's metaphysical conclusion that time *is* extendedness of mind; and the third, from Wittgenstein, challenges the very sensibility that gives rise to philosophical problems like that of time in the first place.

The first argument may be framed as follows: to say that time was created at some particular time *t* is self-contradictory; therefore, time could not have been created in time. Augustine says as much but infers that therefore time must have been created from some atemporal perspective (eternity). This strong inference, however, is not warranted in the sense that saying time was not created in time is perfectly consistent with the notion that time may not have been created at all, that is, that time itself is eternal, that there is no beginning to time.

The argument proceeds on linguistic grounds. Do the phrases "when there was no time" or "before time" make sense, particularly as they are meant to signal something's having taken place, namely God's creation of time? Augustine says, "There was no then, when there was no time," but how can there be no "then" yet still a "when?" "When" is as much a temporally charged term as "then."[33] Moreover, the use of the term "when" seems to indicate that God's creation of time is an event, and an event is understood simply as something that happens in time. This would be the case whether the event of God's creation of time has happened, is still happening, or is always happening.

None of this addresses the issue of God's creative power; it is only to suggest that time and eternity may be coextensive. Augustine may respond that this is no refutation of his position since our ordinary language, thick as it is with temporal imagery, may be inadequate to express the mysterious nature of what God does in eternity. If this is so, as Ronald Suter points out, "one would no longer know what would count as an answer or criticism of Augustine's view," because "whatever hinges primarily on a mystery and the ineffable wisdom of God has a kind of invulnerability, the invulnerability due to the cessation of philosophy."[34]

The second argument challenges the metaphysical claim that time really is extendedness of mind. The argument may be cast as follows: to say that an event is past does not entail that anyone remembers it; to say that an event is present does not entail that anyone perceives it; and to say that an event is future does not entail that anyone anticipates it. This is part of our ordinary understanding of time. Augustine's subjective theory of time proposes that "time is unreal in a world devoid of consciousness, for there can be no past, present, and future events unless they are respectively remembered, perceived, and anticipated."[35] This statement of the theory clearly conflicts with what we logically claim in virtue of our ordinary understanding of time. That is, if the subjective theory of time is true, then we could not hold, without contradiction, that "to say that an event is past, present, or future does not entail that anyone respectively remembers, perceives, or anticipates it."[36] The oddity here, as indicated by Richard M. Gale, is that the metaphysical statement of the subjective theory of time is paradoxical in that it "entails that certain noncontradictory statements of ordinary language are contradictory."[37]

Gale argues further that metaphysical statements about time may be construed as disguised verbal recommendations so that the paradoxes they generate might be said to reveal some aspect of human experience that we might otherwise neglect and "shock us into seeing the world in a different light."[38] In this instance, the paradoxical character of the statement of the subjective theory might serve to heighten our sense of the role of consciousness in temporal experience and reveal that "a world devoid of consciousness would be a rather drab and dull place, lacking that which is most distinctive and significant about human experience—its retention of the past so as to enrich the present and guide us in forming future projects."[39] Understood in this way, the subjective theory importantly gives us a sense of time with a "human face" or an idea of why time matters to creatures like us, but it does not justify the metaphysical claim that time is *in fact* unreal in a world devoid of consciousness.

Augustine undoubtedly means his conclusion in the metaphysical sense; that is, for him time *is* a protraction of the mind, and the past, present, and future are strictly identical with the mental acts of remembering, attending, and anticipating, respectively. In large measure, Augustine is led to this conclusion because, while he conceives of time as an ordered whole, he can find nothing in the nonmental world that can link the nonexistent past and future with a dimensionless present to frame the order of time; consciousness, for him, serves that purpose; it is the "thread by which the long, nonexistent arms of the past and future can be sewn together in the present."⁴⁰ But, as the counterargument goes, this conclusion rests on a misleading analogy between the spatial and the temporal.

While it is perfectly logical to say that the parts of spatial wholes must exist together, it does not necessarily follow that we must say the same about temporal events. As J. N. Findlay puts it:

> We might say we were dealing with two totally different *sorts* of parts and wholes. And we do in fact rule so; for we regard it as nonsense to say of an event that takes time, that its parts are present together. And we recognize the difference between the two sets by talking of *coexistent* parts in the one set of cases, and of successive parts in the other: the successive parts of a whole are, in fact, just those parts of it that *don't* need to be together.⁴¹

Consider the difference between a baseball stadium and a baseball game. It would be absurd to say of the stadium that its parts do not exist together, but not so of the baseball game. The game is a whole, but of a different sort; its parts do not exist together but successively. Now with respect to the game, we might remember in the third inning what happened in the first and anticipate what will happen in the fifth. Our mental acts, while they may contribute to a more interesting time of it at the game, do not collectively constitute the whole (nor are they individually parts) of the game; the innings will proceed in order irrespective of what we and 50,000 other fans may be consciously attending to at any moment during the game.

While the previous arguments are directed toward specific elements in Augustine's account of time, Wittgenstein's brief commentary on time in *The Blue and Brown Books* raises a deeper and more challenging criticism, one that calls into question the very conditions that give rise to philosophical puzzlement generally, a kind of puzzlement "caused by the mystifying use of our language," and the puzzlement about time in particular. Philosophy itself motivates bewilderment through its craving for generality and definition. With this attitude, it tends to view language as functioning according to exact rules, as a kind of calculus. In this way, we are inclined to look for a thing every time a substantive is used. Wittgenstein remarks:

> This is a very one-sided way of looking at language. In practice we very rarely use language as such a calculus. For not only do we not think of the rules of usage—of definitions, etc.—while using language, but when asked to give such rules, in most case we aren't able to do so. We are unable clearly to circumscribe the concepts we use; not because we don't know their real definition, but because there is no real 'definition' to them.⁴²

He suggests further that "the man who is philosophically puzzled sees a law in the way a word is used, and, in trying to apply the law consistently, comes up against cases where it leads to paradoxical results."[43] For Wittgenstein, Augustine's puzzle about time perfectly illustrates how conceptual difficulties emerge when philosophy adopts a rigid view of language and presses for substantive definition.

The *Philosophical Investigations* opens with a passage from the *Confessions* in which Augustine describes language in terms of an object-designation grammar; that is, the individual words of a language name objects and the meaning of a word is the object it designates. Here is the passage:

> When they (my elders) named some object, and accordingly moved towards something, I saw this and I grasped that the thing was called by the sound that they uttered when they meant to point it out. Their intention was shown by their bodily movements, as it were the natural language of all peoples: the expression of the face, the play of the eyes, the movement of other parts of the body, and the tone of voice which expresses our state of mind in seeking, having, rejecting, or avoiding something. Thus, as I heard words repeatedly used in their proper places in various sentences, I gradually learnt to understand what objects they signified; and after I had trained my mouth to form these signs, I used them to express my own desires.[44]

It is just this sense of language that gives rise to Augustine's puzzle about time. In asking the question "What is time?" Augustine is craving for a definition, looking for a thing or substance to which the substantive term "time" refers. "What is time?" looks like any other question of the form "What is *x*?" The problem is, however, that not all such questions function in exactly the same way. It is often the case that a definition clarifies the grammar of a word, Wittgenstein says, but there are instances where we are puzzled by the grammar of a word itself.[45] Such is the case with "time." Here the puzzlement is uniquely philosophical. It is not, for instance, like working at a technical problem in mathematics; the technical language of mathematics is the ordinary mode of the mathematical language-game. Philosophical perplexity arises from the sense that our ordinary language must function in a way analogous, say, to mathematics. It may just be the case, however, that ordinary language is fine the way it is.

As Augustine himself repeatedly recognizes, the word "time" is a perfectly common one and is used intelligibly in ordinary language; his problem emerges in his effort to wrench the term from its ordinary context and give it some extraordinary definition. Further, he knows what time is (what the word "time" means) in its ordinary context, until someone asks him. But why must someone's question be construed as a request for a definition of time? It is not the ordinary use of the concept but rather the notion that time must have a nature beyond whatever is readily grasped by understanding its ordinary use that makes time seem to be a "queer thing." The question about time may be more properly understood as one seeking clarification of ordinary usage. That is precisely the point of Wittgenstein's claim that "it is not new facts about time which we want to know. All the facts that concern us lie open before us."[46] We need perhaps to be reminded of the role(s) the word "time" plays in ordinary language, to bring the word back from its metaphysical heights to its ordinary place.[47]

Wittgenstein does suggest that investigating the grammar of a word could issue in apparent contradictions. This is what happens when we consider the idea of "measuring" time. Augustine was puzzled by the notion of time's measurement because he could find no things to which the terms "past," "present," and "future" could be affixed; that being so, it appeared that time could not be measured. This apparent contradiction emerges from a confusion of two different uses of the term measure. Wittgenstein writes:

> Augustine, we might say, thinks of the process of measuring a *length*: say, the distance between two marks on a travelling band which passes us, and of which we can only see a tiny bit (the present) in front of us. Solving this puzzle will consist in comparing what we mean by "measurement" (the grammar of the word "measurement") when applied to a distance on a travelling band with the grammar of the word when applied to time. The problem may seem simple, but its extreme difficulty is due to the fascination which the analogy between two similar structures in our language can exert on us.[48]

While Wittgenstein does not tell us what measurement of time is, he does tell us what it is not; that is, the measurement of time is not like spatial measurement.

Augustine would agree, I think, that there is an important disanalogy between spatial and temporal measurement. His puzzlement runs deeper and is more the result of the need, the philosophical urge, to provide a definition of the word "time." Although he may rightly reject the definition "Time is the movement of physical bodies" as unsatisfactory, he is compelled to think he must replace it with a different one. So Augustine believes that "Time is the extendedness of mind" is the correct definition and, accordingly, applies the grammar of "measurement" to mental acts. In making this move, Augustine does not succeed in solving the puzzle about time but may, in fact, deepen its complexity. Wittgenstein suggests that we

> compare with this the case of the definition of number. Here the explanation that a number is the same thing as a numeral satisfies the first craving for a definition. And it is very difficult not to ask: "Well if it isn't the numeral, *what is it?*"[49]

The temptation to provide a general definition is certainly understandable, for philosophy has an obsession about closure and conclusion, but it may just be that giving into that temptation generates more perplexing problems. Resisting the temptation leads back to the ordinary, where we may just have to be content with knowing what time is but not knowing how to explain it. I make no pretense that this is a solution to Augustine's puzzle about time, but I would suggest it points to its dissolution.

## NOTES

1. The original version of this chapter was printed under the same title in *Augustine and Philosophy*, edited by Philip Cary, John Doody, and Kim Paffenroth (Lanham: Rowman & Littlefield, 2010).

2. See the editors' introduction to the sources collected in *Time*, edited by Jonathan Westphal and Carl Levenson (Indianapolis, Indiana: Hackett Publishing Company, 1993), vii, which notes that the first nine books of the *Confessions* constitute Augustine's autobiography, in which time plays a central role, but "by Book XI . . . autobiographical themes have given way to a more purely theoretical interest in the problem of time." I have adopted the view here that Augustine's argument about time in Book XI, given the difference between confessional narrative and discursive argumentation, could be analyzed on its own, so I make no attempt at interpreting the concept of time throughout the *Confessions* in such a way so as to reconcile those two forms of writing or to make any claims about the unity of the work. For an alternative approach, see M. B. Pranger, "Time and Narrative in Augustine's *Confessions*," *Journal of Religion* 81, no. 3 (July 2001), 377–393. Pranger expressly reads Augustine's conversion narrative from the viewpoint of the time argument in Book XI. See also James McEvoy, "St. Augustine's Account of Time and Wittgenstein's Criticisms," *Review of Metaphysics* 38 (March 1984), 547–577. McEvoy, 550, writes that "the philosophical discussion of time must have special significance in an autobiography, for the unfolding of a life in acts of freedom, in varying experiences of fragmentation, in rebellion against mortality, and in partial integration through meaning and purpose, point to time as a crucial but ambivalent feature of all human experience." In this regard, he suggests, Augustine's philosophical argument about time may be understood as "an important key to the entire book."

3. Ludwig Wittgenstein, *The Blue and Brown Books* (New York: Harper & Row, 1958), 6.

4. Joan Stambaugh comments: "It has almost become a hallowed tradition when one speaks on the problem of time to quote Augustine." See her "Time, Finitude, and Finality," *Philosophy East and West* 24, no. 2 (April 1974), 129.

5. Augustine, *Confessions*, XI.1 All references to the text in this chapter are from the F. J. Sheed translation (Indianapolis: Hackett, 1993).

6. McEvoy, "St. Augustine's Account of Time and Wittgenstein's Criticisms," 554.

7. There is, of course, profound theological significance to Augustine's sense of eternity. For example, without the otherness of eternity, it would be impossible to make sense of salvation history. It should be noted that discussion of such issues goes beyond the scope of this chapter, as I have limited my comments to Augustine's more straightforwardly philosophical account of time. This, however, ought not be taken to mean that the theological-historical issues are without value to understanding Augustine on time; fuller consideration of them may, in fact, provide a richer notion of Augustine's account of time than I give here. See, for instance, Robert E. Cushman, "Greek and Christian Views of Time," *Journal of Religion* 33, no. 4 (Oct. 1953), 254–265, and Catherine Rau, "Theories of Time in Ancient Philosophy," *Philosophical Review* 64, no. 2 (Oct. 1953), 514–525.

8. *Confessions,* XI.13.

9. *Confessions,* XI.14.

10. *Confessions,* XI.14.

11. *Confessions,* XI.15. Though he is speaking primarily in sensory terms, that is, that it is impossible to perceive such a fleeting instant, Augustine here prefigures the mathematical problem of a durationless instant. For an excellent discussion of the mathematical definition of an instant and the physical understanding of the continuum of instants, see G. J. Whitrow, *The Natural Philosophy of Time* (New York and Evanston: Harper Torchbooks, 1961), especially Chapter III: "Mathematical Time."

12. *Confessions,* XI.16. McEvoy suggests that Augustine attempts to reinstate the commonsensical, ordinary awareness of time and that it would be wrong to conclude that the reduction of "the present to a dimensionless point constitutes a skeptical betrayal of commonsense belief." See McEvoy, "St. Augustine's Account of Time and Wittgenstein's Criticisms," 556.

13. *Confessions,* XI.17.

14. Ronald Suter, "Augustine on Time with Some Criticisms from Wittgenstein," *Revue international de philosophie* 16 (1957), 381, suggests that Augustine considers this move as a counterargument to the nonexistence of the future and past, for "if it could be established that the future and past do exist after all, this might be one way out of Augustine's present predicament."

15. *Confessions,* XI.20.

16. A. N. Prior, "Changes in Events and Changes in Things," in *The Philosophy of Time,* edited by Robin Le Poidevin and Murray MacBeath (Oxford: Oxford University Press, 1993), 41.

17. Prior, "Changes in Events," 41.

18. *Confessions,* XI.20.

19. *Confessions,* XI.20.

20. Suter, "Augustine on Time," 383.

21. *Confessions,* XI.22.

22. *Confessions,* XI.23. See also Suter, "Augustine on Time," 383–385, and McEvoy, "St. Augustine's Account of Time and Wittgenstein's Criticisms," 558–562, for analyses of Augustine on measuring time.

23. *Confessions,* XI.24.

24. See McEvoy, "St. Augustine's Account of Time and Wittgenstein's Criticisms," 558, which notes that "the question of whether time is simply an aspect of the material

universe is for Augustine a natural and fully-integrated step in the dialectic or philosophy of time, for if time really exists in extendedness, and extendedness can be attached to matter, then the philosophy of time will be absorbed into physics." In denying the validity of a physical account of time, Augustine rejects the earlier views of Plato and Aristotle. As Cushman, "Greek and Christian Views of Time," 263, puts it, Augustine "will not consent to the Platonic-Aristotelian equation: time is the measure of motion."

25. *Confessions*, XI.26.
26. McEvoy, "St. Augustine's Account of Time and Wittgenstein's Criticisms," 560.
27. *Confessions*, XI.26.
28. *Confessions*, XI.27. See also McEvoy, "St. Augustine's Account of Time and Wittgenstein's Criticisms," 561, which notes that Augustine uses this example in a parallel text in *De Musica*. Robert J. O'Connell, *Art and Christian Intelligence in St. Augustine* (Cambridge, MA: Harvard University Press, 1978), 72, comments on Augustine's use of sacred music and poetry in *De Musica:* "The entire work concentrates on the temporal 'measures' which govern the composition of poetry .... From this point in his career until the *Confessions*, Augustine invariably begins his discussion of time by taking the example of a line of poetry, preferably as here, the *Deus creator omnium*, inquiring how we 'measure' the timing of it, then passing to a more generalized speculation on the nature of time when compared with God's eternity. The conclusion is always the same: the experience of time indicates that the soul is 'distended,' fallen from the *otium*, the restful contemplation of eternal truth, into the busy *negotium* of temporal activity."

29. *Confessions*, XI.28.
30. Cushman, "Greek and Christian Views of Time," 264, interprets Augustine's conclusion about time in the context of a distinction between nature and history: "But time has directionality only for mind. Time possesses direction only for creatures who possess *anima* or *nous* capable of three distinguishable acts: anticipation, attention, and memory. Teleological time, therefore, does not properly belong to the physical world of mechanical or organic change. From this it should be apparent why Augustine, but neither Plato nor Aristotle, attained to the notion of 'history' as distinct from nature. Nature really possesses no history. Only *anima* is capable of history. It is because, for mind alone, events move or flow in an inalterable direction: out of the future, through the present, into the past. It is this which gives to human experience its promise to come, its realization or non-realization in the present, its happy, or it may be, its bitter memories of the past. Thus, by the inalterability of time flow in human experience, man's duration is susceptible of tragedy or fulfillment. This kind of duration is history or the raw material of historical existence."

31. *Confessions*, XI.27.
32. Augustine's conclusion lends plausibility to the idea that the time discussion in Book XI of the *Confessions* is a key to understanding the whole work; the autobiographical account of Books I–IX may then be understood as rooted in a philosophical account of the subjective nature of time.

33. This line of argumentation is taken in Suter, "Augustine on Time," 386–387.
34. Suter, "Augustine on Time," 387.

35. Richard M. Gale, "Some Metaphysical Statements about Time," *Journal of Philosophy* 60, no. 9 (April 1963), 225.

36. Gale, "Some Metaphysical Statements," 225.

37. Gale, "Some Metaphysical Statements," 227.

38. Gale, "Some Metaphysical Statements," 226.

39. Gale, "Some Metaphysical Statements," 227–228.

40. Gale, "Some Metaphysical Statements," 228.

41. J. N. Findlay, "Time: A Treatment of Some Puzzles," *Australasian Journal of Philosophy* 19 (Dec.,1941), 227–228.

42. Wittgenstein, *Blue and Brown Books*, 25.

43. Wittgenstein, *Blue and Brown Books*, 27.

44. *Confessions,* I.8. See Wittgenstein, *Philosophical Investigations* (New York: MacMillan, 1953), 2.

45. Wittgenstein, *Blue and Brown Books*, 26.

46. Wittgenstein, *Blue and Brown Books*, 6.

47. For a discussion of this aspect of Wittgenstein's analysis, see Berislav Marusic, "Wittgenstein on Time," *Synthesis Philosophica* 16 (2001), 97–101. See also, S. R. Doss, "Copernicus Revisited: Time versus 'Time' versus Time," *Philosophy and Phenomenological Research* 31, no. 2 (Dec. 1970), 193–211.

48. Wittgenstein, *Blue and Brown Books*, 26.

49. Wittgenstein, *Blue and Brown Books*, 2.

*Chapter 3*

# Time after Augustine

James Wetzel

The metaphysics of time, though almost always diverting, is rarely discomforting.[1] I can wonder what time is, come up only with conundrums, and yet still feel intimately acquainted with time by way of my mundane experience. Familiarity in this case breeds contempt of metaphysics. If I were to pose the question of time as Augustine posed it, however, I would find no refuge in time's familiarity, for time's familiarity is part of what has come into question. My ordinary experience of time may not be of time after all. Facing such a possibility is discomforting, but it may also be the beginning of wisdom. In Augustine's hands, metaphysical questions turn back upon their owners. What I ask of time I ask of myself. The wisdom comes, if it comes at all, in coming to understand the demand knowledge of the world has made upon my self-knowledge. There is nothing worth knowing that does not in some way transform the knower. Augustine hints at the transformation called for in the knowledge of time. It is disturbingly profound.

I plan to discuss in some detail the criticism a number of philosophers have made of Augustine's treatment of time: namely, that he confuses a mode of knowing (consciousness of time) with an object of knowledge (time). For now I will suggest that this criticism perpetuates a common misapprehension of Augustine's philosophizing. When he distinguishes inner from outer, spirit from flesh, mind from body, his efforts have little to do with the distinction between subjective and objective, and very much to do with the distinction between reconciliation and alienation, between being at home in the world and a stranger therein. Traversing Augustine's distinctions is a spiritually fraught enterprise, a struggle with the gods, within and without. It is misleading at best, but more likely mistaken, to think of Augustinian inwardness as a retreat to subjectivity. If time is in the mind, as Augustine seems to conclude, it does not follow that time must be an item in a mental inventory or an artifact of immaterial creativity.

Just what does follow, on the other hand, is not easy to determine. Interpreters disagree over whether Augustine offered a definitive answer to the question of time's nature and even more so over whether any putative answer of his stands up to scrutiny. The best interpretations manage to convey some of the religious gravity of Augustine's interest in time.[2] They begin to suggest the fascination and strangeness of philosophy under Augustine's inspiration.

Naturally not all of Augustine's religious concerns can be rendered into philosophy. The truth that faith begins where philosophy ends is a more modern truth than an ancient one, but it holds reasonably well for Augustine. It is hardly of philosophical moment, however, that philosophy has a limit and that something other than philosophy, call it faith if you like, occupies the other side. The philosophical import of a limit to philosophy is not that there is a limit, but that it emerges out of philosophical practice and thus forms part of philosophy's self-definition. Faith has a philosophical genealogy, even for Augustine. His interpreters miss this if they find it too easy to sort out his religious from his philosophical interests. Such ease betrays an idle philosophical imagination, a failure to appreciate the role philosophy can play in the discovery of its own limits. Posed in the right way, the question of time takes philosophy to one of its limits. I believe that Augustine posed the question in the right way. In what follows, I try to follow his lead.

## I

Philosophers who have foraged in Augustine for philosophy generally have found Book XI of the *Confessions* to be of particular promise. Bertrand Russell, who liked his philosophy unmixed with mysticism, lauded this book as "the best purely philosophical work in Saint Augustine's writings."[3] What made it purely philosophical, as far as Russell was concerned, was that Augustine managed for once to put aside his emotional obsession with sin and look at reality dispassionately. The result was supposedly a "better and clearer statement than Kant's of the subjective theory of time."[4] Ludwig Wittgenstein, who liked his mysticism unmixed with philosophy, cited Book XI for its insight into the nature of a philosophical question. There Augustine asks himself, "What is time?" and his immediate reply is to observe that he knows the answer as long as no one raises the question, but when asked for an explanation, he finds himself at a loss.[5] "This could not be said," Wittgenstein comments, "about a question in natural science. Something that we know when no one asks of us, but no longer know when we are supposed to give an account of it, is something that we need to *remind* ourselves of."[6]

I take Wittgenstein and Russell to have adumbrated two basic philosophical approaches to Augustine on time. Inhabit Russell's mindset for a moment. As he sees things, Augustine wants to know what time is, and to this end, he turns his attention to the world outside of his mind's own machinations. Not finding time there as a reality his mind can lay hold of, he turns within and makes time into a creation of his own mind. Augustine's idealism about time is misplaced empiricism. In order to study time, he reduces time to his mind's perception of time, all the while forgetting that his perceptions of time are themselves temporally situated. Regardless of whether Augustine understood himself to be engaged in scientific inquiry, he is, on Russell's way of seeing, refuted by the physics of time.

Wittgenstein's mindset is rather more difficult to inhabit, but in an appropriately modest spirit, I will venture a tentative characterization. If Augustine needs to be reminded of something in order to answer his question concerning time, then he quite properly begins his investigation by directing his attention upon his own mind, or more directly, to his manner of being mindful of time. No competition with a physics of time is in the offing, for Augustine can admit the physicist's way of speaking of time as one possible way—but not the only possible way—of being mindful of time. Augustine calls to mind some of the different ways in which the duration of events may be described. He attends to talk of times divided into long and short, and extended over past, present, and future. These descriptions of time, Wittgenstein insists, are not statements of a philosophical nature.[7] If they were, in calling them to mind Augustine will have succeeded only in perpetuating the vertigo of his moment of departure, when he asks what time is and finds himself estranged from his once familiar world. The impulse to answer a philosophical question philosophically, to make philosophical statements, is the impulse to discover and inhabit a world beyond the world that perplexes, a world more perfect and better integrated than the world of the questioner's ordinary experience. Wittgenstein fights the good fight against this impulse, and he takes Augustine to be an ally. The answer he supposes Augustine to suggest to the philosophical question of time is not a piece of speculation, a subjective theory of time, but a life returned to time, secured from its original estrangement.

To contrast the two approaches I have just sketched, it could be said that Russell has Augustine begin with the world of time, only to lose it over the course of inquiry, whereas Wittgenstein has Augustine first lose his hold on time's reality, then regain it upon reflection. Following Russell, Augustine is engaged in a kind of natural science, though not physics, and following Wittgenstein, Augustine is engaged in a kind of ethical reflection, though not ethical theory. These two readings are far from exhaustive of the possible interpretive approaches to Augustine, and yet they are enough to serve my purposes. I intend to explore Augustine's problem of time, which is the problem not just of Book XI of the *Confessions* but of confession as such, and to suggest along the way why the problem, although philosophical in nature, admits of no philosophical resolution. To these ends, the temptation of Russell's approach to Augustine needs to be overcome, and Wittgenstein's approach needs to be elaborated and qualified.

Russell imagined Augustine to have resolved his problem of time, wrongly as it happens, but resolved in so far as Augustine attempted a resolution. Russell, however, packaged Augustine's problem within a conception of philosophy wholly alien to Augustine's way of thinking. This is not surprising. Augustine mixed philosophy with the mysticism Russell disdained, and true to character Russell sought to disencumber the philosophy from the mysticism. Augustine's own understanding of philosophy changed over the course of his career, but by the time of his *Confessions*, he had tied his philosophy inextricably to the task of confessing. Philosophical problems were for him ultimately problems of confession. Russell missed this connection in Augustine altogether, but not, I think, because Augustine believed in God and Russell did not. There was nothing in Russell's outspoken atheism, which kept him from taking Augustine's theism with philosophical seriousness. Theism, however misguided, marshalled arguments and contended for truth. What really kept him from understanding Augustine was his inability to imagine how philosophy, once demystified, could still take the form of a confession.

Of the great philosophers of the twentieth century, Wittgenstein probably comes closest to sharing Augustine's conception of philosophy, and yet who can say with certainty what Wittgenstein's philosophy was all about? From the *Tractatus* and even more so the *Philosophical Investigations*, it is nevertheless hard not to come away with the impression that Wittgenstein wanted to bring philosophy to an end. In his mind, it was an enterprise doomed to fail, in that it attempted to transgress the logical limits of the language it used, which was, in effect, to transcend the possibilities of meaningful expression. His critique leaves philosophy with a language of exalted nonsense. To speak at all, philosophers are bound to use words whose meanings remain tied to their ordinary contexts of usage, or, better, to the forms of life, which manifest them (meanings are ordinary to those whose lives are ordered by them; the lives so ordered need not be ordinary). When philosophers use their words philosophically, no longer can they mean what they say. The discrepancy between meaning and saying is often the sign of duplicity. It is hard to tell whether Wittgenstein himself sensed something of duplicity in philosophical ambition. If he did, he pressed the charge not least against himself, and the *Investigations* are his confessions. I am not prepared to argue for this;[8]

nevertheless I am convinced that his conception of philosophical perplexity takes in more than a subtle kind of linguistic incompetence. It betokens a restless heart, unable to rest in the world it has been given. Since the world given to us is all the world we have (it includes our possibilities as well as our actualities), Wittgenstein enjoins the philosopher among us, and within us, to look again.

Wittgenstein is Augustinian in his intimation that the need to do philosophy has its profoundest motivation in a disease of mind and will, but in one respect certainly, he and Augustine differ in their conceptions of philosophy. Estrangement from the ordinary is for Wittgenstein where philosophy begins; for Augustine, it is where philosophy ends. Augustine would not have disavowed the philosophical intent of his statements about time in Book XI, Wittgenstein's reading of them notwithstanding. He spoke there of time in order to express and deepen the sense of alienation he was feeling from his habitual truck with things temporal. In confessional philosophy, alienation from the ordinary prefigures confession of sin. To attempt confession and experience alienation is no small achievement, and it is as much as the Augustinian philosopher can hope to achieve.

I am aware of how strange that conception of philosophy must now seem. It should seem strange. Quite some time has passed since philosophers have found it natural and appropriate to begin their philosophical reflections by invoking the aid of the reality they hope to understand. Augustine prays as he reflects and reflects as he prays. He is not a philosopher who happens also to pray, but a philosopher who philosophizes by praying. We grasp his problem of time to whatever extent our conception of philosophy can meet his. My hopes for much of a meeting are perforce modest. Still, I am moved to think that his problem of time can still move us, though we see it through a glass darkly.

## II

The sort of reading Russell gives of Augustine on time is wrongheaded but not stupid. It has a certain initial and obvious appeal, and it is especially apt to seduce interpreters who consider themselves analytically minded. Christopher Kirwan, the Oxford philosopher who has given Augustine his place within the prestigious Routledge series The Arguments of the Philosophers, is a case in point.[9] Kirwan has no trouble identifying what perplexes Augustine about the nature of time. Augustine wonders what enables him to measure stretches of time, and he wonders what enables time to stretch. Kirwan credits Augustine for having recognized that his ability to measure time depends on his ability to retain stretches of time in his memory, but like Russell, he faults Augustine for having identified time with his mind's memory of time. Aside from being implausible on its face, the identification fails to account for time's stretch. For if an extended time is a mystery, an extended memory of time is no less of one. "Nothing in Augustine's argument," Kirwan notes, "recommends his conclusion that times are affections of the mind."[10] Perhaps not. Let's consider the argument.

Augustine's claim that time is for him a mental affection, or a disposition of his mind, is presumably his answer to the question of what time is. That question Augustine poses for himself in chapter 14 of Book XI; its presumptive answer he offers in chapter 27. His argument for his conclusion, or what I am for the moment taking to be his argument and conclusion, will encompass these chapters and what falls in between. Augustine expresses a good deal of initial bemusement over his ability to register the passage of time, because upon reflection, it would seem that he has long been in the practice of measuring what has no substance. The past no longer is, the future is not yet in existence, and the present, wedged between past and future, collapses into a moment without duration. The present has no duration, for were it to endure, it would have either to extend back into the past, which no longer is, or forward into the future, which is yet to be. "So indeed we cannot truly say that time exists," says Augustine at the close of chapter 14, "except in the sense that it tends towards nonexistence (*nisi quia tendit non esse*)."[11] And yet Augustine is hopeful that he measures something when he measures time.

The crucial argumentative transition between time's apparent lack of reality in chapter 14 and time's reemergence in chapter 27 as a mental affection can be found in chapter 20. Augustine turns his attention there to his awareness of time, or to the presence of time in his consciousness. No longer is he content to speak of time solely in terms of the past, present, and future. The past, as we customarily think of it, has passed on, and yet the past, as we are aware of it, remains with us in some fashion. Similarly with the future, the awareness we now have of the future is not in the future, but present. Augustine asks us to put aside the customary talk of time as past, present, and future in order to entertain the thought of a temporally comprehensive present. In words to capture such a thought, he refers us to "a present of things past, a present of things present, and a present of things to come."[12] These three modes of the present dispose the mind to reflect in different ways. We remember what is gone, sense what is here, and expect what is to come. Past, present, and future are present to us as memory, sensation, and expectation.

From this point on it will be convenient to have terms to refer to Augustine's two different ways of speaking about time. Let "intended time" refer to time insofar as time has been retained in the mind. The present of intended time is able to encompass past, present, and future. Let "distended time" refer to time as it has been abstracted from the mind and divided over past, present, and future. These divisions never coincide. The present of distended time, excluding past and future, includes only itself. Distended time has something to do with time's stretch or extension; intended time something to do with time's measurement. Though distinct, these two ways of speaking of time are mutually dependent. Without distended time, there would be no time to be retained. The intended present would be empty. Without intended time, there would be no way to determine the present of distended time. The distended present would be unintelligible. Somehow the intention and distention of time come together to reveal what time is. But how?

In chapter 20, Augustine contends that it is imprecise to speak of time as distended over past, present, and future, as if these designations could really exist apart from the mind that employs them. When he continues this theme in chapter 27, but there apparently as his answer to the question of what time is, Russell and Kirwan conclude (not unreasonably) that Augustine has reduced distention to intention, thereby making time into an artifact of human psychology. The key passage reads as follows:

> It is in you, my mind, that I measure my times *(tempora mea)*. Do not clamor at me, or rather, do not clamor at yourself, with your disorderly mob of affections. In you, I say, I measure times. The affection *(affectionem)*, which times passing make in you and which remains after they have passed, is what is present for me to measure, not the times which have passed to make it. Affection is the very thing I measure when I measure times. Therefore either times are the very times [they are in affection], or I measure not times.[13]

The "times" Augustine measures in his mind are, I presume, past, present, and future. For most of the passage, Augustine is advancing an unexceptional claim. Consciousness of time's passage is impossible unless there is a distinction between the past as no longer present and the past registered in the mind as no longer present. The latter, an affection of the mind, remains present. The same goes for the future *mutatis mutandis.* In other words, intended time is not reducible to distended time. Reduction in the other direction should also be ruled out, but in the last line of the passage, Augustine seems to depend upon it. Past, present, and future are either in his mind's affection, or he does not measure them.

The meaning of the concluding disjunction is not obvious, but whatever it means, it cannot be that Augustine takes exception to the unexceptional claim I have attributed to him. Russell supposed otherwise. He took Augustine to imply that time cannot exist outside of the mind measuring it. On this theory of time, there is no time, but only a timeless present which includes everything remembered (falsely) to have happened and everything expected (misguidedly) to happen. I will refrain from belaboring the absurdity of such a view. Augustine commits himself to this absurdity only if he has conflated the present of intended time with that of distended time. While it is true that I remember only what I can bring to mind, or what becomes present to me psychologically, it is equally true that I need not be remembering now. My remembering admits of distention backward into the past and forward into the future. Augustine seems to have grasped this point well enough. If he had conceived of past and future as folding without remainder into an instantaneous present, what could he have meant by a "present of things present" (*praesens de praesentibus*)? The designation suggests the distinction between temporal awareness (present as "present to mind") and temporal location (present as "happening now"), and I see no reason not to take the suggestion. As Augustine invokes it, the presentness common to past, present, and future refers to what he can know of time. It is not the content of this knowledge, but its mode of acquisition, that is the concern of the passage cited.

Nothing I have said so far gives an adequate response to Russell, Kirwan, and the host of other philosophers who have found in Augustine a challenge to the objectivity of time. Grant for the moment that Augustine never intended to reduce time to his mind's affection. When he associates time and affection in chapter 27, he must mean to claim instead that his awareness of past and future is neither past nor future *qua* awareness. A hard claim to contest, but one hardly to the point, if the point is to answer the question of what time is. Unless more is going on in Book XI, there will be little philosophical motivation to read Augustine other than as a subjectivist about time. For if he is not a subjectivist, he has dropped his question. Needless to say, I think that more is going on.

When Augustine presses his claim that his measure of time is affection, he presses it against his own mind, whose disorder has surfaced to subvert his comprehension of time at the very moment comprehension seems near to hand. "Do not clamor at yourself," he enjoins it, "with your disorderly mob of affections." The philosophical commentaries I have read treat Augustine's internal dialogue as if it were rhetorical flourish. They pass over it. This practice is unremarkable if Augustine simply takes his own admonishment as a matter of course. Clearly, however, he does not. His mind's disorder never ceases to interfere with his efforts at understanding. Thus, does he lament in chapter 29: "I am scattered in times whose order I do not understand. The storms of incoherent events tear to pieces my thoughts, the inmost entrails of my soul."[14] If affections are revelatory of what time is, then Augustine's tell him that time is, after all, *his* tendency not to exist. If this is to reduce time to the subject who experiences time, it is reduction with a vengeance.

The question of interest here, however, is not of whether Augustine has reduced time to his experience of time (he has in some sense) but of what he takes his experience of time to be. There is a world of difference between the world of the ordered mind and the world of the disordered mind. Suppose that my mind were ordered in Augustine's sense of ordered. My experience of the world would then contain the experience of time within it, and I come to know time by acquaintance. A further question of time takes me beyond time's familiarity, toward an extraordinary way of being affected. If I were, say, to think of time as being subject to my mind, that would be for me to think of my mind's affection of time in an extraordinary way. Ordinarily I think of myself as subject to time. To a mind aware of its own disorder, as Augustine confessed his to be, time's familiarity is not only good enough, it is a consummation devoutly to be wished. The question of time connects up with a feeling of lost intimacy. How could something as familiar as time have become so foreign? Asked in this manner, it is not clear which is the object of inquiry: time or perplexity about time.

Soon after Augustine asks himself what time is, he goes on to describe time as the absence of time, that is, as a present stripped of its past and future and having no time of its own. His meditation on time thus begins in paradox. Time distended is no time at all. Later in the meditation, when he shifts to the idiom of intended time and wonders what he has in mind, he is asking himself whether his affection still registers distention. His answer is that it does, but his answer means little apart from the recognition that goes with it. Augustine's manner of being perplexed by time has everything to do with whether his original question admits of an answer.

### III

Although time is of an essence in Book XI, where confession calls for time's reclamation, timelessness is nevertheless what Augustine keeps describing there. His apophatic approach to his main concern, which those of a mystic bent might well appreciate, will be lost on everyone else, unless he can take for granted that time is not wholly unknown to anyone. The assumption is not unreasonable, given that most of us are apt to feel more at sea with the idea of timelessness. For a good bit of his life, Augustine must have felt similarly. But by the *Confessions*, he has come to recognize the experience of timelessness in himself. He invokes it in Book XI when he tries to remind himself of time under the description of that which tends not to exist. What he recalls tends not to exist, but it is his memory of time, and not time itself, which answers to the description. In trying to recall something forgotten, Augustine has managed to recall only the forgetting.[15] His time is neither in his mind nor quite out of it. He suffers from a condition of vertigo best treated by apophatic therapy.

Before I say more about this, I want first to forestall a confusion or two. When I speak of Augustine as having forgotten time, I am not advancing the ridiculous claim that he has forgotten that time exists, or even the less ridiculous claim (but only slightly) that he cannot recall a theory of time he once had. What I am advancing can perhaps best be grasped by way of analogy. When I forget myself, I do not normally forget that I exist. I act or think out of character, as if my motives were those of another person, one disposed to love or to hate in ways very different from my own. Putting aside the possibility of play-acting, my motives will have emerged out of a lapse in self-consciousness not inappropriately described as a forgetting, though a forgetting more likely than most to lead me through a labyrinth of opaque passion. I cannot but be puzzled at myself in retrospect. At least some of my desires seem to lead a life of their own, and yet they are, in a sense I have still to discover, mine.

Freud reminded moderns of psyche's debt to eros. Augustine, being closer to Plato in both time and sensibility, needed no reminding. His meditation on time traffics heavily in eroticized knowledge. Omit eros from his meditation, and the confession it attempts to convey degenerates into idle, somewhat ludicrous, speculation. Except to a mind disposed to want otherwise, there is little to recommend Augustine's conclusion that time is other than the distention, which renders time into an absence. As a claim about time, it is about as exciting as the claim that time exists. His supposed claim of substance, that time is in his mind's affection, fares no better. Either he has bizarrely made himself into the creator of time (if he thinks that his time includes all of time), or he has advanced a near tautology as if it were news, that his awareness of time must be an aspect of his psychology. An alternative to choosing between the two is to read him as raising a question rather than answering one. If time is not time's undoing, not the tendency not to be, how is a mind affected, which wants to see time undone, and reduced to nothingness? That is the question Augustine has made of his question of time. It has the feel of asking a self having forgotten itself, what sort of self are you trying not to be?

With Augustine, insight into motives almost always involves rediscovering the difference between being God and being human. As an intellectual mistake, the conflation is obtuse, but as it is rarely if ever an intellectual mistake, it admits of endless variation and appears to be endlessly tempting. Eros has its own kind of genius, and as any lover knows, eros rules over time. In the confession of Book XI, Augustine tries to see through love's greatest deception, the masquerading of time as eternity. The context being confessional, he can claim at most partial success. He still wants too much to have what passes for time to God.

This is desire without a well-defined object. Augustine speaks of God's relation to time in the opening chapters of Book XI, and he conceives of God as exempt from the passage of time. There is no waiting for God, no dissipation of the present into past or future, but all of time comprehended eternally.

"In the eternal," Augustine surmises, "Nothing is transient, but the whole is present."[16] In light of what he says later on in the Book about his own human psychology of time, he seems here to suggest a theory of God's psychology. Just imagine a mind that has in mind all that ever was or will be and all that ever might have been or might be, and who knows which is which. But at the close of Book XI, he rejects the suggestion outright. "Far be it from you," he says of God, "to know all future and past events in this kind of sense. You know them in a much more wonderful and mysterious manner."[17] The meaning of what has gone before, not only in Book XI but in the earlier books as well, turns on what Augustine's disclaimer is taken to imply.

I take it to imply that there is no analogy between divine and human manners of knowing time. The content of the knowledge may be comparable (as imperfection is comparable to perfection), but the manner of having it is not. Perhaps it is best not to speak at all of a manner of knowing in reference to God, for a mysterious manner retains the impress of a manner, and that is impression enough to be misleading. Augustine speaks as if he has come to know how little he knows of God's manner of knowing, but that cannot be what he means to imply. He has not got into God's mind and got lost; the mysteries he has arrived at knowingly are his own. The other mysteries, the ones he ascribes to God, define the grammar of his theology. They set the limits to what he will entertain as a meaningful claim about God.

Taken epistemologically, the mystery of God's manner of knowing time hints at a uniquely powerful mode of comprehension, far superior to the human. Taken grammatically, it suggests that there is no God-like experience of time for humans to covet. It is not that God has an experience of timelessness instead, but more that time is not a matter of what God experiences. The epistemological reading tempts us to want more than a human experience of time, as in God's "experience" of eternity. The grammatical reading exposes the confusion behind the temptation. Apart from finitude, the experience of time is not intelligible. To eyes that will see, this point of grammar is illuminating. Finitude being no impediment to knowledge, we have no motive not to trust our experience to inform us of what time is. Time is a matter of what we experience. Really to acknowledge this would be to stop viewing time as a puzzle or a burden and accept it as a gift.

Had Augustine been able to do just that, Book XI never would have been a book of confession. The oddness of the situation he describes there is that he finds himself moved to distend time into oblivion, even though he has no intelligible motive to do so.[18] Time is a problem for him because his heart cannot accept what his mind is telling him, that time remains. If there is a meaning to his heart's discontent, it will have to invoke more than the usual human apprehensions about mortality. Death is answered by having time returned; the picture tempting Augustine is of time being snatched away by nothingness. It is no more a usable picture of time than is eternity. Nevertheless Augustine is wed in his own way to both, for part of him seeks to transcend time altogether. In chapter 27, his mind catches his heart torn between its two impossible aspirations for timelessness, one born of a desire to be as God is, the other born of a desire no longer to be human. If in the end, these come to the same desire, it is the desire no longer to be. In the meantime, there is Augustine's struggle to reclaim a human way of living with time, a way of remembering. But the part of himself he needs most to recall to time, the part in love with time's absence, he finds hardest of all to reach. Followed along the lines of this perplexity, his problem of time undergoes its most telling transformation; it becomes the problem of sin.

## IV

If Augustine is confessing that he knows time as his mind knows affection, it is worth considering what he has in mind to know. Affection, and what the mind can know of it, is a concern of the *Confessions* as a whole. His masterpiece of self-revelation, though admittedly multileveled, is above all an experiment in memory, whose object has been to recollect sin. I say "sin" and not "sins" deliberately, for Augustine's interest is more in motive than in act. The sin behind his sins, or his sinful affection, is what he most wants to recollect and confess. But whether perversity of love or of deeds is understood to be his chief concern there, most commentators read it as the record of a prodigious memory. My own judgment is to the contrary. His *Confessions* tell the story of a failed experiment in memory. This is not to say that they fail as art, religious meditation, or philosophy. In these aspects, they warrant their reputation. My claim is only that they fail as the recollection of sinful affection. Augustine was aware of this, and it was the failure he sought to represent.

I will confine my attention to a paradigm case, his attempt in Book II to recall sin out of an act of theft. Augustine has no difficulty calling to mind what might be termed "the sensible description" of the episode in question, or what a third party could have observed at the time and place described. A group of young adolescents, Augustine among them, set out at night to divest a neighbor's pear tree of armfuls of pears. More taken with forbidden fun than with fruit, the boys eat a perfunctory bite or two of the purloined pears and then throw the lot to hogs. Augustine dispenses of sensible description with a sentence or two in chapter 4 of Book II; sensible description passes lightly over questions of motive, and it is motive that weds us to what we do. Augustine cannot confess an action as his own until he can comprehend what good or combination of goods moved him to act. Success here would give him the intelligible description of his action, the description that renders his sin confessable.[19]

Over the next six chapters Augustine agonizes over his inability to understand what moved him to sin. He looks for a motive first in the sensuous delight of pear-eating, but recalls that the pears he and his friends stole were of "untempting color and taste." He then considers the need he had for the approval of peers, to steal so as not to appear cowardly in their eyes. He understands why sin loves company (we take our friends where we can find them), but it remains a mystery to him why company should love sin. Augustine finds himself driven to conclude that no good outside of the good of sin itself could have moved him to sin. But what is the good of sin? He cannot recall. Instead of resolving his puzzle, his appeal to sin's motive tightens the "tangled knottiness" that recollection has already made of his memory. "The confusion repels me," he admits, "I don't want to have it in mind; I don't want to behold it." What sounds like confession is here its antithesis. Augustine has not owned up to his past; he has absented himself from it. Having searched his memory for a lover of sin, he finds in its stead a "space emptied by desire" *(regio egestatis)*.[20] It is no wonder that the result repels him. The affection he begins to recollect having is the love of his own absence.

As his confession of Book II ends, he is still tied to the sin he would, if he could, first claim and then disavow. Sin perplexes him because he can confess sin only as an end of desire, and yet he can recollect sin only as desire without an end. His memory of having tasted forbidden fruit, which is a memory of original sin, introduces the form of unintelligibility which will frame all of his subsequent recollections of sin. Until sin is recollected as sin, it finds its motive somewhere amid the host of material pleasures and social goods taken to be ordinary ends of human desire. Once recollected as sin, it loses this motive. Something more was sought than was once realized, and this something more moves the sinner beyond ordinary desires for material and social goods, or what Augustine calls the "most limited of goods" *(extrema bona)*.[21] These goods continue to be desired, but always immoderately and always for the sake of some other good, whose nature is hard even for the repentant sinner to fathom.

It requires little in the way of psychological acuity, of course, to recognize in Augustine's description of his boyhood prank his obvious motive for having stolen the pears. He wanted to secure the affection of his companions. It takes rather more acuity to recognize why the obvious motive cannot serve as the answer to the question Augustine poses of his past. He wants to know not why he stole, but why he sinned. These are not queries of the same order, or better put, they are queries that speak to different orders of thievery. One act of theft is over and done with; it had pears as its object. In itself it is hardly worth a second thought. Another act of theft, linked symbolically to the trivial theft, is still in the making. Its intended object lies obscured along a *via negativa*; it is not pears or even companions that the thief wants. The pears are discarded; the names of the companions forgotten.

When Augustine takes his recollection of sin's empty-handed thievery to other times, his memories of what he has forgotten or discarded leave him with the dull and persistent pain of absence. In Book IV, he recalls having forgotten a childhood friend, whose death had made him "live by half," and in Book VI, he recalls having discarded the mistress he loved, whose loss had "bloodied his heart." These losses communicate the desperation of a thief who gets nothing from thieving. In Book II, where a kingdom is lost for want of a pear, Augustine sets out the theme upon which all confession thereafter, in all of its intensified expression of longing and grief, is but variation. In Book II, he tries to remember what he wanted out of sin, and as long as he is not reflecting on sin as such, the answers come readily, there and elsewhere. Ordinary motives suffice. He took some pears to keep some friends. He refused to accept a friend's mortality because he could not accept his own. He sent away his lover in order to please his mother. Where is sin's motive in all of this? Faced with this question, Augustine cannot rely on ordinary motives. They leave him in love with the most limited of goods, and out of sin he seeks some further, still sought for, beloved.

Augustine begins his meditation on time by speaking of time as a distention into nothingness. He ends by putting himself in time's place: "Look and see," he asks of God, "the distention is my life."[22] His petition is despairing, even as it seeks the consolation of a faithful despairing. It is despairing because of what Augustine sees. His love has been claimed by sin, and still he cannot recall the love that claims him. Having failed to bring sin into his time, he sees himself taken up into sin's time, into an alienated present, lost to its past and without expectation of a future. The note of consolation sounds in his recognition that sin's time is not time but time's absence. He has described time not as he has been given it, but as he has given it up. If the time given up can somehow be got back, then forgiveness is not impossible, just incomprehensible. To look at time through God's eyes is to see life gathered from death, a distention inverted.

## V

In one of his many odd and intriguing comments about the nature of philosophy, Wittgenstein put forth that philosophical perplexity is always a problem of the first person. The problem takes the form of a confession of alienation, or an admission that "I don't know my way about."[23] In form,

Augustine's problem of time answers to Wittgenstein's description of philosophical perplexity. Sin's resistance to recollection has robbed him of ordinary time and ordinary motives. He confesses in Book XI that he does not know his way about. Philosophy can help him to articulate the emptiness of the time left to him, but it cannot lead him home. The space emptied in him by desire is not filled by yet more desire, not even the desire for wisdom.

Since I write as a philosopher, there is little more I can add, other than a few comments about the limit, which has been reached. In the experience of time's absence, there is no time to follow time's emptiness, and therefore no intelligible hope for a time to come. Augustine nevertheless finds something of hope in his life's distention. In Augustine, memory is a gathering place for time. There the mind takes in time before and time after, albeit in a dim light. Having made affection the measure of his times, Augustine presents himself with a disjunction. Either time returns to him in affection, or his affection is of time's absence. Time is a problem for him because he knows the truth of the disjunction without knowing the truth of either side. The affection he would use to measure time he remembers only as the shadow of an affection. Sin is the dimness in the light. In Augustine, memory is a place of disaffection.

Somewhere between a word and gesture, there is a meaning to a memory thus disaffected. I will try a gesture with words. Affection is not the idiom we would expect Augustine to use to describe how he measures time. Duration is not usually a matter of desire or disposition, and to avoid an odd assimilation of the two, translators have often rendered the *affectio* to be measured as "impression" (as if measuring an impression of time were an easier notion to comprehend). In this case, however, the assimilation is intentional on Augustine's part. Eros still rules over time in his mind. He illustrates this for us in his attempts to recollect sin. Whenever he calls sin to mind, he notices the limitation of material and social goods. They elicit desire, but do not satisfy it, even though they seemed at one time to have provided satisfaction. In memory, where time is retained, satisfaction has resolved itself back into desire. "No longer" becomes "not yet." Time is undone. Desire's reemergence out of sin's recollection coincides, as it would have to, with sin's distention of time. The paradox that results is twofold: time is emptied of duration, and desire is emptied of aim.

There are two ways to envision the requital of a disaffected memory. In one, desire is eliminated, so that there is nothing to tie the mind to a past or a future. Memory is made over into the image of time's absence, that of an eviscerated present, and the mind knows the vacancy of timelessness. In the other, desire is transformed, so that the mind loves only what God loves. In God's love, there is no lack. Whoever loves as God loves lacks for naught and knows the plenitude of time.

The problem with both these ways of requital is that they come too late. Once desire is on the scene, it can be repressed, but never willed not to be. Even the most determined of ascetics understands this, for the ascetic wills the transformation of worldly desire into love of God, and not the simple elimination of worldly desire. But love's transformation cannot be willed any more readily than its elimination. Augustine can neither eliminate nor transform his paradoxical love of having nothing to love, his sin's love of absence. His affection therefore tells him that his time is out. Having commanded his mind to see through the disorder of its affections, to cure its own disaffection, Augustine is finally forced to admit that his mind has been unwilling to obey its own command.

Self-contradiction distends the mind between two illusions of timelessness, between a present having expelled its past and future, and a present having consumed them. The one is needed for the mind to get outside of itself; the other for the exile to be registered as contradiction. The distention is of the mind's own making, the invention of its affections. In the time the mind has not invented, we stand before God, and because God never lacks for a beloved, we who are beloved are given what we need, the time of our lives. "The real discovery," Wittgenstein said of himself, "is the one that makes me capable of stopping doing philosophy when I want to."[24] If I follow Augustine, the real discovery would be to discover that I want to. Then I would understand that I cannot steal what has already been given to me. My time is mine to accept. I await my resolution. Such is the expectancy at philosophy's end.[25]

## NOTES

1. The original version of this chapter was printed in *Religious Studies* 31 (1995), 341–357.

2. I know of two especially good examples: Robert Jordan, "Time and Contingency in St. Augustine," *Review of Metaphysics* 8 (1954–5), 394–417, and John Cavadini, "Time and Ascent in *Confessions* XI," in *Collectanea Augustiniana 2: Presbyter Factus Sum*, edited by Joseph T. Lienhard, S. J., Earl C. Muller, S.J., and Roland J. Teske, S.J. (New York: Peter Lang, 1994), 171–85. In different ways, Jordan and Cavadini argue that Augustine's valuation of eternity does not imply a devaluation of time. Indeed the problem of time lies in our having to acknowledge a time-bound life as a life God could value. Being resentfully mortal, we scarcely believe this possible. That at least is the interpretation of Augustine I take from them. Its deep influence on my own way of reading him will be evident later on.

3. Bertrand Russell, *A History of Western Philosophy* (New York: Simon and Schuster, 1945), 353.

4. Russell, *History*, 355. See also his *Human Knowledge: its Scope and Limits* (New York: Simon and Schuster, 1948), 212.

5. Augustine, *Confessions (Conf.)*, 11.14.17.
6. Wittgenstein, *Philosophical Investigations (PI)*, no. 89. For citations of Wittgenstein, I will be using the third edition of G. E. M. Anscombe's translation (New York: MacMillan, 1953).
7. Wittgenstein, *PI*, no. 90.
8. But see Philip R. Shields, *Logic and Sin in the Writings of Ludwig Wittgenstein* (Chicago: University of Chicago Press, 1993). He finds a religious sense of sin in Wittgenstein's philosophical concern with violations of language. I find it there too, but it goes beyond my present concerns either to assess the elegant case Shields makes for his conclusion, or to advance a case of my own. In the main, I invoke Wittgenstein to serve as foil for Augustine.
9. Christopher Kirwan, *Augustine* (London and New York: Routledge, 1989), especially 182–186.
10. Kirwan, *Augustine*, 185.
11. *Conf.* 11.14.17. Except where otherwise noted, I will be making use of Henry Chadwick's translation of the *Confessions* (New York: Oxford University Press, 1991).
12. *Conf.* 11.20.26.
13. *Conf.* 11.27.36. The bracketed words are my interpolation of what Augustine's Latin implies but does not explicitly state: *Ergo aut ipsa sunt tempora, aut non tempora metior*. Many translators, Chadwick included, have taken the *ipsa* to refer back to *affectionem*, but if that were so, why the plural verb form *sunt*? More likely *ipsa* (neuter plural) corresponded to an ellipsed *tempora*. My thanks to Andrew Keller for help on this point of syntax.
14. *Conf.* 11.29.39.
15. See *Conf.* 10.16.24, where Augustine tries to understand what is remembered in a memory of forgetting.
16. *Conf.* 11.11.13.
17. *Conf.* 11.31.41.
18. In *The Blue and Brown Books* (New York: Harper & Row, 1958), 26–27, Wittgenstein makes mention of Augustine's trouble with time and offers a partial diagnosis. The word "measure" admits of more than one usage, and although we often speak of measuring a length of time, it does not follow that measuring time is just a special application of measuring length. If Augustine is beside himself over the prospect of having to take the measure of what exists only in passing, he appears to have succumbed to a misleading analogy. It is not clear to me whether Wittgenstein intended his remarks to hold as criticism of Augustine. But suppose he did. His criticism is not wrong, but it leaves open the crucial question of motive. What is so seductive about the analogy, which robs time of its measurability?
19. I base the distinction between sensible and intelligible description on Augustine's distinction between sensible and intelligible perception. The latter is his most explicit debt to Platonism. See *City of God* 8.6.
20. *Conf.* 2.10.18. Here and earlier, my translation.
21. *Conf.* 2.5.10. Chadwick gives an elaborate translation of the term: "things which are at the bottom end of the scale good."

22. *Conf.* 1.29.39. My translation.
23. *PI*, no. 123.
24. *PI*, no. 133.
25. Earlier versions of this chapter were presented before the Humanities Colloquium at Colgate University and the Department of Philosophy at Northern Arizona University (NAU). I am thankful to many people for help and encouragement. I would like to give special recognition to Anne Freire Ashbaugh, as well as to George Rudebusch and Dave Sherry, my hosts at NAU.

*Part II*

# TIME, LANGUAGE, AND SONG

*Chapter 4*

# Living as Singing

## *Augustine's Understanding of the Voice of Creatures in the* Confessiones

Makiko Sato

In his *Confessiones*, Augustine several times expresses himself as though mutable things in the world have their own voice. For example, he says that heaven and earth cry out that they did not make themselves (*clamant etiam, quod se ipsa non fecerint*).[1] Why does Augustine speak as if these things have their own voices? Is he just imitating the rhetoric of personification that he saw also in Platonist texts and the Bible? This simply cannot be the case. In the *Confessiones* and especially in book 11, where Augustine presents a theology of time, "voice" is one of the key words of his argument. This chapter addresses three points of Augustine's understanding of the voice of creatures. First, it examines how Augustine describes the voice of mutable things in order to clarify what meaning he finds in our listening to that voice. Second, it explains how Augustine's expression of the voice of mutable things is based on his understanding of the Creation in the Word of God. This will demonstrate that Augustine interprets the Creation as God's speaking, such that the voice of God in Creation and the voice of creatures are related. The second section will also focus on Augustine's ideas about singing in book 11. This section serves to clarify his understanding of the voice of human beings. The third section of the chapter will then examine arguments in books 12 and 13 to illustrate that Augustine's soteriology is based on his understanding of the three kinds of voices. We will see that Augustine presents salvation of the world as a grand chorus of mixed voices.

## LISTENING TO THE VOICE OF MUTABLE THINGS

For Augustine, the heaven and earth that we see are made or created. As he writes in *Confessiones* 11: "See! Heaven and earth exist. They cry out that they were made, for they undergo change and variation."[2] These mutable things are not the Creator.[3] In this quotation, Augustine does not express this idea by just saying that heaven and earth are made. He expresses it as though they are crying aloud with a voice. Similar expressions are found in other passages of *Confessiones*. For example, in the discourse about the mystical experience at Ostia, Augustine says that he and his mother reflected on how all of the transitory things would say, "We did not make ourselves, but He who remains eternally made us."[4] Next, in the discourse about the quest for God in the first half of book 10, Augustine says that "I interrogated the earth [about what Augustine loves when he loves God], and it said: 'Not me,' and everything in the earth confessed the same . . . . And they cried aloud with a mighty voice: 'He [i.e., God] made us.'"[5] Why does Augustine repeatedly describe these things as if they have their own voices? As Carolyn J.-B. Hammond notes regarding these remarks in book 10,[6] Augustine seems to suggest that his dialogue with things was mental rather than verbal when he states that: "My questioning was the scrutiny I gave them, and their replies showed their beauty."[7] But why does Augustine present his internal mental activity in this way as a dialogue with other creatures rather than with himself or God in himself?

Long before Augustine, Plotinus also used a similar sort of personification, saying that "you will hear [the universe saying] that 'God made me.'"[8] Initially, it might seem that Augustine simply adopts such personification as it is found in Platonist texts. In fact, the motif of ascent to God that leads Augustine to discuss the voices of things does come partially, though not exclusively, from Neo-Platonism. In a sermon, Augustine himself explains the discipline of ascent to invisible things through visible things as the logical thought process of "pagan wise people who are called philosophers."[9] He says that the philosophers knew the artificer from his works.[10] At the same time, as many commentators have pointed out, Augustine's statement reflects the words of Psalm 99/100:3.[11] Also, in Job 28:14, "The deep says, 'It [i.e. wisdom] is not in me,' and the sea says, 'It is not with me.'"[12] John Gibb and William Montgomery add their commentary to Augustine's interrogation of the earth in *Confessiones* 10.6.9, saying that "this is yet another version of the Neo-Platonic discipline, with a scriptural colouring."[13] But does the fact that Augustine uses personification here mean that he was merely "coloring" philosophical discourse with scriptural shades?

It would be rash to rush to that conclusion, because Augustine brings in a distinctively Christian understanding of voice when he describes mutable things as possessing their own voices. For there are many kinds of voices that appear in the *Confessiones* aside from the voices of the external world. As Pierre Courcelle has argued,[14] there are references to voices of each of the parts of the body,[15] the voice of conscience,[16] the voice of carnal custom,[17] the voice of Lady Continence,[18] and the voice of the Truth or the Incarnated Word, all of which talk to Augustine.[19] The imperative voiced by the words "*Tolle, lege*," as is well known, induced Augustine's conversion in book 8.[20] In book 11, Augustine mentions the voice of God at the beginning of creation[21] and our voice when we sing.[22] His interpretation of the Creation by, in, and through the *Verbum* seems to be reflected in his focus on the concept of voice. Attention must be given to how the voice of external creatures, our voice, and the voice of God relate to each other in Augustine's argument.

Let us first consider how Augustine describes the voice of mutable things in the first ten books of the *Confessiones*. According to Augustine, before reading some books of the Platonists, he could not hear the voice of things saying that they are made. Rather, when he tried to return to God, he felt as if physical things were saying to him: "Where are you going, [such] a worthless and sordid fellow?"[23] However, according to the admonition given in the Platonist books and under the guidance given by God, Augustine returned to himself, entered into his innermost parts and there heard the voice of God from on high.[24] Augustine ascends from bodies to his inner power of reasoning, crying out that "unchangeable should be preferred to mutable."[25] After this, in the mystical experience at Ostia, the voices of carnal things (*tumultus carnis*), the things preventing him from returning to God, fall silent, and Augustine hears the voice of mutable things say that "We did not make ourselves."[26] These descriptions show that what Augustine hears depends on what he understands. A philosophical understanding of the hierarchy of mutability and immutability taken from the Platonist writings changes what he hears.[27] Therefore, it is not the case that every human being can hear the voice of created things. In fact, in book 10, Augustine says that animals, who do not have reason, see the beauty of things but cannot interrogate them, and that created things will not respond to interrogators who lack judgment.[28] Augustine here discerns three acts of the human mind: sense perception, reason, and the power of judgment.[29] Even if a person possesses sense perception and reason, such a person does not listen to the voice of mutable things saying that they are made, unless she or he has the power to judge. A man or woman does not understand the voice heard if he or she is not familiar with the language of the voice. The voice of mutable things saying that they are made is heard only by those who have all three of the powers of sense perception, reason, and judgment.[30]

But how is the power to judge distinguished from reason? According to Augustine, human beings are subjected to creatures by love, rendering humans unable to judge.³¹ The order of your love directly affects your power to judge. Augustine himself was overcome by earthy things before reading the Platonist books, with the result that he did not hear the voice of things. After reading those books, however, he cried out that "unchangeable should be preferred to changeable," thereby uttering his cry of love for the immutable thing which is God.³² Augustine also says that it is those alone who are attuned to the outward voice of the beauty of creating things that can understand this voice by measuring it up against the truth that resides within.³³ Augustine does not think that listening consists only of listener and speaker. The assistance of the Truth, which is in the innermost being of one's soul, is necessary. This idea accords with the argument in his *De magistro*: "words have force only to the extent that they remind us to look for things; they don't display them for us to know."³⁴ A bit later in the same text, Augustine adds: "Regarding each of the things we understand, we don't consult a speaker who makes sounds outside of us, but the Truth that presides within, over the mind itself, though perhaps words prompt us to consult Him."³⁵ Listening to the voice of things saying that they are made implies the help of the Inner Teacher. Augustine thinks that this listening to the voice of mutable things is not a completely passive event for the listener, because this listening will not happen when the listener does not understand what is being said. At the same time, the listening is not a completely active endeavor by the listener, because the listener does not understand what the speaker says without the help of the Inner Truth. Listening to the voice of things saying that they are made is a collaboration of the three: the external created things, the Inner Truth, and the human listener. This collaboration occurs when the listener's loves are in proper order.

From the aforementioned context, we can make sense of why Augustine repeatedly expresses the idea that mutable things are made as though they were crying aloud with a voice. Augustine persistently asks the same question to various mutable things, from the earth and the sea and the air to all of the creatures in them, even in book 10, when he has already come to love God and agree that God is the Creator of the entire universe. In the sermon mentioned earlier, as well, he repeats the imperative form *interroga* and induces his audience to question the various things they see outside.³⁶ If the purpose was to simply gain knowledge that is understood by reason, then it would be unnecessary to repeatedly ask the question once understanding has been gained. At that point, you would not need to repeatedly listen to the voice of things. But for Augustine, listening to the voice of created things is not just a representation or confirmation of our ideas about the hierarchy of things. He regards listening to their voice as evidence that he holds the right order of love. To listen to the voice of mutable things is an act that properly positions oneself in the collaboration of the things themselves, the Truth itself, and one's own self. Personifying mutable things in order to give them a voice allows Augustine to connect his account of collaborative listening to his philosophy of love.

## OUR VOICE TO SING

Let us now focus on the sentence of *Confessiones* 11.4.6 mentioned in the beginning of the previous section: "See! Heaven and earth exist. They cry out that they were made, for they undergo change (*mutantur*) and variation (*variantur*)." The change that we see in heaven and earth is regarded as the testimony that the thing is made. This understanding accords with the statement in 10.6.9 that "their response [i.e., the voice of things] was their beauty (*species*)." *Species* is often translated as "beauty," but it can be also translated as a form or the way a thing looks. *Species*, just like *forma*, is a literal translation of the Greek word ιδέα.[37] When we perceive a thing, whether it is visible or invisible, we perceive it as something.[38] As far as it is something, the thing exists.[39] *Species* is regarded as what enables the thing to exist and enables us to perceive it. When you perceive a thing that suffers change, you perceive the same thing losing a certain appearance and receiving another appearance. The appearance is the *species* that we perceive. Thus, it can be said that the change tells you that the *species* is given to the thing, because you see that there is something that previously was not present.[40] Therefore, the change is regarded as the testimony that the thing has been created or made to exist. On this understanding, the creation is not a one-time action. The creation is continuing as long as something exists, at least to our eyes. Listening to the voice of mutable things is to witness the creation in the temporal world.

Beauty and form, two ways of translating *species*, are not contradictory in Augustine, as he accepts the idea of a relationship between formal causes and things that he learned from Greek philosophy. He thinks that things participate in "certain original and principal forms," which are "contained in the Divine intelligence."[41] Thus, forms of things are good, true, and beautiful, insofar as they reflect the divine forms, as Augustine expresses in 11.4.6. The fact that Augustine pays attention to the reflection of the supreme *species* in created things leads us to presume that the idea of the creation in the Word, the voice of God, resonates in Augustine's discussion of the voice of mutable things. In fact, in the following chapter, he starts to discuss God's creation in the Word.[42] He compares God's creativity to a human artificer's creativity. Any human artificer gives a form to a creation, but they always create using materials that already exist in the world. God, however, "spoke and they [i.e., heaven and earth] were made, and you made them in your Word."[43] In this context, the Word is not explained as a tool used for the Creation, like a saw or hammer used by some human artificer. Augustine says "in your Word (*in Verbo tuo*)." It is the locus of the formal cause, the same as "the Divine intelligence"[44] from which the *species* that we perceive have come. Augustine, who regards *species* as the voice of things, keeps in mind the refection of the Word in created things. He does not express the voice of things as merely an instance of rhetorical personification.

However, "word" is not necessarily the same as voice.[45] Moreover, even if the Creation in the Word is a kind of voicing, the nature of the voice of God and the nature of the voice of things must be different. At the end of 11.5.7, Augustine declares that the Creation in the Word is a speech of God, saying that "you spoke and they were made (*dixisti et facta sunt*)." He makes it clear that the creation was done by God's voice. Then Augustine questions how God spoke when he made heaven and earth.[46] To this question, he answers that God speaks everything simultaneously and everlastingly.[47] The voice of God does not suffer change, although the things made in the Word suffer change. How then do they relate to each other? Augustine says that he hears God's voice speaking to him "because anyone who teaches us speaks to us, yet anyone who does not teach us does not speak to us, although he or she speaks."[48] Augustine points out that voice is not just making a sound, but telling something to listeners.[49] Thanks to the voice, the listener can learn what is in the speaker's mind. What is in the speaker's mind does not take up a span of time; it is like when an unplayed song is stored in a computer as data. But when the speaker speaks, the contents are sounded out over a span of time, just like when we press "play" and the song on our computer starts playing, each note passing by in time. What is in the speaker's mind and the spoken word are different, but the listener is given the opportunity to learn what is in the speaker's mind. In the same way, even if the nature of the voice is different, the voice of things can say what the eternal voice says to the listener, just like the song sounding temporally expresses what had been stored up as data. Without the voice of things, human beings cannot begin to understand what is in the Divine intelligence. Thus, Augustine finds a positive role for mutability and the voice of mutable things in our salvation.[50]

In the next chapter, after the above argument about the creation in the Word, Augustine explains his own similarity and dissimilarity to the Supreme Being.[51] The dissimilarity is our mutability. Augustine, a human being, is mutable like other creatures. In fact, in this chapter, he says that he will "cry out: 'How magnificent are your works, Lord, you made everything in Wisdom!'", like the heaven and earth cry out about their being made. He also confesses his terror about the dissimilarity.[52] The mutability of created things is a serious concern for him in view of salvation. Therefore, Augustine expresses his hope for salvation by saying that it is God's mercy, not his own initiative, which will redeem his life from corruption.[53] He seems to move his focus away from the state of the wholly other creatures to the condition of himself as a human being. It is a shift of focus to our voice, the voice of human beings. In the next chapter, Augustine will begin the argument concerning time by answering this question: "What was God doing before he made heaven and earth?"[54] At the conclusion of his argument concerning time, in the final chapter of book 11, Augustine again relates our voice and our singing to our life itself. Throughout book 11, Augustine continues thinking through the relationship of the voice of God, the voice of mutable things, and our voice.[55]

Augustine next turns to the question: "How can time (*tempora*) be measured?"[56] Augustine gives the example of a verse from Ambrose's hymn *Deus Creator omnium*.[57] In the verse, there are short syllables and long syllables. A long syllable is twice as long as a short syllable. Augustine explains how he discerns them, mentioning the working of sense perception in the measuring: "As far as the sense-perception is palpable, I measure the long syllable by the short syllable, and perceive the long syllable having twice length by sense."[58] However, when one syllable starts to sound, the other (previous) syllable has already flown away and exists no more. Where is the syllable that we wish to measure? Augustine's answer is that we are measuring not the syllables themselves but "something in one's memory that was fixed to remain there."[59] Augustine then asserts that it is what is in one's mind that makes the measurement possible.[60] But we do not simply listen to this verse from a hymn; we sing it. Augustine thus leads us to think of the situation of our singing. When we sing a song, the power to measure time is actually necessary, since we intend to utter a long sound and decide beforehand the length of the sound we are about to utter.[61] From this, Augustine focuses on the three actions of mind: to expect (*expectare*), to attend (*adtendere*), and to remember (*meminisse*). When singing a familiar song already known, "my expectation is stretched out toward the whole of the song before I start; once I have started singing, however, as much as I pluck off from my expectation into the past, my memory then is stretched out; . . . but my attention is present at hand, through which what has been about to be is transferred to the past."[62] The three actions of the mind enable us to sing. Singing is a feature of our human voice, which is different from the voice of other mutable things that do not have a rational mind, even though their voice, as *species*, also communicates an idea identical to the one motivating this verse in *Deus Creator omnium*.

What does the ability to sing mean for human beings? Augustine articulates what occurs when a person is singing. He says that what occurs in the whole song (*quod in toto cantico*) occurs (*fit*) also in every part and every syllable of the song, likewise in a longer action, which includes the song, similarly in the entire life of a person, which includes all actions, and also in the total history of human beings.[63] If you understand that "what occurs in the whole song" is the measuring of time, then another question arises: Who in the world can measure the totality of history that remains?[64] It should be noticed that Augustine mentions the concept of totality here. When we sing a song, the song is somehow held in mind as a whole thing (*totum canticum*). With the help of the three actions of the mind, we can perform the song appropriately and sing it all the way through to the end. In the same way, we can conceive the concept of totality within the self; just as we hold a whole song in mind, so can we hold our whole life in mind (perhaps confessing it as a biography) and then perform our life by living it through to the end. As we conceive of the idea of the totality of history, we can perform our history by living our own lives, which are placed in that history. By contrasting the ability to conceive of holding a totality and the possibility of performing something uniquely temporal in the world, which is typified by our singing, Augustine finds a similarity between the voice of humans and the voice of God that creates every mutable thing. Our power to sing suggests our similarity to God, which enables us to hope for salvation.

## LIVING AS SINGING

However, God does not measure time in the same way as we do when we sing, because "nothing in the eternal is passing but everything is present."[65] In fact, Augustine emphasizes the difference between the distension of our lives and the unity of God.[66] God does not need to use the three actions of mind that distend to past and future.[67] Moreover, we humans usually do not know exactly how long we will live, although we do know the length of a song. We do not know exactly what will happen in our lives, although we can know all of the contents of a song. Although we conceive a continuity of our personal identity, our self, in our own mind, the totality of that "self" can be vague, even to ourselves.[68] Augustine mentions the image of shapelessness when discussing his knowledge of himself, such as when he writes of being purified and melted down by divine love,[69] or when he confesses that "he will stand and be solid in God, in his form, by divine truth."[70] He describes himself as unformed matter, which could be molded by the divine form. As confirmed in the previous section, Augustine reveals his idea that every creature receives a form (*species*) insofar as it exists as something. A human being too, as a creature, receives a form, like the other mutable things in the world.[71] However, Augustine thinks that receiving the form in order to exist is not enough for our salvation. In fact, even if we exist as something in the mutable world for now, there is no assurance of our future salvation, if our existence is always just given by the Supreme Being. Even if we can conceive a kind of totality or continuity of self in our mind, how can we gain assurance that our life does not disappear in the wind, just like a sound, when we die?

To consider the question, let us focus on how Augustine thinks of himself as an unformed being that needs a divine form.[72] He develops this idea in his argument on *materia informis* in *Confessiones* 12. He interprets the *terra* that God creates in the beginning as *materia informis*.[73] In 12.6.6, Augustine explains the change in his understanding of the term. At first, he thought that "anything that is free from all forms would not exist." Therefore, he thought of *materia informis* as a materiality possessing innumerable and various forms, rather than none whatsoever. This would have been when he sympathized with Manichaeism, because, at that time, he thought that whatever exists must occupy space.[74] But through his reading of Platonist books, he changed his understanding of formlessness. As he writes:

> I paid attention to bodily things themselves and inspected the mutability (*mutabilitas*) of those things more. By the mutability, they desisted from being what they had been and started to be what they were not. I suspected that this transition from form to form occurred through something that was unformed but was not entirely nothing.[75]

Augustine focuses on mutability in mutable things. Mutability is the possibility of suffering changes. Mutability itself is formless because it does not receive any form. But if it is nothing, it cannot be called even "mutability." Therefore, Augustine thinks that the matter that has not received a form is something that has no form but still exists.

This understanding of *materia informis*, which is developed by focusing on the mutability of mutable things, accords with the thought of Plotinus.[76] But Augustine describes a further development of his understanding in the following chapter.[77] He asks, "Where could *materia informis* exist in any way whatever unless it would exist by way of you, by whom everything whatsoever exist?"[78] Answering his own question, he concludes that God made *materia informis* as that which is nearly nothing (*paene nulla res*) from nothing; God would make from it the great things that we sons of men find amazing.[79] As mentioned earlier, Augustine thinks that form (*species*) is given by the Supreme Being to the mutable things.[80] Here, he expresses his idea that not only form, but also matter that could receive form is made by God. In other words, he thinks that mutability is made by God. This seems to accord with what Augustine sees as the positive role of the mutability of things in our salvation, as described earlier. What then is the importance for our salvation of the fact that mutability is made by God?

It is noteworthy that in book 12, Augustine again mentions singing, connecting the relationship of form and matter to the relationship of song and sound. He says that "song is formed sound (*cantus est formatus sonus*)."[81] Certainly, when you just utter sounds at random, it is usually not called a song. When the sound is uttered under a specific form, like a melody, rhythm, or meter, it can be a song. Augustine explains that sound is prior to form in origin. In the same way, although the matter of something is not prior to its form, neither in time nor in value, formless matter is spoken of as though it were prior in time.[82] It is clear that Augustine is not merely using song as an analogy, since he already described God's creation as his voice speaking to us in book 11.[83] Like song, everyday speech is also sound given form (e.g., by grammar). The speaker generates both the form and the sound in the temporal world. The notion that mutability or unformed matter is made by God surely supports the idea that God's creation is his speaking. As we already noted earlier, Augustine thinks that the changing of things is a testimony of God's creation to our eyes. The mutable world is the word spoken by God. To whom is it spoken? To us who can perceive the mutable world. Then, "What is intended to be brought about through speaking?"[84] Augustine responds to this question by saying that speaking is meant to teach or remind the listener; speaking and teaching remain intimately linked.[85] Augustine says that "also when we are reminded by mutable creatures, we are led to the stable truth where we truly learn."[86] He therefore illustrates our salvation through the image of the relationship of teaching and learning between Creator and creatures. Listening to the voice of creatures is necessary for our salvation, because every one of them is a spoken word of God directed to us for our learning.

Augustine's understanding of himself as unformed matter is continued in *Confessiones* 13. In the beginning of the book, Augustine argues that merely being or existing in itself is not enough for us. He emphasizes the difference between living and living in happiness. "I serve you and worship you so that goodness would be given to me from you," he confesses to God.[87] "From you, the one and supreme goodness," he adds, all mutable things receive "their entire being as 'very good.'"[88] But this in no way means that "being" and "being beautiful" are identical.[89] As a result, simply living is not the same as living in happiness.[90] While Augustine's interest here is in how we are formed by God for our salvation, he returns to his concept of voice. With your calls "happening more frequently with various voices," he declares, "you urged me to listen from far off and to be converted and call upon you who were calling me."[91] Augustine's hearing of God's calling leads to his climbing upward through an inward ascent in the heart.[92] Throughout all of those quotations, the Augustinian concept of voice resonates. But we still have not fully answered our question: Why does Augustine think that we need to utter a voice for our salvation? Why do we need to sing? Preceding his reference to "the song of steps," Augustine says, "My love is my weight; I am carried wherever I am carried. By your gift we are kindled and carried upwards: we burn (*inardescimus*) and ascend." The image of the fire of love accords with Augustine's expression in 11.9.11, where he describes his dissimilarity to God. The term *inardescere* is used in both sentences. Augustine thinks that singing is a process of being molded by the divine form. Now ascending "the song of steps," Augustine adopts the voice of the Psalms: "I was glad when they said to me, let us go to the house of the Lord."[93] Psalms are sung together with others, and this singing together influences each person. Not only do we listen to others' voices; we are listened to by others. This means that what we sing can influence the salvation of others. Singing is the appearance of the ordering of our love toward God and neighbors.

What we sing is not only Psalms. Augustine describes the singing of the song of steps as the way of living that leads us to the life lived in true happiness.[94] Let us remember the argument in book 11, where Augustine described what occurs in singing. Just as we sing a song with the three actions of our mind, we can perform our activities and live our own life by way of those same three actions. Just as we listen to a song, we can perceive other people's activities and their lives. Our life is the song that is sung by our voice and heard by others. This goes not only for one life, but also for a community or an entire human generation. Sadly, our voice does not only say that we are made by God. We can also tell a lie and tempt others not to listen to the truth. Therefore, confession, telling the truth, is the song that should be sung and heard.[95] If you tell the truth, your voice must harmonize with God's voice, because every true being is made by the voice of God. Our lives can produce harmony when the truth is lived. As we showed in the first section, Augustine thinks that true listening occurs when the order of our loves is correct and we collaborate with created things, the Truth and ourselves. Thus, we will be able to listen to the harmony of the voices of the world only when the order of our love is correct. Augustine's image of salvation is a grand chorus of mixed voices. It is the chorus of the voices of creatures and the voice of the Creator.

## CONCLUSION

In *De magistro*, singing and speaking are distinguished, since singing does not necessarily have words. In fact, we, who have not been perfectly formed by the divine form, do not perfectly know the words that we should speak. Our words are not enough when compared to the divine Word. However, for this reason, our life might be regarded as singing. Just as children who start to learn a language do so by singing nursery songs, we too sometimes live our lives non-musically, being out of tune. At other times, we might live more harmoniously. We also listen to other people's voices, just as children do when they learn language. Augustine reminds us that we also listen to the voice of other mutable things. In his *De civitate Dei*, Augustine sings the praises of the beauty and utility of God's creation: "the manifold and varied beauty of heaven and earth and sea, the abundance and marvelous quality of light, sun and moon and stars."[96] According to Augustine, the voice of mutable things is their very beauty, their form, and their *species*. But this beauty is not truly seen by sense perception or reason. The beauty, the voice of mutable things, is clearly heard when the order of your love is correct. Are you listening to the voice of creatures? Are you listening to God's creation? Augustine's voice prompts us to listen to and harmonize with the voices beyond time.

## NOTES

1. Augustine, *Confessions (Conf.)*, 11.4.6. For the Latin text, see: CCSL 27; CSEL 33; BA 14.
2. *Conf.* 11.4.6. English translation is by the author.
3. Subsequently in this passage, Augustine clarifies that he is interested in the category of mutable things (properly speaking), not just physical things.
4. *Conf.* 9.10.25.
5. *Conf.* 10.6.9.
6. Augustine, *Confessions*, Vol. 1, Loeb Classical Library 26, tr. Carolyn J.-B. Hammond (Cambridge, MA: Harvard University Press, 2016), 82.
7. *Conf.* 10.6.9. This is Hammond's translation, not the author.
8. Plotinus, *Enneads*, 3.2.3. Ἐπεὶ οὖν τὸ γενόμενον ὁ κόσμος ἐστὶν ὁ σύμπας, τοῦτον θεωρῶν τάχα ἂν ἀκούσαις παρ' αὐτοῦ, ὡς ἐμὲ πεποίηκε θεός. (*Plotini Opera I. Enneades I-III cum vita Porphyrii* (Oxford Classical Texts), edited by P. Henry and H.-R. Schwyzer (Oxford: Clarendon Press, 1964)). English translation provided by the author. Plotinus also personifies time in 3.7.11 and nature in 3.8.4, writing as if both speak.
9. Cf. Augustine, *Sermon (Serm.)* 241.1–2 (CSEL 101).
10. *Serm.* 241.1: *Hesterno die vobis insinuavimus, sapientes Gentium, quos philosophos dicunt, ipsos qui in eis excellentissimi fuerunt, scrutatos fuisse naturam, et de operibus artificem cognovisse.*
11. See, for example, James J. O'Donnell's commentary on the *Confessions*, Vol. 3 (Oxford: Clarendon Press, 1992), 169.
12. This is the phrasing of the NRSV.
13. John Gibb and William Montgomery, *The Confessions of Augustine* (New York and London: Garland, 1980), 279.
14. Pierre Courcelle, *Recherches sur les Confessions de saint Augustin* (Paris: E. de Boccard, 1968), 291–310.
15. *Conf.* 10.10.17.
16. *Conf.* 8.7.18.
17. *Conf.* 3.6.11; 8.11.26.

18. *Conf.* 9.11.27.
19. *Conf.* 4.12.19; 10.6.10; 13.29.44.
20. *Conf.* 8.12.29.
21. *Conf.* 11.6.8; 11.8.10.
22. *Conf.* 11.27.36; 11.31.41.
23. *Conf.* 7.7.11: *Quo is, indigne et sordide?* The "images of physical things" (*imagines corporum*) are the speakers here.
24. *Conf.* 7.10.16: *Et inde admonitus redire ad memet ipsum intraui in intima mea duce te. . . . Et clamasti de longinquo 'Immo uero ego sum qui sum.' Et audiui, sicut auditur in corde.*
25. *Conf.* 7.17.23: *cum sine ulla dubitatione clamaret inconmutabile praeferendum esse mutabili.*
26. *Conf.* 9.10.25. This is said by "everything transitory" (*quidquid transeundo fit*).
27. Listening to the voice of the heaven and earth is not like hearing sound hitting our physical ears. This voice does not speak in words belonging to any specific language. Cf. *De Trinitate* 15.10.19 (CCSL 50A).
28. *Conf.* 10.6.10: *Nec respondent ista interrogantibus nisi iudicantibus.*
29. There are hints of a distinction between sense perception and understanding in the Gospels: e.g., Mk 4:10–12; Mt 7:24–27, 13:13–15; Lk 10:24, 14:35; Jn 3:31–36, 9:27–41.
30. Cf. the note by Aimé Solignac in his introduction to *Saint Augustin: Les Confessions*, tr. E. Tréhorel et G. Bouissou (Paris: Études Augustiniennes, 1996), 556–7: "Pour Augustin, le monde n'apporte à l'esprit une preuve de Dieu que si l'esprit « interroge » le monde et porte un jugement de valeur sur les être qui le composent."
31. *Conf.* 10.6.10.
32. Carol Harrison, *On Music, Sense, Affect and Voice* (London: T&T Clark, 2019), Ch. 3, clearly and beautifully explains the intimate relationship between understanding God and crying out in joy by appealing to Augustine's *enarratio* on Psalm 99:3. "God is 'understood' not intellectually but in the 'cry of the heart,'" she writes, "in the wordless, jubilant sound of praise, not rationally but affectively."
33. *Conf.* 10.6.10.
34. Augustine, *De magistro (mag.)*, tr. Peter King (Indianapolis: Hackett, 1995), 11.36.
35. *mag.* 11.38.
36. *Serm.* 241.2: *Interroga pulchritudinem terrae, interroga pulchritudinem maris, interroga pulchritudinem dilatati et diffusi aeris, interroga pulchritudinem coeli, interroga ordinem siderum, interroga solem fulgore suo diem clarificantem, interroga lunam splendore subsequentis noctis tenebras temperantem, interroga animalia quae moventur in aquis, quae morantur in terris, quae volitant in aere.*
37. Cf. Augustine, *De diversis quaestionibus octoginta tribus* 46.2 (CCSL 44A).
38. Cf. *De diversis quaestionibus octoginta tribus* 6: *Omne quod est, aut corporeum est aut incorporeum; corporeum sensibili, incorporeum autem intelligibili specie continetur. Omne igitur quod est, sine aliqua specie non est.*
39. Cf. *Soliloquia* 2.5.8 : *quidquid est, uerum est* (CSEL 89).

40. Cf. *Confessiones* 11.4.6: *quidquid autem factum non est et tamen est, non est in eo quicquam, quod ante non erat: quod est mutari atque uariari.*

41. *De diversis quaestionibus octoginta tribus* 46.2: *Sunt namque ideae principales quaedam formae vel rationes rerum stabiles atque incommutabiles, quae ipsae formatae non sunt ac per hoc aeternae ac semper eodem modo sese habentes, quae divina intellegentia continentur.*

42. *Conf.* 11.5.7.

43. *Conf.* 11.5.7.

44. "*Divina intellegentia.*" Cf. *De diversis quaestionibus octoginta tribus* 46.2.

45. Augustine clarifies the difference between word, voice, and sound in his *Sermo* 288. He regards voice as a vehicle of thought. On this, see Takeshi Kato, "La voix chez Origéne et saint Augustin," *Augustiniana* 40, no. 1/4 (1990), 245–258. In this chapter, Kato also examines the voice of God that we hear in *Conf.* 11.8.10. He writes: "La voix est un moyen de communication, non seulement entre les hommes mais aussi entre les hommes et Dieu."

46. *Conf.* 11.6.8.

47. *Conf.* 11.7.9.

48. *Conf.* 11.8.10.

49. Regarding Augustine's understanding of creation as God's teaching, see Makiko Sato, "The Word and Our Words: Augustine's View of Words Based on John 1:3," in *The Theory and Practice of the Scriptural Exegesis in Augustine*, ed. N. Kamimura, Research Report: Grant-in-Aid for Scientific Research (C) 23520098, 33–39.

50. In *Conf.* 10.6.10, Augustine quotes Rom. 1:20. Augustine's positive evaluation of mutable things is based on the Pauline doctrine.

51. *Conf.* 11.9.11.

52. Ibid.: *inhorresco et inardesco: inhorresco, in quantum dissimilis ei sum, inardesco, in quantum similis ei sum.* The image of burning love toward God is mentioned again in 11.29.39 and 13.9.10.

53. Ibid. Context makes it clear that Augustine has a soteriological motivation when he argues about time in book 11. Agreeing with Robert Gillet, Hermann-Josef Kaiser says that "Die Seinsrettung besteht darin, daß—*tempora aeternitatem imitantia* (Aug. *De musica* 6.11.29)—der Bezug zum Sein auf Grund des Geschaffenseins der Zeit nicht verlorengeht." See Kaiser, *Augustinus: Zeit und Memoria* (Bonn: H. Bouvier U. Co., 1969), 24.

54. *Conf.* 11.10.12.

55. Carol Harrison, *The Art of Listening in the Early Church* (Oxford: Oxford University Press, 2013), 230, points out that "in exploring Augustine's *Confessions*, book 11, we saw that listening not only exemplified and illustrated the nature of time but, in a real sense, was identical with it."

56. *Conf.* 11.27.34: *Quo pacto igitur metiri poterit?*

57. The verse is the first line of the hymn that Augustine remembered on the day after the funeral of his mother (*Conf.* 9.12.32). He also cites it in *De musica* 6.2.2; 6.9.23; 6.17.57 (CSEL 102). It is notable that what the verse says accords with Augustine's sense that mutable things cry out.

58. *Conf.* 11.27.35.

59. Ibid.
60. *Conf.* 11.27.36. Augustine's answer was already suggested when he explained how God spoke when he made heaven and earth in 11.6.8. He explained God's audible voice elsewhere in Scripture by arguing that the syllables of that audible voice were temporal, which is how "the external ear announced your [God's] words, which are made in time, to the sagacious mind, whose internal ear is set for your eternal Word." As we confirmed in the previous section, Augustine regards sense-perception, reason, and judgment as necessary for listening. Here, in the case of measuring time, the collaboration of sense-perception and mind is also regarded as necessary.
61. *Conf.* 11.27.36.
62. *Conf.* 11.28.38. Ståle Wikshåland points out the change in the meaning of "present" in the chapter where Augustine describes the act of singing. See Wikshåland, "*Tempus Fugit*: Voice, Intentionality, and Formal Invention in Augustine and Monteverdi," *Journal of Aesthetics and Art Criticism* 66, no. 2 (2008), 133: "The present is no longer a point, not even a point of passage; it is *praesens intentio*, a 'present intention.'"
63. Cf. *Conf.* 11.28.38.
64. Carl G. Vaught, *Access to God in Augustine's Confessions: Books X–XIII* (New York, SUNY Press, 2005), 143, asks: What kind of soul "can hold the entire age of human beings together in the present as well?"
65. *Conf.* 11.11.13.
66. *Conf.* 11.29.39. Terms like *distentio* and *distendere* signify that the three powers of mind dilate in different directions when we measure time. David van Dusen's argument that *distentio animi* means a dilation not of mind but of the senses is suggestive, especially when we consider the concept of voice in book 11, since Augustine pays attention to the neutral position of voice between sensible world and inner world. See van Dusen, *The Space of Time: A Sensualist Interpretation of Time in Augustine, Confessions X to XII* (Leiden: Brill, 2014).
67. Cf. *Conf.* 11.30.41.
68. Regarding the mystery of continuity of "self," see Jaroslav Pelikan, *The Mystery of Continuity: Time and History, Memory and Eternity in the Thought of Saint Augustine* (Charlottesville: University Press of Virginia, 1986), 17–33.
69. *Conf.* 11.29.39: *donec in te confluam purgatus et liquidus igne amoris tui.* Augustine also mentions the image of burning love toward God, just as in 11.9.11.
70. *Conf.* 11.30.40: *stabo atque solidabor in te, in forma mea, veritate tua.*
71. "Form" in Augustine should not be interpreted as quiddity in the scholastic sense.
72. See Sato, "The Understanding of the Variability of an Individual in Augustine: Especially in his Interpretation of Formless Matter," in *The Concept of 'Individual' in Western Thought,* ed. Sumio Nakagawa et al. (Tokyo: Keio University Press, 2007. in Japanese), 53–68.
73. *Materia informis* is the expression found in Wisd. 11:18: *Qui fecisti mundum de informi materia.*
74. Cf. *Conf.* 7.1.1.

75. *Conf.* 12.6.6. *intendi in ipsa corpora eorumque mutabilitatem altius inspexi, qua desinunt esse quod fuerant et incipiunt esse quod non erant, eundemque transitum de forma in formam per informe quiddam fieri suspicatus sum, non per omnino nihil.*

76. Cf. Plotinus, *Enneads*, 2.4.6.

77. Augustine himself, in *Conf.* 12.6.6, suggests that he was further developing what he had learned from Platonism here, saying that: "I desired to know, not [just] to suppose (*sed nosse cupiebam, non suspicari*)."

78. *Conf.* 12.7.7: *unde utcumque erat, nisi esset abs te, a quo sunt omnia, in quantumcumque sunt?*

79. *Conf.* 12.8.8: *fecisti mundum de materia informi, quam fecisti de nulla re paene nullam rem, unde faceres magna, quae miramur filii hominum.*

80. Recall the argument in *Conf.* 11.4.6.

81. *Conf.* 12.29.40. *Cantus* signifies also singing.

82. Ibid.

83. Recall the argument in *Conf.* 11.8.10.

84. *mag.* 1.1: *quid tibi uidetur efficere uelle, cum loquimur.*

85. *mag.* 1.2: *uidetur ergo tibi nisi aut docendi aut commemorandi causa non esse institutam locutionem.*

86. *Conf.* 11.8.10.

87. *Conf.* 13.1.1: *seruiam tibi et colam te, ut de te mihi bene sit.*

88. *Conf.* 13.2.2: *formarentur et essent ab uno te summo bono uniuersa bona ualde.*

89. *Conf.* 13.3.3: *corpori non hoc est esse, quod pulchrum esse.*

90. *Conf.* 13.4.5: *uitam; cui non hoc est uiuere, quod beate uiuere.*

91. *Conf.* 13.1.1.

92. *Conf.* 13.9.10. "The song of steps" is rooted in Psalms 119/120 through 133/134. On voice, see also *Conf.* 13.13.14 and 13.20.26.

93. This is a citation of Psalm 120/121.

94. Cf. *Conf.* 13.9.10: "We burn and ascend by your fire, your good fire, as we ascend upwards 'toward the peace of Jerusalem.'"

95. In this way, Augustine's *Confessiones* is itself a song. See Van Dusen, 96–99, containing a section titled "*Confessions* X to XII: Dialectics and Song," which mentions Jean-François Lyotard's view that the *Confessiones* was a song.

96. Augustine, *The City of God Against the Pagans*, tr. William M. Green (Cambridge MA: Harvard University Press, 1972), 22.24.5, 335.

*Chapter 5*

# Time, Mirror of the Soul

Cristiane Negreiros Abbud Ayoub

In Book XI of his *Confessions*, Augustine of Hippo takes an intriguing approach to the question of time. He refers to time in contradictory terms related to presence and evidence. On the one hand, time is something very familiar to us and undeniably present in our lives. Present, evidentiary features discard any possible doubt about its existence, but we can only examine its meanings and effects in us. That is why time can be approached through a clear and direct question: "what is time?" Nevertheless, on the other hand, as soon as we start to investigate it, this appearance of ease dissolves, and time seems never to be present as a reality in itself. The only thing that is clear concerning this question turns out to be that there is no easy and immediate understanding of it. As Augustine stresses, this play of time conditions our awareness, our thoughts, our actions, our decisions, our perceptions, and our feelings. In short: it conditions us.

In this chapter, I will argue that the methodological framework for understanding time in *Confessions* 11 is still philosophically relevant today. Augustine's text invites his readers to think about how humans experience time. I intend to show that, for Augustine, our relation to time resonates with the intention through which we govern our lives. Therefore, in this precise context, time can be said to be a mirror of the soul.

## SOME PREMISES

It is well known that if we want to understand Augustine's conception of time, we need to read Book XI of the *Confessions*. But if we do so, we will get tricked from the start, since the beginning of the book does not focus on time. Instead, Augustine starts out by organizing his thought by making eternity central to his account of reality. Eternity thus becomes the conceptual touchstone in his analysis of time, which is bizarre because, at first sight, the notions of eternity and time seem to be contradictory. Moreover, given this emphasis on eternity rather than on temporality, the first question posed by Augustine's text to its readers could be: Why is it even necessary to investigate time?

This thematic detour is strategic because it avoids a difficulty that could paralyze the investigation of time. Augustine cannot begin his inquiry by questioning the nature of time in itself, because he is a temporal human being. So how could he examine something that is so mixed with his humanity? This aporia cannot be resolved, because human beings are temporal and cannot escape that fact. In this way, Augustine takes this difficulty to be a philosophically relevant part of his question, and human involvement with time indicates the way this research into time should be conducted. In my opinion, this is one possible reason why Augustine, instead of asking "what is time?" considers human involvement with this question and proposes to deal with another kind of question, which concerns the human interpretation of time. In a few words: time is a situation that necessarily involves humankind. To ask about time always means to ask about the human experience of it, not time in itself.

According to Augustine, human involvement with time is evident in everyone's daily life. We refer to it through words and expressions, such as "long or short time(s)" or "past, present and future." This abundant use of "time" terminology and the fact that we organize our everyday lives using it suggests that we must know what we mean when we talk like this. Nonetheless, when we are faced with the question "what is time?", we fall thoughtfully silent, because we can give no ready and clear answer. This pause gives us the experience of another kind of understanding of temporality and of another quality of time, which seemed to shift to another rhythm guided by our reflection. Here, a perplexity is expressed, and in this gap, we become aware that we live in time without knowing what it is. Augustine writes:

> For what is time? Who could find any quick or easy answer to that? Who could even grasp it in his thought clearly enough to put the matter into words? Yet is there anything to which we refer in conversation with more familiarity, any matter of more common experience, than time? And we know perfectly well what we mean when we speak of it, and understand just as well when we hear someone else refer to it. What, then, is time? If no one asks me, I know; if I want to explain it to someone who asks me, I do not know.[1]

The immobility of this vertigo is avoided by Augustine because he does not begin his argument by asking what time is. He foregrounds his reflection on eternity. Yet by starting with eternity, Augustine is by no means putting himself in the place of or speaking on behalf of the eternal God. Instead, he emphasizes the fact that humans do want to know divine eternity. As temporal beings, humans are governed by the unavoidable desire for eternity, which can only be a kind of disproportionate desire.

The strange amplitude of this desire is a hint suggesting that man is not only temporal but also in contact with eternity, which is what drives this desire. The question of our understanding of eternity and of time is, therefore, placed in a new light. The closer we get to knowing eternity, the more satisfied (and happy) we are. The further we are from knowing eternity, the more anguished we become. This will be made sufficiently clear by the end of our explication of Augustine's argument.[2]

In the first part of Book XI of the *Confessions* (11.1–17), eternity is identified with the ever-present Principle (*principium*) of Genesis 1:1. For Augustine, this Principle also goes by the following names: Son, Christ, God, Lord, Truth, Virtue, Wisdom, merciful Mediator, and Creator of the entire universe. It is the light that shines upon us from within, as well as the Word that speaks so intimately to us from within. Commenting on Genesis 1:1, Augustine defends the idea that, if this Principle or "beginning" made all creatures, it has to be prior to them. But since this Principle is eternal by definition, and since this Principle exists before temporal reality, would it be correct to say that eternity exists before time? Yes and no.

If we imagine that eternity existed chronologically before time was created, then the answer must be "no." Indeed, this argument is misplaced, since it inserts eternity into the course of time. And if we were to "temporize" eternity, it would not be eternity, which should be completely timeless. On the other hand, we may answer "yes" to the question above insofar as divine eternity possesses a causal anteriority because it creates all creatures (including time) out of nothing. Thus, the existence of time (and of all creatures) depends on the causal anteriority of eternity, but not on its chronological precedence. Moreover, anteriority is also to be understood in the sense that the human soul must be illuminated by the light of eternity in order even to begin to think about time in an unambiguous way. In this last sense, for Augustine, a meditation on time starts from human contact with eternity. But in what sense could a temporal being have access to eternity or an eternal God? Eternity itself (which is also called by Augustine "Word" and "mercy") makes this possible by establishing the intimate and transcendent presence of Truth in the soul. In this way, the human investigation into time depends on eternal Truth, which is always illuminating us from within.

But how can this investigation be conducted based on human temporal understanding? Eternity must be approached by a process of discrimination. When trying to grasp the meaning of eternity, we are forced to reject thoughts concerning temporality. Now that we have clarified the foundational role played by eternity in Augustine's thought, let us turn back to the question of time proper.

## THE INTERNAL REALITY OF TIME

If we feel time passing and measure time as an object, this suggests that time exists as a creature different from us. However, we cannot know it as a separate, "objective" thing apart from us. The investigation into time depends on our human sensation and measurement of it. So how do we feel time existing in itself?

It is a matter of fact that we experience time as coming from the future, passing through the present, and ultimately becoming past. But how real are these future, present, and past times? Augustine makes it clear that it is what is felt about the future that is real, not the future time itself, which does not yet exist. Despite its nonexistence, however, it is felt as expectation. And this expectation seems to take place in this present. What then about past time? It refers to what has happened and passed away. This past time does not exist in itself anymore as a reality, but its memory remains inside us. Does this mean that time, as a creature, could be real only as present time? At first, this seems plausible. But when we try to hold on to the present existence of time, it seeps into the past, which no longer exists. This indicates that only one *ictus* (moment) can be present, and even this could be divided into three successive times with no fixed existence.

Now if time is so elusive, how can we explain the fact that we count, compare, and ascribe duration to times? What can we say about our custom of talking about future and past events? These times, impermanent in the realm of exteriority, refer to an interior presence. It is just inside of us that the future, present, and past have some reality for the thinking soul. Therefore, in this aspect, time is an inner reality. Augustine develops this insight into a full-fledged picture of temporality.

In memory, there are images of sensations, imaginations, past experiences, and present ideas. Thus, the past consists of the presence of what has passed (outside) and is stored in memory (inside). The future, for its part, also exists only inside of us. In some ways, it mirrors the work of memory (which is the interior reality of past time for us), but by using another disposition of the soul, which Augustine calls "expectation." The present is precisely the *contuitus* (the sight) of the soul. As Augustine puts it:

> This is now limpid and clear: neither future things nor past things exist; and we do not say properly that "there are three times: the past, the present and the

future." But maybe it is properly said: "there are three times: the present of past things, the present of present things, the present of future things." For, in some way, these three times are in the soul, and I do not see them elsewhere. The present of past things is memory; the present of present things is sight [or perception: *contuitus*]; the present of future things is expectation.[3]

Therefore, all human experience of temporality depends on an internal reference, which, once memory has begun its work, is independent of the change of bodies. But how do we measure the duration of times and compare them? The course of time cannot be fixed, because time is always passing and ceasing to be. Two times are not like two beams placed side by side because it is not possible to stabilize the course of time. It thereby becomes impossible to fix two times and compare them as if they were two extensive spatial bodies being used to measure each other. And so how do we measure durations if no unity of time can be stabilized? For Augustine, it is difficult to dissociate temporal duration and local extension, but it is necessary to think about inner time as something with no "spatial" duration.

An alternative to this external extension criterion for measuring time is that we measure time by the distension of something internal. What we measure is our inner attention. Time is the duration of this attention or the distension of the soul. This is what Augustine means by *distentio animi*. But what would it mean for there to be a distention of an incorporeal substance like our soul? *Distentio animi* will be the expression adopted by Augustine to define time. More than this, the philosopher will argue that there are different ways in which we distend or "stretch out" our souls, depending on our will.

## *DISTENTIO ANIMI* AND JOSHUA'S SUN

The meaning of the expression *distentio animi* can be explored by considering each of its words. In the *Oxford Latin Dictionary*, we find a short entry for "*distentio*" with two definitions, both of which clarify the question of time. The first meaning is divided into two complementary aspects and refers both to exteriorization as a stretching out, as well as to an occupation or inhabitation.[4] Therefore, *distentio* is to occupy exteriority, to inhabit the world through the exteriorization of oneself. The second meaning of *distentio* stands for swelling or distention, for example, a gastric or muscle distention. In this meaning it concerns an anti-natural extension outward, which is caused by internal tension, leading to deformation.

*Distentio* is also derived from the verb *distendo*. In the same dictionary, the entry for *distendo* adds the following to the previous meanings: "to stretch asunder," to fragment, to separate into parts, to separate apart, to divide, to put away; to have a certain extent (to occupy a measurable area); to distract, to go outside, to get dispersed; and to be distended by overuse, as happens to a muscle. *Distendo* is a verb comprised of *"dis"* and *"tendo." Tendo* denotes to will, to yearn, to tend to, to have inclination for, to change the course of something toward another direction, to be devoted to something, to insist, to persist and to endeavor.

This semantic arc of *distentio*, in my estimation, suggests that the *distentio animi*, by which Augustine defines time, could be understood as the process of the soul as it willingly inhabits (occupies) the outer world, and that this is accompanied by wear generated by anti-natural and persistent yearning. *Distentio* refers to an exaggerated kind of stretching outward, which we might term "externalization." It is the soul's process of inhabiting the outer world and getting worn out with excessive occupations and preoccupations. This is the result whenever we misdirect our innermost desire to repose in God toward things that cannot quench this thirst. It consists in the attachment of our will to outer and temporal things. In this way, human attention is always running toward impermanent things, enjoying only passing moments of satisfaction, simultaneously loving and fearing the certain loss of the loved temporal thing.

Going beyond this first layer of meaning, temporal *distentio* seems to gain added and unusual significance in light of a reference Augustine makes to Scripture. In Joshua 10:12, Augustine reminds us, God stops the sun and the moon so that a virtuous battle can be completed. Augustine writes:

> For, when the sun stood still at the wish of a certain person, in order that he might complete a victorious battle, the sun was standing still, but time was going on. Indeed, the fight was waged and finished in its own space of time which was enough for it. I see, then, that time is some sort of extension.[5]

It is remarkable that, in the context of *Confessions* 11, this passage marks a change in the text. Until this point, Augustine has refuted some theories, which defined time in respect to solar movement. From this mention of Joshua, Augustine changes the reference of time, as the aforementioned passage leaves no doubt about who has created and orders time: God is the creator and lord of time. Being so, God is not subjected to time himself, which is evident since he can even stop the course of time. Through creating another kind of temporality for just human beings, as Joshua testifies, a just and difficult war could be won. But what is the significance of this reference to Joshua in *Confessions* 11?

In his book *Knowing God and the Soul*, Roland Teske argues that, although some categories are attributed to God in Scripture, this does not mean that God can be categorized. Teske clarifies his position by saying that when

Scripture talks about God changing his actions—and I would add the example mentioned in Joshua, when God altered the speed of the sun—this does not mean that God has changed. God has not changed, because God is not mutable. But rather, the change relates to the change of human perspective in relation to the immutable God. It is we who have changed, not God.

Reading Joshua in light of Teske, let us return to the scene of God stopping the course of the sun so that a just battle could be fought. What made the battle just was that it followed God's command. Fighting that battle meant acting in accordance with God's will. By bringing his will into alignment with God's will, Joshua experienced another mode of temporality, which was characterized by an inner, expansive joy (*delectatio*). This means that, for Augustine, if we direct our love toward God, human temporality can be experienced in another way, insofar as it serves eternity. Because Joshua's willing was driven to serve God through a fair battle, time stopped for Joshua in the sense that he experienced another quality of temporality, which could no longer be measured by the movement of the Sun. This event put Joshua into intimate proximity with justice, with eternity, and with God, all three of which are identical for Augustine. As a result of this interior transformation, it seemed as though Joshua had achieved something incredible, miraculous, or even impossible for any human being to achieve, given how entangled we are in the distress generated by the externalizing of our core desire.

Another consideration to be made about this mention that Augustine makes of Joshua, and which confirms our interpretation, can be drawn if we highlight that this biblical text refers to a typical sacred war chant, the *jubilus*. To Gianfranco Ravasi, in "'Cantate a Dio con arte': il teologico e il musicale nella Bibbia," martial and sacred chant were imbricated in precisely the same passage of Joshua's text quoted by Augustine (Joshua 10:12).[6] Ravasi affirms that sacred war chants are mentioned in one acclamation that is "famosissima di Giosuè ('Sole, fermati in Gabaon et tu, luna, sulla valle di Aialon'—Gs 10,12)."[7] There is in Joshua, according to Ravasi, an "oscillazione tra canto militare e canto liturgico."[8] Ravasi's argument supports my contention that, in this passage of the *Confessions*, Augustine is referring to both a war chant and a sacred chant in his exegesis of this passage of Joshua. This *jubilus* or sacred war chant is associated by Augustine with *delectatio*. This point is going to be elaborated further on in our discussion, when we look at Augustine's treatment of another example of a *jubilus*: Ambrose's *Deus creator omnium*.[9]

Now, it has already been shown that time conditions the way that the soul directs (or misdirects) her fundamental desire to rest in God. We also have said that when (as the first sense of *distentio* indicates) the soul directs its love outwardly, time runs away as the soul wears away. At the same time, however, it remains possible for us to return to the core of our desire and attend to the love in our hearts, where eternity speaks as Principle, Word, and Truth.

Considering these three presuppositions, it can be affirmed that human actions and reflections thus directed also produce an expansion (or dilatation) inside.[10] This results in a kind of spaciousness of the soul, which space is conveyed by God, as Augustine makes clear in this passage: "Enlarge a space for our meditations on the hideouts of your law."[11] Such an amplitude designates, in a certain way, the antonym of the "distensive" disposition of the will, which amounts to an exhausting and hurried prioritization of temporal things. Living with such a spacious soul, we can accomplish so many things and so well (because there is no distraction or exaggeration caused by lack) that in the eyes of others, it may seem that time has stopped for us and our virtuous actions.

Augustine is referring to another temporality, less fleeting and less inattentive, broader and more concentrated. Within this other temporality, we can be more present to ourselves. This, in turn, brings with it a kind of delight, simultaneously clear and difficult to be conveyed in words. One is left with the impression that this spiritualized way of experiencing time is closer to eternity, at least insofar as any mode of temporal experience is capable of approaching the eternal. Eternity is, after all, also God. And if the way for us to access the divine presence lies along an interior path, it is also in this purely spiritual dimension that time admits of another speed, dictated by the virtuous will aligned with the divine will.

The decisive argument in defense of inner temporality is given when Augustine remembers that we not only measure time but also measure silence. We measure silence as if there were sound, but without sound. This means that we measure without external existence or assistance. And if we refer to the measure of silence in terms of extension, since silence is the privation of sound, this "extension" must be understood as spiritually residing in some "place" or some "extension" within us. Therefore, the example of measuring silence shows that we measure the duration of time based on the way our soul occupies her existence with processes of thinking and willing.

If the soul's understanding of her relation to time is itself seated in the soul, what can be said of the three different times discussed above: present, past, and future? The example Augustine uses when explaining this question will also unfold as his response to the question of the relationship between time and life. For him, it is the act of singing that reveals what happens in "all the actions of man." As Augustine writes:

> Suppose I am about to recite a chant which I know. Before I begin, my expectation is directed towards its totality. But when I have begun, as much of it as I have taken into the past becomes the object of my memory. And the life of this act of mine is distended in my memory—because of the words I have already said—and into my expectation—because of those which I am about to say. But

my attention is on what is present, and through it what was future is transferred to become the past. As the action advances further and further, the shorter the expectation and the longer the memory, until all expectation is consumed, the entire action is finished, and it has passed into memory. What occurs in the chant as a whole occurs in its single parts and its single syllables. This happens in a longer action, whose parts are maybe that chant. This happens in a person's whole life, whose parts are all of that person's actions. This happens in the whole history of the "sons of men" (Ps. 30:20), whose parts are all human lives.[12]

When someone sings a well-known song, in the course of their chanting, they have the three times in their mind simultaneously. They know what should be sung in the future and that this has not yet been sung (although it is known and therefore present in memory as something to be produced). As they sing, in the act of singing, they produce a sound in the present, and this passes from the future (the expectation of what they should sing) into the past (which is the knowledge of what has already been sung and that remains in memory). Therefore, while she is singing, the soul is attentive simultaneously to three times. Moreover, she knows that some notes should last shorter or longer than others, and the same happens with the silences. This measuring takes place inside herself and reproduces internally a simultaneous, inner, silent chant. Thus, in order to sing, the soul has to expand her attention internally, so that it encompasses all three inner times. This inner temporality allows the soul to experience in herself a broadened attention and a greater interior magnitude. In singing, the soul is no longer held hostage to exterior time, which flees precipitously. Instead, the soul moves closer to itself, because it is more focused on eternity.

## DEUS CREATOR OMNIUM

Augustine chooses a verse to exemplify how our experience of time mirrors the quality of the human relation to Eternity (God). It is the initial line and the title of a hymn composed by Ambrose of Milan: *Deus creator omnium* or "God, Creator of All."

The reasons why Augustine has elected this verse are not clearly expressed by him. Nonetheless, I will try to elaborate on this matter. In doing so, I do not aim to give a definitive or exhaustive answer; instead, I will try to call our attention to some hermeneutical results that may come out and clarify some details of this verse. The exposition of this interpretation exercise will be developed in three steps. First, we will follow Augustine's initial approach to the verse, which considers its meter without taking into account the meanings of its words. Considering solely the verse's meter, we will assume that, as it is a verse to be sung, Augustine may have given importance to its melismatic feature, which is one of the main characteristics of a *jubilus*. Second, we will guide our study of this verse toward a general consideration of the meaning of its words. Eventually, I will call our attention to the verse's exemplarity in relation to human life.

Beginning with the metric flow of Ambrose's opening line, Augustine mentions that it is an iamb: a verse composed of eight syllables alternating between short and long (*dĕ-ūs crĕ-ā-tor ō-mni-ūm*).[13] To chant its syllables accurately, one necessarily needs to compare them, because their correct duration is defined by their interrelation, that is, the short syllables should last half as long as the long ones, and the long syllables should perdure for twice the time of the short ones. Now, how could the duration of the syllables be compared, if time is something that cannot be fixed?

Chanting the syllables in such a fashion that four syllables would last twice as long as the other four is only possible by comparing them, and this correlation requires some stabilization of the duration of their sounds in one's memory. Before going further in the analysis of the soul's operation required to chant an iamb, let us retain this development and consider just its first step, which is about chanting with a specific rhythm, following some proportions of time and with no attention to the meaning of the verse's words.

Here, Augustine remains silent about the meanings of the words and gives attention only to the duration of the sound of the syllables. This may remind us that chanting without words defines the melismatic chant and the *jubilus*. According to Lorenzo Mammì:

> The Paleo-Christian community experienced a form of singing in which the separation between music and text is programmatic: *jubilus*, a wordless song, the most primitive of the melismatic forms that will later constitute the glory and luxury of the Christian melody. *Jubilus* seems to be an aesthetic achievement of Christianity. Classical thinking ignores the idea of a song that rejects words. Melismatic singing is also foreign to Jewish tradition.[14]

Considering that Augustine emphasizes the meter of the sound apart from the meanings of the words, it is clear that he does separate text and music. For this reason, I venture to suppose that the separation of sound and meaning is programmatic in Augustine's *Confessions* 11, and this allows me to suppose some aspects of *jubilus* in this first approach to *Deus creator omnium*. As mentioned earlier, a *jubilus* was originally a war and sacred chant, and Augustine abstracts from this reality when he emphasizes the aspect of *delectatio* in a *jubilus*. The *delectatio* of *jubilus* is related to another experience of time, which enlarges the human soul and its way of living in time. We have already thought about it when considering Augustine's mention of Joshua.

Further, considering the "formal" aspect of *Deus creator omnium* as an allusion to *jubilus* is a reading that is supported by the internalization of the reality of time, which Augustine defends when he develops his interpretation of the soul's operation as it chants that verse. This chanting requires the comparison between long and short syllables, and this would be impossible if time were only an exterior fleeting reality. Yet, we measure time and chant properly. In this way, Augustine changes the place of the measurement of time's duration to somewhere where it can be understood. For him the comparison of the syllables' duration occurs inside, when the soul gives herself attention. Only in the interior is it possible to attribute stability to time. In memory, the duration of the syllables of a song that is about to be sung makes it possible to reproduce the meter of a chant, since memory gives some permanence to what is kept in it.

The second aspect we would like to consider about *Deus creator omnium*, Augustine's elected example for clarifying time's relation to eternity, is the meaning of this verse: "*Deus creator omnium*" (dĕ-ūs crĕ-ā-tor ō-mni-ūm), which means "*Oh God, creator of all.*" Such a strong verse was not chosen by chance, especially in a text written by Augustine, a writer so discerning that he selected each word with care. I think that the force of this verse's meaning can be considered in at least two ways: in the meaning of the words and in its performative dimension. This performative power is also the third aspect of our analysis of *Deus creator omnium*.

*Deus creator omnium* designates *Deus* (God) as the *creator omnium* (creator of all). This asserts both God's incomparable power (only he is the creator of all) and that nothing would be without being created by him.[15] This radical dependence of every creature on God occupies the last three books of the *Confessions*, which comment on the beginning of the book of Genesis. But what does it refer to in Ambrose's hymn? Or what would the contemporary readers of Augustine think of when he quotes this line? Maybe his readers would remember the chant and its general meaning, which is already summarized in its first eight lines. Ambrose's hymn reads:

| | |
|---|---|
| *Deus creator omnium /* | Maker of all things, God on high, |
| *Polique rector vestiens /* | And ruler of the sky, |
| *Diem decoro lumine /* | clothing the day with beauteous light, |
| *Noctem soporis gratia /* | with slumbers soft, the night; |
| *Artus solutus ut quies /* | Our nerveless bodies to restore |
| *Reddat laboris usui /* | To labor as before; |
| *Mentes fessas allevet /* | Our weariness to chase away, |
| *Luctusque solvat anxios.*[16] | And anxious cares allay.[17] |

God rules the movements in the sky, gifts the day with beautiful light, offers reinvigorating slumber, offers rest (*quies*) to the fatigue of our bodies and spirits, and dissolves the anguish of death. In the hymn, the human experiences of distress are repaired by God, who conveys rest to restore human weariness and anguish. The actions of man (except to pray and to remember God) bring fatigue, while divine actions order the sky and humankind to move in beautiful harmony. The chant also mentions a kind of restoring that we cannot give to ourselves, since only God offers it. The only relevant human action is to drive our loving attention to God, who places everything in natural movement, as the conductor of a universal orchestra. This resonation with the universal natural rhythms is also a characteristic that Augustine attributes to a kind of chant called *jubilus*.[18]

Finally, the third note on the example of singing *Deus creator omnium* concerns the conclusion that Augustine makes: what happens with singing also happens in human life, either in each part (seconds, minutes, hours, days, events) or in its totality (the life of each human being), and even in the totality of human lives (and here there is the absolute universalization of the consideration of time and the human being). Singing, like life, is thought in terms of durations or times. Singing, like life, can be joyful, although stable happiness is impossible during existence in the world. And even if it does lie in the future, it is already present in expectation. Although inexhaustible happiness comes only after death, it is already present in the God-Principle, and the human being can have experiences of delight in this life, even if they are fleeting. This delight accompanies the inner dilation of the soul and produces another, virtuous quality of time, in which the soul, instead of wearing itself out by seeking to maintain the enjoyment of what is impermanent, presents itself to that inner presence, which is invigorating and can dissolve one's fatigue. When referring time to eternity, Augustine thinks of time as a possible place for practicing a virtuous existence, which, although temporal, is known to be directed toward eternity.

## FINAL REMARKS

The question "what is time?" is asked by Augustine in the context of what time means in terms of a life directed toward the fulfillment of the imperative desire for happiness. Time is not addressed by Augustine as a substance. It concerns the bond that human beings establish with God and the world, sometimes through dispersing, distressing, and exhausting pleasure, but some other times through inner delight. Due to this background, life and time are marked by oscillations derived from human love, to the point that the meaning of time is paired with the guidance that the soul attributes to her life.

Time is dealt with as a theme that concerns the quality of human life, and not as something whose greatness is measured quantitatively. A life of fatigue results from frustration and the deviation from an enormous desire for happiness; it is only remedied to the extent that the choices that govern life harmonize with the true meaning of life. With Augustine, one can think that the invigorating rest does not consist of a number of sleeping hours, but of delight.

Augustine's text is attentive to the humanization of time, which cannot be mechanized or dictated by parameters of happiness that do not bring stability. Fatigue stems from the wear and tear of life, a life which is wasted with pleasure on things that are transient and distinct from the intimate principle (eternity). Our rest from everyday wear, warns Augustine, depends on the quality and not the amount of time at rest: only virtuous delight, operating in terms of another temporality, brings us closer to the experience of eternity-truth-happiness. Human beings make themselves available for such an experience by virtuous action, which intends to live happiness. For example, the song that is permeated by this intent anticipates and exemplifies this experience of the soul's delight, even though it is impermanent due to temporality (or human mutability).

## NOTES

1. Augustine, *Confessions* (*Conf.*), tr. Maria Boulding OSB (New York: New City Press, 2012), 11.14.17, 295. The Latin for this passage is: *quid est enim tempus? quis hoc facile breviterque explicaverit? quis hoc ad verbum de illo proferendum vel cogitatione comprehenderit? quid autem familiarius et notius in loquendo commemoramus quam tempus? et intellegimus utique cum id loquimur, intellegimus etiam cum alio loquente id audimus. quid est ergo tempus? si nemo ex me quaerat, scio; si quaerenti explicare velim, nescio.* The Latin version of Augustine's *Confessions* which I chose to quote is the one edited and commented upon by James O'Donnell and A. Mahoney (https://www.stoa.org/hippo/). This edition provides an accurate version of the Latin text and enhances it by adding punctuation and quotation marks. I want to express my gratitude to the editors of this excellent, free, and open access text, due to which the present chapter was made possible.

2. Time can only be understood if we try to contrast it with eternity. Our experience of time depends on degrees of internalization and exteriorization of the things that are present to us (in our memory). Our attention is directed by our love, which may be directed to exteriority or to this innermost reality of eternity, which is a timelessness that transcends humankind.

3. *Conf.* 11.20.26: *quod autem nunc liquet et claret, nec futura sunt nec praeterita, nec proprie dicitur, 'tempora sunt tria, praeteritum, praesens, et futurum,' sed fortasse proprie diceretur, 'tempora sunt tria, praesens de praeteritis, praesens de praesentibus, praesens de futuris.' sunt enim haec in anima tria quaedam et alibi*

*ea non video, praesens de praeteritis memoria, praesens de praesentibus contuitus, praesens de futuris expectatio.* The translation is my own.

4. See the Perseus entry: http://www.perseus.tufts.edu/hopper/morph?l=distentio&la#lexicon.

5. *Conf.* 11.22.30: *quia et cuiusdam voto cum sol stetisset, ut victoriosum proelium perageret, sol stabat, sed tempus ibat. per suum quippe spatium temporis, quod ei sufficeret, illa pugna gesta atque finita est. video igitur tempus quandam esse distentionem.* This translation is taken from that of Vernon J. Bourke (Washington, D.C.: Catholic University of America Press, 2008), 355.

6. Gianfranco Ravasi, "'Cantate a Dio con arte:' il teologico e il musicale nella Bibbia," in *La Musica e la Bibbia: Atti del Convegno Internazionalle di Studi promosso da Biblia e dall'Accademia Musicale Chigiana, Siena 24–26 agosto 1990*, ed. Pasquale Troia (Rome: Garamond, 1992), 65–110, here 86: "Nella Bibbia i canti marziali hanno spesso una venatura religiosa perchè erano connesi a la guerra santa."

7. Gianfranco Ravasi, "'Cantate a Dio con arte:' il teologico e il musicale nella Bibbia," 86.

8. Gianfranco Ravasi, "'Cantate a Dio con arte:' il teologico e il musicale nella Bibbia," 87.

9. See the later section in this chapter entitled *"Deus Creator Omnium."*

10. The meaning of "dilatation" adopted here is inspired by Jean-Louis Chrétien, *La Joie Spacieuse: essai sur la dilatation* (Lonrai: Les Éditions de Minuit, 2007). Chrétien's first chapter (33–63), "Saint Augustin et le grand large du désir", is dedicated to Augustine's use of the term *"dilatatio."*

11. *Conf.* 11.2.3: *largire inde spatium meditationibus nostris in abdita legis tuae.*

12. *Conf.* 11.28.38: *dicturus sum canticum quod novi. antequam incipiam, in totum expectatio mea tenditur, cum autem coepero, quantum ex illa in praeteritum decerpsero, tenditur et memoria mea, atque distenditur vita huius actionis meae in memoriam propter quod dixi et in expectationem propter quod dicturus sum. praesens tamen adest attentio mea, per quam traicitur quod erat futurum ut fiat praeteritum. quod quanto magis agitur et agitur, tanto breviata expectatione prolongatur memoria, donec tota expectatio consumatur, cum tota illa actio finita transierit in memoriam. et quod in toto cantico, hoc in singulis particulis eius fit atque in singulis syllabis eius, hoc in actione longiore, cuius forte particula est illud canticum, hoc in tota vita hominis, cuius partes sunt omnes actiones hominis, hoc in toto saeculo filiorum hominum, cuius partes sunt omnes vitae hominum.* Here I have used, with some modifications, the translation found in Henry Chadwick's translation of Augustine's *Confessions* (Oxford: Oxford University Press, 1992), 243.

13. See *Conf.* 11.27.35.

14. Lorenzo Mammì, *A fugitiva: ensaios sobre música*, 1st edition (São Paulo: Companhia das Letras, 2017), 328–329: "A comunidade paleocristã conheceu uma forma de canto em que o descolamento entre música e texto é programático: o *jubilus*, canto sem palavras, a mais primitiva das formas melismáticas que constituirão, mais tarde, a glória e o luxo da melodia cristã. *Jubilus* parece ser uma conquista estética do cristianismo. O pensamento clássico desconhece a ideia de um canto que dispense as palavras. O canto melismático é estranho também à tradição judaica."

15. This radical dependence of every creature on God occupies the last two books of the *Confessions*.

16. For the Latin text, see Mammì, *A fugitiva*, 340, note 28.

17. For the English translation, see *The British Magazine and Monthly Register of Religious and Ecclesiastical Information, Parochial History, and Documents Respecting the State of the Poor, Progress of Education, etc.*, edited by J. and J.G.F. Rivington (London: J. Petheram, 1840), 390–391. One may find excellent notes on Ambrose's hymns in Arthur Sumner Walpole, *Early Latin Hymns: With Introduction and Notes* (Cambridge: Cambridge University Press, 1922), 44–52.

18. In his *Canticum Novum*, Mammì develops *jubilus* as a chant without words and in resonance with the rhythms of nature. He quotes various works by Augustine, including Sermon 1.8, as well as *Enarrationes in Psalmos* 32.2 and 99.3–6.

*Chapter 6*

# The Inner Word and the Outer World

## Time, Temporality, and Language in Augustine and Gadamer

Matthew W. Knotts

Augustine's account of time is integrally connected with his understanding of creation and eternity. In the fifth book of *De Genesi ad litteram*, Augustine argues that time arises as a result of the creation of formed and formable material realities.[1] Time and eternity are also conceptually linked in that God creates through the utterance of his eternal word. Moreover, this word enters the created world of time and space in order to redeem it.

This set of themes was also relevant to contemporaneous polemics. Augustine articulated a theological concept of the word in order to combat Arians and Photinians.[2] He wished to maintain the *duae natiuitates* of the Son, one eternal and one human.[3] In doing so, he contrasts the divine word, uttered eternally without any passage of time, with our mutable, human words.[4] However, Augustine also envisions a certain likeness between the incarnation of God's eternal word and our utterances from the inner language of thought. This theological concept of the word would also influence later philosophers, most notably Gadamer, in their attempt to understand human language and its relationship to the world. Thus, Augustine's attempt to reconcile time and eternity through his understanding of the inner word provides the basis for understanding our own thought, which is itself suspended between time and timelessness.

### GADAMER'S THEORY OF LANGUAGE

From an early stage Gadamer found the relationship between philosophy and theology intriguing.[5] J. Zimmermann suggests that it is only according to this insight that one can truly appreciate Gadamer's thought,[6] as it was in theology that Gadamer located resources for addressing questions which push us beyond the limits of our human existence.[7] One of his most valuable sources in this respect was Augustine.

The starting point for treatments of Augustine and Gadamer is a chapter in J. Grondin's 1994 monograph *Der Sinn für Hermeneutik*, in which he discusses the Augustinian inspiration behind Gadamer's hermeneutics as presented in *Wahrheit und Methode* (*WM*). Among other things, Grondin argues that Augustine was a major source for Gadamer's hermeneutics, in particular the conception of hermeneutical universality,[8] a point that was even confirmed by Gadamer himself.[9] Gadamer's specific source was Augustine's understanding of the "inner word," in particular as located in *De Trinitate* (*trin.*) 15.[10] As a result, most of the literature dealing with Augustine and Gadamer has focused on whether and to what extent Gadamer was influenced by Augustine or other sources, or to what extent Gadamer accurately read and interpreted Augustine concerning the inner word. In 2009, two monographs appeared, which also dealt explicitly with this question, namely J. Arthos's *The Inner Word in Gadamer's Hermeneutics*[11] and M. Oliva's *Das innere Verbum in Gadamers Hermeneutik*.[12] Both of these monographs included extended discussion of Augustine on the inner word, as well as how this was received by Gadamer. Several articles or chapters have also dealt with this question, such as M. Llanes's 2013 article on the nature of language and thought. Grondin, Zimmermann, Llanes, and Oliva read Gadamer on the inner word in light of Augustine, whereas scholars such as Arthos are more ambivalent. Arthos holds that Augustine is a clear focal point for Gadamer in Part III of *WM*, but that other classical philosophical figures such as Aquinas also contribute to shaping his understanding of hermeneutic universality.[13] Nonetheless, Arthos sees Augustine as anticipating key developments in the hermeneutics of both Heidegger and Gadamer.[14]

Grondin situates Gadamer's approach to language within the tradition of pre-modern metaphysics. In fact, in reacting against the view of language as enjoying some form of subjective dominance over being, Gadamer wishes rather to re-integrate language and being in a more "metaphysical" and participatory manner.[15] Gadamer formulated his revised conception of the inner word as an alternative to other theories of language, namely *Konventionalismus*, according to which language is nothing more than an arbitrary set of signs, and *Abbildungstheorie*, which holds that language enjoys a direct correspondence to objects in the world.[16] Just as Heidegger did, Gadamer perceived resources in Augustine's *trin.*, which allowed one to challenge specifically modern philosophical positions.

By language, Gadamer means the following: "That which can be understood is language. This means that it is of such a nature that of itself it offers itself to be understood."[17] Gadamer sees the world as "language speaking for us."[18] As Grondin writes, "le langage est pour Gadamer celui des choses avant que d'être celui de notre pensée."[19] It is important to note that according to this view, natural human languages are neither generative of nor exhaustive of reality in themselves. Gadamer identifies being with language, the latter of which he describes as "self-presentation," describing his view as "ontological" in nature.[20] The impression of the thing in the world becomes in our mind the inner word, which is later expressed in our natural languages.[21] Therefore, in the words of Llanes, Gadamer's hermeneutics implies that "los seres de esto mundo son, ontológicamente hablando, lenguaje, palabra, verbo."[22] One who speaks is oriented toward the truth, and therefore toward being.[23] Furthermore, when Gadamer speaks of the word (*Wort*), he means it in the sense of that which is possessed of meaning, that which has a content or a message addressed to one.[24] As Grondin explains, "The *Wort* of which Gadamer speaks is not the 'word' understood as a linguistic entity (the plural form of this in German is *Wörter*), but the word which seizes us, which makes sense, which speaks (the plural in German is *Wörte*)."[25] Simply in virtue of be-ing does being speak itself.[26]

Here one finds the significance of Gadamer's emphasis on language as the basis of intelligibility. This being that is constituted by "language" in Gadamer's sense of the term presses upon us and influences us, to the point that it emerges in our (natural) language(s), in our utterances.[27] In this way, being is able to be understood. Through linguistic utterances, the world, which is of itself linguistic and meaningful, is presented in another communicable form.[28] As Eberhard explains, "Reason is our way of participating in the structure of the *logos* of the world. . . . This rational participation takes place in language."[29] Individual contents present themselves as intelligible to us; they are foregrounded from the general whole of our hermeneutical vision.[30] Gadamer understands language as the medium in and through which meaning is manifested and realized.[31] According to Gadamer, "Man's relation to the world is absolutely and fundamentally verbal in nature, and hence intelligible."[32] This emphasis on intelligibility relies upon the notion of a "pre-linguistic" inner word. Let us now consider the antecedents of this view in Christian theology, in particular in Augustine's account of creation.

## CHRISTIAN LOGOS THEOLOGY

Augustine places a strong emphasis on the eternity and the incorporeality of God. One sees this point especially in his consideration of creation throughout his corpus. In the *Confessiones* (*conf.*), for example, Augustine writes that God creates *in principio*, which is to say, within the divine wisdom or word, the Son,[33] which is both generated from (*de te nata*) and equal to God (*aequalis tibi et coaeterna*).[34] For this position, Augustine is informed by Genesis 1 and John 1, texts which he sees as essentially linked.[35] In other words, the *in principio* in both texts is identical with Christ, the eternal word.

Augustine follows an earlier Christian tradition not only of connecting these two biblical books, but also of understanding *in principio* as referring to a reality beyond all time and space. I. Bochet writes that Augustine's references to Genesis 1 and God's creation *in principio* should be understood as God creating in his wisdom.[36,37] According to J. C. M. Van Winden, though this argumentation is found in Ambrose, it traces its roots to the earliest days of Christianity.[38] Thus, one identified Christ with the wisdom of the OT and the logos and the *archê* of the NT.[39] As a result, Van Winden explains, "Man kann daher statt Ἐν ἀρχῇ ἦν ὁ λόγος (Joh. 1, 1) auch lesen Ἀρχὴ ἦν ὁ λόγος. Christus ist also λόγος, σοφία, ἀρχή. Demzufolge kann man auch sagen: ἐν ἀρχῇ = ἐν σοφίᾳ = ἐν λόγῳ = ἐν Χριστῷ."[40]

Moreover, the prologue asserts a timeless aspect to the source of a creation, a point which is easily lost in the rather misleading English translation of *in principio* as "in the beginning." Johannine scholars view the term *in principio* as referring to the transcendent and eternal, and so it should not be understood in a temporal sense.[41] Such a view was well established in the patristic tradition of biblical exegesis. For example, as G. van Riel explains,[42] various Christian authors who later became sources for Augustine, such as Ambrose, Basil, Tertullian, and Filastrius, reacted vehemently against Hermogenes's critique of *in principio* as referring to something material. The fathers countered this reading of Genesis by emphasizing the transcendent character of God as the ground of created reality.[43] Augustine as well robustly maintains a commitment to the eternity and timelessness of the creator.

He also predicates this same timelessness of the Son. Concerning the eternity of the discarnate logos, Augustine declares, "[the Word of God] is neither confined in places, nor stretched out through times, nor varied by short and long quantities, nor woven together out of different sounds, nor ended by silence."[44] In various locations, such as his Christmas *sermones* (*ss*. 184–196), Augustine incorporates Johannine language and themes into his discussion of Christ by describing him as Word (*Verbum*), life (*uita*), and the light of men (*lux hominum*).[45] Augustine opens *s*. 188 by reaffirming the divinity and eternity of the Son with the Father, and that creation was effected in and through the Son, the divine word: "the Son of God just as he is with the Father, equal to him and co-eternal; the one in whom all things were established in heaven and on earth, visible and invisible; the Word of God, and God, the life and light of the human race."[46] Augustine identifies Christ with wisdom and word, describing how God became incarnate and eternal wisdom dwelt on the earth, a point that he immediately substantiates by quoting the opening verse of John.⁴⁷ Though the Son is begotten, he is neither made nor does he begin to be. The Son is never "not," and the Father is never without the Son, even if he begets him.⁴⁸

In his discussion of the Word and its eternal generation, Augustine invokes his conception of the inner word, and its counterpart, the eternal birth of Christ. However, there is a further element to Augustine's theory of the inner word, namely as a more basic capacity for thought that is pre-linguistic. Augustine speaks of the word in the heart as apart from any natural human language, and not as the simple repetition of linguistic utterances within the silence of one's mind (*non cum ipsa uox in silentio cogitatur, quae uel graecae est, uel latinae, uel linguae alterius cuiuslibet*).⁴⁹ Rather, Augustine specifies that he means a word prior to the variety of human language (*ante omnem linguarum diuersitatem*).⁵⁰ In order to articulate a thought, we draw upon an inner mental content (*quiddam mentis nostrae*), which is not entirely formed.⁵¹ As Grondin explains, Augustine holds that "Unser Verbum schöpft immer aus einem impliziten Wissen . . . um seinen Gedanken zum Ausdruck zu verhelfen."⁵² He describes this cordial word as nude (*nuda*), in particular to the one thinking and understanding it (*intellegenti*),⁵³ and suggests that it is clothed (*uestitur*) in the garments of a natural language so that it can be communicated.⁵⁴

Within the Johannine scheme, Christ constitutes the perfect demonstration of the Father in the world.⁵⁵ In virtue of the incarnation, the logos enters the world in a radically novel way. Even though it was present before, the word made flesh constitutes a significantly different form of divine presence.⁵⁶ The Son, the eternal and timeless conditioner of time itself, enters the world and comes to be in time in a human form (*propter nos fieret in tempore, per quem facta sunt tempora*).⁵⁷

## THE AUGUSTINIAN INNER WORD

Gadamer was deeply informed by Augustine in the development of his theory of language. The latter's presentation of the inner word analogy relates the incarnation of the eternal word to the "incarnation" of human thought in outer speech.⁵⁸ As Oliva notes, following G. Bavaud, Augustine distances himself from prior fathers by speaking of the difference between the inner and the outer word of God in terms of incarnation, rather than creation.⁵⁹ That is, the utterance of God's word consists in its manifestation in the physical, material world.⁶⁰ Hence, the creation of the world is proper to the Son's divine nature, whereas his salvific actions are proper to his human nature.⁶¹

According to Oliva, Augustine initially uses the term *uerbum/a* in the plural and as such does not apply it to the divine word.⁶² Once Augustine's conception of *uerba* develops to the point of a cordial word, the term comes to admit of the possibility of a christological dimension.[63] Oliva locates this development in Augustine's thinking to the composition of his *De trinitate* between 399 and 419.[64] Furthermore, these novel ideas, which Augustine introduced in his *trin.* concerning language, are also those that Gadamer appropriated.[65]

Following C. Panaccio, A. Romele presents an analysis similar to Oliva's.[66] This analysis is separated into three phases.[67] The first, which includes works prior to 395, contains no real doctrine of the inner word.[68] In the second phase, one sees a nascent conception of the inner word, in particular in Augustine's *Epistula ad Romanos inchoata expositio*.[69] The third phase begins roughly 417, and Romele notes the eighth book of *trin.* as the turning point.[70] Here one sees a notion of the inner word coming to fruition, which is identified as something anterior to particular worldly languages.[71] However, as Romele stresses, one must recall that this word is formed on the basis of mutable creation.[72] Furthermore, the inner word does not pertain to one's thinking in words, but rather something more basic. Augustine distinguishes between the spoken outer word, the word recited in the soul in a way that imitates outer speech, and then the inner word itself, which he identifies with the image of God.[73]

As Oliva writes, the latent ambiguity in the Latin term *notitia* is also significant.[74] The term *notitia* can either mean a content (*Wissensinhalt*) or the execution or completion of a thought (*Wissensvollzug*).[75] Hence, there are two different senses of the inner word.[76] One refers to the thought within one's mind, either as it is present there or as it is produced by an object.[77] The other sense pertains to the inner word as the capacity to produce speech and other signs, which implies a temporal, "processual" character.[78] The inner word thus also reflects the two main activities of language, namely the apprehension of a particular object, which will later be expressed, as well as one's inner creativity, by means of which it will be expressed.[79]

As Heidegger takes a "de-theologized" approach to Augustine's speculative philosophy and theology, so does Gadamer concerning Augustine's notion of the inner word. Gadamer shows a particular appreciation for Christian thought concerning language. In particular, he locates in early Christian theology a turn toward linking thought with language in an organic and integral unity.[80] The word that one utters is not something distinct from thought, but is the very expression of thought itself: "that which emerges and externalizes itself in utterance is always already a word."[81] The inner word, in particular in its fruition as a realization of a content in the mind, is analogous to the procession of the Son from the Father in the specific sense that the emergence of the inner word does not deprive the mind or the memory of any particular content, but rather represents the flowering of those mental contents[82]: "The inner mental word is just as consubstantial with thought as is God the Son with God the Father."[83]

As Grondin states, Gadamer's philosophy of language does not so much pertain to our statements in a natural language (*Aussage*), but rather with what exceeds our ability to speak in the first place.[84] Indeed, it pertains to our attempt to express what is held within that we struggle to articulate: "Die wesentliche Sprachlichkeit des Verstehens äußert sich weniger in unseren Aussagen als in unserer Suche nach Sprache für das, was wir in der Seele haben und aussagen, ja heraussagen wollen."[85] The essence of language itself is thus constituted by the dynamic process of bringing the unsaid and the unsayable into the realm of the spoken, even if the latter never totally captures or exhausts the former.[86]

For his discussion of the inner word, Gadamer is informed especially by Augustine's discussion of this theme in the fifteenth and final book of *trin*. Herein the bishop of Hippo avers that there is an interior word of the soul, prior to all language, and even to any particular thought itself.[87] As Oliva writes, this independence from any natural language reflects the connection between the inner word and the *imago Dei* within the human soul.[88] The inner word precedes all the words that one utters and is generated (*gignitur*)[89] from the knowledge within oneself and transmitted to the outer world, while that knowledge remains intact in the soul.[90] From our internal knowledge, we generate a word, which is very similar to the thing that we know; the content is manifest in the inner word itself.[91] The spoken articulation of an inner word does not change the word itself but rather conveys it and realizes it.[92] In addition to language, this word is incorporeal, separate from all sounds, which course through temporal intervals.[93] As Augustine puts it, this is the word "that has neither sound nor thought of sound, the one that belongs to the thing we utter inside as we see it and thus not to any language."[94] Our inner words are utterances of thought: "our true most inner word is not spoken except by our thought."[95] One can be said to "speak" by one's thoughts without pronouncing words in sound: "For even if words do not sound, the one who thinks speaks in his heart."[96] This mode of thought, which could be loosely described as a language of its own, is anterior to and is presupposed by all individual languages.[97] This *uerbum in corde* is, according to D. Vessey, "not in any actual language. It is simply *grasping a meaning with our heart*, which could later be externalized in a language."[98] Augustine sees this inner word as a sort of universal human capacity linked with our capacity for reason. The multiplicity of languages is rooted in a more common shared inner word.[99] As Vessey explains, "all humans, by divine inspiration, share the same mentalese: the Word of God."[100] Our capacity for inner thought is also linked with the fact that we are created in the image of God.[101]

Gadamer argues that the inner word within one's mind contains the thing intended; it is not a thought about a thought.[102] The inner word in entering language is neither diminished nor destroyed.[103] Rather, the content of the outer word just is that of the inner word.[104] As Eberhard writes, "[The inner word's] being lies in its revealing and saying the *Sache*."[105] Though one certainly has the capacity to reflect on one's own thoughts as objects, thoughts as such are not necessarily results of one's thinking, but rather reflections of something in the world.[106] Furthermore, Gadamer sees the inner word as the dynamic unity of thought and utterance.[107] The (inner) word is not merely the product of thought but the process of thought being brought to the realization of truth.[108] Gadamer describes the inner word not as any novel product of thought but as the summation of thought, or the logical result of thought, consciously realized by a thinking subject; the inner word follows "*ut conclusio ex principiis*."[109] In a sense, it represents a different perspective on what is already present in one's mind. Theological analogs, when taken with a pinch of salt, can be of use here. For instance, God's act of creativity is not so much something separate from his nature, but rather the expression of his mind in spatio-temporal extension.[110] Similarly, in the Incarnation, God enters the world without forsaking his divine nature.[111] As Gadamer explains:

> The process and emergence of thought is not a process of change (*motus*), not a transition from potentiality into action, but an emergence *ut actus ex actu*. The word is not formed only after the act of knowledge has been completed—in Scholastic terms, after the *intellectus* has been informed by the *species*; it is the act of knowledge itself. Thus the word is simultaneous with this forming (*formatio*) of the intellect.[112]

Hence, it becomes clear why Gadamer states that a word is already present within one prior to any external utterance. The product of one's "inner dialogue" still stands in need of further refinement, which the mind does through *inquisitio* and *cogitatio*, so that its thoughts may be appropriately couched in intelligible form.[113]

According to Grondin, Gadamer does not wish to diminish the significance of the spoken word, but rather to situate it within its proper context.[114] The interplay of both "types" of words is itself the completion of human speaking.[115] As Oliva writes, the inner and the outer word are both "konstitutive Aspekte des Sprachphänomens."[116] Gadamer wishes to return the focus of the theory of language from that which is spoken to that which precedes and motivates the spoken.[117] In other words, Gadamer identifies the original context of speech with conversation (*Gespräch*), and not with the statement (*Aussage*).[118] The latter is an abstraction, which does not correspond to one's lived experience.[119] In order to understand one's words, one must understand them in terms of what makes them meaningful, namely the implicit question to which they respond.[120] Thus, language both originates and finds its completion in collective speech.[121]

The movement of being into human language is what Gadamer has in mind by the notion that hermeneutics deals with an experience or an event. That is, the articulation of meaning in and through language likewise possesses the character of an event.[122] As Lawrence writes, "The breakthrough to a notion of truth in its primordiality is achieved by uncovering our primordial horizon and implies a normatively freighted notion of experience. This is the movement of disclosure, which is the dynamic vector of Gadamer's entire enterprise."[123] We seek to articulate our inner lives, indeed, our experiences, via targeted linguistic formulations. The significance of this observation, according to Gadamer, consists in the fact that the deliberation over a particular word or phrase reflects how language "real-izes" a certain state of affairs, how words make something present in external reality via language. The reality and the word that mediates it are never fully separable.[124] The linguistic formulation of a particular content does not represent something new or different; it is not another thing. Rather, for Gadamer, there is a mere distinction between the thing and the presentation thereof, a distinction that ultimately disappears from the perspective of philosophical hermeneutics.[125]

The doctrine of the inner word also provides a foundation for the universal character of Gadamer's hermeneutics.[126] Every natural language, according to Gadamer, has a common source in the "universal language" of thought.[127] External utterance is always understood with respect to the inner word.[128] In his analysis of Aquinas, Gadamer writes that an inner word does not refer to some finite form of a word from a natural language but rather represents the *forma excogitata*, the fruition of an idea in one's mind.[129] Hence, for Gadamer, the inner word and the word of articulate, external speech are not radically, essentially different.[130] Gadamer conceives of language and understanding as two aspects of the same mental process.[131] His entire philosophy assumes the co-extension of understanding and language, as well as language's "universality" with respect to particular natural languages.[132] Language therefore is not some product or result of thought, something "secondary" to the thought itself.[133] According to Grondin, there is a certain affinity between Augustine and Gadamer with respect to the unspoken, internal source of external, spoken language. Every utterance is always based in and presupposes an "unsaid" source, a source that is never fully exhausted by any finite linguistic utterance.[134]

## THE RECONCILIATION OF TIME AND ETERNITY

Gadamer describes interpretation as *speculative*, insofar as interpretation relies upon the subject matter, yet also realizes something apparently distinct from it.[135] It pertains to the relationship between the world and the speaker. Gadamer's notion of the *Spiegelverhältnis* is applied to language; in language is produced an image that reflects the world and our interaction with it.[136] Hence, the relation is dyadic, produced by the two coming together.[137] As with classical Greek philosophers, Gadamer conceived of thought as somehow integrally connected with the objects toward which it was directed.[138] As Plato would say, our thinking does not arise in a vacuum and then seek the outside world but rather is ultimately founded on a relationship to the world.[139] In this respect, Gadamer sees knowledge as entailing some form of self-knowledge, though he does not situate this within Augustine's theological understanding of this claim.[140] The mind is present to itself precisely in virtue of the various things it thinks.[141] One's own self, and thus knowledge of oneself, is always implicated in knowledge of a particular thing. For this reason, Gadamer sees method as inadequate, insofar as it attempts to nullify the self, which is nothing other than the very means of enquiry. However, one should note that he sees method and science itself as two different things, arguing that the latter must acquire a method of interrogation in order to arrive at truth in a more holistic and indeed reliable way.[142]

For Augustine, true knowledge involves a love of that knowledge. It is always a *notitia cum amore*.[143] Moreover, this understanding along with love is constitutive of an inner word.[144] Augustine's understanding of the inner word as *cum amore notitia* is "erotic," as it arises from the very depths of one's being and is spoken "aus ganzem Herzen."[145] L. Cilleruelo notes how Augustine takes the erotic notion of knowledge from the Platonists and transfigures it, particularly by means of his understanding of *memoria*.[146] Augustine describes the production of an idea in sexual terms, that is, of conceiving, incubating, and ultimately birthing a product of "procreative" activity.[147]

Such thoughts also help us to see that the inner word does not tend toward the purely subjective. The inner word in Augustine's thought establishes the possibility for communication in the sense of abiding with someone, for as the inner word does not leave the speaker behind when it is uttered, so too can it remain with the hearer, even if it also returns to the original speaker.[148] The implication of the *Verbumlehre* is not solipsism but rather the possibility of continuous communication between individuals at a profound level.[149] Thus for the human person, one "ha la capacità," in Ferri's words, "attraverso la sua parola, di muoversi verso l'altro e rimanere nell'altro, pur senza abbandonare se stesso."[150] In this way, the Augustinian inner word is, as Arthos puts it, "trans-subjective."[151] But beyond other persons, our language encourages us to seek its source, namely the divine word.[152] Here Oliva too denies that the inner word has anything to do with solipsism, as the inner word always disposes one to relate to one's divine source, and provides the capacity to do so.[153] Both Augustine and Gadamer hold in some way that the activity of the inner word relates us to others, whether to the external world, other persons, or even God. Indeed, the inner word promises a reconciliation between time and eternity. For Gadamer, his hermeneutical understanding of language offers a bridge across the Cartesian chasm between the inner and the outer world. Augustine sees our atemporal inner word of thought related to the temporal word of external utterance as loosely analogous to the incarnation of the eternal word in time and space.

## CONCLUSION

Grondin argues that Gadamer's hermeneutics must be read in light of Augustine's notion of the inner word, in particular the tenet that in its external utterance it is continuously striving for perfect articulation.[154] By its very nature this striving requires time, and perhaps the effort can only be fully rewarded in eternity. According to Augustine, the word we produce in speech (at least concerning divine matters) only partially resembles the reality about which it is spoken.[155] The inner word, however, can capture a reality *sicuti est*.[156] Indeed, the great virtue of the *uerbum cordis* consists in its adequation to and reflection of the content in question. There are many things we can understand without being able to explain them. Indeed, in my estimation, this experience is what motivates equivocal uses of language in various literary genres such as poetry, as well as the plastic arts. The artist uses a work as a medium for the communication of a cognitive, intelligible truth claim. The medium should not be understood as a mere generic container, but as a unique reflection of the inner word, molded and shaped by it, such that its structure is inherently designed to convey something of the content. The inner word captures something as it is.[157] However, when it is articulated in speech, it is not communicated as it is but as it may be heard and understood by others.[158] One may recall here Augustine's discussion of his search for a *dignum uehiculum* for communicating the grandeur of the incarnation.[159] Hence it is possible that something of the content is lost in the transmission process.[160] The content of the inner word is conveyed to others by means of spoken language, which transmits information through the medium of corporeal sounds and signs.[161] The interior word (*uerbum*) is actualized in and through linguistic utterance: "Hence the word which sounds outside, is the sign of the word which shines within."[162]

## NOTES

1. Augustine, *De Genesi ad Litteram* (*Gn. litt.*) 5.5.12, CSEL 28.1, 145–6: "Factae itaque creaturae motibus coeperunt currere tempora." See also Kurt Flasch,

*Was ist Zeit? Augustinus von Hippo. Das XI. Buch der Confessiones. Historisch-Philosophische Studie* (Frankfurt am Main: Klostermann, 1993), 93.

2. Basil Studer, *Zur Theophanie-Exegese Augustins. Untersuchung zu einem Ambrosius-Zitat in der Schrift* De uidendo Deo *(Ep. 147)*, Studia Anselmiana 59 (Roma: Herder, 1971), 8.

3. Cf. Augustine, Sermon (*s.*) 184.2.3, SPM 1, 76; *s.* 187.1, PL 38, 1001.

4. Cf. *infra* and, for example, *Confessions* (*conf.*) 9.10.24, Loeb 27, 48.

5. Jens Zimmermann, "Confusion of Horizons: Gadamer and the Christian Logos," *Journal of Beliefs and Values* 22.1 (April 2001), 87–98, here 88.

6. Zimmermann, "Confusion of Horizons," 88.

7. Zimmermann, "Confusion of Horizons," 87.

8. Jean Grondin, "Gadamer und Augustin," in *Der Sinn für Hermeneutik* (Darmstadt: Wissenschaftliche Buchgesellschaft, 1994), 24–39, here 31–2.

9. John Arthos, "The Fullness of Understanding? The Career of the Inner Word in Gadamer Scholarship," *Philosophy Today* 55, no. 2 (June 2011), 166–83, here 166.

10. It is also worth noting that although most scholars point to the Stoic distinction between the *logos prophorikos* and the *logos endiathetos* as the source for Augustine's doctrine of the inner word, Gerard Watson argues strenuously against this possibility. See Watson, "St. Augustine and the Inner Word: The Philosophical Background," *The Irish Theological Quarterly* 54 (1988), 81–92, esp. 82, 88.

11. John Arthos, *The Inner Word in Gadamer's Hermeneutics* (Notre Dame, IN: University of Notre Dame Press, 2009). See also Arthos, "'A Limit that Resides in the Word:' Hermeneutic Appropriations of Augustine," in *Augustine for the Philosophers: The Rhetor of Hippo, the Confessions, and the Continentals*, ed. C. Troup, Studies in Rhetoric and Religion 16 (Waco, TX: Baylor University Press, 2014), 93–106.

12. Mirela Oliva, *Das innere Verbum in Gadamers Hermeneutik*, Hermeneutische Untersuchungen zur Theologie 53 (Tübingen: Mohr Siebeck, 2009).

13. Arthos, "The Fullness of Understanding," 178.

14. Arthos, *The Inner Word*, 110; cf. Graziano Ripanti, "L'allegoria o l''intellectus figuratus' nel *De doctrina Christiana* di Agostino," *Revue d'Études Augustiniennes et Patristiques* 18 (1972), 219–232, here 228.

15. Jean Grondin, "La thèse de l'herméneutique sur l'être," *Revue de Métaphysique et de Morale* no. 4 (Oct.-Dec. 2006), 469–481, here 478.

16. Zimmermann, "Confusion of Horizons," 90.

17. Hans-Georg Gadamer, *Truth and Method* (*TM*), trans. J. Weinsheimer and D. Marshall, 2nd rev. ed. (London: Bloomsbury, 2013) 491; *idem*, *Gesammelte Werke* (*GW*), 10 volumes (Tübingen: Mohr Siebeck, 1986–1995) here *GW* 1, 479: "Was verstanden werden kann, ist Sprache. Das will sagen: es ist so, daß es sich von sich aus dem Verstehen darstellt." All English translations of Gadamer are taken from the Weinsheimer and Marshall translation cited *supra* (hereafter cited as *TM*).

18. Grondin, *The Philosophy of Gadamer*, trans. Kathryn Plant (London: Routledge, 2014), 143.

19. Grondin, "La thèse de l'herméneutique sur l'être," 479. For another take on how language exceeds our spoken and written words, consider, for instance,

Alessandro's aria in Handel's *Tolomeo, re d'Egitto* (*Händel-Werke-Verzeichnis* 25): "Non lo dirò col labbro, che tanto ardir non ha. Forse con le faville dell'avide pupille, per dir come tutt'ardo lo sguardo parlerà."

20. Gadamer, *TM*, 502; *GW* 1, 490.

21. María Guadalupe Llanes, "Gadamer y la igualdad sustancial de pensamiento y lenguaje en San Agustín," *Studia Gilsoniana* 2 (2013), 145–159, here 157–8.

22. Llanes, "Gadamer y la igualdad sustancial," 158. See also Vicente Muñiz, *Introducción a la filosofía del lenguaje. Problemas ontológicos* (Barcelona: Anthropos, 1989), 64: "en el hombre habla *la voz del ser*." Muñiz is quoted in Llanes, "Gadamer y la igualdad sustancial," 146.

23. Oliva, *Das innere Verbum in Gadamers Hermeneutik*, 30.

24. Grondin, *The Philosophy of Gadamer*, 144.

25. Grondin, *The Philosophy of Gadamer*, 144.

26. Grondin, *The Philosophy of Gadamer*, 145.

27. Gadamer, *TM*, 502; *GW* 1, 490–1.

28. Gadamer, *TM*, 461; *GW* 1, 448: "sein [i.e., human] Sprechen die Welt zur Sprache bringt."

29. Philippe Eberhard, "Gadamer and Theology," *International Journal of Systematic Theology* 9.3 (July 2007), 283–300, here 296.

30. Gadamer, *TM*, 462; *GW* 1, 449.

31. Gadamer, *TM*, 490; *GW* 1, 478.

32. Gadamer, *TM*, 491; *GW* 1, 479: "Denn sprachlich und damit verständlich ist das menschliche Weltverhältnis schlechthin und von Grund aus."

33. *conf.* 11.9.11, CCSL 27, 199: "Fecisti caelum et terram, in Verbo tuo, in Filio tuo, in Virtute tua, in Sapientia tua, in Veritate tua."

34. *conf.* 13.5.6, CCSL 27, 244.

35. *s.* 1.2, CCSL 41, 3–4. This sermon was composed ca. 391–395.

36. Isabelle Bochet, "Interprétation Scriptuaire et comprehension de soi: du *De doctrina christiana* aux *Confessions* de Saint Augustin," in *Comprendre et interpréter: le paradigme herméneutique de la raison*, ed. J. Greisch (Paris: Beauchesne, 1993), 21–50, here 48.

37. Cf. Gerd Van Riel, "Augustine's Exegesis of 'Heaven and Earth' in *Conf.* XII: Finding Truth Amidst Philosophers, Heretics, and Exegetes," *Quaestio* 7 (2007), 191–228, as well as J.C.M. Van Winden, "Frühchristliche Bibelexegese: 'Der Anfang,'" in *Arche: a Collection of Patristic Studies by J.C.M. van Winden*, ed. J. den Boeft and D. Runia (Leiden: Brill, 1997), 3–48, here 36. See also C. S. De Beer, "MUTHOS, LOGOS, NOUS: In Pursuit of the Ultimate in Human Thought," *Phronimon* 7.1 (2006), 55–68.

38. Van Winden, "Frühchristliche Bibelexegese," 34–6.

39. Van Winden, "Frühchristliche Bibelexegese," 37; cf. Werner Beierwaltes, "Augustins Interpretation von *Sapientia* 11, 21," *Revue d'Etudes Augustiniennes et Patristiques* 15.1–2 (1969), 51–61, here 51–2.

40. Van Winden, "Frühchristliche Bibelexegese," 37. Cf. Michael Theobald, *Im Anfang war das Wort. Textlinguistische Studie zum Johannesprolog* (Stuttgart: Katholisches Bibelwerk, 1983), 111–12.

41. Dirk G. Van der Merwe and Pierre Y. Albalaa, "The Metaphor of Light Embedded in the Johannine Prologue, Part I: the Light Before the Incarnation," *In Luce Verbi* 47, no. 1 (2013), 1–10, here 5.
42. Van Riel, "Augustine's Exegesis," 225.
43. Van Riel, "Augustine's Exegesis," 225.
44. *s.* 187.2, PL 38, 1001: "nec locis concluditur, nec temporibus tenditur, nec morulis breuibus longisque uariatur, nec uocibus texitur, nec silentio terminatur." The translation is taken from *Sermons 184–229Z*, ed. J. Rotelle, O.S.A., trans. E. Hill, O.P., The Works of Saint Augustine: A Translation for the 21st Century (Hyde Park, NY: New City Press, 1992), 28.
45. *s.* 188.2.2, PL 38, 1004.
46. *s.* 188.1.1, PL 38, 1003: "Filium Dei, sicuti est apud Patrem aequalis illi et coaeternus, in quo condita sunt omnia in coelo et in terra, uisibilia et inuisibilia, Verbum Dei et Deum, uitam et lucem hominum." Trans. Hill, 31. See also *s.* 190.1.1, PL 38, 1007–1009: "erat apud Patrem antequam natus esset ex matre."
47. *s.* 196.3, PL 38, 1020: "Dominus Iesus homo esse uoluit propter nos. Non uilescat misericordia; iacet in terra Sapientia. *In principio erat Verbum, et Verbum erat apud Deum, et Deus erat Verbum.*" Trans. Hill, 61.
48. *s.* 196.1, PL 38, 1019; cf. *s.* 195.2.
49. *s.* 187.3, PL 38, 1002; cf. Oliva, *Das innere Verbum in Gadamers Hermeneutik*, 26.
50. *s.* 187.3, PL 38, 1002.
51. Grondin, "Gadamer und Augustin," 31.
52. Grondin, "Gadamer und Augustin," 31.
53. *s.* 187.3, PL 38, 1002. Cf. Carol Harrison, *Beauty and Revelation in the Thought of Saint Augustine* (Oxford: Oxford UP, 1992), 57–8.
54. *s.* 187.3, PL 38, 1002.
55. Van der Merwe and Albalaa, "Part I," 8.
56. Van der Merwe and Albalaa, "Part II," 3.
57. *s.* 188.2.2, PL 38, 1004.
58. Llanes, "Gadamer y la igualdad sustancial," 152; Oliva, *Das innere Verbum in Gadamers Hermeneutik*, 26.
59. Oliva, *Das innere Verbum in Gadamers Hermeneutik*, 18–19.
60. Oliva, *Das innere Verbum in Gadamers Hermeneutik*, 19.
61. Oliva, *Das innere Verbum in Gadamers Hermeneutik*, 19; cf. G. Bavaud, "Un thème augustinien: Le mystère de l'Incarnation, à la lumière de la distinction entre le verbe intérieur et le verbe proféré," *Revue Augustinienne* 9 (1963), 95–101, here 99ff.
62. Oliva, *Das innere Verbum in Gadamers Hermeneutik*, 16–17.
63. Oliva, *Das innere Verbum in Gadamers Hermeneutik*, 17.
64. Oliva, *Das innere Verbum in Gadamers Hermeneutik*, 17.
65. Oliva, *Das innere Verbum in Gadamers Hermeneutik*, 17.
66. Alberto Romele, "The Ineffectiveness of Hermeneutics: Another Augustine's Legacy in Gadamer," *International Journal of Philosophy and Theology* 75, no. 5 (2015), 422–439, here 424–5.
67. Romele, "The Ineffectiveness of Hermeneutics," 424.

68. Romele, "The Ineffectiveness of Hermeneutics," 424.
69. Romele, "The Ineffectiveness of Hermeneutics," 424.
70. Romele, "The Ineffectiveness of Hermeneutics," 424.
71. Romele, "The Ineffectiveness of Hermeneutics," 425.
72. Romele, "The Ineffectiveness of Hermeneutics," 425.
73. Oliva, *Das innere Verbum in Gadamers Hermeneutik*, 26.
74. Oliva, *Das innere Verbum in Gadamers Hermeneutik*, 22. Cf. Arthos, *The Inner Word*, 130–2, and "The Fullness of Understanding," 167.
75. Oliva, *Das innere Verbum in Gadamers Hermeneutik*, 22.
76. Oliva, *Das innere Verbum in Gadamers Hermeneutik*, 27.
77. Oliva, *Das innere Verbum in Gadamers Hermeneutik*, 27.
78. Oliva, *Das innere Verbum in Gadamers Hermeneutik*, 27.
79. Oliva, *Das innere Verbum in Gadamers Hermeneutik*, 22.
80. Gadamer, *TM*, 437–8; *GW* 1, 424–5.
81. Gadamer, *TM*, 437; *GW* 1, 424: 424: "was so heraustritt und sich in der Äußerung äußert, immer schon Wort ist."
82. Gadamer, *TM*, 441–2; *GW* 1, 427–8.
83. Gadamer, *TM*, 438; *GW* 1, 425: "Das innere Wort des Geistes ist mit dem Denken genauso wesensgleich, wie Gottessohn mit Gottvater."
84. Grondin, "Gadamer und Augustin," 38.
85. Grondin, "Gadamer und Augustin," 38.
86. Grondin, "Gadamer und Augustin," 38–9.
87. *trin.* 15.10.19, CCSL 50A, 484–6; Harrison, *Beauty and Revelation*, 57–8.
88. Oliva, *Das innere Verbum in Gadamers Hermeneutik*, 26.
89. *trin.* 15.11.20, CCSL 50A, 488.
90. *trin.* 15.11.20, CCSL 50A, 486–9.
91. *trin.* 15.12.22, CCSL 50A, 493–5.
92. *trin.* 15.11.20, CCSL 50A, 487: "Et sicut uerbum nostrum fit uox, nec mutatur in uocem." Cf. Oliva, *Das innere Verbum in Gadamers Hermeneutik*, 26, and Riccardo Ferri, *Gesù e la verità: Agostino e Tommaso interpreti del Vangelo di Giovanni*, Collana di teología 59 (Rome: Città Nuova, 2003), 48.
93. *trin.* 15.12.22, CCSL 50A, 493–5.
94. *trin.* 15.14.24, CCSL 50A, 497: "Verbum autem nostrum illud quod non habet sonum neque cogitationem soni, sed eius rei quam uidendo intus dicimus, et ideo nullius linguae est." Trans. Hill, 415. One's thoughts are like words of a sort, but these are said to be seen rather than heard when they are interior. See *trin.* 15.10.18.
95. *trin.* 15.15.25, CCSL 50A, p. 499: "uerbum uerum nostrum intimum nisi nostra cogitatione non dicitur." My translation.
96. *trin.* 15.10.17, CCSL 50A, p. 484: "Nam etsi uerba non sonent, in corde suo dicit utique qui cogitat." My translation.
97. Llanes, "Gadamer y la igualdad sustancial," 154; cf. Romele, "The Ineffectiveness of Hermeneutics," 425, 428.
98. David Vessey, "Gadamer, Augustine, Aquinas, and Hermeneutic Universality," *Philosophy Today* 55, no. 2 (May 2011), 158–65, here 160.
99. Zimmermann, "Confusion of Horizons," 95.

100. D. Vessey, "Hermeneutic Universality," 160. Edward Morgan writes of the conversation which obtains between God and the human mind in *The Incarnation of the Word: The Theology of Language of Augustine of Hippo* (London: T&T Clark, 2010), 86. See also Romele, "The Ineffectiveness of Hermeneutics," 422–39.

101. Cf. Oliva, *Das innere Verbum in Gadamers Hermeneutik*, 15, 18.

102. Jens Zimmermann, *Recovering Theological Hermeneutics: An Incarnational-Trinitarian Theory of Interpretation* (Grand Rapids, MI: Baker, 2004), 170; Oliva, *Das innere Verbum in Gadamers Hermeneutik*, 25.

103. Llanes, "Gadamer y la igualdad sustancial," 157.

104. Llanes, "Gadamer y la igualdad sustancial," 156.

105. Eberhard, "Gadamer and Theology," 290.

106. Gadamer, *TM*, 443–4; *GW* 1, 430.

107. Frederick G. Lawrence, "Ontology *of* and *as* Horizon: Gadamer's Rehabilitation of the Metaphysics of Light," *Revista Portuguesa de Filosofia* 56, no. 3–4 (Jul.-Dec. 2000), 389–420, here 408; *TM*, 403.

108. Zimmermann, *Recovering Theological Hermeneutics*, 170.

109. Gadamer, *TM*, 441; *GW* 1, 427.

110. Gadamer, *TM*, 442; *GW* 1, 428.

111. Zimmermann, *Recovering Theological Hermeneutics*, 164.

112. Gadamer, *TM*, 441; *GW* 1, 427–8: "Der Vorgang und Hervorgang des Denkens ist insofern kein Veränderungsvorgang (*motus*), also kein Übergang von Potenz in Akt, sondern ein Hervorgehen *ut actus ex actu*: das Wort wird nicht erst gebildet, nachdem die Erkenntnis vollendet ist, scholastisch gesprochen, nachdem die Information des Intellektes durch die *species* abgeschlossen ist, sondern es ist der Vollzug der Erkenntnis selbst. Insofern ist das Wort mit dieser Bildung (*formatio*) des Intellektes zugleich."

113. Gadamer, *TM*, 442; *GW* 1, 428–9.

114. Grondin, "Gadamer und Augustin," 34.

115. Oliva, *Das innere Verbum in Gadamers Hermeneutik*, 27.

116. Oliva, *Das innere Verbum in Gadamers Hermeneutik*, 27.

117. Grondin, "Gadamer und Augustin," 34.

118. Grondin, "Gadamer und Augustin," 34.

119. Grondin, "Gadamer und Augustin," 34.

120. Grondin, "Gadamer und Augustin," 34.

121. Grondin, "Gadamer und Augustin," 34.

122. Cf. Gadamer, *TM*, 502–4; *GW* 1, 491–3.

123. Lawrence, "*Ontology* of *and* as *Horizon*," 393.

124. Gadamer, *TM*, 435; *GW* 1, 421.

125. Gadamer, *TM*, 491; *GW* 1, 479.

126. Luc Langlois, "L'universalité du *verbum interius*," *Philosophiques* 22.1 (Spring 1995), 137–57, 148.

127. Zimmermann, *Recovering Theological Hermeneutics*, 172, 176.

128. Langlois, "L'universalité du *verbum interius*," 148.

129. Gadamer, *TM*, 440; *GW* 1, 426.

130. Zimmermann, *Recovering Theological Hermeneutics*, 172.

131. Grondin, "La thèse de l'herméneutique sur l'être," 472.
132. Gadamer, *TM*, 490; *GW* 1, 478.
133. Grondin, "La thèse de l'herméneutique sur l'être," 472.
134. Grondin, *The Philosophy of Gadamer*, 146.
135. Gadamer, *TM*, 489; *GW* 1, 476–7.
136. Lawrence, "*Ontology* of *and* as *Horizon*," 415.
137. Gadamer, *TM*, 486; *GW* 1, 474.
138. Gadamer, *TM*, 476; *GW* 1, 464.
139. Gadamer, *TM*, 474–5; *GW* 1, 462–3.
140. Lawrence, "*Ontology* of *and* as *Horizon*," 403. Zimmermann, *Recovering Theological Hermeneutics*, 186, rightly notes that Gadamer's account of knowledge as self-knowledge ignores Augustine's emphasis on linking such knowledge with knowledge of God.
141. Gadamer, *TM*, 499; *GW* 1, 487; Zimmermann, *Recovering Theological Hermeneutics*, 173.
142. Gadamer, *TM*, 506; *GW* 1, 494.
143. Oliva, *Das innere Verbum in Gadamers Hermeneutik*, 21–2.
144. Oliva, *Das innere Verbum in Gadamers Hermeneutik*, 22.
145. Oliva, *Das innere Verbum in Gadamers Hermeneutik*, 22.
146. Lope Cilleruelo, "'Deum uidere' en San Augustin," *Salmanticensis* 12.1 (1965), 3–31, here 6.
147. Cilleruelo, "'Deum uidere' en San Augustin," 6; cf. Oliva, *Das innere Verbum in Gadamers Hermeneutik*, 28.
148. Ferri, *Gesù e la verità*, 47.
149. Ferri, *Gesù e la verità*, 47.
150. Ferri, *Gesù e la verità*, 48.
151. Arthos, *The Inner Word*, 107.
152. Oliva, *Das innere Verbum in Gadamers Hermeneutik*, 24.
153. Oliva, *Das innere Verbum in Gadamers Hermeneutik*, 24.
154. Langlois, "L'universalité du *verbum interius*," 139.
155. Cf. *s.* 120.2, PL 38, 677.
156. *trin.* 15.11.20, CCSL 50A, 486–9.
157. *trin.* 15.11.20, CCSL 50A, 486–9.
158. *trin.* 15.11.20, CCSL 50A, 486–9; cf. Ferri, *Gesù e la verità*, 48.
159. *s.* 120.2, PL 38, 677.
160. This also shows a possible way that art and literature could function; in other words, someone has a profound experience of something that is then communicated equivocally, as it cannot be explained in univocal terms, a notion suggested by Croce and Collingwood. See, for example, R. G. Collingwood, *The Principles of Art* (Oxford: Clarendon, 1967 [1938]).
161. *trin.* 15.10.19, CCSL 50A, 485–6.
162. *trin.* 15.11.20, CCSL 50A, 486: "Proinde uerbum quod foris sonat, signum est uerbi quod intus lucet." My translation.

*Part III*

# TIME, EMBODIMENT, AND GENDER

*Chapter 7*

# Augustinian Temporality and Resurrected Bodies

Paul Ulishney

While the vast majority of scholarship on Augustinian temporality focuses on his famous "psychological" account of time in *Confessions* 11,[1] Augustine did present an alternative (and complementary) account in many other works, which would, in fact, go on to have a very long life in philosophy and theology, especially in the Middle Ages. This alternative account describes the relation of time to the physical world, in which temporality is inextricably linked to mutability and its attendant functions, namely, motion and movement. We can call this Augustine's "physical" account of time. Physical time, which is both independent of and yet congruent with the psychological perception of time, is an essential characteristic of being created and of matter. In this regard, temporality and mutability are to be understood as two sides of the same coin called "createdness." For Augustine, this aspect of createdness is contrasted ontologically with God's uncreated eternal being, which is understood in terms of immutability and stability.

Much scholarship has been devoted to examining the relationship between eternity and time as it pertains to the creation of the world, as well as to Augustine's engagement with Aristotle's and Plotinus's views on the paradoxes of time, especially with reference to the psychological account of *Confessions* 11.[2] I would, however, like to branch out to some overlooked texts and ideas in Augustine's thought that do not seem to receive as much attention. One understudied topic involves investigating the relationship between eternity and time not at the beginning, as it were, but at the end: in Augustine's eschatology. To this end, I will explore the place of temporality in Augustine's speculations about the nature of resurrected bodies. For if temporality is an irreducible characteristic of createdness, and human resurrected bodies are material bodies that will still retain movement,[3] how are we to understand this in light of Augustine's seemingly contradictory description of heaven as comprising an eternal Sabbath, where "we shall be still and see; we shall see and we shall love; we shall love and we shall praise," being "perfectly at rest . . . in stillness" in a "day without end"?[4] And how does this fit with his contrast between time and eternity in *Confessions* 11? There he writes of the stabilization of humanity in the presence of God's eternity:

> Now, though, my years are spent in groaning, and you are my consolation, Lord, for you are my eternal Father. But I became alienated as I entered into time (*at ego in tempora dissilui*), not knowing the order in which it passes, and my thoughts, the innermost parts of my soul (*intima viscera animae meae*), are ripped apart by turbulent vicissitudes, until I flow back together toward you, purged, and shining with the fire of your love.[5]

This chapter will proceed in two sections. First, I will outline Augustine's physical account of time, noting its relationship to his psychological account, along with some important conceptual distinctions at play in the broader grammar of Augustinian temporality. Second, I will turn to some of the sermons Augustine preached on the resurrection of the body in the late winter and Easter season of 411, which constitute some of his most sustained discussion on the nature and activities of resurrected bodies. My argument is that his eschatological speculations require a holistic understanding of both physical and psychological time, resulting in a reading in which heaven does not consist in being liberated from time, but simply no longer experiencing it as distraction.[6]

## CONCEPTUAL DISTINCTIONS AND AUGUSTINE'S PHYSICAL ACCOUNT OF TIME

In 1950, the French historian Henri-Irénée Marrou made a watershed contribution in Augustinian studies by articulating the concept of the "ambivalence" of time in Augustine's view of history.[7] By this he meant that temporality is simultaneously the locus of humanity's distraction from God and the vehicle of its redemption. One example of this ambivalence can be seen in Augustine's use of the verb *extendere* in *Confessions* 11 as a synonym both for the scattering of time in the mind's perception of it after the Fall[8] and for its opposite, *intentio*,[9] the reaching out or turning toward God's stabilizing eternity. Twelve years later, Aimé Solignac built on Marrou by observing that the *regio dissimilitudinis* ("region of dissimilarity," used by Augustine in *Confessions* 7 to describe human life in a fallen world) from which humans turn to God may signify either ontological dissimilarity (mutability and temporality) or spiritual dissimilarity (sin).[10]

The theme of ambivalence and the distinction between ontological dissimilarity and spiritual dissimilarity are crucial, since Augustine's two accounts of time roughly map onto these two kinds of dissimilarity. Physical time corresponds to ontological dissimilarity to God, understood through concepts like mutability, motion, and movement. Psychological time, meanwhile, corresponds to spiritual dissimilarity, using concepts like the passing of days and the instability of the present moment made such by sin. Sometimes, Augustine does not explicitly make clear which type of time he is referring to, but reading the passage usually provides clarity on the matter. When Augustine is referring to physical time, he tends to offer descriptions of motion or the movements of bodies (including many kinds of physical objects) and, given his particular theology of the Fall, the decay that postlapsarian bodies undergo as a result of sin.[11] When he is describing psychological time, he almost always uses the language of time moving from future into present into past, or the passage of time in terms of days—one day begins and ends, and then a different day begins—both of which are fleeting and unstable.[12] Because he uses these same two sets of illustrations in nearly every reference to time, we can safely deduce from the set he employs which kind of time the reader is meant to understand. While physical time is associated with movement and motion of any sort in creation, including human movement, psychological time is restricted to an individual human mind (*animus*). It is crucial to keep in mind that Augustine almost exclusively explores the latter within the context of how the fallen human mind perceives the passage of time in a fallen world. Accordingly, reflecting on psychological time involves a proto-phenomenological method insofar as it is concerned with the passage of time from future, to present, to past, from the perspective of a soul undergoing its changes, rendered such by sin. This means that both physical and psychological time are experienced in and require bodies. One must remember here that Augustine holds a dualist anthropology. He believes that human beings (*personae*) are a composite of body and soul (*anima*, within which is the *animus* or "mind," which is the seat or ruling principle of the soul).[13] Thus, despite some early uncertainty about how exactly they relate to one another, Augustine is at pains to emphasize that the soul or mind and body naturally desire one another, the body being ruled by the mind, and the mind needing the body's "tools" by which it can perform tasks like sensation or perception.[14] The difference in terms of time is that, for a human subject, the physical time of motion remains a fundamental attribute of human beings whether sin is present or absent in bodies, whereas the psychological perception of time undergoes a significant change depending on the type of body (prelapsarian, postlapsarian, resurrection) within which it is perceived.[15]

Sin, therefore, is the primary factor influencing how a human body conceives of and experiences time, since it has the result of fragmenting the psychological perception of time. The effect of sin (or sinlessness) on bodies is of the utmost importance, since it makes a very big difference whether Augustine is describing the experience of time in a prelapsarian, postlapsarian, or resurrected body. One must not therefore conflate time intended to be understood with reference to fallen creatures with time elsewhere predicated of resurrected bodies. Thus, without Solignac's distinction, Augustine's ambivalence toward time might lead one to incorrectly conflate temporality *as such* with sin.[16] But, much like John Rist's observation about matter in Plotinus's ethics, one must recognize the difference between a necessary condition and a sufficient condition for sin: "There would be no moral evil unless the soul were in the presence of matter or material objects; . . . the existence of matter is a necessary but not a sufficient condition for the existence of moral evil."[17] The same can be said about the relationship between temporality and sin for Augustine. While temporality is a necessary condition of sin, it is not on its own a sufficient cause or result of sin.[18] Let us take a few examples to illustrate these principles—which, as they currently stand, might seem a bit too abstract—by turning first to the physical account of time outside of the *Confessions*.

Though it is found elsewhere, Augustine most clearly sets out his physical account of time in *The Literal Meaning of Genesis* and *City of God*. Both of these texts offer more developed reflections on the relationship between eternity and time than that found in *Confessions* 11, in which Augustine had addressed questions like "What was God doing before he created the world?" In *The Literal Meaning of Genesis* Book 5, Augustine begins his exegesis of Genesis 2:4–6 by reaffirming that the second account of creation conforms to the first insofar as both accounts are intended to convey that God created everything in heaven and earth simultaneously, and that the universe was created from nothing. The order of the seven days found in the first account, he argues, is causal and not temporal.[19] Moreover, he writes, "By the expression 'heaven and earth' the author, according to the normal style of the scriptures, clearly wishes the whole of creation to be understood."[20] Thus, the entire universe came into being together in one moment.

Even here, however, we are confronted with difficulties about the relationship between time and eternity. For it is not quite right to refer to it as a "moment," since the act of creating the world cannot itself be a temporal event. As Augustine himself states,

> An event in time happens after one time and before another, after the past and before the future. But at the time of creation there could have been no past, because there was nothing created to provide *the change and movement which is the condition of time*.[21]

As in the *Confessions*, Augustine here demonstrates that the question "What was God doing before he created the world?" is nonsensical and by implication makes the case that the world cannot be co-eternal with God (nor is the act of creating the world eternal), but here he does so by foraying into the concept of physical time. One might be surprised to see, however, that the argument outside of the *Confessions* is that time *is* inextricably bound up with movement and encapsulated within the boundaries of the created things, and as such it follows that "the world was in fact made *with* time," since "at the time of its creation change and motion came into existence."[22] Time is a creature, created together with matter. Together, time and matter necessarily form a mutually interdependent pair. The inextricable link between time and motion is found not just in the movements of the heavenly bodies, but equally in the movement of human bodies. Augustine further details this theme when describing the lives of the first humans and animals in the Garden of Eden:

> And so creatures once made *began to run with their movements along the tracks of time, which means it is pointless to look for times before any creature, as though times could be found before times. If there were no movement, after all, of either the spiritual or bodily creation, by which things to come in the future would succeed things in the past through the present, there would be absolutely no time at all.* But no creature could move, of course, if it did not exist. So it is time that begins from the creation rather than the creation from time, while both are from God . . . . Nor should the statement that time begins from the creation be taken to imply that time is not a creature, *since in fact it is the movement of creatures from one state to another*, with things following each other as regulated by God managing everything he has created.[23]

Thus, we find the physical account of time mapping nicely onto Solignac's first distinction: motion or movement, which can be broadly rendered as "mutability," is understood as a form of time, which sets created things apart from God's eternity and immutability. Temporality and mutability go hand in hand as the singular medium of createdness.

One must notice here, though, that Augustine is not describing fallen creation. He is describing the world before the Fall. There was motion when Adam named the animals in the Garden and they walked to him, or when he and Eve walked around the trees and spoke with the serpent. Therefore, there was time passing due to the motion of their bodies. This physical understanding of time is again underscored by Augustine's repeated contrasts between createdness and God's eternity:

> But above all we have to remember, a point we have already made several times, that God does not work by time-measured movements, so to say, *of mind*

(*animi*) or body (*corporis*), as do human beings and angels, but by the eternal and unchanging, stable formulae of his Word, co-eternal with himself, and by . . . his equally co-eternal Holy Spirit.[24]

For in God, neither the physical nor psychological notions of time are present. But Augustine does not merely make a distinction between the eternity of God and temporality as such. Instead, he makes a distinction between the eternity of God and two types of time: the time of the mind (*animi*) and the time of the body (*corporis*). This neatly maps onto the distinction between psychological and physical time, indicating that Augustine views both as distinct, but also as complementary and equally constitutive of the human *persona*. Again, Augustine is here describing the original, prelapsarian life of Adam and Eve, and thus we can even venture to say that physical temporality is *good*, just like all of God's other creations.

But if time refers to creatures moving between different states, and if "change and movement . . . is the condition of time,"[25] how can this be reconciled with Augustine's earlier statement in *Confessions* 11 that "time is not the movement of a physical object"?[26] While a surface reading of the text would lead one to believe that these two accounts are in conflict with each other, Augustine will make a terminological development in *On the Nature of the Good* which resolves this issue when seen in the light of the development of his thought. In that treatise, Augustine sets out to define what is truly good, which sends him on a journey describing natures or essences. He begins by arguing that God, as the highest good (i.e., the good than which there is none higher) is the only truly eternal and immutable being. By definition, "all other goods are made only *by* him but are not made *of* him. For that which is of him is what he is, but those things which have been made by him are not what he is. And for this reason he alone is immutable, while all the things that he has made are mutable because he has made them from nothing."[27] God did not generate the world's being from his essence (in Latin, *essentia*, Augustine's translation for the Greek οὐσία), but he created it from nothing in an act. As such, it follows that since they were created by the highest good, "every spirit and every body is naturally something good."[28] This treatise was written as an anti-Manichaean tract, and so Augustine's overall argument is concerned with affirming the goodness of matter. While time is not a nature (i.e., not a *thing*) in the way that bodies are, time and motion are inextricably linked such that the movement of physical objects is impossible without time. So Augustine is consistent with his earlier self in pointing out that time *is* not, in its essence, the movement of the physical object, since it is not a nature in the way that bodies are. It is rather, as he states in the *City of God* earlier, the condition for movement and change and therefore necessary for natures to exist at all. As creatures, so to speak, time and movement require each other, such that bodies cannot be what they are without being enveloped in the medium or plane of temporality. It is also important to keep in mind that the earlier given passage from *Confessions* 11 is, in context, Augustine investigating what he calls the lack of "amplitude" (*spatio*) of time. He is taking up the question of Aristotle's paradoxes of time as to whether there truly is such a thing as a "moment," and whether the mind is the sort of thing, which has the ability to measure it objectively.[29]

Thus, bringing the physical account of time to bear on Augustine's anthropology provides us with a better vantage point from which to distinguish between the irreducible temporality of human beings and sin. It is true that sin could only have occurred in or with time, because only something created from nothing could be capable of sinning, but for Augustine, there is no efficient cause for an evil act of will (i.e., evil is not a material substance). Instead, Augustine posits a "deficient cause" (*declinatio*) by which sin came about, locating the origin of sin in the will, which is, in turn, "located," so to speak, in the mind.[30] And where there is creation from nothing, there is time, since it is inextricably bound up in the movement of bodies. Thus, with Rist, we can say of temporality that it is a necessary condition of sin, but not a sufficient one. And as Augustine will say of the Fall, "It will then be found that the evil choice takes its origin not from the fact that the man is a natural being, but from the fact that his natural being is created from nothing."[31] In this passage, "natural being" refers to the fact that human beings comprise matter, in contrast to God's immaterial being. Physical temporality is therefore not the cause or result of sin. It would be overly simplistic to say that, for Augustine, Adam and Eve *fall* into time and leave it there. At the ontological level, physical temporality is simply a constitutive attribute of being created. When we assume there is only one "sense" of time, and conflate the physical and psychological, or read one through the lens of the other, we lose sight of this fact. In that case, our analysis of the role of time in Augustine's broader theology would be diminished. But if we distinguish physical from psychological time, we can connect the former to Solignac's ontological dissimilarity by defining temporality as the irreducibly natural state of any created being and a fundamental marker of ontological dissimilarity from God, such that were it to cease to be temporal, it would cease being what it is, and this is the case regardless of the presence or absence of sin. Temporality, in its physical sense, is inextricably linked to the mutability of bodies, which for humans is motion and movement.

This first distinction leads us in the direction of Augustine's sermons about time and bodily resurrection. Before discussing those sermons directly, however, we should briefly explore the differences between prelapsarian, postlapsarian, and resurrected bodies. Starting with physical time and moving to psychological, instead of the other way around, enables us to better understand what is at stake in such differences, while also helping us to isolate the role played by psychological time in its complementarity to physical time. When describing the creation of Adam and Eve, Augustine first develops a contrast between "ensouled" bodies and "enspirited" bodies, a distinction which addresses in advance the question of whether heaven will be a return to life in Eden or instead eclipse Eden and comprise something better. An important passage in *The Literal Meaning of Genesis* lays out his interpretive framework and is worth quoting in full:

> *It is one thing, after all, not to be able to die, like natures which God created immortal, while it is quite another to be able not to die; and this is the way the first man was created immortal, something to be granted him by means of the tree of life, not by his natural constitution. From this tree of life he was cut off when he had sinned, so that he could die, while if he had not sinned he would have been able not to die.* So then, he was mortal in virtue of the make of his "ensouled" body (*animale corporis*), immortal in virtue of his maker's favor. If the body, you see, was simply "ensouled," then it was certainly mortal, because it was able to die, though it was also immortal for the reason that it was also able not to die. Nor will it enjoy the immortality of not being able to die at all unless it is "enspirited," *which is something we are promised will be ours in the resurrection.* Accordingly, that "ensouled" and thereby mortal body, which would be "enspirited" (*corpus spiritale*) and thereby altogether immortal on account of justice, became on account of sin, not mortal, which it had been before, but dead, which it need not have become, if the man had not sinned.[32]

Adam and Eve, Augustine tells us, were "equipped with an 'ensouled' body"[33] when they were first created, which would eventually have been "changed, if they had remained obedient, into a better and more 'enspirited' condition without death intervening."[34] While these phrases are not in the text of Genesis, Augustine sees them as necessary logical deductions inherent to the drama of creation and redemption. He reads Paul's distinction between fallen human bodies and resurrected bodies in 1 Corinthians 15:44 (the body "is sown embodying the soul, but rises embodying the spirit") back onto the creation narrative.

This passage also gets at another Augustinian motif, which is the distinction between being able not to sin or die and being incapable of sinning or dying. In *On Rebuke and Grace*, he argues that the "human will's first liberty was able not to sin (*posse non peccare*), but the final will is something much greater, as it is not able to sin (*non posse peccare*)."[35] Likewise, the "first immortality," Adam and Eve's ensouled bodies being sustained by the Tree of Life, "was able not to die (*posse non mori*), but the last immortality will be something much greater, as it is not able to die (*non posse mori*)."[36] Thus,

Adam and Eve were created with ensouled bodies, which are by nature mortal, but before the Fall, they were granted immortality as a gift, which was sustained by eating from the Tree of Life. While in these bodies, the introduction of sin into the world was always a possibility, for ensouled bodies are only "able not to die" and "able not to sin," not "incapable of dying" and "incapable of sinning." These ensouled bodies would have, after an unspecified period of time in obedience to God, been transfigured into enspirited bodies, which *are* incapable of dying or sinning, like God is. Because human beings are still created beings, however, Augustine is at pains to say that even enspirited bodies are not immortal *by nature*, which is still only something reserved for God, but by their participation in that divine nature by virtue of the Spirit's vivifying indwelling—hence en*spirit*ed. With the introduction of sin, however, ensouled bodies lost their trial run at immortality and became capable of dying. This capacity for dying took form in the capacity for *deterioration*, because Augustine makes clear that the Fall does not result in being given a new or different body. It is just that the same, ensouled bodies of Adam and Eve are now prone to failure and sickness.[37] He affirms this in *Sermon* 362 when he argues that decay in the body "is signified by the skins with which Adam and Eve were clothed, and then expelled from paradise."[38] This is why physical time "roughly" remains the same in pre- and postlapsarian bodies, in the sense that the mutability which constitutes the temporality of ontological dissimilarity to God remains just as it was before the Fall, despite the fact that the body is now subject to deterioration. More important for Augustine is that when Adam and Eve ate of the fruit from the Tree of the Knowledge of Good and Evil, "*the eyes of them both were opened* (Gn 3:7)—for what, if not for lusting after each other, as a punishment for the sin, a punishment conceived by the death of the flesh itself?" The change that is undergone in the Fall is most drastically realized in the *mind*, which, as we indicated earlier, is the location of the psychological perception of time. Augustine writes that Adam and Eve's ensouled bodies before the Fall were exactly the same as ours are now, except that "they did not have the same lust for carnal pleasure as these bodies of ours do now, derived as they are from the propagation of death."[39]

It is in this context that we ought to place Augustine's reflections on time in *Confessions* 11, where he frames temporality in terms of spiritual dissimilarity to God, the second category that we borrow from Solignac. As seen earlier, the change that human beings undergo as the result of sin is located especially in the mind, for the mind (or will) is what enabled the introduction of sin into the world. If we understand *Confessions* 11 to be a more limited investigation confined to the mental perception of the passage of time in a postlapsarian body, and not *the* authoritative lens through which every possible concept of time must be read, we can begin to see how it complements the physical account described earlier. When Augustine describes how the "innermost parts of his soul are torn into the vicissitudes of time,"[40] he is not reflecting on time *as such*, but specifically on how the scattering of the mind *made such by sin* struggles to focus itself or find stability in the passage of time in the present life. He is referring to the second sense of temporality, spiritual dissimilarity, not the first, ontological dissimilarity. Likewise, in his *Tractates on the Gospel of John*, Augustine preached that when "the fullness of time had come, the one who would set us free from time also came,"[41] clearly using time as a stand-in for the spiritual dissimilarity into which human beings were thrown as a result of sin. He is *not* referring to mere ontological dissimilarity from God. This is evident from the fact that, immediately after he says this, he explains what he means by "time" by referring to the passage of days and the figures of the future, present, and past, which, as we indicated earlier, are his preferred ways of illustrating fallen psychological time. Had he also mentioned concepts like motion and movement and mutability, we would be justified in thinking he was referring to liberation from time as such.

We can, therefore, speak of a prelapsarian body, a postlapsarian body, and a resurrected body, all of which are distinct from one another. Time is experienced differently at each level (physical and psychological) in each of those bodies. We have sufficiently described the first two and established that since temporality understood as ontological dissimilarity to God is a fundamental characteristic of being created, physical time and psychological time were experienced in prelapsarian bodies in the Garden, but came to be experienced as deterioration in the body and scattering in the mind as a result of the Fall. We are now equipped to investigate whether or not physical time and psychological time also remain in resurrected bodies.

## RESURRECTED BODIES IN THE SERMONS OF EARLY 411

*Sermons* 361 and 362 comprise a diptych of homilies focused on the theme of the resurrection of the dead, especially as found in 1 Corinthians 15. According to Edmund Hill, OP, these sermons were preached between February and March in 411 in Hippo Regius, around the same time as the *Parentalia* (pagan celebrations for the dead), thus making it appropriate for Augustine to raise the question in a specifically Christian context.[42] After these sermons, Augustine revisited the theme in his homilies (240–242) during Eastertide a month later. Given how closely they were preached to one another, I will engage with these sermons collectively, as variations on a theme. Augustine used these sermons, especially 361, to provide his audience with apologetic arguments, defending the resurrection of the body against non-Christians' criticisms.[43] While some sermons get preoccupied with simply establishing *that* there will be a resurrection of the dead, all engage, at some level, with questions about the nature and activities of resurrected bodies.

In each instance, Augustine admits the speculative nature of his task but insists that not having absolute knowledge regarding the nature of resurrected bodies makes little difference, since the opinions he offers are simply the logical results of deductions from what the Gospels and Paul say about the resurrected body of Christ.[44] Indeed, Augustine grounds his speculations about the resurrected bodies of Christians with an ecclesiological point about Jesus Christ being the foundation of the Church and, in the Pauline metaphor, the Church's head.[45] He then states that in the light of Christ's bodily resurrection, "What I do say is that what we ought to hope for in the resurrection of the dead is what has already been portrayed in our head, what has been portrayed in the body of our Lord Jesus Christ."[46] As we know from the Scriptural accounts, Christ's body was fully capable of existing in time due to the fact that, as a body, it still possessed the physical temporality of movement and motion. Christians will "rise again like that, to be forever in the state into which we shall be changed by rising again."[47] Thus, Augustine argues that the specific form of resurrected bodies will be the same as the body of Jesus after his own resurrection, when he walked around and ate with his disciples and eventually ascended into heaven. To this, he adds:

> It's because that specific form, however, will have no tendency to decay that the apostle says, "But this I must say, brothers, that flesh and blood shall not gain possession by inheritance of the kingdom of God; nor shall what is perishable gain possession by inheritance of imperishability" (1 Cor. 15:50); to show that by the expression "flesh and blood" he wished us to understand the tendency to decay of a mortal and merely soul-animated body (*animalis corporis*).[48]

After establishing that resurrected human bodies will be like the resurrected body of Christ, Augustine begins to address the roles that physical and psychological time play in resurrected bodies. He starts with physical time by discussing the concept of "decay" in ensouled bodies (*animalis corporis*). "But what is this change?" asks Augustine: "Does it mean the loss of the specific form which now exists, or only the perishability and liability to decay?"[49] He emphatically denies the former, for "when the flesh rises again it will be changed into the kind of body in which there will no longer be any mortal tendency to decay, and which therefore will no longer be properly called flesh and blood."[50] Moreover, he indicates that the resurrected bodies of human beings will still retain their "specific form," which is physical and thus still contains motion and movement: "Much more marvellous is the agility that will mark the spiritual body of the future," and "how fast it will be able to move." The motion and movement and therefore physical time in these bodies still function to distinguish humans from God in terms of ontological dissimilarity, even in heaven. This is underscored in *Sermon* 277, when Augustine argues that even enspirited bodies cannot physically see God:

> Human curiosity, you see, sometimes pokes around, and says to itself, "Do you suppose that by means of that spiritual body we shall see God?" To which a quick answer can be given: God is not to be seen, as though he were spread out in space, and divided by distance. Although he fills heaven and earth, that doesn't mean he is half in heaven and half on earth.[51]

As we can see, the physical temporality of movement and motion *still* functions to indicate ontological dissimilarity to God, since even resurrected bodies with their "ease and agility, swiftness of movement and such health as this body enjoys" cannot see God, for "God is not a body" and is therefore "not to be seen, as though he were spread out in space, and divided by distance. Although he fills heaven and earth, that doesn't mean he is half in heaven and half in earth."[52] In contrast, the bodies that God gives human beings will move with "a wonderful ease, a wonderful lightness,"[53] just like the body of Christ after his resurrection. In heaven, human bodies will occupy a particular place like they do now, such that "you will be wherever you like, but you will not draw away from God," since "wherever you go, you will have your God."[54] Thus, the effects of the Fall on the physical temporality of the body are reversed in resurrected bodies. Physical temporality is not simply done away with or discarded entirely, because even perfected humans necessarily possess bodies, which always are in motion. Here, what we require liberation from is not physical temporality as such, but the effects of decay (and therefore death) that manifest themselves physically in the postlapsarian body.[55]

One must, then, consider how a resurrected body might psychologically experience time. If physical time refers to the nature of resurrected bodies, psychological time refers to their activity. We know that Augustine is switching to discuss psychological time, because he frames the end of the sermon in the passage of time in terms of days coming and going: "We won't just praise him for one day; but just as that day has no end in time, so our praise will have no end at which it stops."[56] Resurrected bodies are no longer in a state of spiritual dissimilarity to God; instead, their spiritual state will be a "wonderful rest,"[57] "leisure," and contemplation.[58] At the end of *Sermon* 362, Augustine depicts this leisurely activity as an eternal Sabbath praising God: "Our whole activity will consist of Amen and Alleluia," and "our praise will have no end at which it stops; and that's why we shall praise him forever and ever."[59] As a result, we shall then say with quite a different, an inexpressibly different feeling of love, "It's true"; and when we say this, we shall of course be saying Amen, but with a kind of never satisfied satisfaction. Because there will be nothing lacking, you see, that's why complete satisfaction; but because what is not lacking will always be giving delight, that's why, if one can so put it, it will be an unsatisfied satisfaction. So just as you will be insatiably satisfied with the truth, so you will be saying with insatiable truth, Amen.[60]

What we see in these passages is not a discarding of psychological time, but rather its healing, in which the time of the mind is not distracted and split into succeeding infinitesimal moments, but stabilized into God's eternal presence, "continuing forever in the contemplation of truth."[61] And this contemplation is not a static one, but a dynamic one. Augustine will go on to explain this contemplation in terms of a "never satisfied satisfaction" (*insatiabilis satietas*), which, understood in the context of the two registers of time, makes perfect sense. Human beings do not suddenly become atemporal in the life to come, for as we saw earlier, only God can be spoken of in this way, and the physical time inherent to human bodies entails that it is impossible for the whole human person to become static. We are left with the following picture: resurrected bodies will retain both aspects of time, physical and psychological, now redeemed and experienced in different ways. Physically, these bodies will not cease to move or have motion, for humans, as created beings, remain irreducibly temporal in the sense of being ontologically dissimilar to God. They will merely no longer decay. This form of immortality that they experience in the physical register is a gift; natural immortality is reserved for God alone. Psychologically, time will no longer be experienced as distraction, as it was when humans were in postlapsarian bodies and in a state of spiritual dissimilarity to God, with the soul being distended into future and past and caught up in the vicissitudes of time flowing from future to present to past. Instead, the minds of the resurrected will be healed such that they can contemplate the divine love as it ought to be experienced, in an eternal, stabilizing presence.

## CONCLUSION

Given how neatly Augustine's descriptions and illustrations of time map onto the distinction between physical and psychological temporality, we are justified in reading his sermons on resurrected bodies in the light of such a distinction. One ought to understand these sermons as explicating this distinction for Augustine's congregation, who would understandably want to learn in detail about what heaven will be like, especially in the context of Lent and

Easter. By studying neglected texts and articulating a more holistic account of Augustinian temporality, which involves two registers (physical and psychological) and three types of bodies (prelapsarian, postlapsarian, and resurrected), one can problematize overly simplistic notions of salvation as liberation from time as such. Instead, a closer reading acknowledges that it is only right to say that humans are liberated from time if by this we mean postlapsarian time. Temporal experience is not simply discarded, but healed and stabilized into a dynamic, insatiably satiated presence. Throughout this process, temporality as a sign of ontological dissimilarity from God always remains in created beings—even perfected ones. This vision does better justice to the anthropological intuitions found in Augustine's corpus, leaving one with a more consistent anthropological picture spanning creation, fall, and resurrection.

## NOTES

1. I will use the terms "time" and "temporality" interchangeably in this chapter, unless otherwise noted.

2. As with any topic within Augustinian scholarship, the secondary literature is labyrinthine, making it easy for one to get lost in it. I will restrict myself throughout this chapter to referencing only a few studies for any given topic mentioned. On this particular topic, see Roland J. Teske, S.J., *Paradoxes of Time in St. Augustine* (Milwaukee: Marquette University Press, 1996); Richard Sorabji, *Time, Creation, and the Continuum* (London: Duckworth, 1983), 29–32, 163–168; and Simo Knuuttila, "Time and Creation in Augustine," in *The Cambridge Companion to Augustine,* 2nd ed., ed. David Vincent Meconi, S.J., and Eleonore Stump (Cambridge: Cambridge University Press, 2014), 81–97.

3. See: Augustine, *The Literal Meaning of Genesis* 5.12 in *The Works of Saint Augustine: A Translation for the 21st Century, On Genesis*, Vol. 1/13, translation and notes by Edmund Hill, O.P., edited by John E. Rotelle O.S.A. (Hyde Park, New York: New City Press, 2002); *Sermons* 242.11 and 277.7–12 in *The Works of Saint Augustine: A Translation for the 21st Century, Sermons (230–272B) on the Liturgical Seasons*, Vol. 3/7, translation and notes by Edmund Hill, O.P., edited by John E. Rotelle, O.S.A. (New Rochelle, New York: New City Press, 1993); and Books 13 and 22 of the *City of God,* trans. Henry Bettenson, in the Penguin Classics series (London: Penguin Books, 2003). With the exception of *City of God* and *Confessions*, all translations of Augustine's work come from *The Works of Saint Augustine: A Translation for the 21st Century* series.

4. Augustine, *City of God* 22.30.

5. Augustine, *Confessions* 11.29.39, Loeb Classical Library 27, edited and translated by Carolyn J.-B. Hammond (Cambridge, Massachusetts: Harvard University Press, 2014).

6. My account of the role of time in heaven contrasts with the reading developed in Roland Teske, S.J., "'*Vocans Temporales, Faciens Aeternos*:' St. Augustine on

Liberation from Time," *Traditio* 41 (1985), 29–47. Teske's account offers insights into the traces of Neoplatonism to be found in Augustine's thought on divine immutability, but his study suffers from a lack of engagement with the relevant texts in the *City of God*, overemphasizes the role of Plotinus's *Enneads* 3.7 in Augustine's understanding of eternity, and assumes that the psychological and physical accounts of time are competitive rather than complementary. He is certainly right in observing that, for such a massive field as Augustinian studies, there has been surprisingly little literature on this topic. My argument also responds to the "paradoxes" of Edenic and resurrected time set forth in Andrea Nightingale's *Once Out of Nature: Augustine on Time and Body* (Chicago: University of Chicago Press, 2011). The conceptual framework of this chapter shares more in common with Nightingale, though she too presupposes the priority of the psychological account and uses the language of "falling into time" or the need for "liberation" from it.

7. H.-I. Marrou, *L'Ambivalence du temps de l'histoire chez saint Augustin* (Paris: Vrin, 1950).

8. Augustine, *Conf.* 11.11.13, 11.15.20, 11.27.34.

9. Augustine, *Conf.* 11.29.39: "Leaving behind my former times, I recollect myself and follow the One. I forget what is past, and instead of being distracted, I reach out (*sed in ea quae ante sunt non distentus sed extentus*), not for what is in the future and so transitory, but for those things which are before me (*non secundum distentionem sed secundum intentionem*)."

10. Aimé Solignac, "Notes Complémentaires à Livre VII," in vol. 13 of *Oeuvres de Saint Augustin: Les Confessions Livres I–VII* (Paris: Brouwer, 1962), 691.

11. See, for example, *Literal Meaning of Genesis* 5.5.12 and *City of God* 11.6. Even *Confessions* 11.24.31 offers a nascent account of physical time, as we will see later.

12. *Conf.* 11 is Augustine's most famous account, but he utilizes nearly the exact same language in *Homilies* [Tractates] *on the Gospel of John* 31.5 in Vol 3/12, translation and notes by Edmund Hill, O.P., edited and with an introduction and notes by Alan Fitzgerald, O.S.A. (Hyde Park, New York: New City Press, 2009).

13. Augustine also describes the mind as *mens* at other points, but in the passages discussed in this chapter he uses the term *animus*. For Augustine's various descriptions of the unity of body and soul, see, for example, *On the Magnitude of the Soul* 30.59 in Vol. 1/23, introduction, translation and notes by Roland J. Teske, S.J., edited by John E. Rotelle, O.S.A. (Hyde Park, New York: New City Press, 1997); *Letter* 137.3.11 in Vol. 2/2, translation and notes by Roland Teske, edited by Boniface Ramsey (Hyde Park, New York: New City Press, 2003); *City of God* 13.24.2; *Literal Meaning of Genesis* 3.16.25 and 12.35.68; *On the Trinity* 15.7.11 in Vol. 1/5, introduction, translation and notes by Edmund Hill, O.P., edited by John E. Rotelle, O.S.A. (Brooklyn, New York: New City Press, 1991).

14. For a summary of the development of Augustine's thought with respect to the relationship between soul and body, see John Rist, *Augustine: Ancient Thought Baptized* (Cambridge: Cambridge University Press, 1996), 97–104.

15. The differences between how prelapsarian, postlapsarian, and resurrected bodies experience change will be discussed further.

16. See, for instance, Teske, "St. Augustine on Liberation from Time," 32–34, 38–41, *et passim*. Teske either interprets Augustine's language about time within the paradigm of the psychological account or assumes that the psychological account trumps the physical.

17. Rist, *Augustine: Ancient Thought Baptized*, 103.

18. Augustine, *City of God* 12.6.

19. Augustine, *Literal Meaning of Genesis* 5.3.6; cf. *Conf.* 11.31.41.

20. Augustine, *Conf.* 5.2.4.

21. Augustine, *City of God* 11.6, emphasis mine. Cf. *Conf.* 11.31.41.

22. Ibid.

23. Augustine, *Literal Meaning of Genesis* 5.5.12 (emphasis mine).

24. Augustine, *Literal Meaning of Genesis* 1.18.36 (emphasis mine).

25. Augustine, *City of God* 11.6.

26. Augustine, *Conf.* 11.24.31.

27. Augustine, *On the Nature of the Good* 1 in *The Manichean Debate*, Vol. 1/19, translation and notes by Roland Teske, S.J., edited by Boniface Ramsey, O.P. (Hyde Park, New York: New City Press, 2006).

28. Ibid.

29. Aristotle, *Physics* 4.10 in *Physics, Volume 1: Books 1–4*, translated by P.H. Wicksteed and F.M. Cornford in the Loeb Classical Library 228 (Cambridge, Massachusetts: Harvard University Press, 1957).

30. See Rist, *Augustine: Ancient Thought Baptized*, 104–108, and Rowan Williams, "Insubstantial Evil," in *On Augustine* (London: Bloomsbury, 2016), 79–105. This move is part of the wider intent of his theodicy, which makes evil a negative rather than a positive reality.

31. Augustine, *City of God* 12.6. The only complication to this would be the fall of Satan and some of the angels with him, but as this chapter is about human bodies, I have chosen to omit Augustine's speculations about the "time" of the angelic fall. For his thoughts, see: *Literal Meaning of Genesis* 11.13.17–17.22; *City of God* 11.13–15.

32. Augustine, *Literal Meaning of Genesis* 6.24.25 (emphasis mine).

33. Augustine, *Literal Meaning of Genesis* 6.18.23–24.

34. Augustine, *Literal Meaning of Genesis* 11.31.40.

35. Augustine, *On Rebuke and Grace* 12.33 in *The Works of Saint Augustine: A Translation for the 21$^{st}$ Century*, Vol. 1/23, introduction, translation and notes by Roland J. Teske, S.J., edited by John E. Rotelle, O.S.A. (Hyde Park, New York: New City Press, 1997).

36. Ibid.

37. See also *City of God* 13.23, where this argument resurfaces. Being handed over to time is explicitly identified with the deterioration of the body, not being handed over to time as if time did not exist before, since Augustine references the passage of time in the Garden just one sentence before.

38. Augustine, *Sermon* 362.12, in *The Works of Saint Augustine: A Translation for the 21$^{st}$ Century, Sermons (341–400) on Various Subjects*, translated by Edmund Hill, O.P. (Hyde Park, New York: New City Press, 1995), 248.

39. Augustine, *Literal Meaning of Genesis* 4.10.16.

40. Augustine, *Conf.* 11.29.39.
41. Augustine, *Homilies on the Gospel of John* 31.5.
42. Augustine, *Sermons (341–400) on Various Subjects*, 267, note 1.
43. The question of the audience to which Augustine preached these sermons—whether a more advanced circle after Mass in the basilica or his normal congregation—need not detain us here.
44. Augustine, *Sermon* 362.5.
45. Ibid., 9.
46. Ibid., 10.
47. Ibid., 12.
48. Ibid., 19. Cf. a similar line of thinking developed in *Sermon* 277.22.
49. Ibid., *Sermon* 362.21.
50. Ibid.
51. Augustine, *Sermon* 277.13.
52. Ibid.
53. Augustine, *Sermon* 242.11.
54. Ibid.
55. See *City of God* 22.29 for another treatment of this idea outside of the sermons.
56. Ibid., *Sermon* 362.31.
57. Augustine, *Sermon* 362.30.
58. Ibid., 362.31.
59. Ibid., 362.31.
60. Ibid., 362.29.
61. Ibid., 362.31.

*Chapter 8*

# Love in the Time of Augustine

## *Rape, Suicide, and Resurrection in* City of God

Patricia Grosse

The first three books of Augustine's *City of God* were written in 413 C.E. as a direct response to a refugee crisis.[1] At this time, Italian Roman refugees fled to Northern Africa, where Augustine, Bishop of Hippo, sought through letters, meetings, and sermons to console them. The refugees despaired at the loss of Rome, the loss of their possessions, the loss of their friends and family, and, for some, the loss of their virginity and chastity. The latter were faced with an impossible choice: suicide or living unchaste lives marked by the violence done to them. Augustine devotes a significant portion of the first book of the *City of God* to these women.

Given his reputation as a misogynist, Augustine is an unlikely resource for a feminist theological reading of violence against women. Indeed, one major claim against feminist readings of the philosophical canon in general and Augustine in particular is that such readings are necessarily anachronistic—readings outside of time. Within the charge of anachronism in feminist readings of the canon is the implication that non-feminist readings are better able to be objective, better able to be *in* the time of Augustine. To bring questions of gender and women into Augustine's theology (and to find in Augustine a possible support for a feminist philosophy of soul, body, love, etc.) is to misinterpret who Augustine (and other figures of the philosophical and theological canon) is *for*.

Augustine's exploration of heavenly bodies is influenced by his experience as what Margaret Miles refers to as a "Rape Crisis Counselor": caught between philosophical calls for perfection and virtue in this life and the very real lived experience of his parishioners, Augustine seeks to uphold women's bodies as perfect in their form at the same time as he seeks to protect them from further domination from men. The *City of God* is a text that seeks not only to console such refugees but also to make a claim about what it is to be human in body and soul; it ranges from discussions of alternative religious myths to current crises, from Christian mythic beginnings to the life of saints in the world that is to come. Augustine's own accounting for the resurrected life in the *City of God* is speculative—he does not claim to have a perfect understanding of the time after time. His eschatology is based on his knowledge of the human psyche, of what is necessary to the human person. The resurrected body at first glance may not seem to be capable of *concupiscentia*.[2] However, Augustine's discussion of women's bodies in the greater context of the *City of God* hints at what is possible in a time after the end of patriarchal divisions.

In this chapter, I seek to contextualize the discussion of resurrected bodies in Augustine's *City of God* in order to expand the presence of *concupiscentia*, the wild side of love, to the bodies of the resurrected. Far from being the evil, unavoidable result of a Fallen World, this desirous, bodily love is fundamental to Augustine's conception of what it is to be a human today, yesterday, and for all time.

I begin this chapter with a discussion of Augustine's relationships within the fractured community he was ministering to at the time of his composing the *City of God*. I am particularly interested, for the purposes of this project, in his response to victims of wartime rape. In this way, I lay the foundation for Augustine's account of postlapsarian bodies and their innate goodness (and the impossibility of their being tainted, though they are corruptible). I then turn in the next section to Augustine's discussion of the resurrection of women's bodies. This section focuses on the way in which Augustine rips sexual activity away from women's bodies in the *City of God* and (as with babies and bathwater) seems to rip *concupiscentia* out of the proper form of the human person entirely. Finally, I explore several important feminist readings of Augustine on the resurrected life, focusing on readings that explore the lack or presence of sexual desire in the next world. Ultimately, Augustine's account of resurrected female flesh arises from intimate knowledge and critique of the suffering of women caused by Roman patriarchy: he upholds women's bodies as perfect in their form at the same time as he seeks to protect them from further domination by men.

## CRISIS THEOLOGY: CONTEXTUALIZING AUGUSTINE'S *CITY OF GOD*

Book I of the *City of God* is replete with women's sufferings. Late Antique Roman society greatly emphasized the importance of the interconnection between virtue and virginity and chastity in Christian women. Augustine himself stressed the importance of holy virginity. As a result of the three-day sack of Rome permitted by Alaric, Augustine's North Africa became a refuge for those seeking to escape the damage wrought by soldiers. The women in the community of refugees were particularly vulnerable. In all societies that hold women's virtue and worth together with their chastity and virginity, rape victims are precariously placed.

It is to the experiences of these precariously placed women that Augustine addresses his remarks in the *City of God*. Augustine does not focus on the men who committed the acts of violence against these women because his focus is on the inherent value of a woman as a person and a child of God. Indeed, his entire argument is centered on the assertion that "whatever anyone else does with the body or to the body, provided that it cannot be avoided without committing sin (*peccato*), involves no blame (*culpam*) to the sufferer."[3]

In "'On Lucretia who slew herself': Rape and Consolation in Augustine's *De ciuitate dei*," Melanie Webb emphasizes Augustine's peculiar response to this crisis. On the one hand, Augustine was faced with "reimagin[ing] the social order in the aftermath of the sack, he was faced with North Africa's distinctive heritage of valorized suicides."[4] Augustine as Bishop was faced with the merging and clashing of different cultures within his dominion—the incoming group traumatized, the incumbent group thinking the appropriate response to trauma to be self-murder. Webb emphasizes that dual nature of Augustine's audience in the *City of God*. He was not only speaking to victims of wartime rape but also attempting to reshape "the perceptions and expectations that Roman North African civil and ecclesial leaders would have of these women."[5] For the audience of the *City of God*, the effects of this sack were very present. The victims of various traumas were new members in the communities to which that audience must minister.

In contrast to Margaret Miles and Virginia Burrus, Webb argues that Augustine does not seek to blame the victims of rape or to actually accuse them of wanting their violation.[6] "Augustine does not understand rape primarily as a sexual encounter, but as torture and bereavement," writes Webb, "Rape, as a result, warrants consolation—a judgment, it seems, that Augustine is the first to make."[7] There is a difference between "enduring" and "consenting." Just as the torture victim doesn't "consent" to be tortured but may choose to endure the torture rather than die, so too the victim of rape does not "consent" to the rape but might choose to endure it. Even arousal during a rape, on Webb's interpretation, does not retroactively create consent—and consent is what matters when it comes to "blame."[8]

Sympathetic to Webb's view, I seek to emphasize the importance of Augustine's biting chastisement of certain views of community members concerning women who were victims of rape. Indeed, Augustine writes that the acts committed against these women caused shame in some of the women because they feared that their community might believe they consented. Augustine is sensitive to this fear of the opinions of others. Yet in the same passage that he says it is understandable for women to kill themselves in order to avoid being brutally raped, Augustine firmly states that no one has the "private right to kill."[9] Suicide, on Augustine's view, is murder. Augustine's compassionate treatment of victims of wartime rape leads to a confusion in these passages. On the one hand, who could blame a person who in fear of torture kills herself? On the other hand, how silly is it to say that women who have been raped ought to kill themselves for the shame, given that suicide is self-murder?

Augustine is rather bitingly chastising men for encouraging women to kill themselves as a response to the shame they ought to feel. He goes on to outline the foolishness of women killing themselves for fear of others' thoughts and at the same time condemns any man who accuses women of being unchaste for being raped. For the female martyrs who killed themselves after being raped, he says that we must assume God gave them direct permission (as with Samson)![10]

In the context of women's bodies as a site for personal and communal trauma, Augustine takes a position, which is grounded in reality: it is monstrous to blame women who kill themselves and monstrous to blame women who don't kill themselves. It is monstrous to put the main virtue of a woman in the performance of certain gender roles, especially when those roles are constantly shifting and contradictory.

To return to Webb: "No philosopher prior to Augustine had ever taken note of rape as an occasion warranting consolation, i.e., as an experience that occasions grief and requires encouragement and support in order that the survivor might continue to live with the dignity that characterized her life prior to the loss."[11] Thus, the opening chapters of the *City of God* are concerned with healing communal trauma, but specifically the trauma that occurred against women. To reiterate: women take precedence in this text because it is women who are in need of a "place" in community, and perhaps it is the community not allowing its own wounds to heal by holding these women apart. Augustine disrupts the prevailing patriarchal culture of his time by saying that women have meaning *completely apart from men*. A woman's virtue is not in her relation to *a* man or even *a group* of men. Women's virtue, like men's virtue, is located in their souls. Of course there are limitations to his thought concerning post-Fall human experience, but these limitations can be fruitfully seen as an invitation to a discussion, for example, on what the world would be like if women were free of the debilitating threat of rape.

In the next section, I will turn to Augustine's account of resurrected bodies in the *City of God*. However, Augustine emphasizes the importance of fleshy resurrected bodies in his later work, as well. For example, in his *Enchiridion on Faith, Hope, and Love*, written in 420 C.E., he writes:

> But, as far as regards the substance [of the resurrected body], even then it shall be flesh. For even after the resurrection (*resurrectionem*) the body (*corpus*) of Christ was called flesh (*caro*) [Luke 24:39]. The apostle, however, says: "It is sown a natural body (*corpus animale*); it is raised a spiritual body (*corpus spiritale*)" [1 Cor. 15:44]; because so perfect shall then be the harmony between flesh and spirit (*concordia carnis et spiritus*), the spirit keeping alive the subjugated flesh without the need of any nourishment, that no part of our nature shall be in discord with another; but as we shall be free from enemies without, so we shall not have ourselves for enemies within (*ita nec intus nos ipsos patiamur inimicos*).[12]

In this way the resurrected human is in harmony with herself—flesh with spirit. Augustine's account of the resurrected body is important for philosophers of the body, since he sees the significance of flesh to the human person. To be human is to be flesh and soul. In the next section, I linger on Augustine's motivations for the desexualization of the spiritual bodies humans possess after the resurrection.

## THE DESEXUALIZATION OF GENDER IN THE WORLD THAT IS TO COME

In Chapter 24 of Book XXII of the *City of God*, Augustine sustains his claim that the human body is not only good but also made to be beautiful. The *entire* human body is made to be beautiful (even inner organs). Not only is the human body good as a created thing, it is also meant to be a thing of beauty. Augustine supports this idea by comparing the bodies of humans to the bodies of animals: "Moreover, even in the body, which is something we have in common with the brute creation—which is in fact weaker than the bodies of any of the lower animals (*cum beluis mortalitate*)—even here what evidence we find of the goodness of God, of the providence of the mighty Creator!"[13] What humans *do not* have in common with animals is particularly important to Augustine's claims about the body. He notes that human bodies are weaker than those of animals. There is symmetry and beauty to the body, to be sure, but there are also useless things that have no purpose other than adornment: men's nipples and beards are examples of this useless adornment. Beards, according to Augustine, can serve no biological, protective function because women don't have them. Moreover, for Augustine, it would make more sense for women to have them because it would protect their faces.[14]

Given the weakness and seeming uselessness of many aspects of the human body, Augustine makes the claim that the human body is meant for enjoyment.[15] In this passage, Augustine discusses the distinction between utility and dignity in terms of the human body. Dignity, in this sense, is related to the beauty (*decorum*) of the body, not just in itself but in others' sensing of that body. The practical is transitory, the beautiful is eternal in Augustine's eyes. The resurrected body is meant to be enjoyed (and *perfruamur* is a grand word to describe this enjoyment, since it can also mean "have full enjoyment of") by other resurrected people *sine ulla libidine*, without any desire. By desire here, it seems that Augustine is referring to sexual desire. So, the resurrected body is meant to be enjoyed but not desired.

In the *City of God* and elsewhere, Augustine stresses that the goal of the Christian afterlife is not a full separation of soul from body. In fact, he goes to great length to, on the one hand, agree that the human body seems in this life to be a great weight and, on the other hand, emphasize the naturalness of the human body. As he writes in Book XIV of *City of God*, "those who imagine that all the ills of the soul derive from the body are mistaken."[16] This line of his I take to be particularly emphatic. The Latin reads: "*Verum tamen quia omnia mala animae ex corpore putant accidisse, in errore sunt.*" I translate this more directly as: "Truly nevertheless those who think all evils of soul happen from the body *are in error*." *Errore* has multiple meanings, many of which connote being physically lost. This passage might as well say that those who think the body the cause of the soul's evils are in a maze. They are turning down corners that do not lead them where they wish to be. The body is corruptible in that it ages, gets hurt, and dies. However, the corruptibility of the body is not, according to Augustine, the fault of the body. Moreover, while the corruptibility of the body is a burden, on Augustine's view, the body itself is not and cannot be conceived of apart from soul, as soul cannot be conceived of apart from body in the next life. In this way, Augustine's dualism stands in stark contrast with modern conceptions of dualism.

Augustine affirms the importance of one's individual body again and again, taking great pains to affirm that, although there is a certain corruptibility to the body that makes it seem to be to blame for libidinal desire, the human body is not to blame for the presence of *concupiscentia*, desire or love, in the human experience. The goal of resurrection is not to escape the body, but to be reborn with the same body. In the midst of a conversation about the burning of demons in Hell, for example, Augustine says as an aside: "the spirit of man, which without doubt is immaterial also, can at this present time be shut up within the framework of a material body, and . . . it will be possible at the judgment for them to be bound to their bodies with an indissoluble connection."[17] Resurrection, for Augustine, is the perfection of the lived body. There are no spiritual bodies that are separate from one's pre-existing physical body.

I have sought to establish that, for Augustine, the human body is: (A) made to be aesthetically pleasing (over and above its usefulness); (B) meant to be (fully) enjoyed by other members of the resurrected community; (C) not responsible for its own corruption; (D) meant to be resurrected and clothed with immortality; and (E) not responsible for *concupiscentia*, though related to the experience of *concupiscentia*. This last point is a matter of contention for readers of Augustine, as it is related to the presence of pleasure and sex in Augustine's conception of the afterlife. In his thoughtful explorations of the possibilities of the world that is to come, he considers the importance of one's actual, gendered body as created by God. Augustine writes in Chapter 17 of Book XXII that what is natural to our bodies will remain in place; it is only our defects that will be erased:

> Now a woman's sex is not a defect; it is natural (*Non est autem uitium sexus femineus, sed natura*). And in the resurrection it will be free of the necessity of intercourse (*concubitu*) and childbirth. However, the female organs will not subserve their former use; they will be part of a new beauty (*decori novo*), which will not excite the lust (*concupiscentia*) of the beholder—there will be no lust in that life (*quae nulla erit*)—but will arouse the praises of God for his wisdom and compassion, in that he not only created out of nothing but freed from corruption that which he had created.[18]

In this way, Augustine desexualizes all humanity in the world that is to come while at the same time maintaining gender difference. Women will be resurrected *as women*, retaining not only what they have in common with men but also their uteruses (as an inner organ and therefore as a God-made thing, a thing of beauty), breasts, and genitalia. Augustine couches this retention in relation to men—women's bodies will not be *used* for sex or *excite* lust in men. I will discuss feminist responses to this aspect of Augustine's eschatology in the next section. Here I linger on the importance of reading passages concerning women's bodies at the end of the *City of God* in relation to the passages concerning women's bodies at the beginning of the text.

Women's bodies are "desexed" upon resurrection and yet remain gendered. Augustine could have easily neutered all humanity and claimed that no bodies would retain their sex organs or "impure" features. He could have claimed women's bodies to be resurrected as men's bodies. He could have also posited a genderless body (or one with no flesh at all). Instead, he emphasizes the importance of the resurrection of women's bodies and emphasizes the fact that women's bodies are not defective. Indeed, he turns the discussion from women's bodies as such to the theological implications of the creation of a woman from a man in the same chapter I cited earlier. This creation becomes a foreshadowing of the relationship between Christ and Church. Again, Augustine's vision of beatitude for humans does not include the marriage between men and women or sexual relationships:

> And though [Christ] might have said, "The woman you are asking about will not be a woman; she will be a man," he did not say this. What he said was, "For in the resurrected life men and women do not marry; they are like the angels of God in heaven" (Matt. 22:29). . . . Thus Christ denies the existence of marriage in the resurrected life; he does not deny the existence of women in heaven.[19]

Augustine could have interpreted the passage in Matthew several ways, many of which could exclude women from resurrected life.

Reading these passages alongside his discussion of raped women in Book I, the impetus becomes clear: raped women are excluded from their community, yes, but all women are excluded, in a way, because of their status as sexual objects in the eyes of men. Augustine responds to this by, on the one hand, chastising his male community members who exclude victims of rape and, on the other hand, emphasizing in his eschatology that women's value does not come from their relationship with any man (but only with God). If Augustine were to allow for marriage or sex in heaven, then he would have to allow for the only kind of marriage and sex he knew in his time period: one that subserviates women and places them at the mercy of the desires of men. The problem is a social one that is instantiated by desire (*libido, cupiditas, concupiscentia*) and sex (*concubitus*).

## GENDERED HEAVENLY BODIES

Before resurrecting desire in Augustine's theology of love, I will contextualize my reading of Augustine by engaging with the scholarship on Augustine's treatment of women and sexuality in the world that is to come, as well as with scholarship that aims to understand human existence in the world in terms of extension. Feminist theology does not necessarily seek to look to important theological texts and figures and read into them gender. As feminist philosopher Sandra Bartky writes in her 1975 essay "Toward a Phenomenology of Feminist Consciousness," "Feminists are not aware of different things than other people; they are aware of the same things differently."[20] In the conclusion to her *Veiled Desire: Augustine on Women*, Kim Power draws similar insights into the reading of gender into theology:

> Thus questions of gender are not peripheral to "mainstream theology." This is consistent with the anthropological research which locates sexual meanings at

the heart of cultural systems. Hence any theological or historical analyses of the early church which ignore gender analysis offer an impoverished theological understanding. There is a poignant irony in the fact that it was Augustine, the man who argued so powerfully, and eventually persuasively, that sexuality belonged in Eden, who also made the desire to be loved by the beloved so suspect and so shameful, rendering it so tainted and dangerous that the erotic could never be permitted to symbolise the divine.[21]

Not only are questions concerning gender helpful for reading theology, they are *essential*. Thus, for Power, Augustine views the present instantiation of human sexuality to be necessary but not ideal. In the ideal future, sexuality (and desirous love) is gotten rid of as something shameful, dangerous, and tainted.

Augustine does not get away lightly with his desexualizing of women in feminist readings of his eschatology. Rosemary Radford Reuther interprets Augustine's desexing as representative of his entrenched focus on masculine desire. She rightly points out that Augustine does not make a claim about the desexualizing of men in the way that he does women. She compares Augustine's desexing of women to the original punishment of Eve: that she be subjugated to Adam and bear children in pain. Reuther writes, "Only eschatologically is gender hierarchy to be overcome, but at the price of the excising in women of all that has to do with their specific female functions, sex and childbearing."[22] Being stripped of sex is not a consolation in Reuther's thinking.

Some feminist thinkers, while firmly condemning Augustine's neutering of women, seek to think along with Augustine and take him further than he would go himself. In "Sex and the City (of God): Is Sex Forfeited or Fulfilled in Augustine's Resurrection of Body?" Margaret Miles problematizes Augustine's theory of embodiment by exploring his eschatology in relation to his historical, personal context. She writes:

> Given Augustine's experience as a rape crisis counselor [*City of God* I.16–20], it is not surprising that he was reluctant to give sex acts a place in resurrection society. Yet he described a pan-sexuality from which the painfully urgent focus on genitally organized sexual object and aim have been eliminated and pleasure has been retained.[23]

In this way, Miles foregrounds her reading of Augustine on the resurrected life within the context of Augustine's writing of the *City of God*. This is an intellectual move I find so compelling that I have difficulty thinking through Augustine on the resurrected body outside of this context. I read Augustine along with Miles in this sense, though I do not follow Miles on each of her claims. She continues:

Augustine tried to imagine the properties and capacities of bodies no longer vulnerable to impotence, disease, or death. Having no concept of "sexuality" with which to work, he nonetheless described what we would call "sexuality" as a property of resurrected bodies in the city of God. As one of the beauties and goods of human life, this "sharp joy" of human experience belongs to the calmer bliss of resurrection. Reading sexuality in Augustine's idea of resurrection bodies begins to sketch a model that can function to correct and shape present ideas of sex and its role in human relationships. The value of imagining ideal sexualities is that only then can one begin to make "good sex" now.[24]

Miles offers a provocative explanation for the desexing of the afterlife: the beginning of the *City of God* is not to be forgotten. In Augustine's time, relationships between sexual partners were often highly unbalanced in the best of circumstances, much more so in the instances of men raping women, reducing them to their sexual function and then blaming them for it. The healing of the wound of the sexual violence of his age seems at first to be a neutering of women, but this desexing can be seen too as Augustine attempting to think through and beyond patriarchal objectification of women. To say the same thing again: Augustine's eschatology is present-thinking. How he thinks of the ideal of human relationships in the world that is to come says more about how he thinks relationships ought to be and can't be in the world that is.

In the post-resurrection world, friendship between men and women need not be hampered by lust and rampant desire. "Lacking the concept, Augustine neither explicitly included nor excluded 'sexuality' as a feature of resurrection bodies," writes Miles, "His descriptions of beauty and enjoyment, however, provide a foundation for identifying in resurrection bodies an implicit sexuality free from the constraints and damages of present sexuality."[25] While there is no procreation in heaven, Miles makes room for sexual intercourse between resurrected bodies. And indeed, if we are to assume the resurrected life involves an experience of pleasure that never objectifies and always participates in joy, perhaps it is possible to imagine a kind of pleasure, separate from current sexuality that crushes one or both partners, that is, orgasmic and eternal.

This is made complicated by the fact that Augustine himself seems to claim that there will be no emotions in heaven. If Augustine is to be taken seriously about emotion in this sense, then how might there be pleasure at all? In "No Time for Sex," Virginia Burrus discusses the relationship between feelings of the will and Augustine's account of heavenly bodies. With reference to the distinction between postlapsarian and resurrected wills, she writes, "Not to desire, rejoice, fear, or grieve would be not only strange but wrong, in this life; even Jesus had emotions! Such movements of the soul will, however, be stilled when time is no more."[26] It is difficult to consider how a life without emotion might be possible; perhaps it is nearly as difficult as it would be to consider a life in eternity.

There is an opening in Augustine's reading of human resurrected bodies for an ordered *concupiscentia*, a *voluptas* (pleasure) that is not overpowering. Burrus relates this to the nature of pleasure in eternity:

> For Augustine, *voluptas* remains balanced at the point between time and eternity, then; it does not quite get us to heaven, though it almost does. Indeed, its potent memory may keep us mired in time. Nonetheless, it *does* disclose something of eternal bliss. For eternity rests in pleasure, albeit a sublime pleasure—a felicity, a delight, a blessedness. And pleasure is not only what satisfies desire; it is also what makes it grow. If an imperfectly recollected Paradise kills desire by giving us exactly what we need before we have a chance to want it, an enticingly anticipated heaven makes us want ever more by always giving us more than we need so that we will continue to want more that we have—and all at once![27]

There is desire and pleasure in eternity, though it seems contradictory to say so. There both will and will not be *concupiscentia*. Following Miles, it is no wonder that Augustine pauses when he considers sex in the next world. By neglecting *concupiscentia*, Augustine is protecting those in this world that are vulnerable to the desires of others. One is invited by this reading to consider what *concupiscentia* might look like if it were not mired in violence and lack of consent.

On my reading of Augustine, *concupiscentia* is necessary and not accidental. It is fundamental to the human person both today and in Eden, as well as in the future time. It was the concept of love in Augustine's historical moment in time that precluded his extension of *concupiscentia* into the world that is to come.

## CONCLUSION

Christian resurrection theologies are important sources for understanding human life and what it could be. How we are to be resurrected tells us a lot about what a given theological system holds to be most (and least) valuable in humans today. Examining Augustine's eschatology in particular offers a deeper understanding of what it is to be human. For Augustine, resurrected bodies are bodies that are clothed in immortality. What is left over after the resurrection is very much ourselves, only perfected. Thus, whether or not sexuality is allowed for heavenly bodies is of the utmost importance. If not, then there is something "unnatural" about desire. If so, then it is necessary to come to understand the link between the sex that was, the sex that will be, and the sex that is to come.

Augustine's speculations are meant to be taken as watery graspings. There is no clear way to know what ecstatic life might be like, so Augustine must be using what he knows about what it is to be human to say what it is to be perfected. And the surprise is: the resurrected life is a lot like life today, since it is inhabited by humans as they are today but perfected.

## NOTES

1. In 410 C.E., Alaric I, King of the Visigoths, himself an Arian Christian, conquered Rome, and allowed his men three days to sack the city. He would have spared it, Church historians say, but he had to give his men what they deserved: three days to rape, steal, and destroy. In this chapter, I will be using Augustine, *Concerning the City of God Against the Pagans*, trans. Henry Bettenson (London: Penguin, 2003). I would like to thank the editors of this volume as well as the anonymous reviewers for comments and suggestions on this chapter. This chapter is derived from the fourth chapter of my doctoral dissertation, *Embodied Love and Extended Desire* (2017). I would like to thank James Wetzel, Sally Scholz, Georg Theiner, Rachel Aumiller, and Sarah Vitale for their helpful comments in previous versions of this chapter.

2. I have emphasized some important conceptual distinctions often made concerning love in Augustine's work in "Love and the Patriarch: Augustine and (Pregnant) Women," *Hypatia: A Journal of Feminist Philosophy*, 32, no. 1 (2017): 119–134. It is important to reiterate that Augustine has a complex relationship with "love" throughout his corpus. One might even say he has a theology of love. Augustine's love is often presented as the juxtaposition of a wild, vicious *concupiscentia* and the stable, unchanging love for God, *caritas*. He has other terms: *cupiditas* (general lust) and *dilectio* (sometimes translated as fondness, but often love as well), for example. *Libido* has a role to play as well. In my work, I use *concupiscentia* as a catchall term for bodily loves. It is the way in which we love things in the world that we do not in fact possess. *Concupiscentia*, even more so than *libido* and *cupiditas*, is considered quite carnal: it is the love that is associated with bodily arousal. *Caritas* is, far from *agape* love, the specific love of a human for God.

3. Augustine, *City of God*, I.16, 26.

4. Melanie Webb, "On Lucretia Who Slew Herself: Rape and Consolation in Augustine's *De ciuitate dei*," *Augustinian Studies* 44, no. 1 (2013), 37–58, here 38.

5. Webb, "On Lucretia Who Slew Herself," 39.

6. Augustine, *City of God*, I:16, 26.

7. Webb, "On Lucretia Who Slew Herself," 41. Webb's essay is an excellent resource for those seeking further understanding of Augustine on the topic of shame and pleasure. Her reading of Augustine's account of the rape and suicide of Lucretia is novel and important for those seeking to understand Augustine's relationship with women, pagan or Christian. Webb does not just read the Lucretia sections of *City of God*, she reads them in their context and in relation to Augustine's account of

Regulus, who was tortured. On her view, the reading of I.16 as Augustine's accusation of lust in the loins of raped women is problematic. Webb, "On Lucretia Who Slew Herself," 48, supports this claim with a reading of the relationship between the will and physical pleasure (not *concupiscentia*): "For Augustine, *uoluptas* (physical pleasure) does not indicate *uoluntas* (will, or consent). While *uoluntas* and *uoluptas* both derive from the verb *uolo* and are thereby conceptually interdependent, by positing *uoluptas* without *uoluntas* Augustine is making a conceptual move similar to our own distinction in English of 'arousal' from 'pleasure' or 'enjoyment.' The English term 'arousal' does not have a clear Latin corollary, particularly not to describe the sexual experiences of women. The structure of Augustine's argument, however, indicates that he is using the term in a way distinct from its implication in one's *uoluntas*. The terms 'pleasure' and 'enjoyment' suggest some positive engagement of *uoluntas*, while "arousal" suggests dissociation of *uoluptas* from *uoluntas*. Augustine's focus, then, is not to distinguish between those who are to be blamed and those who are not to be blamed for their rapes; rather, he suggests that an inbursting of shame does not indicate rightful blame. In other words, in order to be considered innocent of her rape, a woman need not state the distinction between her body's guilt and her mind's innocence as clearly as Lucretia did." For more on Augustine and the will, see James Wetzel's *Augustine and the Limits of Virtue* (Cambridge: Cambridge UP, 1992).

8. Webb, "On Lucretia Who Slew Herself," 54.
9. Augustine, *City of God*, I.17, 26–27.
10. Augustine, *City of God*, I.26, 36–38.
11. Webb, "On Lucretia Who Slew Herself," 57.
12. Augustine, *Enchiridion*, XCI, 106.
13. Augustine, *City of God*, XXII.24, 1073.
14. Augustine, *City of God*, 22.24, 1074.
15. Augustine, *City of God*, XXII.24, 1074.
16. Augustine, *City of God*, XIV.3, 551.
17. Augustine, *City of God*, XXI.10, 986. The context of this quote is quite interesting: Augustine is attempting to make sense of a kind of "mind-body" problem. Demons don't have material bodies, as they are fallen angels and therefore spirit. However, they are said to be damned to a physical Hell-fire. The question becomes, how can the non-physical demon be burned by the physical flame? The answer Augustine gives is the same reason human spirits are connected to the material body: in hopes of being connected to that same body for eternity. It is not a satisfying answer to the "demon-fire" problem, as it is recursive.
18. Augustine, *City of God*, XXII.17, 1057. See also Rosemary Radford Reuther, "Augustine: Sexuality, Gender, and Women," in *Feminist Interpretations of Augustine: Re-reading the Canon*, ed. Judith Chelius Stark (University Park, PA: Pennsylvania State University Press, 2007), 47–67, especially 63: "Since women represent and incarnate the lower realm of sense knowledge, some Christian thinkers debated whether women would be resurrected in a male body, thus losing that which linked them to sin." Augustine is firmly on the "no" side of this debate.
19. Augustine, *City of God*, XXII.17, 1058.

20. Sandra Lee Bartky, "Toward a Phenomenology of Feminist Consciousness," *Social Theory and Practice* 3, no. 4 (1975), 425–439, here 429.

21. Kim Power, *Veiled Desire: Augustine on Women* (New York: Continuum, 1995), 239.

22. Reuther, "Augustine," 64.

23. Margaret Miles, "Sex and the City (of God): Is Sex Forfeited or Fulfilled in Augustine's Resurrection of Body?" *Journal of the American Academy of Religion* 73, no. 2 (2005), 307–327, here 325.

24. Miles, "Sex and the City (of God)," 325.

25. Miles, "Sex and the City (of God)," 309.

26. Burrus, "No Time for Sex," in *Seducing Augustine: Bodies, Desires, Confessions*, ed. Virginia Burrus, Mark D Jordan, and Karmen MacKendrick (New York: Fordham University Press, 2010), 101.

27. Burrus, "No Time for Sex," 114.

*Chapter 9*

# Augustine and the Gendered Self in Time

Megan Loumagne Ulishney

Despite objectionable elements in many of Augustine's statements about gender, this chapter argues that there are other aspects of his thought that subvert his depiction of the static and hierarchical nature of gender.[1] These aspects could be helpfully retrieved for a feminist theological anthropology. Of particular relevance is his notion of the self as a relationally constituted reality that is unfinished and in-process in the realm of temporality. To be human, for Augustine, is to be a material creature immersed in the flux and flow of the temporal realm. In the words of Rowan Williams, it is to be "a moving and changing image."[2] While Augustine does not extend his thinking about the fluidity of the self in time to considerations of gender, and indeed, many of Augustine's assumptions about the nature of gender are radically different from those of people living in the twenty-first century, this chapter creatively extends his thought to include reflection on gender by showing that his thought has some resonances with the contemporary development in feminist theory known as "New Feminist Materialism." New Feminist Materialism is a movement of feminist thought that depicts the gendered human as inextricably entangled in the constant proliferation of temporal change that defines the material world. This chapter places Augustine and New Feminist Materialists in dialogue and, in doing so, suggests that the juxtaposition of their thought will be generative, thereby enabling both sides to mutually correct one another.

## NEW FEMINIST MATERIALISM

New Feminist Materialism is an emerging stream of thought within feminist theory that has arisen as part of a broader "material turn" occurring in a variety of disciplines. Instead of a one-directional focus on the violent material effects of corrupt cultural systems or the ways in which cultural systems constrain and discipline formations of selves, New Feminist Materialists combine this mode of analysis with an equal interest in the ways in which "nature punches back."[3] New Feminist Materialists call for renewed attention to the agency of matter and to the reality that creaturely life is dependent upon and immersed in materiality.[4] The penchant for deconstruction that typified postmodern forms of feminism in the wake of Derrida and Foucault is valued and largely embraced by the New Feminist Materialists. However, they also view this tendency toward deconstruction as incomplete.[5] New Feminist Materialists argue that in their efforts to combat problematic biological essentialisms, postmodern feminists failed to attribute any agency to the material realm in forming social and political realities, thereby reifying a dualism in which matter is regarded as inert and passive, merely written upon by the active shaping forces of mind and culture.

While New Feminist Materialists are not monolithic, their writings typically share the following features: extensive engagement with the natural sciences (especially quantum physics and evolutionary biology), an acknowledgment of the nature of matter as active and generative, and a commitment to taking seriously the "material details of everyday life."[6] For example, Anne Fausto-Sterling exhorts feminists to "accept the body as simultaneously composed of genes, hormones, cells, and organs—all of which shape health and behavior—and of culture and history."[7] Rather than solely interrogating the ways in which discourse and power relations shape bodies (how "culture" becomes "nature"), New Feminist Materialists use developments in evolutionary biology to foreground the ways in which material forces possess their own fecundity and agency. Matter, they argue, "acts, creates, destroys, and transforms."[8]

Material and biological forces in the world impose real constraints upon human becoming since our materiality is often recalcitrant. However, while the reality of these constraints must be acknowledged, according to New Feminist Materialists, when viewed within an evolutionary framework, the possibilities provided by materiality are more significant than the limitations that it presents. The biological, while never completely unbounded, is also the realm of flux, temporality, plasticity, transformation, and "generative surprise."[9] Culture does not write upon nature in a one-directional way. Rather, nature is presented here as alive, energetic, and formative of human and nonhuman life. As a result, nature and culture work together in continuously intersecting feedback loops. This recasts nature as an active agent that is entangled with culture, thereby undermining the nature/culture dichotomy altogether.

Elizabeth Grosz, a key contributor to New Feminist Materialism, draws from a wide range of philosophical sources in her work. For the purposes of this chapter, her feminist retrieval of the works of Charles Darwin and her interest in reading the language of materiality through the lens of a philosophy of time are particularly relevant. Additionally, her 2017 monograph, *The Incorporeal: Ontology, Ethics, and the Limits of Materialism*, is relevant for our purposes. There she aims to develop an "incorporeal" framework for materiality that addresses some of the conceptual limitations of reductive forms of materialism. In doing so, she renders New Feminist Materialism more open to theological insights into creaturely life.

In her analysis of the history of philosophical thinking about nature and materiality, Grosz acknowledges the history of gendered baggage associated with these terms. Forgetfulness or fear of (as well as hostility to) nature and materiality are evident within the Western philosophical tradition, she argues, "in both the desire for the domination of nature and in the control of men over women."[10] The proper response from feminists should not be to seek to dissociate women from the concept of nature, since this will only reinforce a deeply flawed framework. Instead, the task for feminists is threefold: (1) to develop a revitalized understanding of nature in order to emphasize the reality that the natural, the biological, and the material are "imbued with activity, with their own forces and unpredictabilities;" (2) to reconceptualize the notion of culture in order to emphasize its continuity with and dependence upon nature; and finally (3) to undermine the nature/culture distinction altogether.[11] Darwin, evolutionary theory, and a renewed focus on the temporality that haunts creaturely life are key to accomplishing these tasks for Grosz.

As part of her project of reinvigorating feminist philosophical engagement with the material, Grosz turns to Charles Darwin as a fruitful resource for reconceptualizing the concepts of biology, ontology, and sexual difference. Darwin, she argues, provides a framework for affirming the continuity of nature and culture. Nature is not a point of departure that is then left behind upon development of the more sophisticated innovations of culture. Instead, nature should be seen as the source of productivity and creativity that continually informs and permeates cultural developments. She argues that we must recapture an awareness of nature as a "dynamic force of self-differentiation or emergence,"[12] and as "evolving, as alive, as subject to upheaval and transformation . . . construed as unpredictable and open-ended, as a form of perpetual becoming."[13] Furthermore, she argues, nature is haunted by time. Time inhabits all of creaturely life and is an "internal, indeed constitutive, feature of life itself."[14]

In addition to providing a framework for undermining the dichotomy between nature and culture, Darwin also reconfigures the notion of ontology, according to Grosz. She defines ontology as "the philosophical analysis of what exists, what is, and what might be."[15] Darwin's elucidating the reality of all of creaturely life as enmeshed in the ongoing workings of evolutionary processes transforms the notion of ontology away from connotations of stasis and essence to that of "ceaseless becoming."[16] After Darwin, creaturely life becomes defined in terms of "dynamic, collective change."[17] Being is replaced by becoming, essence by existence, and stasis by dynamism. The nature of the human as in a state of continual transformation entails that we can never know our own nature in a comprehensive way, that every attempt to essentialize or categorize humanity will be incomplete and provisional, and that the future of our species cannot be predicted with certainty.[18] Nature is, therefore, the realm of flux, creativity, unpredictability, wonder, and "generative surprise."[19] Evolution does not create blueprints, but rather, it creates possibilities for life to be different than what it has been previously. The human is both a preservation of the past and a "dissipation," she argues, since "the present dissipates its force in producing a future which differs from it."[20] The evolutionary past prefigures and provides resources for the present to draw from in order to develop the future in unique trajectories. The past is also a dynamism and not a stasis since it is always being utilized, harnessed, and "revivified" in novel ways in the present.[21] Grosz argues, "The more clearly we understand our temporal location as beings who straddle the past and the future without the security of a stable and abiding present, the more mobile our possibilities are, and the more transformation becomes conceivable."[22] Thus, the nature of creaturely life as defined by immersion in the temporal can be viewed as providing a generative instability that enables creative differentiation and exploration, as well as the production of the novel.

Central to Grosz's non-reductionist and non-essentialist notion of ontology as ceaseless becoming are the reality of sexual difference and the process of sexual selection. She contends that sexual difference is an ontological and ineliminable aspect of human life that drives the endless proliferation of difference. Sexual difference is given, but it is also "lived, created, invented."[23] Darwin, she argues, "insists that sexual bifurcation, the division of species into (at least) two sexes, is an evolutionary invention of remarkable tenacity and value, for it multiplies difference *ad infinitum*."[24] The multiplication of differences inherent to the processes of evolution is excessive, aesthetic, and artistic, she argues. It exceeds what is necessary for survival. Sexual, racial, and other types of differences produced by the processes of natural and sexual selection make life "more enjoyable, more intense, more noticeable and pleasurable than it would otherwise be."[25]

Through her feminist retrieval of Darwin's insights about evolution, especially regarding sexual difference and sexual selection, Grosz provides important insights for understanding the nature of human life as a dynamism of nature and culture, and as continually immersed in the biological world that is imbued with agency and activity of its own. Grosz's engagement with Darwin's work brings to the fore the fact that human life is not defined by stasis, but is rather totally immersed in an evolutionary milieu, which means that it is in a state of continual transformation and becoming. We cannot know ourselves in fullness now, nor can we predict with certainty what we will become. Human nature always exceeds our ability to categorize and contain it. Sexual difference, as an evolutionary feature of the world, is always in the process of becoming different than it was in the past, in unknown and surprising ways that elicit wonder and joy.

We turn now from the recent contributions of the New Feminist Materialists to a historical examination of Augustine's insights on the nature of gender and of the self immersed in time. While there are aspects of Augustine's thinking about gender that should be corrected in a contemporary approach, he is more complex on gender questions than is sometimes acknowledged, and there are other elements of his anthropological intuitions that can still be retrieved for feminist theological developments in the twenty-first century.

## AUGUSTINE, GENDER, AND THE SELF IN TIME

Augustine has been one of the most significant influences on Christian thinking about the meaning of gender and sexual difference. As Kim Power suggests, Augustine's "resolution of the fourth-century debates about the significance of sexual difference and its place in creation has been perceived as the dominant voice in the Christian discourse of sexuality."[26] Augustine clearly accepted to a large extent the cultural and biological frameworks of his time that viewed women as physically inferior to men and as appropriately subordinated to men because of their nature.[27] He argues that even before the fall, the woman's nature was such that it was proper for her to be "ruled by her husband and to be submissive and subject to him."[28] However, before the fall, this hierarchical relationship was governed by the bond of love. Only after the fall did it become more like the relationship between slave and master. This natural hierarchical ordering of the male ruling over the female is even more necessary after the fall, Augustine argues, because if it is not maintained, "nature will be distorted even more, and sin will be increased."[29] A woman ruling over a man would be the symbolic equivalent of the lower faculties of the bodily desire ruling over the higher faculty of reason, thus resulting in disorder and loss of *harmonia*. However, on the other hand, Augustine is more generous to women than many of his contemporaries. This section provides a brief overview of Augustine's understanding of gender, followed by a brief assessment of some of his more general views on anthropology. While much within his corpus is outdated on the issue of gender, this section also argues that his broader views on the nature of creaturely life contradict and undermine the rigidity with which he depicts the nature of gender, and thus there are elements of his thought that are retrievable for feminist theologians.

Augustine frequently uses representations of women and femininity as ways of referring to fallenness and sin, yet this is counterbalanced by a swing to the opposite extreme in his frequent use of idealized feminine imagery to describe "the eschatological paradise in which he, and all faithful Christians, will find union with God."[30] Augustine has been much derided by feminists for his depiction of women as closer to the material realm in contrast to men who supposedly exist closer to the realm of mind/spirit, as well as for the aspects of his thought that express suspicion of desire, (especially female) bodiliness, and sex. Indeed, as Rosemary Radford Ruether notes, he argues that "those parts of the female body that have to do with sex and childbirth will be transformed, so they become 'fitted to glory rather than to shame,'" although the meaning of this phrase is not entirely clear.[31] It is likely, as Edmund Hill notes, that Augustine accepted the commonplace of his time that "the sexual act itself" is something impure, but it is also true that Augustine in many ways softened this commonplace through his teaching that the corruption of sex is a result of sin rather than being something intrinsic to it by nature.[32] His understanding of women as closer to the realm of bodiliness, affectivity, and desire implies that women are intrinsically more sinful, since sin is cast in terms of disordered desire for Augustine. And yet, conversely, it seems that women are closer to salvation, as well, in their superior strength of affectivity and love, exemplified by Mary Magdalene seeking for Jesus after the crucifixion.

In one of his sermons, Augustine recalls that after the crucifixion, the disciples left Jesus, but Mary was determined to stay close to Jesus. Augustine says, "*Illi minorem curam habuerunt, fortiores sexu, sed minores affectu.*"[33] The disciples, he argues, though members of the "stronger sex," had less *curam* (care) and less affection than the woman. Mary's strength in affectivity motivated her to search for Jesus with greater intensity and *lacrimis*, or "with tears."[34] Augustine interprets Mary Magdalene here in a symbolic way as "woman" (*mulier*) or an image of women generally. Thus, he argues that Mary Magdalene's intensity of affection stemmed from her membership in the sex of Eve. She sought after Jesus, the source of life because of her unity with Eve, who had previously brought ruin into paradise and introduced death. Being stronger in love is no small thing since, for Augustine, love "determines the Christian virtues" and is also the attribute of the Holy Spirit.[35] Augustine does not elaborate upon this notion of female superiority in love in much depth, and so we are left to wonder what implications he might have drawn from this notion for a theology of gender. It is consistent, however, with his general understanding of women as closer to the realm of desire and men as closer to reason.

Additionally, Augustine argues against some of his contemporaries in favor of the notion that women are capable of imaging God in their rational souls.[36] However, this defense of women is again counterbalanced by a linguistic and metaphorical framework in which he uses Adam and Eve as analogies for the masculine and feminine to describe dimensions of the human mind and to argue for the necessity of "masculine" rule over the "feminine" elements of the human mind. In *De Trinitate*, Augustine describes the two functions of the rational human soul as *sapientia* (heavenly wisdom) and *scientia* (temporal knowledge or skill). As Kim Power notes, although both words are linguistically feminine and *sapientia* is depicted as a feminine figure elsewhere within the Christian and Judaic traditions, Augustine argues that *sapientia* is analogically masculine, while *scientia* is analogically feminine.[37] He uses the figures of Adam and Eve in order to explain that just as Eve was created as an assistant for Adam, so *scientia* exists as a helper for *sapientia* and must be ruled and subdued by *sapientia*, because *sapientia* is concerned with higher things such as the contemplation of God.[38] The feminine *scientia* is concerned with temporal matters and cannot image God unless it is united with masculine *sapientia*. Importantly, Augustine argues that both *sapientia* and *scientia* are present in every human mind regardless of a person's sex. It seems that his motivation in doing this was, ironically, to try to defend the notion that women could image God against certain interlocutors who argued otherwise, often on the basis of the supposedly inferior physical constitution of women (treated as "obvious" by the received medical information of his day). In order to defend woman's ability to image God, Augustine argues that sexual difference is only in the body and not in the mind or soul. As he says in *De Genesi ad Litteram*, "Now the expression, 'in His image,' can apply only to the soul, and the expression, 'male and female,' can be properly understood as referring only to the body."[39] For Augustine, the mind and the soul have no sex. Therefore, since women also have *sapientia* in their rational souls, they could also image God. While Augustine's defending of the woman's ability to image God is certainly praiseworthy, and despite his protestations that he was using the concepts of masculine and feminine analogically, in his association of the masculine with *sapientia* and the feminine with *scientia*, he was nevertheless reinforcing the cultural dominance of the male and the stereotype that women are closer to nature, closer to bodiliness, and thus more vulnerable to the perversions of fleshly concupiscence. In arguing that sexual difference is only in the body, Augustine perpetuates a two-substance dualism and the impression that somehow the personal and sexual history of a body has no relation to the life of the soul. Also, as John Rist notes, Augustine "apparently never considered whether a soul designed and habituated to look after a male body might be different from a soul looking after a female body."[40] In a contemporary context, we might raise further questions about the relationship between a nonbinary or intersex body and the soul.

Augustine has significantly shaped Christian thinking about gender and sexual difference. His thinking about the meaning of gender was significantly shaped by the cultural, philosophical, geographic, political, and biological context of his time, as well as by his Biblical exegesis. While Augustine's influence on Christian perceptions of gender has been problematic in many ways, it is important to acknowledge that when placed alongside some of his contemporaries, as Elizabeth Clark has argued, Augustine expresses "*relatively . . . prosexual, promarital, and proreproductive theories.*"[41] Additionally, in contrast to the fixed and hierarchical views of gender expressed by Augustine, his broader views on the nature of creaturely life depict the realm of materiality as defined by the constant flux and flow of creatures in time. We turn now to a brief analysis of these elements of his thought.

In a way similar to the New Feminist Materialists, Augustine also understands creaturely life to be defined by movement, incomplete knowledge, and the flux and flow of temporality. As Rowan Williams notes, "Augustine's is a universe in motion," and self-knowledge is "knowledge of the unknowing and unfinished self."[42] Augustine's *Confessions*, in particular, presents the self as split apart and scattered through time, constantly eluding comprehension. Our participation in a history of sin is one reason for the unstable and fragmentary nature of creaturely life, according to Augustine. Sin is that which divides and scatters, and salvation is accomplished by becoming united with the unified Christ, who is the perfect unity of the divine and the human. As Luigi Gioia argues, in Augustine's thought, "Christ alone is 'the one' (*unum*) who can heal the scattering effects of sinfulness," adding that "through love and faith we adhere to 'the one' Christ, the Mediator through whom we are reconciled with God, and are able to cling to the One, enjoy the One and remain forever one."[43] After the primal sin, Augustine argues that human nature became "discordant." In the *Confessions*, he notes that before Christ, he "was tossed about and split, scattered and boiled dry."[44]

However, the temporality and mutability that define creaturely life are not simplistically a result of sin. For Augustine, *disordered and chaotic* motion is the result of sin, but motion itself is constitutive of what it means to be a creature. Likely influenced by the Stoics who saw the universe as being "in a constant state of making and unmaking," Augustine suggests in *De Genesi ad Litteram* that God implants into the world seed-like agencies, *rationes seminales*, so that creation continually unfolds over time, thus rendering it constantly in motion.[45] He states, "The motion we now see in creatures, measured by the lapse of time as each fulfils its proper function, comes to creatures from those *rationes seminales* implanted in them, which God scattered as seeds at the moment of creation."[46] Augustine, then, agrees with the New Feminist Materialists that temporality and changeability are essential components of what it means to be a creature. To be a material being is to exist in an unfinished state, with imperfect knowledge of one's identity and future. This other side of Augustine undermines his depiction of the nature of gender and sexual difference as knowable and fixed. It could be helpfully retrieved for new trajectories in feminist theologies of gender. We turn now to place Augustine and the New Feminist Materialists in dialogue in order to allow them to be mutually corrective to one another.

## AUGUSTINE AND THE NEW FEMINIST MATERIALISTS IN DIALOGUE

The New Feminist Materialists helpfully illuminate the nature of creatures as negotiating a variety of "in between" places in the realm of temporality. This approach to thinking about creaturely life more adequately avoids the tendency toward dualism that at times entraps Augustine. For the New Feminist Materialists, the human exists "in the middle" of nature and culture. Every person is a collection of dynamically fluctuating physiological, psychological, social, and other systems that achieve various forms of coherence and stability over the course of a lifetime. Thus, the New Feminist Materialists can assist theologians in more adequately characterizing what Michele Saracino refers to as "our hybrid reality."[47] We must begin to develop frameworks in theology for portraying "the plural and enmeshed qualities of human existence—in other words to claim its hybridity" in order to have theological anthropologies that reflect that complexity of creaturely life. The New Feminist Materialists provide some tools to accomplish this task.

Additionally, while Augustine would likely agree with the New Feminist Materialists regarding the nature of the body as both a memorial to the past and a site of development that is open to the future, the New Feminist Materialists provide more helpful tools for conceptualizing creaturely life as a blend of "givenness" and construction (both social and individual). Demonstrating that every creature exists in the midst of a matrix of "interdependencies," they work against not only the myths of both essentialism and determinism but also the fantasies of autonomy and self-creation.[48] Our bodies are products of an accumulation of events, forces, and processes in our evolutionary past that we do not control. As Augustine would also argue, we carry in our bodies the effects of choices made by our ancestors, the effects of traumas and triumphs they experienced, and the influences of the families and communities in which we were raised. On the other hand, as we have learned from Grosz, the past we carry within us is not static, but is constantly providing resources that we use in the present to develop new behaviors and trajectories for us as individuals, for our communities, and for our species. These insights into creaturely life are helpful for new developments in theologies of gender.

Locating the body as a site "in between" the past and the future means that our sexed traits always remain in some continuity with what has come before. Much of what our bodies look like in terms of bodily sexual differentiation is the result of inherited genetic, epigenetic, hormonal, and environmental influences. In many crucial ways, we do not make ourselves who we are. Rather, we receive our identities from others. However, since both sexual difference and gender identity are, to a certain extent, lived and developed over the course of a lifetime, and since we constantly draw from the resources of the past to develop the new, sexual difference and gender identity will also continue to develop in a myriad of unpredictable, surprising, and sometimes unexpected ways. The approach to sexual difference of the New Feminist Materialists expresses an appreciation for both the recalcitrance and the plasticity of the materiality of sexual difference. Since, as they emphasize, sexual difference is a biological reality that is immersed in the flux and flow of the evolutionary world, it cannot be depicted in terms of stasis and essence without reifying a soul/body dualism, which causes problems for Augustine's approach to gender.

New Feminist Materialism helps theologians to develop an appreciation for the material dynamism and complexity of sexual difference, as well as the multilayered processes through which humans come to understand the meaning of our bodies in dialogue with cultural norms. These insights from the New Feminist Materialists can assist theologians in creating more expansive categories for thinking theologically about the nature of sex and gender. New Feminist Materialism also brings renewed attention to the ways in which biology (understood in terms of a dynamic relationship between nature and culture) can be a source of liberation, renewal, and transformation. The dynamism of sexual difference and the multiplicity of causal influences shaping its development also remind us to be circumspect about the extent to which we can understand the nature of sexual difference.

The meaning of our bodies will always exceed our comprehension and defy our abilities to categorize and contain them. This is a gift for theology, in that it opens up our theologies of sexual difference and gender to uncertainty and wonder. New Feminist Materialism gives theology a great gift in turn by demonstrating that the elements of life we might be tempted to consider basic, simple, fundamental, and knowable are ineluctably mysterious.

While the New Feminist Materialists have certain correctives to offer to Augustine, Augustine also presents resources that could helpfully contribute to New Feminist Materialist thought. One area in which Augustine can offer a corrective to the New Feminist Materialists is in providing a metaphysics that can render comprehensible their approach to materiality. For the New Feminist Materialists, their desire to avoid invoking the divine results in the processes of "life," particularly in the writings of Grosz, being imbued with an almost magical ability to transform and direct the movements of evolution. However, this is done without any openness to the possibility of a divine presence in the world or a providential ordering of nature. Yet the question arises of whether, despite every explicit intention, Grosz succeeds in eliminating the divine from the material world or instead simply gives it another name, such as the mysterious and wonderful creative energy of "life" or "ideality." Where a New Feminist Materialist would attribute the forward movements of transformation within evolution to the vague agency of "life," Augustine would, without necessarily ascribing to a view of divine intervention that overrides the processes of evolution, suggest that God is involved in the temporal movements of evolution, holding these processes together in love, and that it is God who provides the "incorporeal conditions" for materiality that Grosz seeks.

One reason for Grosz's rejection of the possibility of God in her work is her assumption that to affirm a divine being is to necessarily embrace the notion of, as she describes, "an independent God who exists separately from the world," or a "creator God conceived as the external force of coherence and direction of the world."[49] She rejects this concept of God because it establishes a dualism between ideality and materiality. This characterization of God as an "independent" being who is "separate" from the world, however, is not at all reflective of the concept of God affirmed by the incarnational theology of Augustine. In the framework of Augustine, the divine is that which became flesh. In this theology, the material has its existence only through the divine; it is saturated with and held together by the divine. Note Augustine's depiction of the God-world relationship in *Confessions*: "For he did not create and then depart; the things derived from him have their being in him."[50]

This is not to say that creation is a "piece" of God, since God does not have a material body. However, it is to say that God does not exist in rivalry with the world, outside the world, or "above" the world. As Rowan Williams notes, the world is "a limited and fluid whole that is not God, yet is saturated with God."[51] Thus, the notion of a divinity who is "separate" from the material world is one that would not be recognizable to Augustine. Rather, for him, the material world is so imbued with God that it is "sacramental." This deepens the New Feminist Materialist claim that human life is defined by "hybridity" by extending hybridity to also acknowledge the "constant exchange between the sacred and the everyday."[52] Augustine's understanding of the Incarnation that shapes his view of creation could thus provide a potent resource for New Feminist Materialists, like Grosz, who are in search of an "incorporeal" grounding to provide meaning and direction to the material world and a framework to conceive of "the mutual inherence of materiality and incorporeality."[53] Indeed, in Christ is the hypostatic union of the human and the divine natures, and thus Christology could provide a conceptual model of this mutual inherence that Grosz seeks.

For New Feminist Materialists who engage with theology, the primary tendency is to embrace process theology, thereby collapsing God into the flux and flow of material processes. This is reflected in the writings of Susan Hekman, for example. Hekman argues that New Feminist Materialism opens up new possibilities for engagement between feminist philosophers and theologians, but only if the theology being engaged with is process theology, since she argues that traditional theologies that focus on substance and being are hopelessly androcentric.[54] Hekman states that within a framework informed by process theology, "everything is in flux: there are no enduring substances but only processes of becoming."[55] Within this framework, God is included in these processes of endless becoming as "creative activity rather than passive matter, by evolutionary becoming rather than changeless enduring. He is an in-the-world being who intervenes selectively in world processes."[56] Like Hekman, Catherine Keller finds the sovereign God of traditional theism unsatisfactory. The Christian tradition promotes, she argues, a picture of a "biblical lord of great if somewhat unpredictable power" and an "immutable, unilateral All-Power clothed in the attributes of a single male Person (or two; or . . . )."[57] This God is "a bully God, a blustering warrior" and "a detached omnipotence."[58] She argues instead for a process metaphysic in which "becoming is not outside of God nor God outside of becoming."[59] This is a God who is vulnerable and enmeshed in "potentialities of an indeterminate creativity."[60] She sees this concept of God as subverting the distant, cold, immutable, male God of classical theism with its allegedly accompanying "legitimation of domination" in favor of the "tehomic deity" who is "enmeshed in the vulnerabilities and potentialities of an indeterminate creativity."[61] The "tehomic deity" does not dominate or control, but rather lures, persuades, and "suckles."[62]

There are attractive features of Hekman's and Keller's notion of God as endless becoming, including its promotion of more stereotypically feminine qualities that could offer an important corrective to the male-centric Judeo-Christian theological tradition. Additionally, its valuing of creativity, exploration, and process over perfection, control, and order is compelling. However, the cost of this revision to the orthodox concept of God is not worth the potential benefits, and there are other ways of achieving the ends hoped for by Hekman and Keller by working within the concept of God expressed by figures like Augustine. The main inadequacy with the notion of a God of "endless becoming" is that it, again, does not actually provide an adequate conceptual grounding for materialism. Even Grosz acknowledges that,

"Without ideality, a plan, a map, a model, an ideal, a direction, or a theme, materiality could not materialize itself."[63] The collapse of God into material processes of becoming fails to adequately account for the reality that God is not a creature like us. As we have seen with Augustine, there is an infinite *difference* between God and the material world, even while the material world is permeated with the presence of God, and so it is able to reveal something about God. To be in motion, in flux, and in process are features of creaturely life that reveal God to us through their difference from that which defines divine life.[64] This does not entail, despite the claims of Keller and Hekman, that we therefore affirm the notion of a "distant," "separate," or "unaffected" divinity who has no intimate relation to creation. Rather, as discussed earlier, the God described by Augustine is the source of everything that exists, and thus creation exists "in" God. This God became incarnate in Christ, and far from being "unaffected" by creation, took on the sufferings of creation in order to be united with everything that is genuinely human. Indeed, as Augustine argues, God is "more inward to me than my most inward part and higher than my highest."[65] However, it is important to retain as well the transcendence of God, even as we affirm God's immanence. As Rowan Williams argues, "God could not (logically) be simultaneously the cause of a whole interlocking system and a member of it, and so we can never talk of features in common between God and the world."[66] God is not one process among other processes of becoming, but is rather the source and foundation of all processes, the guarantee of their coherence and meaningfulness. As Williams continues:

> For there to be a world, a limited whole, there must be coherence, a convergence on stability, though it is a stability that continues to alter and reinvent itself at every moment, as time advances: there is no question of "imposing" anything from "outside" or "above," since there is no above or outside the universe in the sense of a rival system acting casually on it from a competing position.[67]

There is continuity in the world by virtue of the relationship of creation to Creator. This continuity enables us to know and speak of God, albeit imperfectly and only analogically. However, there is also always a fundamental discontinuity between God and the world in the sense that God is not a process in the world like other processes. Without a notion of a loving Creator who sustains and is intimately present to the processes of nature, but who also ultimately transcends them, it becomes difficult to share the optimism of Keller and the New Feminist Materialists about the future of evolution and the transformative potential of material processes.

The optimism about "process" and "becoming" that is expressed by Keller and the New Feminist Materialists brings us to another area in which

Augustine could offer a helpful corrective to New Feminist Materialists. A notion of sin, even of "inherited" sin, would temper the optimism expressed by some of the New Feminist Materialists, including Grosz, about the possibility of the ongoing movement of material forces leading to the transformation of oppressive and corrupt structures. Grosz speaks of "a fleeting humanity whose destiny is self-overcoming," and the power of "Life," which "magnifies and extends matter," just as "matter in turn intensifies and transforms life."[68] The evolutionary movement of materiality, she argues, "opens up feminist and other political struggles to what is beyond current comprehension and control, to becoming unrecognizable, becoming other, becoming artistic."[69]

Grosz has no conceptual grounding within her framework to affirm anything more than the fact that the world is in flux and that this sometimes produces novelty and diversity. She views the instability and "ceaseless becoming" of the world as a hopeful reality that ensures that everything that is subordinated, marginalized, and oppressed is only this way temporarily. She is right to assert that the processes of becoming may potentially lead humanity to "becoming other and becoming artistic." However, with only the resources of materialism, we have no assurances that the processes of becoming will lead to greater flourishing or liberation. Indeed, they may simply lead to new and different forms of oppression. A robust notion of systemic, "inherited" sin can help theologians to develop an appreciation for how persistent and recalcitrant sinful structures can be. Sedimented distortions and "discreations" are not easily uprooted.[70] The belief in human sinfulness and the need for redemption that is expressed within the theology of Augustine would temper some of the unbounded enthusiasm for the processes of nature that is present in New Feminist Materialist writings. A concept of sin is an essential element of a realistic description of the situation of creaturely life in the twenty-first century. As Augustine argues, inherited sin strikes at the foundation of all of human existence. We cannot understand ourselves adequately without including a notion of inherited, systemic sin, even though sin still does not get to have the final word in terms of determining the meaning of human life.

## CONCLUSION

This chapter has brought together an unlikely pair of sources in Augustine and the New Feminist Materialists. Such a juxtaposition has enabled us to draw out what is useful from each source, while still allowing them to be mutually corrective to one another. It has developed a theological anthropology that integrates analysis of the body's sexed, material dynamism with reflection on its history of participation in inherited sin. Drawing from both the New Feminist Materialists and Augustine, it argues that the body is dynamic, continually evolving in different sexed ways, infected by sin and yet saturated with the divine. It is constrained by the past but also utilizes the past to develop resources for the future. The ongoing development and evolution of the body invites creative participation on the part of humans, while simultaneously encouraging us to remain circumspect about the extent to which we can ever claim to understand comprehensively the meaning of our bodies as sexed.

The work of the New Feminist Materialists was thus read through Augustine's incarnational lens so that matter is not just imbued with activity and creativity in its own right, but rather is created by God, lovingly sustained by God, and permeated with God's presence, all without collapsing the infinite difference between God and the world. This theology of matter rejects process theology, since God's transcendence of the material is necessary for its existence, coherence, and meaning. God transcends materiality without being "separate" from it. In Christ, materiality is brought into union with the divine, making it sacramental and a privileged site for divine revelation.

## NOTES

1. In this chapter, I will be referring to Augustine, *Confessions (Conf.)*, tr. Henry Chadwick (Oxford: Oxford University Press, 1998).
2. Rowan Williams, *On Augustine* (London: Bloomsbury Continuum, 2016), 75.
3. *Material Feminisms*, eds. Stacy Alaimo and Susan Hekman (Bloomington: Indiana University Press, 2008), 7.
4. Samantha Frost, "The Implications of the New Materialisms for Feminist Epistemology," in *Feminist Epistemology and Philosophy of Science: Power in Knowledge*, ed. H. E. Grasswick (Dordrecht: Springer, 2011), 69: "'new materialist' work challenges the linear models of causation that underlie constructivist analyses of the ways power shapes subjects and objects of knowledge."
5. Michel Foucault, in *The History of Sexuality: Volume I: An Introduction*, tr. Robert Hurley (New York: Pantheon, 1978), 155, argued that power, not biology, should be the primary object of analysis, since sex and sexuality have been "organized by power in its grip on bodies and their materiality, their forces, energies, sensations, and pleasures."
6. Diana H. Coole and Samantha Frost, *New Materialisms: Ontology, Agency, and Politics* (Durham: Duke University Press, 2010), 7.
7. Anne Fausto-Sterling, "The Bare Bones of Sex: Part 1 - Sex and Gender," *Signs* 30, no. 2 (2005), 1495.
8. Catherine Keller and Mary-Jane Rubenstein, *Entangled Worlds: Religion, Science, and New Materialisms* (New York: Fordham University Press, 2018), 1.

9. Elizabeth Grosz, *Time Travels: Feminism, Nature, and Power* (Durham: Duke University Press, 2005), 18.

10. Grosz, "The Nature of Sexual Difference: Irigaray and Darwin," *Angelaki 17*, no. 2 (2012), 75.

11. Grosz, *Time Travels*, 8.

12. Grosz, *Time Travels*, 49.

13. Ibid.

14. Grosz, *The Nick of Time: Politics, Evolution, and the Untimely* (London: Duke University Press, 2004), 5.

15. Grosz, *Time Travels*, 36.

16. Ibid.

17. Ibid.

18. Ibid., 41.

19. Ibid., 18.

20. Ibid., 4.

21. Ibid., 181.

22. Grosz, *The Nick of Time*, 14.

23. Grosz, "The Nature of Sexual Difference," 73.

24. Grosz, *Becoming Undone*, 104.

25. Ibid., 131.

26. Kim Power, *Veiled Desire: Augustine's Writing on Women* (London: Darton, Longman, & Todd, 1995), 5.

27. E. Ann Matter, "Women," in *Augustine through the Ages: An Encyclopedia*, ed. Allan D. Fitzgerald, OSA (Grand Rapids: Eerdmans, 2009), 887.

28. Augustine, *De Genesi ad Litteram (De Gen.)*, in the *Corpus Augustinianum Gissense (CAG)*, ed. Cornelius Mayer, (Charlottesville, VA: 2000), 11.37.

29. Ibid.

30. Felecia McDuffie, "Augustine's Rhetoric of the Feminine in the *Confessions*: Woman as Mother, Woman as Other," in *Feminist Interpretations of Augustine*, ed. Judith Stark (University Park, PA: Pennsylvania State University Press, 2007), 98.

31. Rosemary Radford Ruether, "Sexuality, Gender, and Women," in *Feminist Interpretations of Augustine*, ed. Judith Stark (University Park, PA: Pennsylvania State University Press, 2007), 63.

32. Augustine, *The Trinity (De Trin.)*, 2nd edition, ed. John E. Rotelle, trans. Edmund Hill (New York: New City Press, 1991), 325.

33. Describing the early moments after the resurrection, Augustine says that while the male disciples ("the stronger sex") left, "mulier [Maria] stetit, et coepit corpus Iesu lacrimis quaerere, coepit ad monumentum plorare; *illi minorem curam habuerunt, fortiores sexu, sed minores affectu.* mulier plus quaerebat Iesum, quia ipsa prior in paradiso perdiderat Iesum: quia per illam mors intrauerat, plus uitam quaerebat. et tamen quomodo quaerebat?" See the *Sermones Moriniani ex collectione Guelferbytana* in the *CAG*, 14. My thanks to Jenny Rallens for her input on my translation of this passage and for her expertise in capturing some of the nuances in Augustine's Latin.

34. One is led to wonder if Augustine's belief in the greater affectivity of women, alongside the image of Mary Magdalene searching for Jesus with tears, was shaped in

any way by his memory of his mother Monica weeping and praying for his conversion or of her Dido-like weeping on the shore as his ship departed for Rome, as recounted in *Conf.* 5.8.14–15.

35. John Rist, *Augustine: Ancient Thought Baptized* (Cambridge: Cambridge University Press, 1994), 119.

36. Note Augustine's statement in *De Trin.* 12.3.10: "what was made to the image of God is the human nature that is realized in each sex, and it does not exclude the female from the image of God."

37. Power, *Veiled Desire*, 135; Augustine, *De Trin.* 12.5.

38. *De Trin.* 12.3, 12.25.

39. Augustine, *The Literal Meaning of Genesis*, Vol. 1, tr. and ed. John H. Taylor (New York: Paulist Press, 1982), 12.35.

40. Rist, *Augustine: Ancient Thought Baptized*, 120.

41. Elizabeth A. Clark, "Theory and Practice in Late Ancient Asceticism: Jerome, Chrysostom, and Augustine," *Journal of Feminist Studies in Religion* 5, no. 2 (1989), 25.

42. Williams, *On Augustine*, 10.

43. Luigi Gioia, *The Theological Epistemology of Augustine's De Trinitate* (Oxford: Oxford University Press, 2008), 125–126.

44. Augustine, *Confessions*, as translated by Chadwick, 2.2.

45. Ernan McMullin, "Darwin and the Other Christian Tradition," *Zygon* 46, no. 2 (2011), 295.

46. Augustine, *The Literal Meaning of Genesis*, 4, 33, 51.

47. Michele Saracino, "Moving Beyond the 'One True Story,'" *Frontiers in Catholic Feminist Theology: Shoulder to Shoulder*, eds. Susan Abraham and Elena Procario-Foley (Minneapolis: Fortress Press, 2009), 10.

48. Ibid., 78.

49. Grosz, *The Incorporeal: Ontology, Ethics, and the Limits of Materialism* (New York: Colombia University Press, 2017), 13.

50. Augustine, *Conf.* 4.12, as translated by Chadwick, 63, emphasis mine.

51. Williams, *On Augustine*, 75.

52. Saracino, "Moving beyond the 'One True Story,'" 13.

53. Grosz, *The Incorporeal*, 14.

54. Susan Hekman, "Feminist New Materialism and Process Theology: Beginning the Dialogue," *Feminist Theology* 25, no. 2 (Jan. 2017), 198–207.

55. Hekman, "Feminist New Materialism," 200.

56. Ibid., 201.

57. Catherine Keller, *The Face of the Deep: A Theology of Becoming* (London: Routledge, 2003), 15–16.

58. Ibid., 139–140.

59. Ibid., 164, 181.

60. Ibid., 226.

61. Ibid., 226, 230.

62. Ibid., 226.

63. Grosz, *The Incorporeal*, 12.

64. Williams, *On Augustine*, 67.
65. Augustine, *Conf.*, as translated by Chadwick, 3.6.11.
66. Williams, *On Augustine*, 67.
67. Ibid.
68. Grosz, *Becoming Undone*, 24, 39.
69. Grosz, *Time Travels*, 5.
70. Keller, *The Face of the Deep*, 112.

*Part IV*

# AUGUSTINIAN TEMPORALITY IN THE MIDDLE AGES

*Chapter 10*

# Augustine and Avicenna on the Puzzle of Time without Time

Celia Hatherly

There is a remarkable coincidence in Augustine and Avicenna's investigations into the nature of time. Despite the fact that Avicenna wrote in Arabic and Persian, was born in Central Asia more than 500 years after the death of Augustine, and had no access to Augustine's philosophical works, both consider a strikingly similar objection to the ontological dependence of time on the motion of the heavens. The objection, as found in Avicenna, is as follows:

> One might ask: Do you think that if that motion [i.e. eternal, circular motion] did not exist, time would vanish such that the other motions different from it would be without priority (*taqaddum*) and posteriority (*ta'aḫḫur*)?[1]

And in Augustine:

> I once heard a learned man say that the motions of the sun, moon, and stars constituted time; and I did not agree. For why should not the motions of all bodies constitute time? What if the lights of heaven should cease, and a potter's wheel still turn round: would there be no time by which we might measure those rotations and say either that it turned at equal intervals, or, if it moved now more slowly and now more quickly, that some rotations were longer and others shorter? And while we were saying this, would we not also be speaking in time?[2]

Both versions of the objection (which I shall henceforth call the Time without Time objection) share a common structure. Both assume that there can be terrestrial motions in the absence of celestial motion. Both also assume that these remaining terrestrial motions would retain properties necessary to ensure the existence of time. In Avicenna's case, these terrestrial motions must retain their division into the prior and the posterior, for, as Avicenna claimed earlier in his treatise on time, "you know that being divisible into the prior (*mutaqaddim*) and the posterior (*muta'aḫḫir*) is a necessary concomitant of motion."[3] Given this division of motion into the prior and the posterior, it seems that time too must exist, since, following Aristotle, Avicenna defines time as "the number of motion when it is differentiated into what is prior and what is posterior."[4] Thus, if terrestrial motions can exist without celestial motion, time can exist in the absence of celestial motion. In Augustine's case, terrestrial motions guarantee the existence of time because their durations can still be measured and compared to each other, for "when a body is moved, I measure by time how long it was moving from the time when it began to be moved until it stopped."[5] Thus, in the absence of celestial motion, the remaining terrestrial motions would still be measured by time. In structure, then, Avicenna and Augustine's versions of the Time without Time objection are essentially the same. This similarity is even more remarkable given that there is no clear line of transmission connecting the two.

The source for Avicenna's version of the Time without Time objection appears to be Alexander of Aphrodisias. Avicenna would have had access to his version of the objection because several of the Arabic translations of Aristotle's *Physics IV* included Alexander's commentary.[6] Unfortunately, the Greek originals and Arabic translations of these commentaries have been lost, but fragments of Alexander's comments can still be found in the works of Simiplicius. In one such fragment, Alexander objects to the theory of time found in Plato's *Timaeus* as interpreted by Galen.[7] On Galen's reading of the text, Plato identifies time with the ordered motion of the heavens. This ordered motion, however, was preceded in time by the chaotic and disordered motions. Thus, for Plato, time comes to be after motion, since time begins only after the Demiurge imposed order on the motion of the cosmos.[8] Against this view, Simplicius records that Alexander argued:

> If all movement is in time, it is clear that the faulty and irregular movement is also in time. If, then, such time was before the heaven came to be, it is clear that time was also before the circular motion of the heaven. If, then, this is time, there would be time before time.[9]

From this quotation, we can see that Alexander's objection has the same structure as both Augustine's and Avicenna's. Like theirs, Alexander's turns on the premises that (1) there can be motion in the absence of celestial motion and (2) this motion takes place in time. This structural similarity is what makes Alexander the likeliest source for Avicenna's Time without Time objection even though Avicenna's target is not a Platonic theory of time, but his own Aristotelian theory of time as the magnitude of the motion of the heavens.[10] This change of target, however, presents no difficulty because, due to its structure, the Time without Time objection works just as well against Aristotle as against Plato.[11]

Now, given the similarity between Alexander's objection and Augustine's, it would be unsurprising if Alexander turned out to be the ultimate source of Augustine's objection as well. In fact, Alexander's version of the Time without Time objection is closer to Augustine's than to Avicenna's, since both Alexander and Augustine object to making time the motion of the heavens rather than its measure. The secondary literature on Augustine's version, however, offers two immediate sources for his version, only one of which traces back to Alexander.

The immediate source that can be traced back to Alexander is Basil of Caesarea's *Adversus Eunomium*. John F. Callahan first proposed this work as the immediate source of Augustine's version (despite the lack of a known Latin translation) because of the striking similarities between the objections in the *Adversus Eunomium* and the *Confessions*.[12] In the *Adversus Eunomium*, Basil argues against Eunomius, a fourth-century advocate of Arianism, who claimed that time is the motion of the stars. Basil, however, insists that this cannot be true and objects to Eunomius' claim by pointing to the account of creation in Genesis, which asserts that the motion of the Sun and stars began only on the fourth day of creation. Thus, the identification of time with celestial motion would imply that there was no time during the first three days of creation. Thus, Basil, like Augustine, thinks that there can be time without celestial motion and so time cannot be identical with it. Furthermore, like Augustine, Basil holds that the existence of any motion, great or small, is sufficient for the existence of time. Finally, if Callahan is correct that Basil is Augustine's immediate source, then Alexander of Aphrodisias is the common ultimate source for both Augustine and Avicenna, for as Mark Del Cogliano has shown, Basil of Caesarea grounded his objection to Eunomius in his understanding of Alexander's commentary on Aristotle's *Physics*.[13]

Jason Carter, however, has suggested that Augustine's version is borrowed from the Neo-Pythagorean astrologer Nigidius Figulus because both compare celestial motion to that of a potter's wheel.[14] Thus, according to Carter, there is no need to suppose Augustine had access to an unknown Latin translation of the *Adversus Eunomium*, when we know from Augustine's *City of God* that he was familiar with Nigidius Figulus's potter's wheel example. If, however, Carter is correct, there will be no earlier version of the Time without Time objection to which both Augustine and Avicenna had access, since Avicenna obviously had no access to the work of Nigidius Figulus. It is, of course, also possible that the line of transmission is not clear because there is no line of transmission, for it seems perfectly possible that the Time without Time objection is obvious to any philosopher considering a theory of time that makes time dependent on a single privileged motion.

Regardless of how Avicenna and Augustine came to consider the puzzle of Time without Time, understanding their different approaches to the puzzle is of both philosophical and historical interest. It is of philosophical interest because Augustine and Avicenna disagree about whether the objection is successful. Augustine thinks that it is and so dismisses the idea that time is ontologically dependent on celestial motion.[15] Avicenna, however, is at pains to show why it is not successful. Thus, looking at Augustine and Avicenna's assessments of the strength of the objection can give us deeper insight into what philosophical commitments are necessary in order to make a theory like Plato's or Aristotle's coherent. Second, assessments of the strength of the objection will also make clearer what was driving two different and independent traditions in the development of the ancient Greek philosophy of time, one that accepted and built on Aristotle's theory and another that rejected it. This opposition is of particular historical interest given that later Medieval Latin philosophers would have to adjudicate between Augustine's rejection and Avicenna's acceptance of Aristotle's theory of time. Thus, my aim for this article is to lay out why it is that Avicenna thinks the Time without Time objection does not work. As we shall see, it is because, unlike Augustine, Avicenna thinks that time and motion must be eternal.

## AVICENNA'S THEORY OF TIME

Before examining Avicenna's response to the Time without Time objection, we must understand what he thinks time is. As quoted earlier, time, for Avicenna, is "the number of motion when it is differentiated into what is prior and what is posterior."[16] This definition appears to be circular but is not because "the prior and the posterior are found in [motion] only as a result of relation of the prior and the posterior in distance."[17] That is, it is not circular because "prior" and "posterior" are spatial as well as temporal terms. Indeed, for Avicenna, priority and posteriority in motion is in the first instance a matter of being spatially closer or farther away for the starting point of the motion.[18] To get a sense of what this means, consider a train trip from Ottawa to Vancouver. This trip, like all motions for Avicenna, is defined as the actualization of a potentiality and thus is goal-oriented. So, Vancouver is the end of the trip not because the train arrived in Vancouver at the latest time. Instead, Vancouver is the end of the trip because the goal of the trip is to actualize the train's potentiality to be in Vancouver. Furthermore, the other stages of the trip can be ordered into prior and posterior without using time, for during the trip, the train passes through one spatial position and then through another until it reaches Vancouver, its destination. The order in which the train passes through these spatial positions is determined by the order inherent in the positions itself. Thus, given that, from East to West, the provinces between Ottawa and Vancouver are Manitoba, Saskatchewan, and Alberta, it is necessarily the case that the train's motion through Manitoba is prior to its motion through Alberta. This necessary priority, moreover, is explained entirely due to the goal-oriented nature of the train trip and Canadian geography. Thus, the priority of motion that Avicenna mentions in his version of the Time without Time puzzle is not temporal. The existence of motion, however, entails the existence of time as well since

> time, owing to what it is in itself, is essentially a magnitude, possessing [the states] of being prior and posterior, the posterior part of which does not exist together with what is prior, as might be found in other types of [things that might] be prior and posterior.[19]

Thus, time is a magnitude ordered into prior and posterior states that do not coexist. Furthermore, whenever motion exists, such a magnitude will as well. The reason is that all motion through distance is divided into the prior and the posterior as a result of its goal-directed nature and the order inherent in any spatial magnitude. Furthermore, as Avicenna claimed earlier, "The prior part of the motion will not exist together with its later part in the way that the prior and posterior parts in distance exist together."[20] That is, it is a necessary feature of motion that its prior and posterior states do not coexist. Indeed, it is this inability to coexist that differentiates prior and posterior states of motion from those of position. There must be magnitude that separates them, and this magnitude is time. Thus, it seems that Avicenna's account of time does fall prey to the Time without Time objection and that the motion of any body through space produces time, regardless of whether this motion is terrestrial or celestial.

## AVICENNA AND THE PUZZLE OF TOO MANY TIMES

Avicenna, however, cannot allow that any and all motions can cause the existence of time and not only because of the Time without Time objection. Instead, he must find a way to claim that only the eternal motion of the spheres can. To understand why, we need to see how Avicenna thinks that the puzzle of Time without Time works in conjunction with another objection to identifying time with the magnitude of motion. This puzzle (which I henceforth call the Too Many Times puzzle) tries to show, first, that if time is the magnitude of motion, then there are as many numerically distinct times as there are motions. Second, it argues that two numerically distinct times cannot be simultaneous and, therefore, no two motions can be simultaneous.[21] We must consider these two objections because Avicenna raises the problem of Time without Time in the context of responding to the Too Many Times puzzle. Indeed, as we shall see in the penultimate section, Avicenna's response to the two are intricately connected because both are based on the same mistake: thinking that time can depend on a motion with finite duration.

Returning to the Too Many Times puzzle, in order to establish its first step, Avicenna reports that his opponents

> say [1] that there inevitably belongs to a motion, insofar as it is a motion, a certain amount of time and [2] that this motion, insofar as it is a motion, does not require that another body that is distinct from its body is also moved (there perhaps being a requirement for this in some cases is not due to it being motion but [due to] its existence requiring of [the body] that moves [it] that [this body] moves; but this is neither a condition of motion insofar as it is a motion nor one of its necessary concomitants.) [3] So, given these [assumptions], any motion that you posit as existing, insofar as it is a motion, necessitates that a time belongs to it; but [this motion], insofar as it is a motion, does not necessitate that there is another motion. [4] If that is the case, then each motion is accompanied by a private time that does not apply to any other motion, just as each is accompanied by a private place.[22]

In this passage, the objector reveals why there must be as many times as there are motions: every motion possesses its own private time. Thus, just as two moving bodies do not, and indeed cannot, occupy the same place, so too must every motion occupy its own time. To establish this, the objector considers how the relationship between motion and time differs from the relationship between two numerically distinct motions. In the case of the relationship between motion and time, [1] the existence of time is a logical consequence of the existence of motion. As we saw earlier, motion is just the ordered succession of spatial states that do not coexist, and time just is the magnitude of change between these states. Thus, it appears to follow from the definition of motion that it exists in time. Nevertheless, [2] it does not follow from the definition of motion that if one body moves, another must move as well. Granted, as the objector points out, one motion might need the motion of another body to exist, but it does not need it to be motion. Thus, [3] while the existence of time is a logical consequence of the existence of a motion, the existence of another motion is not. Thus, the existence of any motion is sufficient for the existence of a time and it is sufficient for said time to be independent of the existence of another motion. From this, it follows that the times that belong to each motion will be only generically rather than numerically the same. So, just as it follows from the nature of motion that they all traverse *a* distance but not the *same* distance, so too it follows from the nature of motion they traverse *a* time but not the *same* time.

The next step in the objection is to show that if the times of distinct motions are numerically distinct, it is impossible for two motions to be simultaneous. The reasoning for this conclusion goes as follows:

> So, [1] when motions are together, their times must also be together, [2] and their [times'] togetherness must be with respect to place, subject, rank, nature, or anything else but togetherness in time. [3] However, every one of these ways [of being together] fails to prevent some of [these times] from being before and some after—that is, some of them existing while others do not. [4] So, it remains that their togetherness is togetherness in time, where togetherness in time is the occurrence of many things in a single time, or a single instant which is a single limit of time. [5] This necessitates that the many times would have a single time; but [6] the reason for each of these times [being] together with them [the many times] is, in this sense, just like the reason that they are joined together in [the single time], [7] in which case there would necessarily be an infinite number of simultaneous times.[23]

The argument in this passage begins with two assumptions: [1] two motions are simultaneous (together or *ma'*) if and only if their times are simultaneous; and [2] the simultaneity of two times is not a matter of the two times' existence at the same time. This second assumption, of course, stems from the objector's prior conclusion that the times of two motions are not numerically identical. If this is the case, their simultaneity cannot be explained by their existence at the numerically same time. The objector, however, quickly shows that assumption [2] cannot be correct, given that simultaneity cannot be explained in terms of any other kind of sameness, for [3] no other kind of sameness necessitates that the two times and motions coexist. For example, two times or motions are not simultaneous because they occur in the same place. Indeed, the only way that, say, Socrates and Plato can move through the same place is if their movements are not simultaneous. Likewise, two motions are not simultaneous because they occur in the same subject. So, a walk to the Athenian agora and a walk to the Areopagus are not simultaneous because they both occur in Socrates. Again, the two motions can occur in Socrates only if they are not simultaneous. Thus, as the objector concludes, [4] simultaneity must mean existing at the same time, and so [5] the times of two motions can be simultaneous only if they exist at the same time. As the objector argues, however, two times that are genetically identical but numerically distinct can never be simultaneous. The reasoning seems to be that the times of two motions can only be simultaneous if (a) they are numerically identical or (b) they are both simultaneous with a third time. Now, since the times of two motions cannot be numerically identical, it follows that they can be simultaneous only if they are both simultaneous with a third time. This third time, however, is not numerically identical with the first two, so [6] there must be a fourth time that explains why the third time is simultaneous with the first and second. This same problem would occur again and again. Thus, the objector concludes that [7] one could posit an infinite number of times without ever explaining why the first two were simultaneous. Thus, the definition of time as the magnitude of motion cannot be correct since it leads to the absurd conclusion that no two motions can ever be simultaneous.[24]

We can now see how the Time without Time objection works in conjunction with the Too Many Times objection and why Avicenna raised the latter in the course of responding to the former. He did this because his version of the Time without Time objection seeks to block his answer to the Too Many Times objection. As we shall see in the next section, Avicenna tried to avoid the Too Many Times objection by making time the magnitude of a single privileged motion: the motion of the spheres. Hence, the point of the Time without Time objection is to show that this solution does not work because it is possible for terrestrial motion to exist and generate time in the absence of celestial motion. Thus, the two objections together try to put Avicenna in a double bind: he must either accept that there are as many independent times as there are motions or accept that there can be motion without time. In the next section, I examine how Avicenna tries to get out of this bind.

## AVICENNA'S SOLUTION TO THE TWO PUZZLES

Given that the puzzle of Time without Time is raised in the context of responding to the puzzle of Too Many Times, it is unsurprising that we can only understand Avicenna's response to the former in the light of his response to the latter. In his view, the latter puzzle arises only because of a misunderstanding in what it means for time to be the magnitude of motion. In particular, it is based on the failure to make two important distinctions. Thus, the way to respond to it is to

> [1] distinguish between someone saying that time is a magnitude (*miqdār*) of every motion and someone saying that its individual existence depends on every motion. [2] Furthermore, there is a distinction between someone saying that the essence of time is connected to motion as one of its accidents and someone saying that time is connected to the essence of motion as an accident of the essence of motion, because [according to] the first sense, certain things accidentally

belong to something, while [according to] the second, certain things are dependent upon something.²⁵

According to the first distinction, time's status as the magnitude of every motion does not entail that it has ontological dependence on every motion. Thus, time is not an accident of motion in the same way that whiteness is an accident of bodies. In the case of whiteness, a group of five bodies can be white only if there are five individual instances of whiteness, each of which depends ontologically on the body in which it inheres. Time, however, can be the magnitude (*miqdār*) of every motion without depending on every motion because

> it is not a condition of what measures that it be something accidental to and subsist with the thing; rather, it might measure something distinct [from itself] by being brought next to and juxtaposed with what is distinct from it.²⁶

To understand Avicenna's reasoning in this quotation, we need to understand that the Arabic word *miqdār*, which I have translated as "magnitude," can also mean "measure."²⁷ Indeed, the term was used by the Arabic translators of Aristotle to render both μέτρον (measure) and μέγεθος (continuous quantity). Thus, in the aforementioned quotation, Avicenna takes time's role as the *miqdār* of motion to mean that time is the μέτρον (measure) of motion and thus not ontologically dependent on it. However, in the *Metaphysics of the Healing*, Avicenna frequently uses *miqdār* to refer to μέγεθος, as when, for example, he writes:

> [Now,] it has become evident that this magnitude (*miqdār*) is in matter and that it increases and decreases while substance continues to exist. [Magnitude] is, hence, necessarily an accident. But it is one of the accidents that attaches to matter and to something in matter, because this magnitude does not separate from matter.²⁸

Thus, Avicenna uses *miqdār* to refer to either a magnitude, that is, a continuous quantity existing in a body, or to the measure of that quantity. Furthermore, in his treatise on time, Avicenna plays with this ambiguity in the definition of time as the *miqdār* of motion by claiming that

> what was demonstrated for us concerning time is only that it depends upon motion and is a certain disposition (*hay'a*) of it, while, concerning motion, it is only that every motion is measured (*tuqaddar*) by time.²⁹

In this passage, we can see that Avicenna makes time as both the μέγεθος and μέτρον of motion. It is the former because it is ontologically dependent on motion and because time is a disposition of motion just as motion, whiteness, and blackness are dispositions of body.[30] It is the latter because every motion is measured by time. Thus, Avicenna's understanding of time's status as a magnitude appears to be similar to the modern understanding of the meter. The meter is the base unit of length in the International System of Units (SI) and so is the unit that determines the length of all other bodies. Furthermore, the meter is itself the length of a particular body, namely the international prototype meter, which is a bar of platinum-iridium alloy kept in a vault near Paris. Thus, like time, the meter both determines the length of every extended body and is the length of one body in particular.

Now in the case of the meter, the decision to make the meter dependent on a particular bar of platinum-iridium was arbitrary. In fact, the meter isn't defined as the length of that bar anymore but as the length of the path traveled by light in vacuum during 1/299792458 of a second. For Avicenna, however, the choice of making time the μέγεθος of the motion of the heavens is not arbitrary at all. This brings us to Avicenna's second distinction, which claims that while time is essentially an accident of motion, it is not the case that every motion essentially possesses time as an accident. The latter does not follow from the former because "it is not the case that when the thing itself depends upon the nature of a given thing, the nature of the thing must not be devoid of it."[31] That is, it is not the case that every motion by nature possesses time as an accident just because time by nature exists as an accident of motion. Indeed, as Avicenna argues, only eternal celestial motion can possess time as an accident because

> time does not depend on motions that have a beginning and an end; so how could time be dependent upon them? If time were to belong to them, then it would be divided by two instants, but we have forbidden that. Of course, when time exists (due to a motion that has a character such that it is fitting for the existence of time to be dependent on it and this motion is motion that is continuous and is not delimited by actual extreme limits) all the other motions will be measured by it.[32]

When Avicenna speaks in this passage of the impossibility of motion being "divided by two instants," he is referring to the impossibility of time having a beginning or an end. From this impossibility, it follows that time cannot be an accident of terrestrial motion, for if time ontologically depends on terrestrial motions, it will exist only as long as those motions do. Thus, given that all terrestrial motions begin and end, if time depends on these motions, time will as well. As Avicenna claimed earlier, however, time cannot begin or end and so it cannot depend on terrestrial motion.

With these two distinctions in mind, we can now appreciate how Avicenna responds to the problems of Too Many Times and of Time without Time.

The former relied on the claim that time is a necessary consequence of the existence of every motion. This cannot be the case, however, because given that time cannot begin or end, it cannot be the consequence of finite motion. Granted, every motion possesses a magnitude between its prior and posterior states. This magnitude, however, cannot itself be time since time is, by definition, an infinite magnitude and they are finite. Thus, while these magnitudes are *measured* by time, they cannot *be* time. This distinction, moreover, allows Avicenna to respond to the problem of Time without Time.[33] This problem also relied on the claim that time is a necessary consequence of the existence of every motion. However, for Avicenna, what is necessary is that these motions are *measured* by time, not that time is a quantity inhering in these motions. Thus, it is Avicenna's understanding of what it means for time to be a magnitude, along with his insistence on the necessary eternity of time, that allows him to respond to the problems of Too Many Times and Time without Time. His insistence on its eternity, however, represents a significant disagreement with Augustine. In the final section, I discuss why Augustine thinks that time can begin, and Avicenna thinks that it cannot.

## AVICENNA AND AUGUSTINE ON THE ETERNITY OF TIME

Augustine addressed the question of whether time has a beginning in the context of addressing what God was doing before the first moment of creation and why he created at that moment (and not an earlier or later one).[34] Augustine's answer to these arguments against the temporal beginning of the cosmos is grounded in the distinction between time and timelessness. Time depends on movement, and since God is unmoving, there is no time before creation.[35] Thus, for Augustine, time was created when the cosmos was created. The questions "Why not sooner?" or "What was God doing before?" make no sense because, as Augustine says to God, "You have made time itself. Time could not elapse before you made time. But if time did not exist before heaven and earth, why do people ask what you were doing then? There was no 'then' when there was no time."[36] Thus, Augustine dismisses the question of what God was doing before the creation by pointing out that there was no *before* before creation.[37] To put it another way, Augustine resolves these objections to the temporal beginning of the cosmos by insisting on the beginning of time.

Avicenna argues, by contrast, that time cannot have a beginning because such a beginning is impossible.[38] The reason is that if time began, then:

[1] time has no before and [2], since it has no before, [time] could not have been non-existent and then existed, for, if had been non-existent and then existed,

its existence would be after its non-existence, and so its non-existence would be before its existence. [3] Therefore, it must have a before, and that before must mean something other than the non-existence that describes it, according to what we stated elsewhere. So, this species of before-ness is predicated of something that exists but is not this time. [4] Thus, before this time, there was [another] time that is continuous with it.[39]

The aforementioned argument works by pointing out that [1] if time began a thousand years ago, then we cannot speak about what happened before a thousand years ago. This claim, however, leads to a contradiction because, as Avicenna argues, [2] if time began a thousand years ago, then we must speak about what happened before a thousand years ago, for to begin is to exist after not existing. Thus, if time began, something must have preceded time.[40] Moreover, what preceded time cannot be merely the nonexistence of time. To explain why, [3] Avicenna refers to a prior discussion in which he gives time the job of ordering nontemporal states into a temporal sequence, or as he puts it:

when something is said to be before and that thing is not time (but, for example, is motion, humans, and the like), [its being before] means that it exists together with a certain thing that is in some state such that when that state is compared with the state of something later, it is inseparable from [that state] if the thing in [the former state] is essentially before. That is, this inseparability belongs to [time] essentially.[41]

Thus, time has the job of ordering nontemporal states because time and time alone has prior states that are essentially earlier than its posterior ones. This reasoning, moreover, contains a background assumption that is key to understanding Avicenna's argument against the beginning of time: that there must be an explanation for why one state is earlier than another.[42] Thus, for example, there must be an explanation for why the birth of Augustine happened before the birth of Avicenna. This factor moreover cannot be the existence of Avicenna and the nonexistence of Augustine at some time because, as Avicenna explains:

this factor cannot merely be some relation to nonexistence (or existence), since the existing thing's relation to the non-existing thing might be one of being later just as easily as being earlier (and the same holds with regard to existence).[43]

Thus, something needs to explain why Augustine lived and died before Avicenna because, in and of themselves, Augustine's life and death are not necessarily prior to Avicenna's. Thus, if we consider only Avicenna *qua*

Avicenna and Augustine *qua* Augustine, we could not know who lived and died prior to whom. Instead, as Avicenna explained, to determine who lived first, we need to know that Augustine coexisted with a state that is essentially prior to the state with which Avicenna coexisted. These states will be the states of a body in motion, since, as we have already seen, Avicenna thinks that motion is inherently ordered into prior and posterior states. In other words, these states will be states of time.

With this in mind, we can return to Avicenna's argument for why time cannot begin. Remember that for time to have a beginning, its nonexistence must be temporally prior to its existence. Furthermore, as we now know, there must be an explanation for why its nonexistence is prior to its existence. This explanation, moreover, cannot be the nonexistence of time itself because the nonexistence of time does not, in and of itself, entail that it is temporally prior (rather than posterior) to the existence of time. Thus, if time's nonexistence is prior to its existence, then, necessarily, time's nonexistence coexists with a state that is essentially temporally prior to a state with which time's existence coexists. These states, however, will just be time since time is what "turns out to essentially have a before and an after," and so time cannot begin.

Given the aforementioned argument, it is obvious that Avicenna would reject Augustine's answer to the question about what God was doing before he created the cosmos. Again, Augustine's response hinged on the view that God created time when he created the cosmos. Thus, we cannot ask what God was doing before creation, because before creation, there was no time and without time there can be no before. Now, Avicenna would agree that without time there can be no before. Rather than resolving an objection to the temporal beginning of the cosmos, however, this just creates a new one, since Avicenna defines a beginning as existence *after* nonexistence. Thus, to deny that there was a before prior to the beginning of the world is simply to deny that it began. According to Avicenna, then, it is logically impossible for time to begin. Furthermore, time's inability to begin was a key part of what allowed Avicenna to resolve his version of the Time without Time objection. Thus, it seems that the ultimate explanation for why Avicenna differs from Augustine in his assessment of the strength of this objection is his different view on whether time can begin.

## NOTES

1. Avicenna, *The Physics of the Healing*, tr. Jon McGinnis (Provo: Brigham Young University Press, 2009), 2.13.3, 251. Translation modified.

2. Augustine, *Confessions* (*Conf.*), tr. William Watt (Cambridge MA: Harvard UP, 1992), 11.23.

3. Avicenna, *Physics of the Healing*, 2.11.3, 232. I have followed Andreas Lammer in translating *mutaqaddim* and *muta'aḫḫir* as "prior" and "posterior" rather than as "earlier" and "latter" as Jon McGinnis does in order to highlight that these are not temporal terms.

4. Avicenna, *Physics of the Healing*, 2.11.3, 232. As we shall see, Avicenna like Aristotle refers to time as a number (ἀριθμός / *'adad*) and as a measure or magnitude (μέτρον / *miqdār*). Avicenna, like many late ancient commentators, used the two terms interchangeably. However, some contemporary scholars have argued that Aristotle did not and so his ultimately defining time as the number of motion is of philosophical significance. See: Julia Annas, "Aristotle, Number, and Time," *Philosophical Quarterly* 25 (1975), 97–113; Richard Sorabji, *Time, Creation, and the Continuum* (Chicago, University of Chicago Press, 1983), 84–89; Ursula Coope, *Time for Aristotle* (New York: Oxford University Press, 2005), chs. 5–6; and Tony Roark, *Aristotle on Time: A Study of the Physics* (Cambridge: Cambridge University Press, 2011), ch. 6.

5. *Conf.* 11.24.

6. For a detailed history of the transmission of the works of Alexander of Aphrodisias into Arabic along with an overview of the scholarship on this transmission, see Andreas Lammer, *The Elements of Avicenna's Physics: Greek Sources and Arabic Innovations* (Berlin and Boston: De Gruyter, 2018), 10–19, 22–25.

7. See Galen's paraphrase of the *Timaeus* in the *Compendium Timaei Platonis alioquorumque dialogorum synopsis quae extant fragmenta*, ed. Paul Kraus and Richard Walzer (London: Warburg Institute, 1951), 7. For a discussion, see Robert W. Sharples's annotated translation of Alexander of Aphrodisias' "On Time," *Phronesis* 27, no. 1 (1982), 58–81, here 72–78, and Peter Adamson, "Galen and al-Rāzī on Time," in *Medieval Arabic Thought: Essays in Honour of Fritz Zimmermann*, ed. Rotraud Hansberger, Muhammad Afifi al-Akiti, and Charles Burnett (London and Turin: Warburg Institute and Nino Aragno Editore, 2012), 1–14, here 7–8.

8. Whether Galen's interpretation of the *Timaeus* is correct is a matter of scholarly debate. For an overview of various contemporary interpretations, see Roark, *Aristotle on Time*, 22–33. For an overview of the *Timaeus*'s three main ancient interpretations, see Sorabji, *Time, Creation, and the Continuum*, 268–276.

9. Alexander *apud* Simplicius, *In Aristotelis Physicorum libros quattuor priores commentaria*, ed. Hermann Diels (Berlin: Verlag Georg Reimer, 1982), 703.

10. I have not found any philosopher prior to Avicenna who used the Time without Time objection against Aristotle's theory of time. Granted, Alexander's *Treatise on Time* (which was extant in Arabic) contains an objection to Aristotle's theory, which partially resembles Avicenna's. In this work, Alexander reports that previous philosophers objected to Aristotle by claiming that "if we were to think of the sphere standing still, its standing still would be in time; and since its standing still would be in time, its movement would be in time" (93.22). This objection, however, differs from the Time without Time objection in that the latter is grounded in the intuition that the motion of other bodies is sufficient to generate time, while the former is grounded in the intuition that time exists independently of motion. Given this difference, Alexander's objection to Aristotle is at best a partial prefiguring of Avicenna's.

11. Arabic philosophers took the identification of time with the number of the motion of the spheres to be part of the canonical Aristotelian definition on the authority of Alexander. See Sharples, "On Time," 61–62.

12. John Callahan, "Basil of Caesarea: A New Source for St. Augustine's Theory of Time," *Harvard Studies in Classical Philology* 63 (1958), 437–454, here 439–444.

13. Mark Del Cogliano, "Basil of Caesarea versus Eunomius of Cyzicus on the Nature of Time: A Patristic Reception of the Critique of Plato," *Vigiliae Christianae* 68, no. 5 (2014), 498–532, here 521–531.

14. Jason Carter, "St. Augustine on Time, Time Numbers, and Enduring Objects," *Vivarium* 49, no. 4 (2011), 301–323, here 314, note 39.

15. I shall not attempt to answer in this article whether Augustine makes time a distention of the soul. For arguments for and against this identification, see Robert Jordan, "Time and Contingency in St. Augustine," *Review of Metaphysics* 8 (1955), 394–417; Roland Teske, SJ, "The World-Soul and Time in St. Augustine," *Augustinian Studies* 14 (1983), 75–92; James Wetzel, "Time After Augustine," *Religious Studies* 31, no. 3 (1995), 341–357; Katherine Rogers, "St. Augustine on Time and Eternity," *American Catholic Philosophical Quarterly* 70, no. 2 (1996), 207–223; and Carter, "St. Augustine on Time."

16. Avicenna, *Physics of the Healing*, 2.11.3, 232. Translation modified. According to McGinnis, Avicenna also identifies time with a moving object's possibility of traversing more or less distance at higher or lower speeds. See McGinnis, *Avicenna* (New York: Oxford University Press, 2010), 198. However, Lammer, *Elements*, 431–438, argues that Avicenna does not identify time with the possibility itself, but with the magnitude in which that possibility obtains.

17. Avicenna, *Physics of the Healing*, 2.11.3, 232. Translation modified. The first known charge of circularity against Aristotle's definition of time was leveled by Galen and reported by Simplicius. See Simplicius, *In Phys.*, 718.13–18. Whether any Arabic philosophers prior to Avicenna also objected to Aristotle in this way is considered in Lammer, *Elements*, 463.

18. Avicenna's account of priority and posteriority in motion resembles Coope's and Roark's modern interpretations of Aristotle's. See Coope, *Time for Aristotle*, 69–75, and Roark, *Aristotle on Time*, chs. 4–5. For a critique of this reading of Aristotle, see John Bowin, "Aristotle on the Order and Direction of Time," *Apeiron* 42, no. 1 (2009), 33–62, here 57. McGinnis and Lammer have both argued that Avicenna shared this understanding, and my understanding of Avicenna's definition of time is very much indebted to their work. See McGinnis, "Review of *Aristotle on Time: A Study of the Physics* by Tony Roark," *Philosophy in Review* 32, no. 6 (2012), 518–520, and Lammer, *Elements*, 2018.

19. Avicenna, *Physics of the Healing*, 2.11.3, 23. Translation modified. Lammer, *Elements*, 471, offers the following alternative translation: "time is through itself (*li-ḏātihī*) a magnitude for that (*li-mā*) which in itself (*fī ḏātihī*) has a priority and posteriority (*taqaddum wa-taʾaḫḫur*) of which the posterior does not exist together with the prior as what may be found in other types of priority and posteriority." Lammer, *Elements*, 465, justifies this alternate translation on the grounds that "if time is the magnitude of motion when differentiated into the prior and posterior and if time is

what essentially possesses the prior and posterior—i.e., if 'prior' and 'posterior' are essentially temporal terms—then the definition is hopelessly circular." However, all that follows from McGinnis's translation is that time is defined in terms of priority and posteriority (which are atemporal terms), *not that* priority and posteriority are defined by time.

20. Avicenna, *Physics of the Healing*, 2.11.3, 23.

21. To my knowledge, this puzzle has not yet been discussed in the secondary literature on Avicenna's theory of time.

22. Avicenna, *Physics of the Healing*, 2.10.4, 221. Translation my own.

23. Avicenna, *Physics of the Healing*, 2.10.4, 221–2. Translation my own.

24. Thus, Avicenna's Too Many Times objection appears to be structurally similar to Teske's objection to the Augustinian identification of time as a distention of the mind. See Teske, "World-Soul and Time," 89: "If one interprets Augustine's definition of time in terms of the distention of individual souls, then it would seem that there could be no common temporal frame of reference within which we can date all real events; rather there would seem to be as many distinct temporal series as there are distinct distended souls."

25. Avicenna, *Physics of the Healing*, 2.13.2, 250. Translation my own.

26. Avicenna, *Physics of the Healing*, 2.13.2, 250–1.

27. For a longer discussion of Avicenna's use of the term *miqdār* as well and that of earlier Arabic philosophers and translators of Aristotle, see Lammer, *Elements*, 443–462.

28. Avicenna, *The Metaphysics of the Healing*, tr. Michael E. Marmura (Provo: Brigham Young University Press, 2005), 3.4.2, 84. Translation modified.

29. Avicenna, *Physics of the Healing*, 2.13.2, 251.

30. Avicenna, *Physics of the Healing*, 2.11.2, 231. Translation modified.

31. Avicenna, *Physics of the Healing*, 2.13.2, 251.

32. Avicenna, *Physics of the Healing*, 2.13.3, 251. Translation my own.

33. Avicenna, *Physics of the Healing*, 2.13.3, 251–52, also replies to the Time without Time objection by arguing that without the circular motion of the outermost sphere, there would not be any other motion. For a discussion of the other solution, see Lammer, *Elements*, 502–4.

34. For an overview of Ancient and Medieval arguments for the world's age drawn from the nature of time, see McGinnis, "Creation and Eternity in Medieval Philosophy," in *A Companion to the Philosophy of Time*, eds. Heather Dyke and Adrian Bardo (Chichester: Wiley-Blackwell, 2013), 73–86. This work covers Augustine's argument in the *Confessions* and several of Avicenna's arguments not discussed in this article.

35. *Conf.* 11.13.

36. *Conf.* 11.13.

37. For a fuller explication, see Simo Knuuttila, "Time and Creation in Augustine," in *The Cambridge Companion to Augustine*, eds. Eleonore Stump and Norman Kretzmann (Cambridge: Cambridge University Press, 2001), 103–15.

38. For a discussion of why time cannot end, as well as a thorough discussion of Avicenna's theory of the instant, see McGinnis, "Ibn Sīnā on the Now," *American Catholic Philosophical Quarterly* 73, no. 1 (1999), 73–106.

39. Avicenna, *Physics of the Healing*, 2.12.1, 237–38. Translation my own.

40. This argument seems to be an elaboration of a brief remark in Aristotle's *Metaphysics*, tr. William David Ross, in *Aristotle: The Complete Works of Aristotle*, ed. Jonathan Barnes, Vol. 2. (Princeton: Princeton University Press, 1995), 12.6, 1071b8: "it is impossible that movement should either have come into being or cease to be (for it must always have existed), or that time should. For there could not be a before and an after if time did not exist."

41. Avicenna, *Physics of the Healing*, 2.11.5, 234. Translation modified.

42. My understanding of this facet of Avicenna's theory of time is indebted to Lammer, *Elements*, 473–484.

43. Avicenna, *Physics of the Healing*, 2.11.5, 235. Translation modified. McGinnis and Lammer disagree about the role this passage plays in Avicenna's exposition of his theory of time. McGinnis, "Time and Time Again: A Study of Aristotle and Ibn Sīnā's Temporal Theories," PhD dissertation (Philadelphia: University of Pennsylvania, 1999), 236–238, regards this passage as "a response to a potential objection . . . that existence and nonexistence are sufficient conditions to explain priority and posteriority," while Lammer, *Elements*, 485–491, argues that it aims to establish the existence of time, something McGinnis argues Avicenna accomplished much earlier in *Physics of the Healing* 2.11. For Lammer's objection to McGinnis's view, see Lammer, *Elements*, 431–438.

*Chapter 11*

# The Timing of Creation
## *Aquinas's Reception of Augustine*
Daniel W. Houck

In recent years, there has been a growing interest in the reception of Augustine's thought, including, in particular, that of Thomas Aquinas.[1] Though there have been scattered studies and popular articles on aspects of Thomas's reception of Augustine's account of creation—including, notably, a published dissertation on the concept of "seminal reasons" (*rationes seminales*) in Augustine's thought that features a detailed comparison of Thomas and the Bishop of Hippo, and a brief article by the Dominican theologian John Baptist Ku comparing Thomas's account of Genesis 1 with Augustine's—further work is needed.[2] It is needed not only for historical purposes but also for constructive ones. There has been a great deal of debate over whether Augustine's account of creation is congenial to synthesis with an evolutionary perspective.[3] If it is, and Thomas is open to Augustine's perspective, then the principles of two of the most significant theologians in the premodern era would be open to the modern theory of evolution. This is not generally acknowledged in the field of systematic theology, let alone in the broader, popular understanding of the history of theology and science.

The question of "the timing of creation" is not a single question but encompasses many sub-questions, such as the age of the universe, the nature of the days in Genesis (are they twenty-four hour days, or symbolic of larger periods of time, or something else entirely?), the relation between the creation of "the heavens and the earth" in Gen. 1:1 and the formlessness in Gen. 1:2, and the timing of the creation of the rest of the creatures mentioned in the opening chapter of Genesis. This chapter aims to focus on the specific question of how Thomas, in his later writings (in particular, the *De potentia* and *Summa theologiae*), engaged Augustine's account of the timing of the creation of species and what we might call "cosmic development," with an eye toward Thomas's reception of—what he took to be the closely related issue of—Augustine's hermeneutical principles pertaining to "theology and science." As the focus of this chapter is reception history, it brackets the question of the veracity of Thomas's treatment of Augustine. It is "Thomas's Augustine" with which we will primarily be concerned.

## THE HERMENEUTICS OF THE TIMING OF CREATION IN THE *DE POTENTIA*

Thomas discusses Augustine's account of the timing of creation in the fourth question of his treatise *De potentia*, written circa 1265–1266, in Rome, around the time of the *Prima Pars*, but possibly slightly earlier.[4] The most important part of the treatise for present purposes is the first article of the fourth question, which asks whether the creation of formless matter preceded, in duration, the creation of things. The article begins with twenty-three objections arguing that "formless matter precedes informed things not in duration but only in nature" and eight objections arguing to the contrary. What exactly does this question mean? It seems to be formulated from the perspective of one who holds that "prime matter" could exist without form, before being formed into this or that particular thing (e.g., a dog or a house). Thomas, however, clarifies his own view in the body of the article. It is absurd to hold that matter could ever be *completely* formless; matter, in order actually to exist, must have some form. The real question, then, is not whether prime matter can exist without form, but rather whether the specific forms of things that were created *in potentia* and thus in a *relatively* "formless" state could preexist receiving their proper forms, or all things instead received their forms right away, and the relative lack of form is simply an absence of beauty (*naturae complementum et decorem*). Thomas identifies the former as Augustine's view, the latter as Basil the Great's (i.e., Basil of Caesarea's). His response comes in two parts. The first is a formal discussion of some key hermeneutical principles; the second addresses the material question at hand.

Thomas begins by discussing and developing two hermeneutical principles from Augustine's *Confessions*.[5] Thomas frames the distinction between these principles as follows. The first principle relates to the truth of the matter (*rerum veritate*); the second relates to the sense of the text (*sensu litterae*). Each principle involves avoiding two errors. Regarding the truth of the matter itself, the first error to avoid is saying what is false, especially if it contradicts the faith. Second, one should not assert one's theological opinion as though it were an article of faith.[6] "As Augustine says (*Conf.* 10)," according to Thomas, "when a man thinks his false opinions to be the teaching of godliness, and dares obstinately to dogmatise about matters of which he is ignorant, he becomes a stumbling block to others."[7] This occurs because the faith looks ridiculous to those who know the truth: "The reason why he says that such an one is a stumbling block is because the faith is made ridiculous to the unbeliever when a simple-minded believer asserts as an article of faith that which is demonstrably false, as again Augustine says in his commentary (*Gen. ad lit.* 1)."[8]

Regarding the sense of the text, the first error is to offer an interpretation of Scripture that is clearly false. Scripture is from the Holy Spirit, and cannot teach falsehood; therefore, any interpretation that is clearly false cannot be a genuine interpretation of Scripture.[9] The second error is to force an interpretation of the text that excludes other interpretations that are actually or *possibly* true, *salva circumstantia litterae*.[10] This phrase seems to mean, roughly, the way the words run.[11] For example (mine, not Thomas's), if the text says the earth was "formless and void," and one confusedly thought the text said "full of form," one's interpretation would be baseless, as the "letter" would not be saved but rather lost. But Thomas clearly is *not* suggesting that the multiplicity of legitimate interpretations need to be grounded in the intent of the human author. He argues:

> It is part of the dignity of Holy Writ that under the one literal sense many others are contained. It is thus that the sacred text not only adapts itself to man's various intelligence, so that each one marvels to find his thoughts expressed in the words of Holy Writ (*hoc enim ad dignitatem divinae Scripturae pertinet, ut sub una littera multos sensus contineat, ut sic et diversis intellectibus hominum conveniat, ut unusquisque miretur se in divina Scriptura posse invenire veritatem quam mente conceperit*); but also is all the more easily defended against unbelievers in that when one finds his own interpretation of Scripture to be false he can fall back upon some other. Hence it is not inconceivable that Moses and the other authors of the Holy Books were given to know the various truths that men would discover in the text, and that they expressed them under one literary style, so that each truth is the sense intended by the author. *And then even if commentators adapt certain truths to the sacred text that were not understood by the author*, without doubt the Holy Spirit understood them, since he is the principal author of Holy Scripture. Consequently every truth that can be adapted to the sacred text without prejudice to the literal sense, is the sense of Holy Scripture.[12]

Several things are noteworthy here. First, as is well known, Thomas holds that there are a multiplicity of senses contained under the literal. Second, the text adapts itself to different levels of knowledge, so that we "marvel to find our thoughts expressed in Scripture," as the translation of the Dominican Fathers puts it. What is Thomas suggesting here? Is the idea that one has a given thought, and then marvels that that same thought can be found in the biblical text? If so, does Thomas's idea here imply that different cultures—with different approaches to and views of the natural sciences, for example—can impose their knowledge onto the biblical text and "marvel" to find their own ideas expressed in it? This seems unlikely, as a consideration of the parenthetical Latin should indicate. Thomas says that readers marvel that they find the truth that their minds conceive (*veritatem quam mente conceperit*); the implication seems to be that readers can discover different truths in Scripture, not that they can or should read Scripture to discover what they already knew. In any case, Thomas is open to the possibility that Moses *knew* that different people, at different times and places, would find different truths in the text, as well as the possibility that Moses had no idea what these various truths were, and only the Spirit guards the text. What did Thomas mean by interpretations that are possibly true? This seems to be an exhortation to "epistemic humility." At times, multiple, incompatible interpretations of a text will arise that are consistent with the way the words run, but one won't *know* which one is right. Only the interpretations that are true can be part of the literal sense, however.

Thomas then turns to the material question. He argues that both the Basilian and Augustinian interpretations are compatible with the way the words of Genesis run, and neither is incompatible with the truth of faith (*quorum nullus fidei veritati repugnat*).[13] Before turning to Augustine's account, Thomas first sums up the absurd stance of those who tried to argue that Genesis was referring to matter without any form whatsoever. This, he argues, is impossible, due to the fact that truly formless matter

> cannot exist in nature unless it receive formation from some form: since whatever exists in nature exists actually, and actual existence comes to a thing from its form which is its act, so that nature does not contain a thing without a form. Moreover, since nothing can be included in a genus that is not contained specifically in some division of the genus, matter cannot be a being unless it be determined to some specific mode of being, and this cannot be without a form. Consequently if formless matter be understood in this sense it could not possibly precede its formation in point of duration, but only by priority of nature, inasmuch as that from which something is made naturally precedes that which is made from it.[14]

If matter exists, it exists actually; and actual existence only comes to something from its form in act. Strictly speaking, then, formless matter in that sense couldn't precede its formation in duration, but only in priority of nature. There is, according to this priority of nature, an "idea" of prime matter, which is presupposed in every actually existing material thing, insofar as no material object could exist without matter. Thomas identifies this with Augustine's view.

By contrast, another perspective argues that the formless state of matter merely refers to the absence of "natural finish and comeliness." According to Thomas,

> This would seem in keeping with the wise ordering of its Maker who in producing things out of nothing did not at once bring them from nothingness to the ultimate perfection of their nature, but at first gave them a kind of imperfect being, and afterwards perfected them: thus showing not only that they received their being from God so as to refute those who assert that matter is uncreated; but also that they derive their perfection from him, so as to refute those who ascribe the formation of this lower world to other causes. Such was the view of Basil the Great, Gregory and others who followed them. *Since, however, neither opinion is in conflict with revealed truth, and since both are compatible with the context, while admitting that either may be held, we must now deal with the arguments advanced on both sides.*[15]

By Thomas's lights, Augustine's hermeneutical principles imply that Augustine's own *material* conclusions on the interpretation of Genesis's claim that the earth was formless and void should be held loosely. Nothing essential to the faith is at stake here, because in either case God created the world *ex nihilo*.

We can sum up Thomas's arguments from *De potentia*, q. 4, a. 1, as follows. The Fathers held conflicting views of the meaning of Genesis 1:2. Some, including Augustine, held that "formlessness" implied that there were seminal reasons implanted in the first creatures, by virtue of which they grew into their mature state over time. Others, including Basil of Caesarea, held that creatures were created in their "perfect" or completed state, and merely decorated later. But neither interpretation contradicts Scripture, and neither is absurd. Augustine's material conclusion regarding the timing of creation has been relativized by Thomas, by appealing to Augustine's own formal hermeneutical principles. Yet for Thomas, the material view of Augustine has in no way been ruled out as impossible or even problematic from a biblical perspective.

## THE TIMING OF CREATION IN THE *SUMMA THEOLOGIAE*

The discussion of creation in the *Summa theologiae* is more complex than that found in *De potentia*. It is therefore worth setting the former in context briefly before proceeding. After his treatise on God (qq. 2–43), Thomas devotes the rest of the *Pars prima* to a discussion of the procession of creatures from God (qq. 44–119). This includes a discussion of the production of creatures (i.e., the concept of creation itself) in qq. 44–46, the "distinction" of creatures (i.e., different discussions of different types of creatures, beginning with spiritual creatures, angels, then moving to corporeal creatures such as the nonhuman animals, and then finally the creature who is both spiritual and corporeal, the human being) in qq. 47–102, and finally the government of creatures in qq. 103–119. Here I move through some salient points of Thomas's discussion of the creation of the corporeal creature (*creatura corporali*), qq. 65–74, keeping an eye on his use of Augustine.

We can begin with Question 66, which starts with the problem of whether the formlessness of matter preceded, in time, its formation. (The same question is asked in Thomas's disputed question in *De potentia*.) The first objection in Article 1 cites Augustine to the effect that it did.[16] The Augustinian position argues that Gen. 1:2 (wherein the earth was formless and empty) should be understood in terms of "the formlessness of matter, as Augustine says (*Confess.* 12.12)."[17] In the *corpus*, Thomas responds to this objection by arguing that Augustine only holds that the formlessness of matter precedes its form in nature, not in duration: "Augustine, for instance (*Gen. ad lit.* 1.15), believes that the formlessness of matter was not prior in time to its formation, but only in origin or the order of nature."[18] This is in substance the same argument Thomas gave in *De potentia*.

Another important text on the timing of creation is Article 4 of Question 67, in which Thomas asks whether the production of light is fittingly assigned to the first day. He notes a disagreement between Augustine—who takes the creation of light to refer to angels—and Basil, who holds that angels are passed over, because Genesis focuses on the creation of material things. Thomas notes that there are two reasons why we should think that light was created on the first day, the second of which is salient for present purposes. "Light is a common quality," writes Thomas, "For light is common to terrestrial and celestial bodies. But as in knowledge we proceed from general principles, so do we in work of every kind."[19] Because light is more general, and it's fitting to move from the general to the particular, it makes sense to start with light and only later produce various terrestrial and celestial bodies. In the course of making his argument, Thomas notes that it's fitting for individual organisms to develop through transformation. Likewise, it's fitting for the cosmos itself to begin with light and develop from there. "For the living thing is generated before the animal, and the animal before the man, as is shown in *De Gener. Anim.* 2.3," continues Thomas, "It was fitting, then, as an evidence of the Divine wisdom, that among the works of distinction the production of light should take first place, since light is a form of the primary body, and because it is a more common quality."[20] It is noteworthy that Thomas holds that "cosmic development"—development from the more general to the more particular—is a fitting means for God to use in creation. He does not get this idea from Augustine though, at least not explicitly. It seems to come from the Aristotelian tradition, since the quotation regarding the analogous case of the development of individual organisms is from Aristotle's *On the Generation of Animals*. Thomas, then, explicitly holds that there is a meaningful analogy between the development of individual organisms and cosmic development; if the former is fitting, so is the latter. Could this analogy be developed further in an evolutionary context? That is, if Thomas thought that the movement from the creation of light to the creation of more specific bodies could be meaningfully compared to the movement an individual organism undergoes in its various stages of life, why shouldn't the same comparison be drawn between an individual organism and various stages of evolutionary development?

Also of note in this question is that Thomas quotes Augustine's principle that we should not look for miracles in creation: "As to this, however, Augustine remarks (*Gen. ad lit.* i) that in the first founding of the order of nature we must not look for miracles, but for what is in accordance with nature."[21] This Augustinian principle endorsed by Thomas, in conjunction with the aforementioned hermeneutical principles from *De potentia*, would seem to have implications for how contemporary theologians should handle evolutionary theory, especially the question of the evolution of humanity (which is thought, by many, to create far more theological difficulties than the hypothesis of the evolution of nonhuman animals or vegetative life). It is often argued, for example, that Christian theology can accept evolution of nonhuman animals without any major difficulties, but that we must posit an exception in the case of the creation of human beings. Perhaps, for instance, God supernaturally created human beings who then interbred with nonhuman animals, that is, biologically human beings who lacked the rational soul.[22] If it is true, however, that the sciences indicate—*sans* the hypothesis of a miracle or at least a supernatural intervention—that humans have evolved, wouldn't denying their evolution require positing a miracle in the "founding of nature" *pace* the hermeneutical principle of Augustine here endorsed by Thomas?

Another important issue is addressed in Question 69, which discusses the third day of creation, the gathering of the waters and the production of plants. Thomas notes that Augustine consistently maintained the simultaneity of creation.[23] Other writers, however, argue that there is a difference in the timing of the gathering of the waters and the production of plants, and so on, but not in such a way as to imply that completely formless matter ever existed. Thomas leaves the different opinions juxtaposed, not appearing to prefer one side or the other. Article 2 addresses the production of plants, and Thomas's engagement with Augustine here is worth quoting at length:

But concerning the production of plants, Augustine's opinion differs from that of others. For other commentators, in accordance with the surface meaning of the text, consider that the plants were produced in act in their various species on this third day; whereas Augustine (*Gen. ad lit.* 5.5; 5.3) says that the earth is said to have then produced plants and trees in their causes, that is, it received then the power to produce them. He supports this view by the authority of Scripture, for it is said (Genesis 2:4–5): "These are the generations of the heaven and the earth, when they were created, in the day that . . . God made the heaven and the earth, and every plant of the field before it sprung up in the earth, and every herb of the ground before it grew." Therefore, the production of plants in their causes, within the earth, took place before they sprang up from the earth's surface. And this is confirmed by reason, as follows. In these first days God created all things in their origin or causes, and from this work He subsequently rested. Yet afterwards, by governing His creatures, in the work of propagation, "He worketh until now." Now the production of plants from out the earth is a work of propagation, and therefore they were not produced in act on the third day, but in their causes only. However, in accordance with other writers, it may be said that the first constitution of species belongs to the work of the six days, but the reproduction among them of like from like, to the government of the universe. And Scripture indicates this in the words, "before it sprung up in the earth," and "before it grew," that is, before like was produced from like; just as now happens in the natural course by the production of seed. Wherefore Scripture says pointedly (Genesis 1:11): "Let the earth bring forth the green herb, and such as may seed," as indicating the production of perfection of perfect species, from which the seed of others should arise. Nor does the question where the seminal power may reside, whether in root, stem, or fruit, affect the argument."[24]

While some writers think that various species of plants were separately created on the third day, Augustine argues that they were merely created in their causes, that is, with the power to develop into their proper species. Thomas does grant that the "surface meaning" (*superficies litterae*) of the text goes against Augustine, but it would be wrong, I think, to read too much into this, as though Thomas thought Augustine's view contradicts Scripture. For Augustine, too, is able to "confirm" his view with Scripture (*confirmat auctoritate Scripturae*), as well as reason (*confirmat autem hoc etiam ratione*). Thomas again contextualizes Augustine, admitting the legitimacy and possibility of his views, without however arguing they are the only option.

Interestingly, though not citing Augustine, Thomas appears to draw on the Bishop of Hippo's openness to development by admitting that new species could be formed, in principle, *after* the six days of creation:

Species, also, that are new, if any such appear, existed beforehand in various active powers; so that animals, and perhaps even new species of animals, are produced by putrefaction by the power which the stars and elements received at the beginning. Again, animals of new kinds arise occasionally from the connection of individuals belonging to different species, as the mule is the offspring of an ass and a mare; but even these existed previously in their causes, in the works of the six days.[25]

New species that are formed after the six days nevertheless existed causally during the six days (*praecesserunt causaliter in operibus sex dierum*). God is said to "rest" after the initial six days because everything had been made in its causes.[26] If Thomas held that this was not a major problem theologically, if it occurred by "putrefaction" or crossbreeding, what would have stopped him from holding that it occurred through evolution?

## CONCLUSION

This preliminary inquiry into Thomas's reception of Augustine's account of the timing of creation has revealed several things. Thomas appears to have adopted, without reservation, several salient hermeneutical principles of Augustine. First, one should not expose the faith to ridicule by offering interpretations of Scripture that contradict what is "known" to be true by even those outside the faith. Second, since Scripture has a divine author, it is open to a multiplicity of true meanings. Third, one should not have recourse to miraculous works of God when endeavoring to explain creation; one should instead seek to understand the work of God through nature. Materially, Thomas was open to Augustine's view of simultaneous creation and argued—though without directly citing Augustine—that new species could continue to be formed after the six days of creation had been completed, as long as the power of the causes of these species has been created initially. (He was also, to be sure, open to the more "literal" view of Basil of Caesarea.) We also saw Thomas draw on Aristotle to compare "cosmic development" (the fittingness of light being created before other earthly or heavenly bodies) to the development of an individual organism.

Future research could proceed along a number of different lines. Historically, one could ask whether Thomas has accurately represented Augustine's thought, hermeneutically or with respect to his view of the Bishop of Hippo's exegetical conclusions. If Thomas's views are accurate as far as they go, might there be development in Augustine's thought on these issues that Thomas doesn't sufficiently acknowledge? Moreover, what would a study of Thomas's early engagement with Augustine in his *Sentences* commentary and elsewhere add to the discussion here, focused as it was on Thomas's mature works? Constructively, one could draw on Thomas's Augustinian hermeneutics to address a number of different issues, including, I've suggested, the evolution of the human being. This controversial question, however, would also require engaging Augustine's and Thomas's accounts of the rational soul, church tradition, and ecclesial authority, in addition to their biblical hermeneutics.

## NOTES

1. See, for example, *Aquinas the Augustinian*, ed. Michael Dauphinais, Barry David, and Matthew Levering (Washington, DC: CUA Press, 2007). This learned volume engages topics such as the image of God, original sin, and the Trinity. There is no contribution, however, focused on the doctrine of creation.

2. Michael J. McKeough, *The Meaning of the Rationes Seminales in St. Augustine* (Washington, DC: Catholic University of America Doctoral Dissertation, 1926); John Baptist Ku, "Interpreting Genesis 1 with St. Thomas Aquinas," http://www.thomistic evolution.org/disputed-questions/interpreting-genesis-1-with-st-thomas-aquinas/#rf7-207. For a discussion of Thomas's and Augustine's doctrines of creation in relation to their doctrines of God, see Janet Soskice, "Aquinas and Augustine on Creation and God as 'Eternal Being,'" *New Blackfriars* 95, no. 1056 (2014): 190–207.

3. For an early argument to the effect that Augustine's account of creation is congenial to evolution, see J. A. Zahm, *Evolution and Dogma* (Chicago: McBride, 1896). For a discussion of Zahm's life, thought, and career in its historical context, see John P. Slattery, *Faith and Science at Notre Dame: John Zahm, Evolution, and the Catholic Church* (Notre Dame: University of Notre Dame Press, 2019). For a discussion of Roman Catholic engagement with Darwin in the final quarter of the nineteenth century that contains detailed discussion of appeals to authorities—including Augustine and Thomas in particular—see *Negotiating Darwin: The Vatican Confronts Evolution, 1877–1902*, ed. Mariano Artigas, Rafael A. Martinez, and Thomas F. Glick (Baltimore: The Johns Hopkins University Press, 2006). For a recent, wide-ranging engagement with both the reception history and contemporary prospects of retrieval of Augustine's thought, see *Augustine and Science*, edited by John Doody, Adam Goldstein, and Kim Paffenroth (Lanham, MD: Rowman & Littlefield, 2012).

4. "Chronological List of Aquinas's Writings," in *The Oxford Handbook of Aquinas*, ed. Brian Davies and Eleonore Stump (Oxford: Oxford University Press, 2012): https://www.oxfordhandbooks.com/view/10.1093/oxfordhb/9780195326093.001.0001/oxfordhb-9780195326093-miscMatter-46.

5. Thomas Aquinas, *Summa theologiae* [*STh*], trans. Fathers of the English Dominican Province (London: Burns, Oates, and Washbourne, 1920) I, q. 68, a. 1, where Thomas cites the hermeneutical principles discussed in this paragraph in the context of arguing that theologians should be open to different interpretations of the meaning of the making of the firmament on the second day of creation. Translations

of the *Summa theologiae* in this chapter have been supplemented with the Latin from https://www.corpusthomisticum.org/iopera.html.

6. Thomas Aquinas, *De potentia*, trans. Fathers of the English Dominican Province (London: Burns, Oates, and Washbourne, 1932–34) q. IV, a. 1. Translations of the *De potentia* in this chapter have been supplemented with the Latin from https://www.corpusthomisticum.org/iopera.html.

7. *De potentia*, q. IV, a. 1.

8. *De potentia*, q. IV, a. 1. Note that Augustine and Thomas are only speaking of *demonstrably false* views. Whether or to what extent this principle could be applied in the context of modern sciences, relying on (for example) inferences to the best explanation as opposed to "demonstrations" in the classical sense, is, as far as I am concerned, an open question. Prima facie, though, it seems to me that a strong case could be made that Augustine's principles should be extended beyond strict demonstrations. The reason *why* Augustine urges caution is precisely the risk of ridicule that Christians expose the faith to when they pontificate on matters they know little to nothing of; and of course, this risk is acute in a modern context, in which scientific "knowledge" is not held to be restricted to disciplines in which strict demonstrations are possible, such as mathematics.

9. *De potentia*, q. IV, a. 1.

10. *De potentia*, q. IV, a. 1.

11. Gregory W. Lee, *Today When You Hear His Voice: Scripture, the Covenants, and the People of God* (Grand Rapids, MI: Eerdmans, 2016): "So far as I can discern, the phrase originated with Bruce Marshall as a loose translation of Thomas's reference in *De potentia* to the *litterae circumstantia*, a genitive Latin construction which does not, in and of itself, provide a particularly high degree of specificity on the proper controls for interpretation." Lee cites Bruce D. Marshall, "Absorbing the World: Christianity and the Universe of Truths," in *Theology and Dialogue: Essays in Conversation with George Lindbeck* (Notre Dame, IN: University of Notre Dame Press, 1990), 101, n. 38.

12. *De potentia*, q. IV, a. 1, emphasis mine.

13. *De potentia*, q. IV, a. 1.

14. *De potentia*, q. IV, a. 1.

15. *De potentia*, q. IV, a. 1, emphasis mine.

16. *STh* I, q. 66, a. 1, ob. 1: *Dicitur enim Gen. 1, terra erat inanis et vacua, sive invisibilis et incomposita, secundum aliam litteram; per quod designatur informitas materiae, ut Augustinus dicit.* An editorial note from the Fathers of the English Dominican Province notes that the reference is *Confessions* 12.12.

17. *STh* I, q. 66, a. 1, ob. 1.

18. *STh* I, q. 66, a. 1, *corpus*.

19. *STh* I, q. 67, a. 4.

20. *STh* I, q. 67, a. 4.

21. *STh* I, q. 67, a. 4, ad 2.

22. Kenneth W. Kemp, "Science, Theology, and Monogenesis," *American Catholic Philosophical Quarterly* 85 (2011): 217–36.

23. *STh* I, q. 69, a. 1, *corpus*: "It is necessary to reply differently to this question according to the different interpretations given by Augustine and other holy writers.

In all these works, according to Augustine (*Gen. ad lit.* 1.15; 4.22, 4.34; *De Gen. Contr. Manich.* 1.5.7), there is no order of duration, but only of origin and nature. He says that the formless spiritual and formless corporeal natures were created first of all, and that the latter are at first indicated by the words 'earth' and 'water.' Not that this formlessness preceded formation, in time, but only in origin; nor yet that one formation preceded another in duration, but merely in the order of nature." See also *STh* I, q. 69, a. 1: "Therefore the words, 'Let the waters be gathered together, and the dry land appear,' mean that corporeal matter was impressed with the substantial form of water, so as to have such movement, and with the substantial form of earth, so as to have such an appearance."

24. *STh* I, q. 69, a. 2.
25. *STh* I, q. 73, a. 1, ad 3.
26. *STh* I, q. 73, a. 2:

"First, because He ceased from creating new creatures on that day, for, as said above (Article 1, Reply to Objection 3), He made nothing afterwards that had not existed previously, in some degree, in the first works; secondly, because He Himself had no need of the things that He had made, but was happy in the fruition of Himself. Hence, when all things were made He is not said to have rested 'in' His works, as though needing them for His own happiness, but to have rested 'from' them, as in fact resting in Himself, as He suffices for Himself and fulfils His own desire. And even though from all eternity He rested in Himself, yet the rest in Himself, which He took after He had finished His works, is that rest which belongs to the seventh day. And this, says Augustine, is the meaning of God's resting from His works on that day (*Gen. ad lit.* 4)."

*Chapter 12*

# Augustine's Dilemma

## *Divine Eternity and the Reality of Temporal Passage*

Brendan Case

"No one," exclaimed Bonaventure of Bagnoregio, "described the nature of time and matter better than Augustine, when he inquired and disputed in his book of *Confessions*."[1] He would have heartily agreed with Brian Leftow's assessment, that "Augustine's thinking [about eternity] was the core that determined the broad outlines of all that later medieval philosophical theology made of the concept of God."[2] In this area of his thought, as in so many others, Augustine's heirs were offered an embarrassment of riches. Indeed, I will argue that there are at least two distinct theories of time in Augustine: the first, which was worked out on the ground of creaturely finitude, is "tensed," taking time's passage through a real present as metaphysically basic. (In the wake of McTaggart's seminal essay, "The Unreality of Time," we have learned to call this an "A-theory," or "presentism.") A second theory of time, by contrast, is implied in Augustine's account of divine eternity and is "tenseless" (a "B-theory," or "eternalism"), taking all times' exposure to God's gaze as implying their equal reality.[3] Augustine bequeaths these two theories to his heirs, and later scholastic reflection on time is in large part a struggle, first to articulate and then to resolve the dilemma they impose.[4] In what follows, I briefly expound each of these aspects of Augustine's thought, and then consider two attempts to unify them: first John Duns Scotus's and Francisco Suarez's bid to develop an interpretation of divine eternity as consistent with an A-theory of time, and then John Wyclif's suggestion that the perspective of divine eternity entails that all times are a-temporally perduring.

## AUGUSTINE'S DILEMMA: TEMPORAL PASSAGE AND THE ETERNITY OF DIVINE KNOWLEDGE

Augustine illustrates the difficulties in joining eternity's stillness to time's flight in his most detailed treatment of time, in *Confessions* 11.[5] His discussion there is bracketed by meditations on divine eternity and opens by defining the latter by contrast with the former: the most basic fact about time is its passage, Augustine insists. Its every moment is momentary: "No times are co-eternal with you, because you remain forever; but should these continue, they would not be times."[6] And times are fleeting, for Augustine, because they are the motions of bodies, which are themselves in constant change.[7] Temporal passage means that neither the past, because it has passed away, nor the future, because it is yet to be, exist at present, which seems to be all there is.[8]

What is this present? Any moment you might point to as "now" (this year, this day, this hour, this minute) can be subdivided into further moments, and exactly to that extent, "it is divided into the past and future; but the present has no space."[9] And yet, we all know what we mean when we say that a day is longer than an hour, or that a meeting was shorter than usual. But if no time exists except the infinitesimal present, where is the space, which time occupies, that it might be long or short? As David van Dusen puts it, "Augustine's time-question in *Confessions* XI.14–29 can be stated in a way that is acute, but not complex: How is it that temporal presence is dimensive (*spatium temporis*) when present-time has no space (*punctum temporis*)?"[10] Augustine's solution, in short, is to suggest that space might be found for time within the soul, which makes the present to be present through perception, the past through memory, and the future through anticipation.[11] The set of bodily motions which constituted yesterday's meeting coexist only in the space opened up by the soul's "distention (*distentio*),"[12] as it embraces and unifies them in memory, having measured their passage in itself.[13]

Given a commitment to time's passage through the specious present, where else might have Augustine located temporal extension besides the anticipating and remembering intellect?[14] In the order of temporal passage, past and future are equally nonexistent, while in the order of divine eternity, both are equally present. Only the finite soul is, as Pegueroles puts it, "a mean between the flowing instant of the body and the full instant of the infinite Spirit."[15] Since no two moments coexist, the unity-in-distinction of the parts in a temporal series can be present only to the measuring soul, which intends them as such. This says nothing at all, however, about the ideality of "times" with respect to their causes, which are for Augustine entirely independent of my consciousness or yours, but only about the ideality of "time" as a measure of "times."[16]

As we noted earlier, however, Augustine's treatment of time in *Confessions* 11 is bracketed by discussions of divine eternity. "For what was spoken [by

God in the act of creation] was not finished, and another spoken until all were spoken," Augustine insists, "but all things at once and forever. For otherwise have we time and change, and not a true eternity, nor a true immortality."[17] Time, as we have seen earlier, is the measure of creaturely change, and so, as time's opposite, eternity is changelessness,[18] and so in some sense identical with God,[19] in comparison with whom time's changes are mere wisps and ghosts.[20]

Relating these two discourses is not at all straightforward, for, as van Dusen rightly observes, "Augustine writes under a speculative canopy of eternity, but *without recourse to eternity* . . . . Within the space that his time-investigation occupies, Augustine not only proceeds 'in time'—as he himself confesses (XI.25.32)—but also, *methodologically*, 'from below.'"[21] Augustine's presentist account of time's passage is worked out by way of contrast with divine eternity, but not in terms of any specifiable relation to it. And it is precisely here that the difficulties arise, for he acknowledges that creation as it is known and willed by God is in some sense a world without time:

> But far be it that you, creator of the universe, creator of souls and bodies—far be it that you should know all things as future and past. Far, far more wonderfully, and far more secretly do you know them . . . . As, then, you in the beginning knew heaven and the earth without any change of your knowledge, so in the beginning you made heaven and earth without any distention of your action (*sine distentione actionis tuae*).[22]

He makes a similar point in his slightly earlier work, *On 83 Different Questions*: "Every past thing no longer is, and every future thing is not yet. But with God, nothing is absent, and so neither past nor future, but everything is present with God."[23] What God knows, he must know in his divine eternity. But if God knows everything that is, then everything must in some sense be folded within that eternal present of his eternity. (Aristotle famously seized one horn of the dilemma, by denying that God's knowledge is directed beyond himself at all—the future and past can simply not exist in a strong sense, for God is the self-enclosed "thinking thinking of thinking," and stands to the world only as its indifferent final cause.[24])

Augustine attempts to avoid the contradiction between these two perspectives by specifying the objects of God's eternal knowledge as the "divine ideas." So, he suggests that "everything, which begins to be and ceases to be, then begins to be and then ceases to be, when it is known to have had to begin or to cease in the eternal concept (*aeterna ratione*), where nothing either begins or ceases."[25] He says more about these "eternal concepts" in *On 83 Different Questions*: "For there are principal ideas, certain forms or concepts which are stable and immutable, which are not the things formed, and so are eternal and ... are contained in the divine understanding. And although they neither arise nor perish, nonetheless everything which can arise or perish is said to be formed in accord with them."[26] God directly knows the divine ideas, whose "moving image" (so to speak) the created order is.

But appealing to the divine ideas would only help in this case if Augustine were willing to limit divine knowledge to the ideas themselves—but he clearly is not so willing. Even if the ideas are that through which God knows creatures,[27] Augustine often refers to creatures as the objects of God's knowledge, and can even insist, in a more theoretical mode, that the ultimate objects of divine knowledge are in fact the creatures themselves, and not merely their archetypes. For instance, in a discussion of divine "foreknowledge" in his *Questions to Simplicianus* (written the year before *Confessions*, in 396 CE), Augustine insists, "For if the knowledge of God has the very things themselves (*res ipsas habet*), they are not future but present to him," since otherwise "he knows them twice, in one way according to the foreknowledge of future things, but in another according to present knowledge."[28] (Augustine takes for granted that God knows things in themselves; the question is whether he has an additional, "prior" knowledge of them—this would presumably be knowledge of the divine ideas alone.) And in that case, "something would temporally modify the knowledge of God, which is most absurd and false .... So, it is best if we do not speak of God's foreknowledge, but only of his knowledge."[29] Here, God's eternal perspective takes in, not only his ideas, but "the things themselves," and so presses Augustine toward a version of eternalism.

## AQUINAS: SHARPENING THE HORNS OF AUGUSTINE'S DILEMMA

Augustine's dilemma reappears in many of his heirs. Thomas Aquinas, for instance, seems to have been torn between an intuitive presentism about temporal passage, and an eternalist conception of time, viewed from the perspective of divine eternity. On the one hand, he takes over Boethius's definition of eternity as time's opposite,[30] the former consisting not only in the succession of before and after (as opposed to eternity's "all-at-once" (*simul*) character), but also in "the 'now' of time, which is imperfect" (as opposed to eternity's "perfect possession").[31] "The flux of the very 'now,'" Aquinas writes, "insofar as it alternates in aspect, is time:" time's deficiency in comparison with eternity isn't merely that it is composite, but also that it exists only one slice (defined by the extensionless "now") at a time. There is always a fact of the matter about which time is (approximately) "now," which is why, as Aquinas notes in his commentary on Aristotle's *Physics*, "we do not say that the

Trojan war happened 'now,' because, although time is continuous, it is not near to the present now."[32]

Nonetheless, Aquinas goes further yet than Augustine in embracing the apparently eternalist implications of God's knowledge of all temporal truths. As he puts the matter in the *Summa contra Gentiles*, "whatever is found in any part of time coexists with what is eternal as being present to it, although with respect to some other time it be past or future," on analogy with the way in which all the points on the circumference of a circle are identically related to their common center, even if they are distant from one another.[33] This is not, he emphasizes, merely a function of God's knowing creatures' eternal archetypes, but rather of his knowing creatures, even those future to us, as they actually exist.[34]

At times these two positions collide in a single text, as in Aquinas's commentary on *De Interpretatione* I, where Aristotle argues for the indeterminacy of future contingents.[35] In his gloss, Aquinas maintains both that man "does not know future things in themselves, because they do not yet exist, but can know them in their causes," and that God "in every way eternally sees all of those things which are in any time, as the human eye sees Socrates sitting in himself, not in his cause."[36] William Lane Craig nicely summarizes the interpretive difficulty:

> What Aquinas's doctrine of God's eternity and knowledge of future contingents was seen to imply seems to be positively affirmed by Aquinas, namely, that the past, present, and future are all ontologically on a par with each other. Accordingly, Thomas held to what contemporary philosophers of space and time call a B-theory of time. Nevertheless, I find it inconceivable that he consciously adhered to such a theory of time. For him becoming was not mind-dependent, but real, and it was only because of God's eternal being that all things were present to Him.[37]

As we have seen, Augustine's dilemma grew only more acute as it was taken up by Aquinas. In the remainder of the chapter, we'll consider two scholastic strategies for resolving that dilemma, whether (with John Duns Scotus and Francisco Suarez) in favor of a more consistent presentism, or (with John Wyclif) in favor of a consistent eternalism.

## SCOTUS'S EXPOSURE OF AUGUSTINE'S DILEMMA

To my knowledge, Scotus was the first to bring Augustine's dilemma—the inconsistency between a real and changing present and God's changeless vision of all times—into clear view and to insist on a decision between its horns. He begins his discussion of the relation between time and eternity by considering whether God might know the truth of propositions about future contingents through the divine ideas (Augustine's half-hearted solution). He concludes that God could not so know them, assuming that he has ideas of possible creatures as well as actual ones, because the difference between them is located, not in the ideas themselves, but rather in God's will to create some and not others.[38]

Scotus then turns to the eternalist position we saw Aquinas developing, according to which "God has certain knowledge about future contingents in this way, because all the flux of time is present to eternity . . . just as the immense ['measureless,' *immensum*] is present in every place, so too the eternal is present at once to every time."[39] He explains this using Aquinas's preferred analogy of center and circumference: "If flowing time (*tempus fluans*) were posited to be the circumference of a circle, and the now of eternity (*nunc aeternitatis*) to be its center, whatever flux there might be in time, and each of its parts, would always be present to the center."[40]

Scotus criticizes this position on several grounds, one of which is that it requires throwing over the view that all that exists is the "*nunc temporis*," the specious present. As he observes, "If an effect has being in itself, with respect to the first cause, it simply is in itself, because with respect to nothing does it have being more truly. So, that which is said to be such with respect to the first cause, can simply be said to be such."[41] If creaturehood is being known and willed by God,[42] then the future contingents, which God beholds in themselves, are created, full stop. "If," that is, "something future is in act with respect to God, it simply is in act, and so it is impossible that it afterward be put in act."

On the center-circumference view of time, talk of any creatures as "not yet" is necessarily deprived of ontological commitment, reduced to the status of an indexical. But insofar as some creature—"my act of sitting" (*sessio mea*), Scotus proposes—is future in the strong sense of "not-yet-existing," that eternalist view has the odd consequence "that what was already produced by God, would again be produced in being, and so would be produced in being twice."[43] Notice that Scotus here closely parallels Augustine's own dilemma about foreknowledge from the *Questions to Simplicianus* (either "foreknowledge" of creatures or actual knowledge of them), though where Augustine (at least in this text) accepts the latter horn, with its apparently eternalist implications, Scotus prefers the former as required by his understanding of time.

At bottom, Scotus's interrogation of the eternalist position aims to force a decision about the "not yet" of future things: "eternity will not be a basis for coexisting with something, unless it exists, because that which is not cannot coexist with anything."[44] Do future contingents "already" exist (albeit in their own time), or do they "not yet" exist? At least in this passage, Scotus himself happily seizes the latter horn of the dilemma, and denies that God's certitude even about present events requires acquaintance with the events themselves; rather, "because the divine intellect does not receive any certitude from some object other than his essence," even in the case of "my sitting now, the divine intellect does not have any certitude caused by the sitting itself, for the sitting does not move his intellect."[45]

And this, he insists, is the authentically Augustinian position; after all, Augustine insisted (in *De Genesi ad litteram* 5.2 and *De civitate Dei* 10.12) that God does not "otherwise know things he has made than he knows things he is going to make."[46] As we saw earlier, Augustine does indeed often claim that God's knowledge of creatures derives from his apprehension of their divine ideas (to which Scotus adds God's knowledge of his own will regarding them); but, as we also saw, Augustine is restless at best with the idea that God might not know creatures themselves, but only (so to speak) an a-temporal, holographic representation of them.

In this passage of the *Lectura*, at least, Scotus is a staunch advocate for reconciling divine eternity to presentism. Richard Cross, however, has argued that elsewhere in the *Lectura* and in the later *Ordinatio*, Scotus rejects this presentism in favor of a consistently eternalist theory of time.[47] A key text for Cross is Scotus's insistence that "the divine intellect not only eternally understands the soul of Antichrist as possible in all time before it was created, but it understands it to be, as existing in act in that instant of creation in which it exists (*intellexit esse, ut actu existentem pro illo instanti creationis pro quo existet*)."[48] The fact that God understands the Antichrist's soul to be *actual* in its own time surely requires, Cross insists, that that soul actually exist, and this "certainly entails a B-theory of time, according to which none of time is ontologically privileged."[49]

It looks to me, however, as though a more modest reading of this text is possible, which is consistent with the *Lectura*'s rigorous presentism. After all, as we just saw earlier, Scotus is adamant that God's knowledge even of existing things derives none of its certitude from the things themselves, but only from the divine essence; on that view, God can know, given his knowledge of the divine ideas and of his will to create, that the Antichrist exists actually at time $t$, but only potentially at time $t_1$, quite apart from whether the order of creatures itself presently includes the Antichrist or not.

## SUAREZ'S AUGUSTINIAN PRESENTISM

Nonetheless, even if the *Lectura*'s discussion of time and eternity was simply a passing fancy for Scotus, his exposure there of Augustine's dilemma had a tremendous influence on later attempts to relate time and eternity. For instance, in an *opusculum*, *On the Absolute Knowledge of Future Contingents*, the great Jesuit Francisco Suarez cites Scotus as a key authority for rejecting the apparently eternalist implications of Aquinas's and Augustine's approaches, and for interpreting divine eternity in consistently presentist terms.[50] Suarez's solution to Augustine's dilemma is to follow Scotus, who denied that times "always coexist with the divine eternity, or (what comes to the same thing) are always present to it according to a real coexistence, and so concluded that this kind of existence could not be the basis for [God's] knowing future things."[51]

Rather than describing all times as coexisting with divine eternity, Suarez insists that "created things do not exist or coexist in eternity, insofar as we are speaking about things, but rather exist successively, insofar as they successively come to be and exist."[52] To be a creature is to exist in a succession of creatures, one after another, each possessed of "its own existence and duration," which is strictly limited and passing, before it possesses a relation to divine eternity.[53]

He immediately anticipates perhaps the most difficult objection to this view, which is that it introduces succession into eternity, since it posits that creatures coexist successively with it.[54] He concedes creatures' successive coexistence with God, but denies that this introduces succession into eternity, which remains unchanged despite creatures' changing relations to it.[55] The key, Suarez takes it, is to recognize that God is related to creatures only logically, by an "extrinsic denomination," so that their successive changes "do not indicate succession in God."[56] In a striking image, he compares the divine eternity to "a tree remaining immobile in a river, which is successively present or locally near to the flowing waters, not by any succession which is in the tree, but rather in the waters."[57]

The sensible analogy founders, of course, on the fact of divine simplicity, which allows for every moment of time to coexist, albeit "inadequately," with one and the same "moment" of eternity. This occurs, Suarez suggests, in something like the way that the whole of the divine essence is present in each spatial part of creation, albeit not adequately, since God could be present with equal fullness to each part even if their total were multiplied indefinitely.[58] Suarez's proposal of a whole (the divine essence), which exists in many times (Robert Pasnau has recently dubbed this property "holochronicity"), was less well-known, thought it too had precedents in, for example, Anselm.[59] In Suarez's mind, this coexistence of divine eternity with every moment of time no more implies the simultaneous coexistence of those moments than the divine essence's coexistence with every part of space implies their contiguity. Rather, "all things, when they exist, coexist with that entire [eternity]; but it does not follow from this that they always coexist with it."[60]

And so, Suarez concludes, God cannot know future contingents by way of their real coexistence with his divine eternity, since what is future does not yet exist except potentially. Nonetheless, even he cannot resist the lure of eternalist language when he comes to describe the character of divine knowledge. Future contingents, he grants, do exist "objectively, in the order of the eternal knowledge of God, inasmuch as his eternal gaze falls at once on all times, as if they were in the act of existence."[61] But how can even God see what does not exist?

Suarez grants that there is a problem here: "as divine power cannot make that which is not in itself makeable, so neither can divine knowledge know that which is in itself unknowable, nor bring a certain judgment to bear about that which is in every way uncertain."[62] He insists that it can be resolved simply by showing that it involves no contradiction, and so is docile (even if unknowably so) to divine omnipotence. But here again, the logic of his position presses him inexorably back toward eternalism: "We can say that this future, although it does not exist eternally, nonetheless has a certain mode of being, inasmuch as it can sufficiently found the truth of an eternal judgment or enunciation, and terminate the act of understanding."[63] This qualified being, he says, is in fact the "the very being which the thing will have in its time."[64] Future events don't actually *exist*; they only have a certain (but carefully unspecified) mode of *being*, which is sufficient for God's almighty powers of intellection to get them in view. But if appeals to divine omnipotence are generally a counsel of despair, we might wonder whether better results could be had by taking seriously the intuition—which even Suarez's relentless pursuit of presentism can't seem to leave behind—that the true measure of a time's existence is given by its relation to the divine eternity.

## WYCLIF'S AUGUSTINIAN ETERNALISM

For a particularly robust attempt to develop such an account of time out of distinctively Augustinian resources, we can now turn back to John Wyclif, particularly in his early *De Ente Predicamentali*.[65] Sadly, his later controversial writings about the nature of the sacraments and papal authority left him branded a heretic, which perhaps explains the almost total subsequent neglect of his philosophical reflections on time.[66] Wyclif develops three arguments for eternalism, the most interesting of which for our purposes is his insistence that this theory of time is entailed by God's knowledge of creatures.

"It is clear," Wyclif maintains, "that many things exist outside the present instant."[67] His initial warrant for this position is one that Suarez would have shared: "For . . . God, by his most infinite brightness, comprehends all things at once, and so all the parts of time, as they are most truly through him, since the divine essence represents all things uniformly and invariably."[68]

But Wyclif departs from the theistic presentist in insisting that these divine cognitive attitudes toward actual creatures require that the creatures actually exist. Since, he maintains, loving a thing entails not only willing it as good for oneself but also willing it as available (*fundabile bonum*), "it follows that if God loves anything, then it has being."[69]

Not that everything beloved by God need be in every time; rather, everything beloved by God need be in its own time, "one before, and another after." And this is why, Wyclif notes, "with God all things are present, as Augustine ... says ... It is clear, then, that if the parts of time are with God, then they truly are (*si partes temporis sunt apud Deum, tunc vere sunt*)."[70] For Wyclif, then, time's contrast with eternity is defined solely by its compositeness, and not by its passage (cf. note 29 of this chapter for this distinction), since all times equally perdure before the divine gaze.

As Wyclif notes, his is clearly an Augustinian position, if less clearly Augustine's own. He points out that in places Augustine at least strongly implies that, from God's perspective, the past and the future are on an ontological par. So, in *Confessions* 11, Augustine "says himself to know that past and future time, wherever they are, are presences. So, he calls past time, the presence of the past, and future time, the presence of the future."[71] Wyclif likewise cites Augustine's discussion of time in the seventeenth of the *83 Different Questions* (a text we have also noted earlier), where he argues, "'Every past no longer is, every future is not yet; therefore, every past and future do not exist. Therefore there is neither past nor future, but all is present with God.'"

"Behold," Wyclif exclaims, "the decision of the question. And there is no doubt but that if something is with God, then it truly is."[72] As Pasnau suggests, in glossing Wyclif, "at least on its face, Wyclif's point seems a reasonable one. For as long as we think of our temporal frame of reference and God's eternal frame of reference as at least equally valid, it is hard to see what basis there could be for giving a privileged metaphysical status to what is, for us, the present."[73]

As should be evident from our discussion earlier, Wyclif's reading of Augustine is one-sided, but he taps into an important tension in Augustine's thinking about time: the presence of past and future is a function *both* of the transcendental conditions for human thought, *and* of the transcendental conditions for creaturehood itself, in God's perspective on things. Wyclif's innovation is to identify the a-temporal order known by God with the order of creatures themselves, and then to downgrade talk about time's apparent motion to the status of a well-founded phenomenon, available to creatures with the right sensory and cognitive equipment.

As we saw earlier, Suarez's principal motivation for resisting the eternalist implications of God's knowledge was the apparent absurdities they introduced into our ordinary conceptions of temporal becoming, in particular, that what hasn't yet happened doesn't yet exist, and what already happened no longer exists, though its effects might. Wyclif, by contrast, develops an ingenious set of arguments for the view that these ordinary intuitions about the nature of causality in particular require an "amplification of the word 'present.'"[74] Only an eternalist account of time, he insists, is compatible with realism about efficient and final causality. He observes, "from modes of speech which are necessary in connection with causes, time, and many similar things, we are required to posit something to exist outside the present instant (*aliquid esse extra presens instans*)."[75] This necessity extends, by way of efficient causality, to the reality of past events, and by way of final causality, to the reality of future events.

Wyclif first discusses efficient causality, noting, "according to the Philosopher (*Physics* I, 56), matter, form, and privation are intrinsic principles of a composite, and so privation is an efficient cause, albeit only accidentally."[76] (He stipulates that "A" will refer to a causal privation, and "B" to a caused composite.) The idea here is that privation A (being uncultured, say) constitutes a kind of gap in B's being, into which a positive determination (being cultured) can be fitted. It supplies a condition of possibility for B's coming-to-be-thus, even if it does so indirectly (per accidens), by *not* being, rather than directly. Now, Wyclif relates privations-as-causes to the nature of time as follows: "And it is clear that if A causes or stands as a principle to B, then both of them exist. But it is obvious that it involves a contradiction for those to exist together in the same instant; so, it must be the case that one is temporally prior to the other."[77] The impossibility of A and B's coexistence follows from the law of noncontradiction: B can't be both uncultured and cultured in the same respect at the same time. A and its contrary are noncompossible, and so they must occupy distinct times in the history of the substance, which possesses them.[78]

Wyclif draws a radical conclusion from the truth of this conditional, however: for B to exist, so too must A, even if at a different time, since "cause and caused ... are related, such that each requires the other to exist, and both perish together."[79] A sufficient account of B's existing, Wyclif reasons, must appeal to all of its causes—otherwise why refer to them as causes? But, on the presentist view of time, A (the privation-as-accidental-cause) no longer exists, and so it can no longer figure in an explanation of B. As Pasnau puts it, "Since generation must build on that prior state [i.e., of privation], the prior state figures as a cause. But then, Wyclif reasons, if it is a cause in generation, it must exist, even if it is in the past. Hence past things exist."[80]

We should notice that Wyclif will not be moved by objections of the form, "My grandfather clearly contributed to causing me by way of causing my father, but he died long before I was born, and so no longer exists." His point is that this relation too is only possible on the assumption that your grandfather's time *also* exists in a region of time appropriately (i.e., causally) continuous with yours. At the very least, the commonsense objection extends the definition of causality in a puzzling way: surely the hardheaded objector would have no sympathy for the man who steps off a cliff, protesting all the while, "There used to be a bridge here!" Wyclif's proposal applies this logic across the modes of causality.

Now, it is possible to accept Wyclif's conclusions about the necessary reality of prior causes and maintain an ontological commitment to a real present, if you adopt a "moving spotlight" theory of time, according to which an indeterminate future is forever leaping through the film of the present, only to be frozen in the amber of the past.[81] Wyclif has a further set of arguments against this view, however, in the form of a parallel discussion of final causality, "by virtue of which a movement or operation is caused." "For," he observes, "nature and every orderly agent acts outwardly for the sake of an end, which exercises final causality over such a work; as an alteration is for the sake of a substantial form which is to be generated, or a walk is for the sake of sought-after health."[82] The second example is the simpler of the two and perhaps easier to account for on presentism: after all, we're justified in saying that health is the point of a walk only insofar as health is included among the intentions of the walker *at the time of his walking*. (I can intend to improve my health by walking even if it turns out that I have a congenital heart defect which the exercise aggravates.)

The case of natural change, however, is stranger and more pressing: alterations occur "in order to generate a substantial form." Water molecules of a neutral pH when heated at sea level to 100 degrees Celsius *necessarily* change state, from a liquid to a gas. (For the moment, at least, let's seal any Humean escape hatches.) The process of heating seems to *aim* at the outcome of gaseousness, like an arrow at its target;[83] indeed, we can specify necessary and sufficient conditions for boiling water only because they invariably issue in this outcome. But how can this be, Wyclif wonders, if there's nothing yet for it to aim at? Wyclif essentially applies the axiom regarding the simultaneity of cause and effect in the opposite direction: "It is obvious that all such things are impossible, unless a thing is more extended than in the present instant; and so not all things which exist temporally exist in the present instant."[84] Unless we can form true statements about future events ("If present conditions remain unaltered, that water will be boiling in five minutes"), how can it be that final causality genuinely contributes to an explanation of things?

## CONCLUSION

With Wyclif, we have reached the end of our road in this consideration of Augustine's dilemma regarding time's relation to eternity. As we have seen,

Augustine's brilliant speculations about each posed a problem, both for himself and for his heirs: an eternal and immutable God seemingly cannot know creatures as they pass into and out of existence through the film of the present; if God knows them, then either eternity must in some sense be assimilated to time, as in Augustine's presentist interpreters, such as Duns Scotus or Suarez, or time must be assimilated to eternity, as in Wyclif. Despite Augustine's legacy as the great theorist of temporal passage, then, it is equally true that a short route to a B-theory can be found in his reflections on the eternity of God's knowledge of creatures.[85]

## NOTES

1. *Epistola de tribus quaestionibus*, n. 12 (Quaracchi ed., vol. VIII, 335b). Unless otherwise noted, all translations are my own.

2. Brian Leftow, *Time and Eternity* (Ithaca, NY: Cornell University Press, 1991), 73.

3. The labels "A-theory" and "B-theory" come from James McTaggart's seminal essay, "The Unreality of Time," *Mind* 17, no. 68 (Oct., 1908), 457–474. Various kinds of B-theory have become something of a *cause célèbre* among Anglophone philosophers following McTaggart's arguments against the reality of temporal passage. Though McTaggart makes no reference to Einstein's "The Electrodynamics of Moving Bodies" (1905), eternalism's rise has been particularly aided by the apparent "geometrization" of time in both special and general relativity. On this, see also: Hilary Putnam, "Time and Physical Geometry," *Journal of Philosophy* 64, no. 8 (Apr., 1967), 240–247; Palle Yourgrau, *The Disappearance of Time: Kurt Gödel and the Idealistic Tradition in Philosophy* (New York: Cambridge University Press, 1991), 7–8; Idem., *A World without Time: The Forgotten Legacy of Gödel and Einstein* (New York: Basic Books, 2005), 6.

4. As David van Dusen rightly observes in an excellent recent interpretation Augustine's account of time, "The scholastic reception of *Confessions* XI [is] a sophisticated and conflicted reception-history which has yet to be written" (*The Space of Time: A Sensualist Interpretation of Time in* Confessions X–XII (New York: Oxford University Press, 2014), 38). This chapter is an initial and partial attempt at filling this gap.

5. As I have no intention of advancing a novel interpretation of *Confessions* 11, I will not over-burden this chapter with a full litany of Augustine's commentators. The best recent study as of my writing in late 2019, and the one I follow most closely, is David van Dusen's *The Space of Time* (see note 4 of this chapter). I've also learned much from: William Lane Craig, *Divine Foreknowledge and the Problem of Future Contingents* (New York: Brill, 1988), 59–78; Brian Leftow, *Time and Eternity*; Juan Pegueroles, *El Pensamiento filosófico de San Agustín* (Barcelona: Editorial Labor, 1972); Gerard O'Daly, *Augustine's Philosophy of Mind* (Berkeley, CA: University of

California Press, 1987); and James O'Donnell's indispensable notes and commentary on the *Confessions*: https://www.stoa.org/hippo/noframe_entry.html.

6. Quotations of *Confessions* in the body of the text are adapted from the translation by J.G. Pilkington (cf. *Nicene and Post-Nicene Fathers*, vol. 1; ed. Philip Schaff; Buffalo, NY: Christian Literature, 1887), though usually modified in light of the Latin given in *Confessiones* (JP Migne; PL 32) 11.14.17. Hereafter, cited as *Conf.*

7. *Conf.* 11.23.29: "Why should not rather the motions of all bodies be time?" See also *Conf.* 12.11.14: "Without variance of motion there are no times, and there is no variance of motion where there is no determination." Van Dusen, in *The Space of Time*, has convincingly shown that this "physical" account of time can be seamlessly united with Augustine's famously "psychological" conception of it in *Confessions* 11: in short, "times" are bodily motions (11.23.29), while "time" is that "distention of the soul (*distentio animi*)" "by which we measure the movements of all bodies" (= times) (11.23.30, cf. *The Space of Time*, 111).

8. *Conf.* 11.14.17.
9. *Conf.* 11.15.20.
10. Van Dusen, *Space of Time*, 246.
11. *Conf.* 11.20.26, 11.28.37.
12. *Conf.* 11.26.33.
13. *Conf.* 11.27.36.

14. Aristotle also observes that it is only in the present that sensation can perceive what is, hope anticipate the future, and memory recollect the past. See *De Memoria* I.449b, quoted in Van Dusen, *The Space of Time*, 7. Augustine might have encountered this Aristotelian notion by way of Cicero, *De Inventione* II.53.160–61, and *Tusculan Disputations* I.10.22. For discussion of these passages, see van Dusen, *The Space of Time*, 7, n. 2.

15. Pegueroles, *Pensamiento filosófico*, 64: "*El espíritu creado está a medio camino entre el instante fluyente del cuerpo y el instante pleno del Espíritu infinito*," viz., God himself, who alone is eternal and immutable.

16. Van Dusen, *Space of Time*, 113: "When Augustine pursues . . . his question of 'time,' he is *solely* and *stipulatively* concerned with the condition of possibility of temporal *mensuration*—and that 'the soul' (*anima-animus*) is this condition of possibility, in *Confessions* XI, is a perfectly Aristotelian *and* Epicurean conclusion. The question of the condition of possibility of temporal *succession*—which is for Augustine, as for Lucretius, 'the movement of *all* bodies'—is hereafter, for Augustine, a question of 'times.'"

17. *Conf.* 11.7.9.

18. *83 Div. Qu.* 19, in Leftow, *Time and Eternity*, 75: "What is unchangeable is eternal, for it always exists in the same state." This is the point at which to note a possible escape route between the horns of Augustine's dilemma: one might, with some contemporary theologians and philosophers of religion, deny divine immutability and simplicity. See, for example, William Lane Craig, *Time and Eternity: Exploring God's Relationship to Time* (Wheaton, IL: Crossway, 2001), 29–31. There isn't space here to defend the adherence of Augustine and his heirs to these classical "perfections" of deity. This has been ably done elsewhere, especially by Paul Gavrilyuk in

*The Suffering of the Impassible God* (New York: Oxford University Press, 2004). In any case, our interest at present is in a survey of the Augustinian tradition, not in the conclusions we might draw from it today.

19. *Enarrationes in Psalmos* 101. s. 2.10, quoted in O'Donnell, *Confessions*, ad 11.1.1 "Eternity is the very substance of God."

20. *Sermo* 7.7 (PL 38), in Leftow, *Time and Eternity*, 73: "Being is a name for immutability."

21. Van Dusen, *Space of Time*, 12, 14–15. Cf. O'Daly's comment in *Augustine's Philosophy of Mind*, 152, that, "perhaps uniquely among ancient Platonists, Augustine does not attempt to understand time with reference to its supposed *paradeigma* or model, eternity."

22. *Conf.* 11.31.41.

23. *83 Div. Qu.* 17 (ed. JP Migne; PL 40): http://www.augustinus.it/latino/ottantatre _questioni/index2.htm.

24. Aristotle's clearest denial that God exercises any immediate providence over the world is the famous description, in *Metaphysics* (LCL 287; trans. Hugh Tredennick; Cambridge, MA: Harvard UP, 1933), of God as "thinking thinking of thinking" (L, 1074b), who stands to the cosmos only as its final and not efficient cause: "κινεῖ δὲ ὧδε τὸ ὀρεκτὸν καὶ τὸ νοητόν· κινεῖ οὐ κινούμενα" (L, 1072a26).

25. *Conf.* 11.8.10.

26. *83 Div. Qu.* 46.2.

27. For this way of specifying the theory of the divine ideas, see Aquinas, *De Veritate* (Textum Leoninum, 1970; https://www.corpusthomisticum.org/qdv01.html) q. 3, art. 1, ad 2; Bonaventure, *In I Sent.*, d. 35, art. un., qu. 1; I, 600.

28. A key issue connected with the problem of divine foreknowledge of future contingent events is of course its compossibility with human freedom. This is the pressing issue in Augustine's dispute with Cicero in Book V of *De civitate Dei*, for instance. Mercifully, weighing in on the merits of libertarian or compatibilist conceptions of freedom and their relations to various theories of time and of eternity would require another essay altogether. Craig's entire *Divine Foreknowledge and the Problem of Future Contingents* is given over to a thorough historical exposition of this issue.

29. *De Div. Qu. ad Simpl.* 2.2.2. Years later, in *de civ. Dei*, Augustine describes divine foreknowledge in terms of God's exact knowledge of "the order of causes," in the sense that God knows, about the disposition of the world $x$ at time $t$, that it will issue in the further disposition $y$ at time $t+1$ (5.9). I take it that this isn't inconsistent with Augustine's denial of foreknowledge in *Ad Simplicianum*; rather, Augustine chose in *De civitate Dei* to defend a weaker position than in the former work, arguing not that God a-temporally knows all creatures, but that God knows, merely on the basis of knowing what is happening in my present, what will happen in my future.

30. Boethius, *De consolatione philosophiae*, 5.6.4: "Eternity is the all-at-once and perfect possession of a boundless life (*Aeternitas igitur est interminabilis uitae tota simul et perfecta possessio*)." Boethius, ibid., explicates this definition by contrasting it with time's passage ("for whatever is in time proceeds, as present, from the past to

the future") and with time's compositeness ("nothing constituted in time can embrace the whole space of its life all at once").

31. *Summa Theologiae* (Textum Leoninum Romae, 1888; https://www.corpusthomisticum.org/sth0000.html) 1.10.2 ad 5.

32. *In IV libros Physicorum* (Textum Leoninum Taurini, 1954; https://www.corpusthomisticum.org/cpy011.html), lect. 21, no. 614.

33. *Summa contra Gentiles* (Textum Leoninum Taurini, 1961; https://www.corpusthomisticum.org/scg1001.html) 1.67.7. This image is likely inspired by Boethius, *De consolatione philosophiae*, 4.6.17: "So, as reasoning is related to understanding, that which is begotten to that which is, time to eternity, a circle to its midpoint, so is the mobile series to the stable simplicity of providence (*Igitur uti est ad intellectum ratiocinatio, ad id quod est id quod gignitur, ad aeternitatem tempus, ad punctum medium circulus, ita est fati series mobilis ad prouidentiae stabilem simplicitatem*)."

34. *Summa Theologiae* 1.14.13, corp.: "All things that are in time are present to God from eternity, not only because He has the types of things present within Him, as some say; but because His glance is carried from eternity over all things as they are in their mode of being present (*prout sunt in sua praesentialitate*)."

35. Aristotle, *De Interpretatione* (LCL 321; trans. Harold Cook; Cambridge, MA: Harvard UP, 1938) 1.9, 18a29–30, begins this seminal passage with the anodyne observation, "With regard to things which are or are coming to be, an affirmation or denial is necessarily either true or false." In statements about the past or present, the Law of the Excluded Middle applies: my statement that a sea-battle occurred yesterday or is occurring today is either true or false. But he then denies that this Law can hold for statements about future contingents: if my saying today, "There will be a sea-battle tomorrow" is true, then the sea-battle is in the can, its existence fixed for all times, and so occurs by necessity, not by choice. See ibid. 1.9, 18a34–b30. But in that case, according to ibid., 1.9, 18b29, why would the admirals or their sailors bother planning ahead or making an effort to fight? Tomorrow's putative sea-battle necessarily either will or won't happen, but neither outcome is itself necessary, because the present is yet in potency to both, a potency which only free human decisions can reduce to a particular actuality, at least according to ibid., 1.9, 19a29–30. On Aristotle's view, the statement "there will be a sea-battle tomorrow" is like the statement, "Lear had three sons, all of whom died as infants." Both have no truth-value, because the world is blurred, indeterminate in a strong sense, in the regions where one could be found. For an extended defense of this reading of *De Interpretatione* as endorsing the metaphysical indeterminacy of future contingents, and not merely their epistemic opacity, see Craig, *Divine Foreknowledge and the Problem of Future Contingents*, 1–58.

36. *Expositio libri Perihermeneias* (Textum Leoninum Taurini, 1955; https://www.corpusthomisticum.org/cpe.html) I, lect. 14, cap. 19–20.

37. Craig, *Divine Foreknowledge and the Problem of Future Contingents*, 118.

38. *Lectura* I, d. 39, qu. un. (Città del Vaticano: Typis Polyglottis Vaticanis, 1960), vol. 16, p. 762.

39. Ibid.

40. Ibid.

41. Ibid., 763.
42. *Summa Theologiae* 1.14.8: God's "knowledge is the cause of things, insofar as it has his will conjoined to it (*secundum quod habet voluntatem coniunctam*)."
43. *Lectura* I, d. 39, qu. un., p. 763.
44. Ibid.
45. Ibid.
46. Ibid.
47. Cross, "Scotus on Timelessness and Eternity," *Faith and Philosophy* 14 (1): 3–25 (1997); cf. Cross, *The Physics of John Duns Scotus* (Oxford: Clarendon, 1998), 242–46.
48. *Lect.* I, d. 30, qu. 2 (v. 16, p. 706); cf. also *Ordinatio* 1.1–2, n. 41 (Città del Vaticano: Typis Polyglottis Vaticanis, 1963), v. 6, p. 187–88.
49. Cross, *The Physics of John Duns Scotus*, 244.
50. Suarez, *De Scientia Dei Contingentium Futurorum Absolutorum*, in *Opera Omnia*, vol. 11 (ed. Carolo Berton; Paris, 1858) 7.1, 320b–321a, cites Aquinas, *Summa Theologiae* 1.14.14 and *Conf.* 11.18 in particular.
51. Ibid. 7.4, 322ab.
52. Ibid. 7.16, 325a.
53. Ibid., 325b.
54. Ibid. 7.17, 325b.
55. Ibid.
56. Ibid.
57. Ibid. A similar image, though with a different import, appears in John Duns Scotus, *Lectura*, I, d. 39, 762.
58. Cf. Suarez, *De Scientia Dei* 7.11, 322b–323a, and the parallel discussion in Scotus, *Lectura*, I, d. 39, 763. The latter property—a whole's existing entirely in each of its parts—was widely discussed in late ancient and medieval philosophy, in reference both to divine ubiquity and to the soul's existence in the body. In the seventeenth century, Henry More dubbed this property "holenmerism." See here Robert Pasnau, *Metaphysical Themes: 1274–1671* (Oxford: Oxford UP, 2013), 337–40.
59. Cf. Pasnau, "On Existing All at Once," in *God, Eternity, and Time*, ed. Christian Tapp and Edmund Runggaldier (Burlington, VT: Ashgate, 2011), 11; cf. Anselm, *Monologion* 22, discussed in ibid., 20–21.
60. Suarez, *De Scientia Dei* 7.20, 327a. Suarez's idea of time's successive asymmetric relations to eternity is similar to what Eleonore Stump and Norman Kretzmann have called "eternal-temporal simultaneity," according to which every moment of time is successively simultaneous with the whole of eternity, without thereby being simultaneous with each other. See Stump and Kretzmann, "Eternity," *Journal of Philosophy*, 78, no. 8 (1981), 429–458.
61. Suarez, *De Scientia Dei* 7.18, 325b.
62. Ibid. 8.5, 328b.
63. Ibid., 8.8, 329b.
64. Ibid., 329ab.
65. Rudolf Beer, who edited and published the only surviving manuscript of this work, argued that Wyclif intended it to be "the fifth division of the first book"

of his great unfinished *Summa de Ente*. See Beer's "Introduction" to *De Ente Predicamentali* (London: Trubner & Co., 1891), viii. In it, Wyclif discusses each of the ten Aristotelian categories, including time. Beer assigns the treatise to a date of ca. 1360, prior to Wyclif's more controversial ventures into political and sacramental theology. Wyclif's treatment of time was first brought to my attention by the excellent discussion in Robert Pasnau, *Metaphysical Themes*, 389–91.

66. As Pasnau, 390, observes, "So far as I can find, Wyclif's important views on this subject have never before been noticed."

67. Wyclif, *De Ente Predicamentali*, cap. 22, 218): "*Patet . . . multa esse extra instans presens.*" Wyclif makes frequent reference in this paragraph to Thomas Bradwardine, whose presentism he is reducing to absurdity; for simplicity's sake, I have eliminated those references from my exposition.

68. Ibid., 218–19.
69. Ibid., 219.
70. Ibid.
71. Ibid., 192.
72. Ibid.
73. Pasnau, *Metaphysical Themes*, 390.
74. Ibid., 20, 189.
75. Ibid., 19, 184.
76. Ibid.
77. Ibid., 19, 184.
78. Ibid., 186.
79. Ibid., 184–5.
80. Pasnau, *Metaphysical Themes*, 390.
81. Cf., for example, Bradford Skow, "Relativity and the Moving Spotlight," *Journal of Philosophy* 106 (2009), 666–678, here 666–67.
82. *De Ente Predicamentali* 19, 185.
83. Cf. Aquinas's "fifth way" to God in *ST* 1.2.3.
84. Wyclif, *De Ente Predicamentali* 19, 185.
85. For a recent development of an Augustinian eternalism independently of Wyclif, see Paul J. Griffiths, *Decreation: The Last Things of All Creatures* (Waco, TX: Baylor University Press, 2015), §16.

*Chapter 13*

# Thomas Bradwardine
## *A Fourteenth-Century Augustinian View of Time*

Sarah Hogarth Rossiter

Thomas Bradwardine is a figure who for many years enjoyed relative obscurity, at least among historians of philosophy. For much of the twentieth century, this fourteenth-century English cleric tended only to be discussed, if at all, by historians of Reformation thought, who often saw in Bradwardine's emphasis on the sovereignty of God a prototype for Calvinism.[1] Less frequently, passing references may have been made to his pioneering work in physics and mathematics, as one of the famed "Oxford Calculators."[2] More recently, some scholars have become interested in more explicitly philosophical and logical aspects of Bradwardine's writing, including his remarkably original solution to the Liar Paradox, as well as his views on modality in general and contingency in particular. But the revival of interest in Bradwardine as a philosopher in the past twenty to thirty years is due at least partly to a particular interest in his philosophy of time, prompted largely by the analysis of Edith Wilks Dolnikowski.[3] In this chapter, I will introduce readers to the life and work of this fascinating and little-known figure, explaining how his thought represents a significant strand in the thread of Augustinianism running through the early fourteenth century. I will begin with a brief biography of his eventful life and historical context. I will then explain why an examination of this figure may be of particular relevance in a volume on time in the Augustinian tradition, which will include an explanation of what I take to be characteristic of Augustinian views on the subject of time. As we eventually turn to the examination of Bradwardine's own account of time, it will be important to consider first a prominent *non*-Augustinian view to which he is responding, namely, that of William Ockham.

As we come to the summary and assessment of Bradwardine's own view of time, outlining its inherently Augustinian elements, I will argue, *pace*

Dolnikowski, that it is indeed appropriate to view Bradwardine's philosophy as fundamentally reactionary in nature, against what he perceives to be heretical pelagianism in the thinking of Ockham. In my concluding remarks, I will speak briefly of the reception of Bradwardine's views of time in the decades and centuries that followed.

## WHO IS THOMAS BRADWARDINE?

In my overview of Thomas Bradwardine's life, I am relying largely on the work of Jean-François Genest and Heiko Oberman.[4] Bradwardine was probably born in the last decade or so of the thirteenth century, somewhere in Sussex, most likely in the diocese of Chichester. Though little is known about his exact provenance or year of birth, he rose to such prominence in adulthood that we know with a great deal of certainty the exact date and circumstances of his untimely death on August 26, 1349.

Bradwardine's life spanned a time of extreme religious and political upheaval: this was the ecclesiastically tumultuous time of the Avignon Papacy, during which the French crown exerted unprecedented control over matters of the Church and gave rise to competing claims to the papal tiara; it was also a period of fierce and bitter disputes, often with serious political implications, between the Franciscan order and the Papacy about interpretations of Apostolic poverty and the care of mendicant religious communities by the Church; and, finally, it was the beginning of the so-called Hundred Years' War, a period of intermittent conflict and conquest of France by England, sparked by rival claims to the French throne, which would continue off and on for more than a century. The first and last of these events would have a direct impact on Bradwardine's life, while the second shaped the later life of his contemporary, William Ockham (who probably died between 1347 and 1349). There is one final major historical event that would exert a fateful influence on Bradwardine's life: the Black Death.

Bradwardine's birth may have been obscure, but we know that he rose to prominence as a scholar in Oxford in the 1320s and 1330s. As a fellow at Merton College, he was part of a rich intellectual community that made significant discoveries in the fields of mathematics and physics. During his early career at Oxford, Bradwardine established his reputation as a talented member of the "Oxford Calculators," writing treatises in the areas of geometry, mathematics, and physics that received considerable attention. He was also a notable logician, devising a unique and influential solution to the Liar Paradox, which still has advocates even in the twenty-first century.[5] It was during his tenure at Oxford that Bradwardine became a strong intellectual opponent of Ockham. Bradwardine and Ockham may not have worked in precisely the same circles—Ockham being a Franciscan, Bradwardine a secular cleric—but Oxford in the 1320s was not a large place. Undoubtedly, Bradwardine became familiar with Ockham's much-discussed and highly controversial commentary on the *Sentences* of Peter Lombard.[6] Bradwardine makes explicit reference to the positions of this work in his early-career treatise on future contingents (*De futuris contingentibus*).[7] In particular, Bradwardine objected strongly to those elements of Ockham's teaching that he perceived as undermining the authority and power of God.

Gradually, Bradwardine's work became focused on more theological matters, culminating in his most well-known contribution, *De causa Dei contra pelagium*, or: *In the Defence of God against the Pelagians*.[8] There can be little doubt that William Ockham and his followers were the "Pelagians" that Bradwardine had in mind. In this work, Bradwardine emphasizes the primary importance of God's will and action in the work of salvation, alongside the necessity of God's extension of grace for our salvation. Thus, *contra* the "Pelagians," human creatures are dependent upon God's action for their salvation, and apart from God's will and grace, they can do nothing to merit salvation. There is much in this work of Bradwardine's that anticipates the emphases of various Reformation theologians, particularly John Calvin and John Knox, and various historians of theology have pointed to the probable influence Bradwardine had on these later thinkers.

In the 1340s, Bradwardine's life took on an increasingly ecclesiastical and political focus, and he became chaplain and confessor to the King, Edward III, whom he accompanied on campaigns in France. In 1348, Bradwardine was appointed Archbishop of Canterbury. Edward, however, not wanting to lose Bradwardine's services as confessor, prevented his ascension to the See of Canterbury, having John de Ufford made Archbishop instead. But even before his consecration as Archbishop, Ufford succumbed to the plague, which was at the height of its spread into Western Europe and onto the island of Great Britain. Edward did not seek to prevent Bradwardine's appointment a second time, and in June of 1349, in Avignon, Bradwardine was consecrated Archbishop of Canterbury, ascending to the most powerful ecclesial position in England. But Bradwardine fared little better than his unlucky predecessor: on the 26th of August, 1349, while traveling back to Canterbury from Avignon, he, too, died of plague. He is buried at Canterbury.

## BRADWARDINE AND AUGUSTINIAN APPROACHES TO TIME

There are two reasons why it is appropriate to include a study of Bradwardine in a volume on Augustine and time. The first is that there is a tradition in the literature on Bradwardine of viewing him as a primary conduit of Augustinian thought in the fourteenth century. This is seen perhaps most prominently in the very title of Oberman's influential study, *Archbishop Thomas Bradwardine: A Fourteenth-Century Augustinian*. In general, moreover, Augustine scholarship has been the context in which some of the most prominent discussion of Bradwardine's work has taken place.[9]

The view of Bradwardine as an Augustinian is certainly bolstered by his own self-identification as a champion in the cause of Christian orthodoxy against a resurgence of the old heresy of Pelagius. It is easy to see in this branding a kind of self-conscious posturing as a type of Augustine. And it is certainly the case that many prominent strands of Augustinian thought find expression in the work of Bradwardine, particularly his emphasis on the sovereignty of God and the prevenience of God's grace for any and all human action that is pleasing to God. Thus, Bradwardine stands as a prominent representative of Augustinianism in his own century. However, it is somewhat simplistic to draw too straight or direct a line from Augustine to Bradwardine, since much of Bradwardine's Augustinianism comes to him via Anselm of Canterbury.

The second reason to include him in this study is that there has been some considerable interest in Bradwardine's philosophy of time sparked by Dolnikowski's extensive monograph study of the topic. This interest also springs from scholarship on the related topics of contingency and necessity, which are very closely linked to discussions of free will (and thus, to discussions of God's knowledge of things past, present, and future). Calvin Normore has suggested that Bradwardine exhibited a comparatively radical view of contingency and necessity by which God *could* have made even necessary things otherwise, making his view a kind of proto-Cartesianism.[10] However, Gloria Frost has challenged this reading of Bradwardine as a radical voluntarist, arguing that Bradwardine's understanding of possibility and necessity is grounded rather in the "repugnance" or "non-repugnance" of objects or propositions relative to the necessity of God.[11] These terms—"repugnance" and "non-repugnance"—can be broadly read by a contemporary audience, without much distortion, as corresponding to the logical notions of "contradiction" and "consistency." In my own work, I have previously examined Bradwardine's treatment of this topic in a more obscure early work called the *De futuris contingentibus* (*On future contingents*).[12] Given this interest in Bradwardine's treatment of time in an Augustinian context, it is natural to include a study of such a figure in this present volume.

## WHAT IS AN "AUGUSTINIAN" VIEW OF TIME?

Before we turn to examining Bradwardine's own account of time, we ought first to establish what characteristically "Augustinian" elements we might expect to find. In other words, what is it that makes an account of time like that of Augustine?[13] I contend that there are two main features that set Augustine apart from his ancient predecessors and that recur prominently in the thinkers he influenced. The first of these is the notion of time as *created*.[14] Following Aristotle, Augustine sees time and motion as inextricably linked: time is the measure of motion, and motion occurs in and through time. Each could not exist without the other, despite being conceptually distinct from one another.[15] However, in a radical departure from Aristotle and much of the ancient Greek philosophical tradition, Augustine rejects the eternality of the universe. Instead, he posits, the universe came into existence *ex nihilo* by the Word of God, and time along with it. Thus, time is *a part of* creation, and prior to creation, time did not exist.

Since, however, God is strictly prior to creation, this position leads to many questions about the relationship between God and time. And this is where we find the second characteristic that is particularly Augustinian: on Augustine's account, God exists *apart from* time, inhabiting a sort of eternity that is more than mere *perpetuity*. Because time is a product of God's creation, God is prior to time, and exists not only apart from time but entirely independent of it. God is not bound by the constraints of time that we creatures experience. This is not necessarily to say that God has no interaction with time, but that his existence is prior to and does not depend upon time.[16] In the presence of time, God is not bound by its linear succession.

This view of God's relationship to time has many implications for the understanding of God's particular kind of necessary being, as well as the way in which God relates to the created order and its creatures. First of all, it addresses the problem of God's apparently arbitrary choice to create the universe at one point in time rather than another. According to this reported criticism, if God is unchanging, any beginning point set out for the universe would seem to be arbitrary. Why should God decide at some moment to create a universe, when for all the moments preceding God did not deem that to be the thing to do? Particularly for a view of God as unchanging, this would seem to imply a contradiction, namely, between God's *not* willing creation at many moments of time, and then *willing* creation at another moment in time.[17] Augustine's view of time as created offers a solution to this problem for the creationist: for if time does not exist prior to creation, then there is no succession of moments "prior" to creation in which this apparent contradiction might occur. God's being is strictly prior, as efficient cause, to the movement of the universe, and thus prior to time—but not "prior" in a temporal sense, since there *is* no time before time. In whatever sense, then, that we can speak of God preceding time, it is only through statements concerning God's essence (God's changelessness, necessity, goodness, etc.) as timelessly eternal. We cannot, however, speak of any pre-creation succession of God's actions, including the act of creation itself, since such a succession requires the existence of time. In this way, Augustine believes that the apparent logical problems entailed by positing a created beginning of the universe are resolved.[18]

Augustine is also noted for providing an extension of Aristotle's account of time, which brings into focus the phenomenological aspects of temporality, from the psychology of temporal experience to matters of human volition. Much of Augustine's discussion of memory in *Confessions* 10 concerns our own phenomenological relationship to the passage of time. Another important implication of God's timeless eternity in Augustine is the role it serves in providing an apparent resolution to the problems of human free will in relation to Divine omniscience. There are different possible formulations of this family of problems and subtle differences in the many and various contexts in which it may arise. But in essence, all have at their heart the observation that there is an apparent contradiction between upholding the following two theses: (a) God eternally knows all things—past, present, and future—and (b) human beings have the power to act freely, or without compulsion, in at least some circumstances. The contradiction lies in the fact that God's knowledge of future events would seem to entail that they cannot turn out otherwise than as he foreknows that they will; thus, it would appear that a person could never act freely, since God eternally foreknows every action that that person will take before she takes it, meaning that there is at least some sense in which she cannot act otherwise (since then God would be mistaken). Augustine's conception of God as outside of or beyond temporality provides a resolution to this apparent contradiction that is quite possibly the most historically influential solution to the problem of free will and divine foreknowledge in the literature.

For Augustine, God's timelessness means that God has knowledge now of events that are future to us, not because he "foresees" them in time, but precisely because all of created time is eternally a part of God's unchanging present. It is not as though God knows at time $t_1$ what will occur at $t_2$, and so because of God's knowledge that precedes $t_2$ the events of $t_2$ are now forced to turn out as previously predicted, as though God is some kind of soothsayer; rather, *both* $t_1$ and $t_2$ are simultaneously present to God, and so God's knowledge of what occurs in them is a sort of merely passive observation. An analogy often used to understand this interpretation of God's foreknowledge, and explicitly developed by Boethius, is that of a person who has climbed to the top of a high hill, and can survey the winding road below her for a great distance in both directions along the road. A traveler is making his slow way along the road from the west, say, and cannot see the highway robbers ahead; but the person atop the hill can simultaneously see the traveler, and the highway robbers, and indeed is aware of everything the traveler will encounter along the road long before the traveler himself is aware of them. But the observer's "foreknowledge" of these events does not have any causal powers in "making" these events come about; rather, she merely observes what is before her, through the benefit of her broader perspective on the scene.[19]

As a minor aside, I note here that there are some shortcomings to the metaphor as described, most notably due to the fact that the observer does not actually simultaneously see each and every step along the traveler's way *as* he takes it. It could be improved, perhaps, by thinking of the way in which stories are often told in medieval and early renaissance art, with various scenes from different times in a saint's, or Christ's, life presented as vignettes within a single large tableau. To take one example for illustrative purposes: consider Hans Memling's *Scenes from the Passion of Christ*, painted around 1470. In a single large scene, the figure of Jesus appears again and again, at various stages along the way: from his entry into Jerusalem, cleansing of the Temple, last supper, and agony in the garden; to his arrest, trial, scourging, carrying the cross, and crucifixion; to his burial, harrowing of Hell, and finally his resurrection. All these scenes and more are before the viewer and *present* to the viewer all at once.

Augustine's view of time, as characterized by the features outlined in this section, was in many ways the dominant view in the Latin West throughout much of the Middle Ages. Strong echoes of these ideas are to be found, for instance, in the profoundly influential works of Boethius, Anselm of Canterbury, and Thomas Aquinas. But they were not universally received, and especially in the fourteenth century, an increasing number of adherents of alternative theories are to be found. In what follows, we will explore the thought of one prominent detractor.

## TEMPORALITY IN WILLIAM OCKHAM

I have already noted that Ockham constituted a major opposing force and impetus for Bradwardine's philosophical thought. It therefore behooves me to take an interlude to outline Ockham's views on the matter, so that we may understand what Bradwardine is responding to in particular. Ockham's position is also important from a contemporary standpoint, since a number of influential philosophers of religion—most notably, Marilyn McCord Adams and Alvin Plantinga—have in recent decades taken up and defended versions of Ockham's solution to the problem.[20] This has generated significant debate for and against Ockham's solution and its merit as a viable solution.

It is going to help our understanding of what follows if we first take a brief diversion to discuss Ockham's understanding of the content of a proposition. In the late medieval period, there is a great deal of contention about how exactly propositions and their terms are to be understood and what precisely they represent. At the risk of trying to dissect the problem with too dull a knife, the disagreement may be broadly understood along the lines of nominalism versus realism, concerning both universals and the signification of terms. Ockham is widely recognized as a nominalist, explicitly rejecting the so-called moderate realism of many of his prominent contemporaries and proximate predecessors. Some scholars have even gone so far as to label Ockham an "extreme nominalist."[21] The "moderate realism" against which Ockham protests largely follows the tradition begun by Aristotle. This form of realism does not follow the Platonist doctrine that universals "really" exist as separate heavenly entities independent from the particulars that they inform, but it nonetheless maintains that universal properties really do exist and inhere in their particulars. It therefore ascribes a certain metaphysical reality and independence to these species and genera, which we term "universals." Though there is variation in the exact expression and understanding of this doctrine, this basic principle—that universals are real—informs the understanding of many of the most prominent thinkers leading into the late thirteenth and early fourteenth centuries, including Thomas Aquinas and John Duns Scotus.[22]

Ockham's well-documented nominalism, therefore, stands at odds with many of his prominent contemporaries. Adams summarizes a central tenet of Ockham's approach, which she sees as continuous with that of Henry of Harclay,[23] in the following way: "Everything that exists in reality is essentially singular—i.e., logically incapable of existing in, as a constituent of, numerically many simultaneously."[24] Unlike Harclay, however, Ockham derives as a consequence that "universals are nothing other than names."[25] This understanding of Ockham on universals is chiefly to be found in his *Ordinatio* I, dist. 2, question 4[26] but is also supported by his commentary on Aristotle's *De interpretatione*.[27] Ockham's nominalism will help us later to understand some of his arguments about propositions with respect to time, which are otherwise somewhat puzzling. In particular, it is a consequence of his anti-realism that, when it comes to understanding propositions, Ockham does not see the terms as representing anything more than the bare particulars to which they refer, whenever they are uttered.[28] A proposition does not take on any fixed existence of its own apart from the words uttered and their immediate referents.

Where this will become particularly relevant in the following discussion is in understanding Ockham's interpretation of propositions as they relate to the passage of time. It may be generally assumed that when a proposition is uttered with a time referent, such as "Justin Trudeau is *now* the Prime Minister of Canada," or "*Yesterday*, the last petal fell from the last tulip in my garden" (uttered at 10 a.m., say, on April 30, 2020), that the proposition automatically ever hereafter bears the meaning imposed by the referents at the time of its utterance. Thus, the first proposition, for instance, is eternally equivalent to the proposition, "Justin Trudeau is Prime Minister of Canada at 10 a.m. on 30 April 2020," and by this token, is determinately true. But Ockham does not take propositions to have enduring referential content in this way. On Ockham's view, propositions never mean anything more than what the bare referents of the words themselves would imply at the moment of their utterance. Propositions are never more nor less than a string of words—words which name things, but which may name different things at different times, depending on the context. Thus, for Ockham, a proposition whose truth or falsity depends on a particular moment in time may change in truth-value as time elapses. "Justin Trudeau is Prime Minister of Canada" is true as I write this, but fifty years from now, when Trudeau (presumably) is no longer prime minister, the proposition will correspondingly cease to be true. This is an idiosyncratic way of understanding the truth of propositions over time, but it is an understanding that Ockham adheres to in a remarkably consistent way. And as we shall see in what follows, it is important for understanding much of what he says concerning God's foreknowledge of future contingents.

Ockham's most sustained and focused discussion of the topic of future contingents occurs in his treatise *On Predestination, God's Foreknowledge, and Future Contingents* (PPD), written sometime between 1319 (the year that Ockham completed his *Sentences* commentary) and 1324 (the year that Ockham was summoned before the Pope in Avignon to answer for charges of heresy).[29] I will confine the discussion that follows to this treatise, which is composed of five questions, the most substantial and significant of which is the second. In this second question, Ockham argues that God's knowledge of future events is *determinate* (though his understanding of what makes something "determinate" is rather non-standard), *certain*, and *infallible*.[30] At the same time, however, he argues that God's knowledge is only *immutable* in a certain sense.[31] In one sense, Ockham contends, immutability may be taken to mean that the *content* of knowledge does not change; but this kind of immutability would seem to be a defect, because the content of our knowledge *ought* to change along with changing states of affairs. If it is true on 1 March that it is raining in New Westminster, then it is appropriate if the set of propositions that make up my knowledge should include "It is raining in New Westminster." But if it ceases to rain the following day, yet my "knowledge" continues to include the proposition "It is raining in New Westminster," then my knowledge of this fact is no longer knowledge at all, but a mistaken belief. Thus, Ockham claims, it is wrong to say that God's knowledge is immutable with respect to its content. However, Ockham does concede that one may speak of immutability with respect to the *amount* of knowledge one has. In that case, God's knowledge would be immutable, since when any proposition ceases to be true, it is immediately replaced by the negation of that proposition. When "It is raining in New Westminster" ceases to be true, that proposition passes from God's knowledge and is replaced by the proposition "It is not raining in New Westminster." As we shall shortly discover, it is one of Bradwardine's chief criticisms of Ockham that his view fails to adequately account for the immutability of God's knowledge in particular and hence undermines God's immutability in general.

After addressing whether God's foreknowledge is determinate, certain, infallible, and immutable (to which Ockham's answers are "yes" in a somewhat unorthodox manner, "yes," "yes," and "yes in one sense, but not in another"), Ockham turns to the question that causes Bradwardine most consternation. Contrary to the general thrust of received views on the matter, Ockham denies (with qualification) that God's knowledge is *necessary*.[32] Once again, though, and in true scholastic fashion, Ockham sets up a distinction: God's knowledge of future contingent events may be said to be necessary in the *way* that it knows things (it is necessary, for instance, that *if* a proposition is true, then God knows it); but it is not necessary with respect to *what* it knows. This is so, Ockham argues, because knowledge of contingent things cannot possibly be necessary, as the objects of that knowledge are not necessary. On this view, God's knowledge of future contingent events is itself contingent.

But how can Ockham simultaneously hold that God's knowledge is immutable and non-necessary? How is it that God's knowledge may simultaneously be said to be immutable—that is, never changing—and yet not necessary? Ockham would have it that, although God's knowledge is immutable, God's knowledge *might have been* otherwise than it is. Contingent factors (namely, the contingent events in the world) contribute to God's knowledge being as it is. Because many of the things that God knows could be otherwise than they are, God's knowledge could be otherwise than it is. What this means is that, though God's knowledge is unchangingly *as* it is—that is, immutable—it is nevertheless non-necessary, in the sense that *it could have been* otherwise.

In this way, Ockham denies the necessity of God's knowledge, while affirming both its immutability and its perfect consistency with the truth about the world. God's knowledge is non-necessary precisely because events in the world are non-necessary. *Had* things been other than they are (and the property of something to be such that it could-have-been-otherwise is precisely what it means, on Ockham's model, for it to be contingent), then God's knowledge would correspondingly have been otherwise than it is. So it would be nonsense, thinks Ockham, to assert that God's knowledge is necessary. Necessity is not a perfection of knowledge, because knowledge that was necessary could, on account of its necessity, fail to correspond in appropriate ways to the contingent reality of the world around us. Ockham does not see any inconsistency at all between the assertion that God is unchanging, eternal, and immutable, and the claim that God's knowledge is not necessary, for something can be ever-unchanging, and yet still could have been otherwise.

We should find this claim somewhat novel and surprising in a medieval context, for it directly contradicts the long-standing "Principle of Plenitude." This is the notion that everything that *can* happen, will indeed happen, given sufficient time. On this view of contingency, a state of affairs is contingent if at some point in time—assuming time stretches infinitely far forward— that state of affairs is realized, and at another point in time, it is not. But on Ockham's view, simply because something is never (or never will be) *in fact* the case, it does not follow that it is impossible for that thing to be.[33] Even if something never *in fact* transpires throughout the whole history of the world, Ockham maintains that it *could have* been otherwise, and, in this sense, the event may yet be contingent. This is precisely the situation we're dealing with with respect to God's knowledge of contingent events.

## BRADWARDINE'S REJECTION OF OCKHAM

Bradwardine rejects Ockham's view of God's foreknowledge as contingent, primarily because of his own intuition that this kind of knowledge is not genuine knowledge at all. He therefore sees Ockham to be seriously undermining an important attribute of God, which particularly relates to God's Providence. In his rejection of this view, Bradwardine is implicitly setting up his own view of time. But rather than his better-known work *De causa Dei*, the text I wish to primarily focus on here is *De futuris contingentibus* (DFC).[34] In this earlier treatise, Bradwardine begins by setting out and examining nine positions on the topic of God's foreknowledge of future contingent events.[35] Almost all of the nine opinions receive brief, terse replies. But to the eighth, Bradwardine devotes fifteen or more pages of text: this eighth position is that of William Ockham. Bradwardine's concentrated attention on this one view seems not to spring so much from finding it a particularly difficult or subtle position to reject, but rather, from an impulse to show us just how entirely bad the view really is.

One way of understanding Ockham's position that helps us to understand Bradwardine's deep suspicion of it is to observe that, for Ockham, what is most important in his development of a solution is the preservation of the true contingency of future events. That future contingents are truly contingent is, as it were, taken as a given, and the rest of the account developed accordingly to correspond with this fact. It seems that Ockham's position unfolds around the central tenet of future contingents, such that he is saying, "In light of this, what is to be said of God's knowledge of future contingents?" From this perspective, it seems that concerning any future contingent event A, Ockham would have it concerning God's *knowledge* of A that, because A is contingent, God's knowledge of A is also contingent. Ockham's claim is that knowledge of future events cannot be ascribed the same properties as knowledge of present or past events. Because the subject matter of the knowledge in question is future and contingent, Ockham would have it that God's knowledge of these things is itself future and contingent in some special sense. Through this assertion, Ockham blocks the conclusion that God's foreknowledge of A entails the necessity of A: for if God's knowledge of A is future and contingent, we cannot ascribe to it the sort of necessity generally thought to inhere in past and present knowledge. Since the knowledge itself is not necessary, it therefore does not in any way follow that its subject, A, is necessary. But to make this work, it was necessary for Ockham to deny necessity of God's knowledge.

Bradwardine summarizes Ockham's view by saying, "something is going to happen contingently *ad utrumlibet* and is foreknown by God in this present instant, but . . . it is possible, even for this present instant, that it could not be going to be, nor foreknown by God."[36] This solution raises some important epistemological and logical problems. But despite these other issues, what Bradwardine is primarily concerned with are the ways this solution seems to undermine the absolute omniscience of God, and thus, God's relationship to time. His chief complaint against Ockham's solution is that attributing to God a kind of knowledge that is contingent undermines God's immutability. Contingent knowledge, at least on Bradwardine's understanding of contingency (recall the Principle of Plenitude), must be knowledge that could come into or out of existence: for God to have such knowledge would imply that God might know A at time $t_1$, and cease to know A at $t_2$. Loss of knowledge seems, to Bradwardine, to constitute a substantial change in the knower, leading to the unacceptable consequence that God is mutable. The first objection Bradwardine levels against Ockham's position runs as follows:

> Consider the following: it follows that it is possible that something would be going to be that is not now going to be. This consequent is false, since, if it were so [the following argument could be made]: Suppose that it is now that instant [in the future], and [suppose] that A would [happen]; it may then be argued as follows: A is now going to be, and previously A was not going to be, therefore it is changed from not-going-to-be to going-to-be; and it is not changed because of a change in itself (since it did not exist before now); it is therefore the case that, if A is changed, it is because of a change in something else. This consequent is false, since in the same way that it has just been argued concerning possibility that A can be changed from not-going-to-be to going-to-be, so too could it be argued concerning [A's] essence.[37]

If it were the case, argues Bradwardine, that something could come to be that was previously not going to be, as would seem to follow from Ockham's claim that God's foreknowledge is contingent, then *something* must change between the time when the thing was not going to be and the time that it came to be, *other than the thing itself*. This is because prior to the thing's coming to be, nothing of it exists *to* undergo change. We see in this objection premonitions of things to come: for in what "other" thing might that change occur than God?

The connexion to God's mutability is drawn out more strongly in the second objection, several paragraphs later:

> If God has foreknowledge of *ad utrumlibet* future contingents, it follows that God can will and promise the opposite of what is now known, promised, and willed by him. This consequent is false, since in this way God could be changed with respect to knowledge, will, and promises, which is contrary to what is said in Malachi 3[:6]: "I am the LORD, and I do not change"; and so it follows that [if] it will not be just as God has promised or has willed it to be, then God is changed.[38]

Bradwardine is arguing that God's foreknowledge, as understood by Ockham, leads to the consequence that key aspects of God's nature—namely, God's knowledge, God's will, and God's promise-making—are mutable. This is so because, Bradwardine reasons, on Ockham's model, things may turn out otherwise than they were at one point going to turn out. So suppose at time $t_1$, some future event A was not going to happen. Then at $t_1$, God knew that A would not happen, perhaps willed that A would not happen, perhaps even *promised* that A would not happen. Because of A's contingency, Bradwardine's Ockham may suppose that A *does* in fact happen, say at time $t_2$. Were A to happen at $t_2$, after it had been the case at $t_1$ that A was not going to happen—along with God's corresponding knowledge, will, and perhaps even promises—then at $t_2$ God's knowledge, will, and promises are substantially different, and consequently, God will have changed. This, as Bradwardine attests, is contrary not only to the Classical or Neoplatonist notions of God but also to the character and person of God as presented in the Jewish and Christian canons of Scripture—and indeed, the Augustinian conception of God.

A further fourteen objections follow in Bradwardine's treatise, but these two suffice to give a general idea of the thrust of Bradwardine's complaints. In these objections, we see the importance Bradwardine places on the immutability of God's knowledge with respect to the passage of time. As a result, we should conclude that Bradwardine's impetus is primarily reactionary, intended to demonstrate the heretical error he perceives Ockham to be making.

## CONCLUSION: BRADWARDINE'S LEGACY

It is important to note that, though largely overlooked in more recent centuries of scholarship (a deficiency only recently experiencing correction), Bradwardine was an influential thinker in his own day and in the decades immediately following his death. Among the most striking pieces of evidence for this fact is the mention that is made of Bradwardine in "The Nun's Priest's Tale" of Chaucer's classic work of Middle English literature, *The Canterbury Tales*. Writing about forty years after Bradwardine's death, Chaucer is intellectually engaged in the philosophical problems of his day, and his interest in these topics is apparent even in an otherwise very silly fable concerning some chickens and a fox.

> But I cannot sift it to the bran [as grain]
> As can the holy doctor, Augustine,
> Or Boethius, or the Bishop Bradwardine,
> Whether God's worthy foreknowledge
> Compels me by need to do something—
> By "need" I mean *simple* necessity;
> Or if I am granted free choice
> To do something or not to do it,
> Despite God's foreknowing it before I was ever made;
> Or if his knowing does not compel at all,
> Except by *conditional* necessity.
> But I will have nothing to do with such matters;
> *My* tale is of a cock, as you will hear.[39]

Here, Bradwardine is mentioned alongside Boethius and Augustine himself as one who is particularly skilled in untangling the complexities of the relationship between God's foreknowledge and our free actions in time. Implicitly, he is being identified as in continuity with Augustine's legacy. Leff and Oberman have particularly highlighted Bradwardine's influence on the development of the ideas of pre-Reformation thinkers, and in particular, how his thought came to indirectly influence the likes of John Calvin and John Knox via John Wycliffe.

By the Enlightenment, Bradwardine and his work had mostly faded from the collective intellectual memory. But in these past fifty years or so, his significance as a mathematician, physicist, logician, philosopher, and theologian is being rediscovered. In this context, it is fitting to have considered his place as a conduit of Augustinian thought in the fourteenth century. In particular, we have seen how he may be recognized, like Augustine, as a champion of the sovereignty of God over the whole created order, including over time itself, in opposition to Pelagians ancient and medieval.

# NOTES

1. The classic studies here are: Gordon Leff, *Bradwardine and the Pelagians: A Study of His De Causa Dei and Its Opponents* (New York: Cambridge University Press, 1957); Heiko Oberman, *Archbishop Thomas Bradwardine: A Fourteenth-Century Augustinian* (Utrecht: Kemink & Zoon, 1958).
2. Clifford Truesdell, *Essays in The History of Mechanics* (New York: Springer, 1968), 30.
3. Edith Wilks Dolnikowski, *Thomas Bradwardine: A View of Time and a Vision of Eternity in Fourteenth-Century Thought* (Leiden: Brill, 1995).
4. See: Oberman, *Archbishop Thomas Bradwardine*; Jean-François Genest, "Le De futuris contingentibus de Thomas Bradwardine," *Recherches Augustiniennes* 14 (1979), 249–336, here 251.
5. There is currently a vast literature on this topic, with contributions by Stephen Read, Graham Priest, Catarina Dutilh Novaes, and others. A good place to start is Stephen Read, "The Liar Paradox from John Buridan back to Thomas Bradwardine," *Vivarium* 40, no. 2 (2002), 189–218; and Read, "Bradwardine's Revenge," in *Revenge of the Liar: New Essays on the Paradox*, ed. J. C. Beall (Oxford: Oxford UP, 2007), 250–61.
6. The particular treatise of import is Ockham's *De praedestinatione et de prescientia Dei respectu futurorum contingentium*, or *Predestination, God's Foreknowledge, and Future Contingents* (hereafter PPD), 2nd ed., tr. and ed. Marilyn McCord Adams and Norman Kretzmann (Indianapolis: Hackett, 1983).
7. All translations from *De futuris contingentibus* in this chapter will be my own.
8. Thomas Bradwardine, *De causa Dei contra Pelagium et de virtute causarum*, ed. Henry Seville (London: 1618; Reprint, Frankfurt: Minerva, 1964). There is currently an inexpensive reprint-of-the-reprint available on demand from Nabu Public Domain Reprints, with an erroneous attribution of authorship to Henry Seville.
9. Recall Genest, "Le *De futuris contingentibus*," 251.
10. Calvin Normore, "Descartes's Possibilities," in *René Descartes: Critical Assessments*, ed. G. J. D. Moyal (New York: Routledge, 1991), Vol. III, 68–83.
11. Gloria Frost, "Thomas Bradwardine on God and the Foundations of Modality," *British Journal for the History of Philosophy* 21, no. 2 (2012), 368–380.
12. Sarah Hogarth Rossiter, "Foreknowledge, Free Will, and the Divine Power Distinction in Thomas Bradwardine's *De futuris contingentibus*" (Doctoral Dissertation, Western University 2017): https://ir.lib.uwo.ca/etd/4432.
13. A good primer on this topic is Simo Knuuttila, "Time and Creation in Augustine," in *The Cambridge Companion to Augustine*, ed. Eleonore Stump and Norman Kretzmann (Cambridge: Cambridge UP, 2001), 103–115.
14. Augustine of Hippo, *The City of God against the Pagans*, translated by Robert W. Dyson (Cambridge: Cambridge UP, 1998), 11.6.
15. Augustine of Hippo, *Confessions*, translated by Henry Chadwick (Oxford: Oxford UP, 1991), 11.24.31.

16. As some contemporary philosophers have pointed out, there may be problems with understanding how such interaction between an inhabitant of timeless eternity and the world in time could occur. This problem is, in some sense, rather like the Cartesian problem of mind-body dualism, insofar as it seems a puzzle to understand how entities operating on entirely different principles or "planes of existence" from one another could in any way affect, or be affected by, each other. But this puzzle is quite far beyond the scope of our present study.

17. An historical overview of this criticism may be found in Richard Sorabji, *Time, Creation, and the Continuum: Theories in Antiquity and the Early Middle Ages* (Ithaca: Cornell UP, 1983).

18. For discussion, see Knuuttila, "Time and Creation," 105–107, as well as three works by Augustine: *De Genesi contra Manichaeos*, edited by Dorothy Weber, CSEL 91 (Vienna: Verlag der Österreichischen Akademieder Wissenschaften, 1998) 1.2.3–4; *Confessions* 11.10.12, 11.12.14, 11.30.40; *City of God* 11.4–5.

19. Linda Zagzebski has cited Boethius as the originator of this metaphor, which has strong resonance with Augustine's own discussions of divine foreknowledge. See Linda Zagzebski, "Foreknowledge and Free Will," *Stanford Encyclopedia of Philosophy* (Summer 2017 Edition), ed. Edward N. Zalta: https://plato.stanford.edu/archives/sum2017/entries/free-will-foreknowledge/

20. See Adams' introduction to her translation (with Kretzmann) of Ockham, *Predestination, God's Foreknowledge, and Future Contingents*, as well as her enormous two-volume study of Ockham's philosophy, *William Ockham* (South Bend, Indiana: Notre Dame, 1987). William Lane Craig has provided a more succinct summary in *The Problem of Divine Foreknowledge and Future Contingents from Aristotle to Suarez* (Leiden: Brill, 1988), 146–68. For Alvin Plantinga's treatment of the topic, see "On Ockham's Way Out," *Faith and Philosophy: Journal of the Society of Christian Philosophers* 3 (July 1986), 235–69.

21. Joseph A. Magno, "Ockham's Extreme Nominalism," *Thomist: A Speculative Quarterly* 43 (July 1979), 414–49.

22. An eminently useful overview of the discussion of the problem leading up to the thirteenth and fourteenth centuries, which particularly sets up Ockham's response to the same, can be found in Adams, *William Ockham*. In particular, chapters 1, 2, and 4 are helpful in understanding Ockham's context, Ockham's rejection of the dominant view of his contemporaries, and Ockham's own nominalist response. Adams has also written a more concise overview of the topic in "Universals in the Early Fourteenth Century," in *The Cambridge History of Later Medieval Philosophy*, ed. Norman Kretzmann, Anthony Kenny, and Jan Pinborg (Cambridge: Cambridge UP, 1982), 411–39.

23. Henry of Harclay was a student of Duns Scotus and near-contemporary of Ockham and Bradwardine at Oxford, where he served as University Chancellor for the last few years of his life until his death in 1317.

24. Adams, "Universals in the Early Fourteenth Century," 429 and 434.

25. Adams, "Universals in the Early Fourteenth Century," 434; Adams, *William Ockham*, 13.

26. William Ockham, *Opera Theologica* II, *Opera philosophica et theologica,* ed. Gedeon Gál *et al.*, 17 volumes (St. Bonaventure, N.Y.: The Franciscan Institute, 1967–88), 117ff.

27. Ockham, *Opera Philosophica* II (as above), 363ff.

28. A classic text outlining Ockham's theory of propositions is that of Philotheus Boehner, O.F.M., "A Medieval Theory of Supposition," *Franciscan Studies* 18, no. 3–4 (September–December 1958), 240–89.

29. Ockham never again left the Continent after that point, spending the remainder of his life embroiled in and writing about political controversies, both religious and secular, until his death in 1347. On this, see Adams' introduction to PPD, 1–2.

30. PPD q. 2, art. i–ii.

31. PPD q. 2, art. iii.

32. PPD q. 2, art. iv.

33. In this respect, Ockham is following the trail generally considered to be first broken by John Duns Scotus. See Knuuttila, "Time and Creation."

34. Thomas Bradwardine, *De futuris contingentibus* (hereafter DFC), ed. J.-F. Genest, *Recherches Augustiniennes* 14 (1979), 280–336. Translations of this text are my own and can be found in the appendix of Hogarth Rossiter, "Foreknowledge, Free Will, and the Divine Power Distinction."

35. DFC 3a–40g.

36. DFC 21: *aliquod est futurum contingens ad utrumlibet et prescitum a Deo in isto instanti presenti, et quod tamen possibile est pro isto instanti presenti quod non sit futurum nec prescitum a Deo.* "*Ad utrumlibet,*" "in either [of two] ways," is a technical term in medieval discussions of modality that can be understood broadly to distinguish a sort of genuine contingency from things that are *technically* contingent, but for all intents and purposes *almost* necessary (*ut in pluribus*) or *almost* impossible (*ut raro*). For example, flipping a heads on a single coin toss is an event that is contingent *ad utrumlibet*, whereas flipping 100 consecutive heads might be said to be contingent only *ut raro*.

37. DFC 22a: *[S]ic: sequitur quod possibile est quod aliquod sit futurum quod nunc non est futurum. Consequens est falsum, quia, si sic, ponatur illud instans in esse, et sit A, et arguitur sic: A est futurum nunc, et prius non fuit futurum, igitur mutatur de non futuro ad futurum; et non sic mutatur propter mutacionem in seipso, cum non sit adhuc; igitur oportet quod, si A mutatur, sit propter mutacionem in alio. Consequens est falsum, quia sic arguitur de possibili quod A potest mutari de non futuro ad futurum sicut arguitur de inesse.*

38. DFC 23a: *[S]i Deus habet prescienciam futurorum contingencium ad utrumlibet, sequitur quod Deus potest velle et promittere oppositum nunc sciti, promissi et voliti ab eo. Consequens est falsum, quia sic Deus potest mutari de scitis, volitis et promissis, quod est contra illud Malachie 3:« Ego Dominus et non mutor »; et ita sequitur quod non erit sic sicut Deus promisit vel voluit fore, igitur Deus mutatur.*

39. Geoffrey Chaucer, "The Nun's Priest's Tale," lines 474–86: "But I ne kan nat bulte it to the bren / As kan the hooly doctour Augustyn, / Or Boece, or the Bisshop Bradwardyn, / Wheither that Goddes worthy forwityng / Streyneth me nedely for

to doon a thyng, - / "Nedely" clepe I symple necessitee; / Or elles, if free choys be graunted me / To do that same thyng, or do it noght, / Though God forwoot it, er that I was wroght; / Or if his wityng streyneth never a deel / But by necessitee condicioneel. / I wol not han to do of swich mateere; / My tale is of a Cok, as ye may heere." Chaucer, *The Canterbury Tales: Fifteen Tales and the General Prologue*, 2nd edition, ed. V.A. Kolve and Glending Olson (New York: W.W. Norton, 2005). The translation into modern English is my own.

*Chapter 14*

# Time after Time

## *Gregory of Rimini, Contingents Past and Future, and Augustinian Critique*

Matthew Vanderpoel

The fourteenth century, typically presented as a critical and fractious century in Latin Christian thought after the heights of the scholastic project in the thirteenth, has nevertheless denied any easy generalization to historians for decades. Central in virtually any telling of the era's scholastic thought, however, is Gregory of Rimini, an Augustinian friar deeply invested in preserving the substance of his order's namesake's thought, an innovative thinker central to the spread of cutting-edge philosophy from Oxford to Paris, and a widely read author whose traces can be seen in virtually all university theologians of the latter half of the fourteenth and the whole fifteenth century.

This chapter analyzes Gregory of Rimini's method as a thinker, taking his treatment(s) of past contingents as a concise case study. I will argue Gregory models a distinctive, and distinctly Augustinian, strand of academic critique within the later Middle Ages. Gregory is in fact a radical thinker who seeks to critically intervene in philosophical and theological method by contesting binary frameworks, challenging teleological thinking, and construing new assemblages for analytic inquiry. This interpretive reorientation throws into relief axes of Gregory's radicalism that have been under-acknowledged due to scholars' inertial perception of Augustinianism as a "conservative" discourse amid late-medieval universities.

To that end, we will first look at Gregory's provocative argument, rehearsed under Distinctions 42–44 of the first redaction of his *Sentences* commentary: not only is the past not necessary in a strong sense but God can also actually change a past thing. Next, Gregory will be historiographically contextualized within the intellectual landscape of fourteenth-century Europe. Then, particular attention will be called to *how* Gregory uses quotation and authority in his argument on past contingents. Finally, Gregory's interventions in scholastic method will be refracted onto the study of late-medieval theology more broadly, pointing to a number of avenues for future research.

Gregory, taken on his own terms, may push us to reorient our understanding of fourteenth-century thought more broadly. In doing this, I follow in a longer historiographic tradition that figures Gregory as particularly instructive for any attempted synthesis of fourteenth-century scholasticism. On the one hand, his insistent combination of terminist methods and Augustinian partisanship has rendered him a challenging limit case for most taxonomies. On the other hand, Gregory's prominence (both among his contemporaries and in his reception) mitigates against placing him near the periphery. Damasus Trapp, for instance, centered Gregory's Augustinianism to counter early-twentieth-century narratives that saw the era as one of ascendant speculation.[1] Shortly thereafter, Heiko Oberman advanced a modified form of Trapp's thesis, arguing that Gregory forces us to recognize the existence of a substantive "right-wing" faction within the larger umbrella movement of "nominalism" characteristic of the era.[2] Numerous other scholars have turned to Gregory to ground arguments about his era more broadly or to serve as a benchmark for reading one of his contemporaries on more specific issues.[3]

This pattern of interventionist, if not downright revisionist, readings of Gregory is suggestive in itself. Gregory's idiosyncratic and complicated place within the intellectual discourses of his time and place(s) is a function of his own critical posture. I intend, accordingly, for the historiographic and theoretical upshots of this chapter to echo, *mutatis mutandis*, Gregory's own. Let us turn now to him.

## SITUATING TIME AND GOD IN GREGORY

Gregory of Rimini, an Augustinian friar born sometime around 1300, had a rather itinerant career teaching in various Augustinian *studia* in Italy, studying theology and lecturing at Paris, and ultimately becoming the prior general of the Augustinians shortly before his death in late 1358. Most importantly for our purposes, he lectured on Peter Lombard's *Sentences* in Paris probably from 1343 to 1344 and revised his commentary thereon in the subsequent few years. The *Sentences* was a comprehensive series of questions, authorities, and arguments on virtually all topics pertinent to academic theology, and it served, alongside the Bible, as the anchor of theological study in the medieval university. Typically, as part of the requirements for the Master's degree, one would have to lecture and comment on the *Sentences*. In the later Middle Ages especially, these commentaries dilated on the opening questions of the *Sentences*, serving as methodological prolegomena to theological inquiry. Gregory's commentary on books I and II of the *Sentences* survives in a number of manuscripts and underwent a number of printings during the early-modern era. This commentary stands as an outstanding contribution to both philosophy and theology.

Perhaps the most studied aspect of Gregory's commentary is his treatment of future contingents vis-à-vis divine foreknowledge. Largely precipitated by the innovative work of Peter Auriol, who claimed that future contingents (e.g., "Socrates will play a synthesizer") are neither true nor false and thus cannot be known to be true by God, the question of how God could meaningfully know future states of affairs without rendering them necessary in a deterministic fashion became increasingly pressing and widely engaged in the middle of the fourteenth century. Gregory provides a particularly lucid and precise defense of a compatibilist position (sc. that God can know the future without it being necessary) that is a starting point for many later thinkers. However, he follows up on this discussion with a consideration of a less common problem: Can God change a past event? Relatedly, are past events necessary or contingent? Gregory is not content to treat the question of temporal contingency from only its usual vantage point.

Gregory's exploration of past contingents is framed by his larger consideration of a scholastic commonplace: the idea of God's ordained and absolute power. In privileging this distinction, Gregory is in good company. As a result, it has served as something of a third rail of fourteenth-century intellectual history. Earlier scholarship saw it as a stark principle that carved out space for divine tyranny, subjecting the created order and human life to the threat of an arbitrary and unrestrained God. This view, rightly, became the object of incisive criticism by historians of Christianity and of philosophy. The corrective, by and large, has argued that the category of absolute power itself presumes that of ordained power and that the former was never understood as superseding the latter.[4] Gregory's own definition, found in an appendical digression between hypothetical arguments and counterarguments about the limits of God *de potentia absoluta*, bears this out.

Nestled amid his discussion of God changing the past, Gregory gives his definition of the ordained and absolute power of God. The ordained and absolute power of God are not to be understood as two distinct powers, he tells us. Each is one way of talking about God's singular power. With this proviso out of the way, he gives a tidy definition:

> God can do, according to God's ordained power, whatever God is able to while abiding by God's own eternal law and decree. And this decree is no different than God's will, by which God has willed eternally that God will do these or those things in this or that way. However, what is meant by God being able to

do something according to God's absolute power is what God is able to do, simply and absolutely.[5]

Gregory illustrates his point by turning to Christ's words in John 10:18, where Christ claims the authority to take up his own spirit despite the eternal decree that dictates he will indeed lay it down. Even if the events are not co-possible, they are not both impossible in that God could have chosen either option.[6] As a result of using this example, technical language notwithstanding, the point is fairly intuitive. We can clarify further. For example, by his absolute power, Socrates is able to go to the library. However, if we are talking about a specific time, when Socrates happens to be getting ready for a fun night at the discotheque, we understand that by his ordained power, Socrates cannot go to the library. He has already decided to do something else that precludes that option. The distinction of absolute and ordained power, at least as presented here, largely boils down to a common-sense distinction between what one could do and what one is going to do. This is not so much scholastic hair-splitting as it is an application of phenomenology of the will and possibility.

The overarching question that gets Gregory to the topic of past contingency is fairly straightforward: "whether God is able to make anything possible, according to God's absolute power."[7] Apparently relying on the Lombard, whom he cites, Gregory sketches some arguments to the effect that God cannot make anything possible: God cannot act contrary to God's will, God must not do certain sorts of actions, and God cannot do something that is not good.[8] Arguing the contrary, Gregory shows the ample biblical and patristic sources affirming God's omnipotence. Gregory wryly implies that it certainly takes some creativity to explain away the "all" (*omne*) from "all powerful" (*omnipotens*).[9] With this traditional scholastic set-up, Gregory prepares to offer his own answer.

After clarifying that the previous answers all equivocate a bit on terms like "possible" and "make," Gregory asserts that the proposition "God is able to make any possible enunciable true" is true or false depending on how we construe the terms.[10] Similar to our Socrates example given earlier, Gregory explains that while God has the potential to do just about anything, when one is specifically talking about *positively* accomplishing something, God is not able to make any possible state of affairs true (given God's decrees, the necessity of certain enunciables like "God exists," etc.). In illustrating this distinction between positive and negative doing, Gregory gives an example that looks ahead to his later discussion on past contingents: can God make something that was not be? Gregory says God can only do this in the *negative* sense, that is, by not prohibiting something or by not making it happen actively. Thus, God can make something that was not be by no longer positively making it the case.

He cites Augustine in *City of God* 12.17 for evidence: "God has made it that things, which God established, would formerly not be the case—while they were not—and later would be the case—when they began to be."[11] The upshot is that God may be said to do or be able to do many things that God does not always or actively accomplish in fact. Because many such propositions about possibility and divine power are true, from a certain point of view, Gregory's digression here illustrates a methodological response: one must not only identify the terms at stake but also cycle through a variety of different perspectives to discern the matter at issue. Indeed, the passage cited of Augustine itself is part of a larger argument that humans cannot simply apply their own creaturely frame of reference to the Deity.

Shortly thereafter, Gregory cites a string of Augustinian statements from various texts to unpack the argument that God's omnipotence must be understood as encompassing both positive and negative doing, depending on the specifics. Crucially, the Augustinian citations all take a slightly different tack in describing the question. The first (from *De diversis quaestionibus octoginta tribus* 3) asserts that God does not make humans worse; we do not hold a wise man accountable for the scope of evil, how much less so should we God.[12] The second (from *De libero arbitrio* 3.16.46) argues that blaming the Creator for sin would absolve the human sinner, and the third (from *Enchiridion* 24.96) rather directly posits that not willing to not let something be is as viable an option as willing to do something.[13] While the overall structure of the commentary's organization suggests a deductive argumentation through arguments and counterarguments, the substance of Gregory's writing here relies on a synthesizing reading of selections approaching a topic from different angles (sc., the relationship of God to evil, human responsibility, and types of accomplishing something). While the reliance on Augustine in this project is certainly largely a function of Gregory's position as an Augustinian hermit, it also suggests that Augustine, for Gregory, serves as a methodological model of this synthesizing, nonlinear approach to theology.

Shortly thereafter, Gregory raises the question of God's ability to make a past thing to not have been. Thanks to the editors' meticulous work preparing the recent critical edition, we now know that this entire section was removed by Gregory in his later editing of his commentary; the ramifications of that redaction will be considered later in this chapter. Gregory offers a rather provocative opening assertion: "God is able to make any past thing to not have been."[14] Unpacking this statement gives something of a representative summary of Gregory's views on contingency, divine freedom, time, and a number of other commonplaces in late-medieval scholasticism.

Gregory's first argument for this proposition considers whether such an action would result in a contradiction. If a past thing could not have been without any subsequent contradiction, then of course that possibility is open to God. He walks through his thinking: "Now, [the proposition] 'Adam was not' does not say that Adam was *and* was not, nor do any more contradictions follow from this statement than do if one says that the Antichrist or some other thing—which in truth will be—will not be."[15] Here, he echoes his earlier example of Christ being able to take up his spirit, even though he was in fact going to die. Gregory points out that we trust, because of divine revelation, that certain things will happen, and yet we do not understand that the future is necessary in any way that restricts human will.

Up to this point, Gregory has been limiting his discussion to the contingency of the past in a relatively abstract sense. He has argued that while God has made the created order to proceed a certain way in time, God could have *de potentia absoluta* made the created order differently. This is, on the face of it, a rather soft sense of contingency—virtually no one would argue to the contrary. Yet he signals he may be up to something more. Gregory here posits an at least logical similarity between the contingency of past and future things, implying that the past-ness of the past does not render it—at least in this aspect—significantly different from the future. Asserting that the past is contingent in this stronger sense would have been a minority opinion in Gregory's day, though not unprecedented.[16]

But in his second argument, Gregory may up the ante. He distills the first argument into a syllogism: "[It is possible that] God did not want to make Adam; therefore God did not make Adam, and, further, therefore Adam was not."[17] Shifting some of the verb tenses, then, he introduces a new phrasing: "It is possible that Adam was not; therefore, God is able to make it that Adam will not have been."[18] The shift in language, from the perfect tense to the present, stands out. The temporal juxtapositions accrue as he concludes this line of reasoning:

> Anything that God was able to will from eternity, God is *now* able to have willed from eternity, and what God was able to not will, God is able not to have willed. Therefore, although God did will from eternity to produce Adam, God is nevertheless able to not have willed that and is able to have willed not to create, just like God was able to from eternity.[19]

It seems clear that here, at least, Gregory has shifted to consider that (*de potentia absoluta* of course) God could in some form of the present eternally will what in some form of the past God had not eternally willed. The fact that Gregory immediately turns to unpack this at much greater length signals he is aware of the boldness of this proposition. Indeed, this is such a strong assertion for mid-fourteenth-century Paris, that scholars still disagree about whether and to what extent we should take Gregory at his word here. It remains possible that the scope of power over the past for Gregory is limited to past propositions about future events.[20]

Of particular interest is how Gregory argues this position. He goes on to offer an additional thesis on the question: "Every future thing is able, by the absolute power of God, not to be; therefore every past thing is able by the [absolute] power of God not to have been."[21] Gregory blurs the distinction between past contingents and future contingents to posit God's freedom in the past. Such a distinction relies on the situated perspective of human life in time, which clearly would not constrain God in the same way.

Let us consider Gregory's next argument about the necessity of the past. He cites Anselm who in *Cur deus homo* 2.17 asserts that necessity does not accomplish things, but rather the will of God does.[22] Gregory is eager to draw out the consequences of Anselm's viewpoint. He pounces on a potential contradiction: "For just as often as he says something incorrectly is said to be impossible for God—like God may make something that has past not be past—he then says something, which God established God would not do in the future, before it has happened, is impossible in the way something, which God has done, is not able to not have been done."[23] Gregory sees two options. The first would be to simply declare all these situations impossible, but apparently Gregory is not totally satisfied with that solution. The second is that the impossibility identified here would be conditional. Gregory lays it out formally as such, "If God proposes God will do A, A will happen, and yet the consequent is simply contingent. And Anselm thinks similarly about the past."[24] Immediately afterward, Gregory goes on to spell out that according to this understanding of consequent necessity, one can say that the past, present, and future are all necessary. This necessity, though, coexists with contingency.[25]

However, this defense of (a soft form of) God being able to change the past is present only in the earliest redaction of Gregory's *Sentences* commentary.[26] The removal almost certainly was a result of the investigation of John of Mirecourt's theses on God's power over temporal contingents that were condemned in 1347.[27] Gregory may have felt it expedient to self-censor his views.

## SITUATING GREGORY IN TIME

How does potential self-censorship inflect our interpretation of Gregory's place in the larger arc of late-medieval theology? This requires us to revisit the historiographic landscape.

At least in the orbit of university faculties of arts and theology, fourteenth-century thought was dominated by an array of nettlesome disputed questions, often overlapping though at times diverging: nominalism versus realism, terminism versus modism, Ockhamism versus old-style Aristotelianism. In the middle of the fourteenth century, these lines started to come into focus, eventually being standardized as a division between the old and new approaches (*via antiqua* and *via moderna*) in the early fifteenth century.[28] In all these questions, however, the implicit issue is to what extent a given late-medieval thinker diverges from earlier medieval views. Thus, persisting from the first pejorative usages of *modernus* in contrast to the established, to the *antiquus*, right up through contemporary scholarship, the study of fourteenth-century theology in particular is superimposed onto a backdrop where novel radicalism competes with traditional conservatism. To be sure, individual figures often resist easy categorization in such a facile schema. Nevertheless, it forms the latent basis for interpretation.

Perhaps the most meticulous and groundbreaking treatment of Gregory of Rimini is offered in numerous articles written by and in the *Sentences*-commentary edition edited by Damasus Trapp. Trapp pushed back against an older, and rather under-supported, formulation that Gregory was the *antesignanus nominalistarum*: the standard-bearer of the nominalists. On the contrary, Trapp argued, Gregory was the pivotal figure behind the 1347 condemnations of nominalism in Paris.[29] While later scholars have convincingly shown that Gregory was not, in fact, pushing the condemnations of 1347,[30] Trapp's reading has stuck in other ways.

First, while seeking to disentangle Gregory from association with what he considered "the mania of the logico-critical" thinkers of the fourteenth century,[31] Trapp nevertheless placed Gregory at the heart of a major trend in the era's scholasticism: an historico-critical attitude, marked by attentive care for sources and for common sense. In so doing, Trapp positions Gregory as a golden mean between overly radical and disappointingly diffident scholastics of the fourteenth century, beset on all sides unfairly. In his memorable prose, he describes it so: "The sinister halo of Gregory probably came from a fusion of two strong animosities, the animosity of the Antiqui against one of the outstanding Moderni, and the animosity of sympathizers of Mirecourt against the promoter of the condemnations [of 1347]."[32] In so doing, Trapp aims to salvage Gregory as a licit authority for theological research by those who reject certain tenets of Ockham and his followers on dogmatic grounds.

This sober-minded Gregory appears in many other scholarly accounts. For instance, Heiko Oberman gives Gregory pride of place in his famous delineation of the "schools" of nominalism. Here, Gregory is put in the "right-wing" school, which avoids the perceived excesses of radical nominalists (again, Mirecourt is the exemplary villain) and suggests an implicitly commendable continuity between Gregory and the traditional authorities of Latin Christianity. Even beyond Oberman's description of Gregory, it is clear the article as a whole seeks to differentiate most fourteenth-century scholastics from the "radical" modernists. While Oberman is less hyperbolic in his language than Trapp, and although he remains less than convinced of the explanatory purchase of Trapp's delineation of two critical attitudes,[33] he still contrasts Gregory to the "left-wing school of Nominalism," centered in England and tending toward skepticism.[34] Gregory is to be placed in the right-wing school that "takes an Augustinian stand, in contrast to the Pelagian trends we observed in the English left-wing."[35] Thus, while Oberman tries to nuance Trapp's two attitudes into four schools, his overarching structure still is staged as a push and pull between radicalism and more traditional Christian thought.

In the wake of such approaches, William Courtenay suggested that "the nominalism of the fourteenth century, if we are to really understand it, must be studied nominalistically"—that is, by recognizing the difficulty of fitting individuals neatly into schools or even under more abstract labels like "Ockhamist" or "nominalist."[36] Courtenay, crucially, notes that diverging views cannot be taken to stand for partisan opposition.[37] The fourteenth century's diversity is not sufficient grounds for labeling it a century of partisan crisis. In a similar vein, Zenon Kaluza has shown that much of the supposed factionalism of the fourteenth century, in Paris at least, results from overreading the era's own heuristics for categorizing systems of thought.[38]

These interventions pose a question: How should we understand the intellectual project of a figure like Gregory? Was he a conservative voice of reason resisting a critical age? Or was he instead an idiosyncratic thinker forced to watch what he said? A tentative, although productive, answer may be found, I suggest, within the *method* of Gregory's discussion of the question of whether God may change the past. Specifically, Gregory is distinguished by his use of quotations as case studies. That is to say, Gregory often does not cite an authority simply to provide a premise or justify an argument. Rather, Gregory frequently uses a passage from an authority to draw out the explanatory force of a distinction he has already specified.

For example, as we noted earlier, Gregory drew on a number of quotes from Augustine to illustrate that whether something is impossible to God depends upon whether one construes God's doing as a positive accomplishment or a negative allowance. To be sure, none of the citations seem to presume, much less draw out, the distinction Gregory has. Instead, Gregory quotes the *Enchiridion*: "[for God] it is as easy to perform what he wills as it is to not permit what he does not will."[39] In the original context, Augustine is arguing from a privative metaphysics of evil to establish that God never wills evil. The force of the quote there is that if evil actually had existence, God could still prevent it from existing. In Gregory's hands however, Augustine's line becomes a test case: Does a distinction between positive and negative doing cohere with, or at least not contradict, the authority in this passage?

To be clear, Gregory is not misreading or misrepresenting Augustine in this case. Rather, Gregory aims to show that his rather scholastic subtlety accords with a wide range of Augustinian statements on related topics. Instead of finding a place where Augustine defines impossibility or various modes of doing, Gregory devises a definition and then sees if it measures up in a variety of different Augustinian contexts.

Gregory's usage of Anselm to delineate the necessity of the past as merely consequent is more of the same. The cited passage of Anselm, as we saw earlier, does not pass muster by fourteenth-century standards of argumentation; Anselm treats necessity as a force driving things rather than a description of things. Nevertheless, Gregory reads Anselm with commendable charity, discerning how his language could be understood to provide a form of internal consistency. Gregory acknowledges at least two possible such readings, but then explores the one that coheres with his own stated position. Gregory reads other sources not simply as authorities, not as viewpoints to be criticized, and not as necessarily asking the same questions he is.

We have not quite come full circle back to a modified form of Trapp's historico-critical reading of Gregory. Despite his clear fondness for the historico-critical thinkers of the fourteenth century, especially the Augustinians, Trapp also sounds notes of disquiet:

> Interest in the sources is a very healthy sign and symptom in a theology which deals with historical revelation, historically closed and historically developed. But as soon as past developments come under consideration the theologian must take a stand, otherwise he is only a recording device; if many past developments come under the lens of the theological observer, a historico-critical judgment must be formulated many times.
>
> In the early decades of a historical movement the enthusiasm of quoting, of looking over the shoulder of ancient or more recent predecessors, may become a fashion, pedantic and affected, perhaps eclectic.[40]

Trapp sees even the careful, attentive historical work done among the Moderni as suspect, running the risk of being overly dismissive on the one hand or becoming a passive "recording device" on the other.

Gregory, though, has shown that he aims to move beyond any such continuum of conservative versus radical. Further, Gregory's discussion of God's ability to change the past has also demonstrated, in his nuanced engagement with quotations, that he is not simply invested in his own personal solutions to the question. The subtlety of his distinctions and his bold formulations instead function to generate new forms of intellectual connection. His quotations draw in past authorities as interlocutors to wrestle with, not raw material to be culled for arguments. Though a nominalist, Gregory did not understand his own intellectual place nominalistically, but rather sought to integrate himself into a larger constellation of thinkers asking hard questions across different universities, different orders, and even different times. In so doing, even within the highly codified generic form of a *Sentences* commentary, Gregory's writing resonates with Augustine's vast, largely occasional corpora of writings. Indeed, this topical breadth and flexible thinking, dynamically brought to bear even on precise questions, suggests that it may not be simply Gregorian, but also Augustinian.

## CONCLUSION

Looking from such a vantage point beyond Gregory to the fourteenth-century intellectual landscape more broadly, his irenic approach to inquiry suggests a number of new ways that the era's intellectual history could be approached. First, scholars' growing discomfort with delineating partisan schools of thought may meaningfully point toward looking more concretely for alternative assemblages of thinkers. While more focused studies of individuals' influences and interlocutors certainly have and will continue to further this end, Gregory's creative use of historical sources suggests that new ways of construing late-medieval scholastics' relationship to their forebears, offering more fulsome models of reception, would be welcome. Second, Gregory's relatively daring formulations about the contingency of the past—formulations that had to be curtailed in the context of 1347's condemnations—further illustrate the need for more study about censure and self-censorship in the university contexts of the era. In particular, research about informal modes of content regulation is called for beyond formal condemnations or heresy proceedings. Third, Gregory's profile continues to call for larger, revisionist study of the Augustinian order in the later Middle Ages. Informed by norms of the Reformation era, the Augustinians continue to be taken as conservatives relative to their colleagues, but the evidence for such a framing only grows thinner.

In sum, received narratives about the decline of medieval thought after the high scholasticism of Thomas, Albert, and Bonaventure, continue to color scholars' reading of fourteenth-century theologians. Looking carefully at individual thinkers is essential to more accurate understandings of the numerous intellectual currents that crisscrossed Europe and its universities on the eve of modernity, but we ought also to look to those very thinkers for new ways of modeling connection, influence, and reception in late-medieval thought. Gregory, a reader and writer in the mold of Augustine, provides an exceptional starting point.

## NOTES

1. Damasus Trapp, "Augustinian Theology of the 14th Century: Notes on Editions, Marginalia, Opinions and Book-Lore," *Augustiniana* 6 (1956), 150–52, 82 ff.

2. Heiko A. Oberman, "Some Notes on the Theology of Nominalism: With Attention to Its Relation to the Renaissance," *Harvard Theological Review* 53, no. 1 (1960), 55.

3. Daniela Ciammetti, *Necessità e contingenza in Gregorio da Rimini*, Philosophica (Pisa: ETS, 2011). This monograph convincingly positions Gregory as *the* standout luminary on questions of necessity and contingency in his era. See also the earlier study by Francesco Fiorentino, *Gregorio da Rimini: contingenza, futuro e scienza nel pensiero tardo-medievale* (Roma: Antonianum, 2004). On more focused topics, John T. Slotemaker has turned, in part, to Gregory's attentive reading of Augustine on the psychological analogy of the Trinity to challenge the claim that the view may be generally attributed to theologians of the Middle Ages: "Reading Augustine in the Fourteenth Century: Gregory of Rimini and Pierre d'Ailly on the *Imago Trinitatis*," in *Studia Patristica: Papers Presented at the Sixteenth International Conference on Patristic Studies held in Oxford 2011*, ed. Markus Vinzent (Leuven: Peeters Publishing, 2013). Likewise, C. L. Loewe notes the unprecedented sophistication and influence of Gregory's discussion of intension and remission within the fourteenth century: "Gregory of Rimini on the Intension and Remission of Corporeal Forms," *Recherches de théologie et philosophie médiévales* 81, no. 2 (2014), 273–330. From another angle, James Halverson's monograph on predestination in Peter Auriol devotes considerable attention to tracing influence and reaction in Gregory's reception of Auriol: *Peter Aureol on Predestination: A Challenge to Late Medieval Thought*, Studies in the History of Christian Thought (Leiden: Brill, 1998), 134–57. Kathryn Tachau's magisterial study of high- and late-medieval semantics gives thoughtful treatment to Gregory's epistemology: *Vision and Certitude in the Age of Ockham: Optics, Epistemology, and the Foundations of Semantics, 1250–1345* (Leiden: Brill, 1988).

4. The classical study remains: William J. Courtenay, *Capacity and Volition: A History of the Distinction of Absolute and Ordained Power* (Bergamo: Lubrina, 1990). Francis Oakley gives a lucid, concise summary in: "The Absolute and Ordained Power of God in Sixteenth- and Seventeenth-Century Theology," *Journal of the History of Ideas* 59, no. 3 (1998), 440–49.

5. Gregory of Rimini, *Gregorii Ariminensis, OESA, Lectura super primum et secundum sententiarum*, vol. III, ed. Adolf Damasus Trapp et al. (Berlin: W. de Gruyter, 1984), 368: "dicitur deus ad intellectum recte intelligentium posse de sua potentia ordinata, quod potest stante sua ordinatione et lege aeterna, quae non est aliud quam eius voluntas, qua aeternaliter voluit haec vel illa et taliter vel taliter se

facturum, illud autem dicitur posse de potentia absoluta, quod simpliciter et absolute potest." All translations of Gregory in this chapter are my own.

6. Gregory of Rimini, *Lectura super primum et secundum sententiarum*, III, 368: "Sunt enim haec incompossibilia 'deus proposuit se moriturum' et 'deus non morietur' referendo ad tempus idem. Quamvis autem ista sint incompossibilia, quia tamen illa ordinatio non est necessaria, id est non est necessarium sic deum ordinasse, quin immo possibile est ipsum ordinasse et voluisse oppositum."

7. Gregory of Rimini, *Lectura super primum et secundum sententiarum*, III, 355: "Utrum omne possibile fieri deus de sua absoluta potentia possit facere."

8. Gregory of Rimini, *Lectura super primum et secundum sententiarum*, III, 355.

9. Gregory of Rimini, *Lectura super primum et secundum sententiarum*, III: "sicut nec illud signum 'omne' inclusum in illo nomine 'omnipotens' videtur aliud posse distribuere in proposito."

10. Gregory of Rimini, *Lectura super primum et secundum sententiarum*, III, 358: "Prima est quod omne possibile enuntiabile deus potest facere esse verum, accipiendo facere communiter ad primum et ad secundum modum. Secunda est quod non omne eiusmodi possibile deus potest facere esse verum, primo modo accipiendo facere."

11. Gregory of Rimini, *Lectura super primum et secundum sententiarum*, III, 358: "Hoc modo loquitur Augustinus 12 De civitate dei capitulo 17, cum ait: 'Res, quas deus condidit, et ut prius non essent, egit, quamdiu non fuerunt, et ut posterius essent, quando esse coeperunt.'"

12. Gregory of Rimini, *Lectura super primum et secundum sententiarum*, III, 359: "tamen deus non potest facere Petrum peccare, quia, sicut dicit Augustinus 83 Quaestionum quaestione 3, 'deo auctore non fit homo deterior;' est enim haec 'tanta culpa, quae in sapientem quamvis hominem cadere nequeat,' multo autem minus in deum."

13. Gregory of Rimini, *Lectura super primum et secundum sententiarum*, III, 359: "Unde Augustinus 3 De libero arbitrio capitulo 37: 'Si peccatum, inquit, tribuere volueris conditori, peccantem purgabis, qui nihil praeter sui conditoris instituta commisit; qui, si recte defenditur, non peccavit.' . . . Omnipotenti enim bono, uta it Augustinus Enchiridio 104, 'quam facile est quod vult esse facere, tam facile est quod non vult esse non sinere. Hoc nisi credamus, periclitatur ipsum nostrae fidei initium, qua nos in deum patrem omnipotentem credere confitemur.'"

14. Gregory of Rimini, *Lectura super primum et secundum sententiarum*, III, 362: "Tertia conclusio est quod quamlibet rem praeteritam potest deus facere non fuisse."

15. Gregory of Rimini, *Lectura super primum et secundum sententiarum*, III, 362: "Non enim dicens quod Adam non fuit dicit Adam fuisse et non fuisse, aut aliqua contradictoria sequuntur dictum suum non plus, quam sequatur, si dicatur quod Antichristus aut aliquod aliud, quod secundum veritatem est futurum, non erit."

16. Richard Gaskin offers Peter Damian, Gilbert of Poitiers, and William of Auxerre as candidates for such a view: "Peter of Ailly and Other Fourteenth-Century Thinkers on Divine Power and the Necessity of the Past," *Archiv für Geschichte der Philosophie* 73, no. 3 (2009), 274. Thomas Bradwardine is often also associated with such a view; the fullest study is: Edith Wilks Dolnikowski, *Thomas Bradwardine: A View of Time and a Vision of Eternity in Fourteenth-Century Thought* (Leiden; New

York: E.J. Brill, 1995). Chris Schabel, however, contests whether any medieval held to this position at all: Christopher Schabel, "Redating Pierre d'Ailly's Early Writings and Revisiting his Position on the Necessity of the Past and the Future," in *Pierre d'Ailly: Un Esprit Universel à l'Aube du XVe Siècle*, ed. Jean-Patrice Boudet et al., Actes de colloque (Paris: Inscriptions et Belles-Lettres, 2019), 62–63. This disagreement will be revisited further.

17. Gregory of Rimini, *Lectura super primum et secundum sententiarum*, III, 362: "Deus non voluit Adam producere; igitur deus non produxit Adam, et ultra, igitur Adam non fuit."

18. Gregory of Rimini, *Lectura super primum et secundum sententiarum*, III, 362: "Possibile est Adam non fuisse; igitur deus potest facere quod Adam non fuerit."

19. Gregory of Rimini, *Lectura super primum et secundum sententiarum*, III, 362: "Quod autem primum antecedens sit possibile, probatur, quia omne, quod deus potuit ab aeterno velle, potest nunc ab aeterno voluisse, et quod potuit non velle, potest non voluisse. Quamvis igitur ab aeterno voluerit producere Adam, potest tamen non voluisse, et potest voluisse non producere, sicut et ab aeterno potuit." Emphasis mine.

20. Christopher Schabel has argued—with further argument forthcoming—that discussions of God's ability to make the past not have been pertain to linguistic concessions designed to preserve compatibilism. In his discussion of Pierre d'Ailly (who relies heavily on Gregory), Schabel notes that Pierre thinks human freedom means that, even if there is a true proposition about a future action of ours, we are able to make it false. Accordingly, some true past events (namely, past propositions about yet future actions) may be made false. Nevertheless, Pierre specifies that if the past propositions are merely about the past, they are not able to be made impossible. See Schabel, "Redating Pierre d'Ailly's Early Writings and Revisiting his Position on the Necessity of the Past and the Future," 72–82. See also his earlier treatment of Rimini on this point: *Theology at Paris, 1316–1345: Peter Auriol and the Problem of Divine Foreknowledge and Future Contingents* (Aldershot; Burlington, VT: Ashgate, 2001), 271–72. A conference presentation on this same question is forthcoming with Vrin, originally given May 12, 2016, at Conférences Pierre Abélard 2016, Université Paris-Sorbonne: "Y a-t-il eu des auteurs scolastiques ayant soutenu que Dieu pouvait défaire le passé?"

21. Gregory of Rimini, *Lectura super primum et secundum sententiarum*, III, 364: "Omne futurum potest per dei potentiam absolutam non fore; ergo omne praeteritum potest per dei potentiam non fuisse."

22. Gregory of Rimini, *Lectura super primum et secundum sententiarum*, III, 364.

23. Gregory of Rimini, *Lectura super primum et secundum sententiarum*, III, 365: "Tum quia dicit non recte dici impossibile deo esse, ut, quod est praeteritum, faciat non esse praeteritum. Tum quia dicit ita impossibile esse aliquid, quod deus proposuit se facturum non esse futurum, antequam fiat, sicut illud, quod fecit, non potest non esse factum."

24. Gregory of Rimini, *Lectura super primum et secundum sententiarum*, III, 365: "si deus proponit se facturum A, A erit, et tamen consequens est simpliciter contingens. Et similiter intelligit de praeterito."

25. Here, Gregory seems to be assuming a similar set of outlooks to his earlier argument on future contingents where he provides what M. J. F. M. Hoenen has called a "logico-semantic approach" to the problem, using logic to define God's foreknowledge as certain even if the future events under consideration are contingent. See Hoenen, *Marsilius of Inghen: Divine Knowledge in Late Medieval Thought* (Leiden: Brill, 1992), 203–04.

26. The editors of the critical edition of the *Sentences* commentary of Gregory provide good manuscript evidence that some of the *additiones* are in fact original material later excised: Gregory of Rimini, *Lectura super primum et secundum sententiarum*, III, xxxiv–xxxix. As for external evidence, identifying the discussion of the past's contingency as removed material fits both with the scrutiny such propositions might have faced after the 1347 condemnations of Autrecourt and Mirecourt as well as with the version of Gregory's arguments known to later thinkers, for example, Pierre d'Ailly. See: William J. Courtenay, "John of Mirecourt and Gregory of Rimini on Whether God Can Undo the Past: Bradwardine and Buckingham," *Recherches de théologie ancienne et médiévale* 40, no. Janvier-Décembre (1973), 162.

27. See the corrigenda in the reprint of Courtenay's article on the topic: William J. Courtenay, "John of Mirecourt and Gregory of Rimini on Whether God Can Undo the Past: Bradwardine and Buckingham," in *Covenant and Causality in Medieval Thought: Studies in Philosophy, Theology and Economic Practice* (London: Variorum Reprints, 1984), 174a.

28. William Courtenay has traced the shifting notions of *antiqui* and *moderni* through the fourteenth century, before their eventual reification in the "split between Wycliffite/Hussite realism on the one side and the terminism of Pierre d'Ailly and Jean Gerson on the other," a split first identified by N. W. Gilbert. See: "Antiqui and Moderni in Late Medieval Thought," *Journal of the History of Ideas* 48, no. 1 (1987), 3; N. W. Gilbert, "Ockham, Wyclif, and the 'Via Moderna'," in *Antiqui und Moderni: Traditionsbewusstsein und Fortschrittsbewusstsein im späten Mittelalter*, ed. Albert Zimmermann, Miscellanea mediaevalia (Berlin: de Gruyter, 1974).

29. Trapp, "Augustinian Theology," 181–82.

30. Once again, see: Courtenay, "Whether God can undo the past."

31. Trapp, "Augustinian Theology," 151.

32. Trapp, "Augustinian Theology," 190.

33. Oberman, "Some Notes on the Theology of Nominalism: With Attention to Its Relation to the Renaissance," 52: "It is too early to pass final judgment on these [Trapp's] suggestions; but, even though it might be possible to make a real distinction between the historico- and logico-critical attitudes, this will not lead us to a better grasp of the essence of Nominalism."

34. Oberman, "Some Notes on the Theology of Nominalism: With Attention to Its Relation to the Renaissance," 54.

35. Oberman, "Some Notes on the Theology of Nominalism: With Attention to Its Relation to the Renaissance," 55.

36. "Late Medieval Nominalism Revisited: 1972–1982," *Journal of the History of Ideas* 44, no. 1 (1983), 164.

37. He gives, as an example, Wodeham's devising of the *complexe significabile* as object of knowledge in contradistinction to Ockham's identification of demonstrative conclusion as the object of knowledge. While these two views each had their own proponents and successors, Wodeham and Ockham nevertheless were "personally and professionally close." See Courtenay, "Late Medieval Nominalism Revisited: 1972–1982," 162–64.

38. Zenon Kaluza, *Les querelles doctrinales à Paris: nominalistes et realistes aux confins du XIVe et du XVe siècles* (Bergamo: Lubrina, 1988).

39. Gregory of Rimini, *Lectura super primum et secundum sententiarum*, III, 359: "quam facile est quod vult esse facere, tam facile est quod non vult esse non sinere."

40. Trapp, "Augustinian Theology," 185.

*Part V*

# AUGUSTINIAN AND BUDDHIST TEMPORALITIES

*Chapter 15*

# Non-Presentism in Antiquity
## *South Asian Buddhist Perspectives*
Sonam Kachru

When meeting Buddhist practitioners in majority-white communities in America[1] one will sooner or later run into advice which seems to accord the present—or "the now," "the here and now," or "the moment"—a particular sort of privilege. Some will think that there's nothing odd about this. After all, have not Buddhists always privileged the present?[2]

Have they? "We are not sure," said Eihei Dōgen in *The Eternal Mirror* (*Kokyō*), "of what these myriad images (*banshō*) of the present are made."[3] That suggests to me that privileging the present may not always have been readily intelligible. Consider two sorts of privilege. Ontological presentism is the thesis that the present alone is real. Practical presentism recommends that the present alone is worth attending to. As we'll see, these may align: one might believe that one ought only to attend to what exists and the present uniquely exists. But ontological and practical presentism need not align: one might think that the present uniquely exists and yet find value in allowing one's attention to dwell on the past or on the future. One might recommend dwelling on the present without pressing any claims regarding the ontological status or even definition of the present.[4]

My thesis is this: Neither ontological nor practical presentism was ever (a) exhaustive or (b) paradigmatic of South Asian Buddhist attitudes to time in antiquity.[5] Some might find this surprising. Surely there are good reasons to believe that what Pierre Hadot took to be true of Hellenistic spiritual exercises holds of ancient Buddhism: Attention to the present is key.[6] Nevertheless, to make the case for (a) and to suggest the truth of (b) I will attempt to indicate, all too cursorily, some of the vast range of attitudes to time and temporality which an undue emphasis on ontological and practical presentism has concealed. Presentism can be a desert landscape. The "attentional landscapes" of Buddhist thought and practice are far more lush environments.

Discussing such attentional landscapes, we shall all too briefly touch on the self-evidence of thinking (e.g., with Derrida)[7] that only temporally present items can be experientially present, such that modes of engaging with past and future or non-actual possibilities (e.g., other worlds) cannot be experientially present.[8] We shall also consider more metaphysical concerns with the existence of past and future and the definition of the present, touching on some but not all of the difficulties involved in individuating the present.[9] To get a sense of the lay of the land, I'll begin by stipulating some working definitions of ontological and practical presentism.

## ONTOLOGICAL PRESENTISM

Ontological presentism in the Buddhist case confines reality to the present. This involves two claims. First, what is temporally present is *paradigmatic* of what it means to exist: to exist just means to be present, and vice versa. Second, reality is exhausted by the concept of concrete particulars.[10]

One may demur on either point. We will meet with Buddhists from the tradition of Sarvāstivāda who consider that part of reality which consists in concrete and spatio-temporally connected events to be a four-dimensional array of events of many times.[11] In contemporary Anglophone metaphysics, such a view is sometimes called eternalism. But we must be able to distinguish those who maintain that concrete particulars (whether past, present, or future) exist from those who say that we should not conflate reality with an array of particulars in the first place.

The Buddhist four-dimensionalist typically holds that reality is a non-univocal concept: it is comprised of paradigmatically temporal items (like the event of registering sensory input) as well as paradigmatically non-temporal items (like nirvana or space). The Buddhist eternalist, however, maintains that reality is a univocal notion: a mode of presence not bound up with past, present, or future.

The aforementioned context offers some scope for disagreement among Buddhists, whether presentist, four-dimensionalist, or eternalist. All Buddhist philosophers we shall meet here, however, agree on this much: concepts of time (e.g., "past," "present," and "future") used in speaking of concrete particulars do not track an independent substance. Instead, these are ways of bringing what contemporary metaphysicians call tropes or property particulars (Pāli: *dhammā*; Sanskrit: *dharmāḥ*)[12] under descriptions.[13] More accurately, concepts of time are ways of bringing the dynamic and serial occurrence of property particulars under a description. Let's assume a property particular, denoted by B (for "being blue," where $B_n$ indicates it is happening now, perhaps only relative to some observer).

Temporal concepts are ways of organizing talk of the occurrence of B, which, to keep things simple, we'll treat as preceded by some instance of the property particular blue and as succeeded for a while by another instance of the same:

$$\ldots B_{n-1}, \ldots B_{n-1}, B_n, B_{n+1}, \ldots B_{n+m}, \ldots$$

Buddhists speak of this as a dynamic, connected sequence (*saṃtāna*).[14] Some Buddhist philosophers take the sequence to be a necessary unit for applying temporal concepts. Others maintain that an individual moment of a sequence is sufficient, though they typically appeal to some further structure. For example, some think that each instance bears properties, which cause the instance to come into being, abide, and cease.[15] According to the thesis of momentariness, we are to understand that each instance of a property particular ends as soon as it begins, to be succeeded by the next instance given the right conditions. On the view described just earlier, each "moment," then, may have a dynamic profile capable of supporting temporal designation. Others deny this, taking the sequence of moments and not any single evanescent moment to be the only item in the metaphysical neighborhood with any such structure capable of yielding dynamic variation.

Those who think that moments are sufficient for the application of temporal concepts may be called "thin presentists;" and those who maintain that a sequence is necessary, "thick" or "serial presentists." This distinction helps us get a grip on some debates important to Buddhist presentism. Consider the question: Whether or not there exists such a thing as a thin present, do we ever perceive it? For Theravada, it is the present constituted as a sequence (*santati-paccuppanna*)—and not the moment (*khana*)—which we *see*.[16] As this shows, explicit invocations of what in Anglophone letters came to be called a "specious present" are common to Buddhist presentists.[17] For Buddhist philosophers working in Sanskrit, the combination of the momentariness of events with the fact that experiences take time entailed different points of emphasis concerning the specious or serial present. Typically, attention is thereby paid not only to the temporal properties of content but also to the temporal properties exemplified by the vehicles of content, the episodes of awareness themselves.[18] For example, what we *can claim to know* in perception might not only have something like a sequence rather than a moment in view, but it might be such as to require experiential memory, as Vasubandhu argued.[19] Later, Dharmottara was to make the point in metaphysical (and not only epistemic) terms: what we can intend in any kind of conscious experience necessarily involves a sequence of moments. Such sequences are not strictly of a piece with what there is, being constructed by the conceptual capacities of epistemic subjects.[20]

There are other questions. Some philosophers, like Vasubandhu, say that phenomenological accounts of what we can experience are left untouched by differences between those who describe concrete particulars as enduring and those who hold momentariness to be true.[21] That is, we could never experientially realize the metaphysical description of momentariness in ordinary experience. (It was maintained that the moment-to-moment perceptual experience of momentariness could be thought to be a refinement, consequent to arduous practice of meditation, of our everyday experience of impermanence.[22]) Interestingly, it is the Buddhist four-dimensionalists who maintain that we can be in strictly perceptual contact with a thinly specified present.[23]

The difference between thin and thick presentism—and the questions described earlier—are particularly important for the trajectory of Buddhist thought after the fifth century in South Asia. They are important, that is, when Buddhist thought was to become predominantly presentist. But for the period we are interested in, the difference between thin and thick presentism is not the most important distinction to draw. As Vasubandhu defines it, the view that contrasts with four-dimensionalism is not presentism exactly, but rather a view that affirms "the existence of the present and that part of the past which has not yet given forth its result."[24] On this view, *what exists* cannot be settled by a blanket appeal to a temporal position: it requires case-by-case analysis. Let's call this non-naïve presentism. Understanding it will help us see what is at stake in the debates between presentists and non-presentists.

It may not be obvious why this should count as presentism. Vasubandhu's view allows the present to share existence with even parts of the remote past. How remote? In Sanskrit, one can use the aorist tense (instead of the imperfect or perfect) to indicate something that is past but whose processes or effects are still felt in the present. It is this aorist that is used by some Buddhists to describe the possibility of experiential memory of past lives.[25] That's pretty remote from the present. Shouldn't it effectively count as a variety of non-presentism? No. The view that existence should be tied to causal efficacy is the key to the presentist's privileging of the present: to exist, says the presentist, is the same as being present because to exist means to be causally efficacious.[26] And it is not only this principle which non-naïve presentism preserves.

We only have to ask: Where is the past that is taken to exist by non-naïve presentism? The presentist locates that part of the past, which exists in a special location and in a certain way: it exists in the moments of the life of a person as receptacles of unactualized dispositions seeded from the past.[27] The four-dimensionalist thinks of the person at a time much more thinly, without appeal to traces of the past or unactualized dispositions of any kind. So understood, a person does not bear his or her lived history moment to moment.

Instead, a person is stretched out over time: at any moment, they consist only in a set of categorical properties and sets of real relations holding between the present and different temporal parts of the person.[28] Differently directed temporal attitudes such as memory and expectation are, on this view, held to be such real relations, as we shall see further.

My use of "stretching" earlier in the text is derived from the Sanskrit verbal root *"tan,"* meaning to extend or to stretch; this is the root from which the word for a connected sequence, *santāna*, is derived. Persons are thought by both Buddhist presentists and four-dimensionalists to be connected psychophysical sequences. Such usage allows one comparative salience. As Sean Hannan reminds me, Augustine too (in *Confessions* 11) thinks of temporality in general (and human temporal experience in particular) in terms of *distentio animi* or the "stretching-apart of the soul or mind" into its pasts, presents, and futures.[29] Though there are non-naïve Buddhist presentists as well as naïve Buddhist presentists,[30] and though it is the naïve presentist who captures the verbal formulation of presentism most simply, it is the non-naïve presentist who shows us how it is that, to use now an Augustinian as well as a Buddhist image, one sort of account of the stretching of persons might most decisively differ from another.

Presentists, fundamentally, believe that what there is involves change and that what there is changes.[31] The naïve presentist would have this happen only by virtue of changes in what is present; for the non-naïve Buddhist presentist, any change in the present can potentially change which parts of the past exist. Thus, the process of stretching out might be said to be actual but not, strictly speaking, the products at different times. Against the four-dimensionalist, the presentist says that we are not *actually* stretched out in real relations holding between myself now and the items that were or will be in connection with me in different temporal locations. What the four-dimensionalist believes, however, she can only believe because she does not think that changes in what is present involve any changes in *what there is*.

## PRACTICAL PRESENTISM

One might enjoin others to inhabit the present or to direct one's attention to the present without ontological commitment. One might count on intuitive understanding: "Live in the moment!" "Be mindful of the present!" "Just be!" Such talk is not new. In 1934, one could read the following in *The Buddhist Bible* under "Sacred Aphorisms:" "Do not dwell in the past, do not dream of the future: concentrate the mind on the present moment."[32] In his "The Aunt and the Sluggard," first published in 1916 in *The Strand Magazine*, P. G. Wodehouse invented the poet Rockmetteller (Rocky) Todd who could capitalize on the ability of men's magazines (like *The Strand Magazine!*) to peddle neo-Stoic bromides in an era characterized by what G. K. Chesterton, thinking of Fitzgerald's Omar Khayyam, called "carpe diem religion."[33] Todd writes the way Fitzgerald's Khayyam sounds: "Be Today! Be!" He even had an argument: "The past is dead / Tomorrow is not born."[34]

Familiarity aside, it is not obvious what is intended by such injunctions. Strictly speaking, Buddhist philosophers recognize that there is a distinction between sensory and non-sensory experience. The distinction is based on temporal restriction: the contents of strictly sensory experience, unlike experiences in which cognitive capacities have played a role, are restricted to the present, whereas, as Vasubandhu says in verse 1.23a of his *Treasury of Metaphysics*, cognitive awareness "has a non-restricted field: being sometimes in the present; sometimes in any of the three times; and sometimes not in time at all."[35] To ask one to restrict awareness to the present sounds like it is implying that one can only ever enjoy sensory experience or, perhaps, that sensory experience is the paradigm for felicitous experience. Each would have been a curious thing for a classical Buddhist philosopher to maintain.

We need more plausible candidates for being in the present. To that end, this section offers a distinction between the concept of "being mentally present" in the moment and a conception of "presence," which marks out some experiences as more valuable than others. In the next section, I'll take up the difference between what I will call specific and covering imperatives. This will allow us to attempt successively deeper and more textually fine-grained account of Practical Early Buddhist Presentism. (In what follows, readers may wish to keep in mind parallels with Augustine's apparent rejection of Stoic present-mindedness in *Conf.* 11.)[36]

Consider, briefly, the range of things it might mean to be present in the moment. It might mean, among other things, any of the following: not letting *some object* drop out of view; vigilance against distraction, or calling to mind *the task* one is engaged in or its importance; not letting one's attention over time be guided;[37] metacognitive monitoring of experience; or forgoing metacognitive thought or guidance for absorption in a nonautomatic activity.[38] This is enough to show that the phrase can mean too many things and that some of its meanings are in tension.

Consider: Is one "present" during sex? It is hard to argue with those who claim that we are least likely to have our thoughts wander—and so least likely to count as distracted—when having sex.[39] But were we to treat the mind so concentrated as paradigmatic of a mind present, we would not be able to predict the young monk Samiddhi's response to the goddess who tried to seduce him as he stood only in his underrobe having just finished his bath. In a verse alive with complex wordplay,[40] the goddess teases the beautiful young man, effectively saying to him: "Don't miss the present opportunity to have the time of your life, when it is appropriate, given your youth." She goes on to say: "Don't overlook the here and now—what is right before your eyes—for what *takes time*," meaning by that last the deferred goals of ascetic cultivation of self-control.

The goddess could very well claim to endorse the practical presentism of *The Buddhist Bible*, believing "being present" to be an intuitive, uncontested norm. Against this the monk recalls that absorption in sex and sensual experience more generally are, in effect, censorious modes of being in time, and time so spent is a kind of death. Non-distraction is insufficient. Indeed, the monk's way of being present is the opposite of "letting be." It is the exercise of vigilance, which requires guidance set by a task and the exertion of excruciatingly fine metacognitive control. The point is not to forgo speaking of being present "here and now." The point, instead, is this: "being present" is a normative and not empirical conception. And it is either a banal conception or one which is potentially historically and culturally variable; when interesting, it is almost certainly contested.

This suggests a problem when "being present" connotes *presence* as some unmediated or direct mode of experiential contact with what there is or with what matters most.[41] The normative notion of being present to which Samiddhi appealed meant something like this: "Be vigilant with respect to one's overarching commitments at the level of the intelligibility of one's form of life, the only one which can free one from time understood as death." But such vigilance is different from enjoying presence in the sense of having some subset of everything that now exists somehow "show up" in just the right way without one's imposing any kind of normative conceptual or practical frame on what there is.

To be sure, premodern Buddhists have at times invoked something like presence. Those ways of talking have a history and a long history of contestation.[42] But it is by no means obvious that early Buddhism prioritized this way of thinking about practice. Even the meditative cultivations, which do pick out ongoing and dynamically variable processes as sites of attention—like breath—are understood as task-dependent and concept-dependent forms of guidance. Practice often involves description-dependent acknowledgment of what one is attending to and why. And the range of possible sites of attention is not exhausted by "present" items, nor are the modes of engagements with possible sites of attention restricted to those which are normatively "silent."

In fact, contemporary students of Buddhist meditation have too often privileged the concrete. Consider the following two ways to acknowledge why doing justice to Buddhist practices requires consideration of spheres of possible attention whose intelligibility and value are not confined to the concrete. The first involves a reconstructed argument from Vasubandhu. Though a presentist, he argues against presence by clarifying the relationship between concreteness and the intelligibility afforded by language. The second involves a reconstruction of a meta-perspective on meditation from the *Pratyutpannasamādhisūtra,* an influential text which redefines what it means to speak of "presence" and "the here and now."

Many objects of attention in early Buddhist meditation are description-dependent. Vasubandhu helps us see why this fact calls into question the intelligibility of talk of presence. The argument has two parts. First, Vasubandhu argues that one cannot, at one and the same time, keep in view language understood as semantic value and language as the empirically describable concrete items (e.g., physical features of voice), which serve as the causal occasions for the conveyance of semantic value. Semantic value, *what we understand,* cannot be described as having temporal parts. But this makes it categorically unlike the making or receiving of articulate sounds, which, being a process, intrinsically takes time.[43] The argument concludes thus: if these are two incommensurable ways of describing the same thing, it would be a categorical mistake to seek to relate them (as cause and effect, or as ground and explanandum, or what have you). But if that is so, we should not think, then, that something with semantic value could be "confined" in something concrete like the present moment.

Second, to endorse talk of presence in the case of something which involves language is to think that some use of language is capable of capturing the present and only the present. Wittgenstein, for one, once spoke of something like this in terms of a "phenomenological language," a language capable of modeling and recording immediate experience.[44] What would that involve? Vasubandhu considers the possibility that semantic value might just consist in a set of things present, which enjoy real and isomorphic relations with our use of bits of language, as a phenomenological language would require.[45] But how would our descriptions exclude past and future and remain confined to the present? Perhaps by saying that there is one use of language by which we come to mean present things and only present things, while another variety of use does duty for our ability to mean things past and future. Vasubandhu says that is not the case. The possibility of reference to past and future is internal to all use of language and is included in our ability to mean anything at all, including the present.

These two arguments suggest that to inhabit language is to inhabit an order of intelligibility and generality that is not describable in terms of real and isomorphic relations holding between empirical bits of things. Nor should we speak of such an order of intelligibility in the same way we speak of processes: which is to say, we should not think of them in temporal terms at all.[46] The argument easily extends to anything that is description-dependent, like the practices of attention with which we began. The point can be made more starkly if we add to generality the issue of modality, something we have only touched on above in our appeal to past and future. In fact, the influential *Pratyutpannasamādhisutra* makes modality an explicit topic of concern and offers us another way to question the meaning of presence.[47]

Some think back to a country of origin. Some think of places experienced in a dream. Think of what is happening in such cases, says the *Pratyutpannasamādhisūtra*,[48] as the mind's getting in touch with what, from our perspective, might be considered alternative contexts of possible experience. The text offers cases of pasts remembered, alternate presents dreamt, and futures anticipated as preliminary examples[49]: for, if temporal modality is any clue, we are often in such experiential contact with other contexts. But along with the familiar cases earlier, there might also be other worlds: radically different sets of possible experiences with their own alternating contexts. What if, as this text argues, these are not only mere possibilities but alternative "here and nows" with which, through practice and in certain contexts (e.g., in dreams), we might be able to get into experiential contact?

If "being present" means "made experientially real," then the "present" appealed to by the presentist need not behave as a categorical reference to one moment, which is the case. It might, instead, index merely one frame of counter-factual possibility among many. Presentism and talk of experiential presence can come apart. By "the experientially present," not all Buddhists intended for us to think of the temporal present. In fact, to speak of other "here and nows," which can be made present (*pratyutpanna*) or real in experience is a good candidate for a covering theory of what Buddhist meditative praxis—when capaciously construed—historically involved: the enactment of doctrinally specified possibilities.[50] On this view, meditation involves not perception but imagination; it is perhaps less like a process of disinterested seeing and more like wishful seeing.[51]

These arguments show that some Buddhists were in a position to appreciate how some varieties of presentism are forms of actualism, confining reality to what is the case.[52] If counter-factual frames for possible experience, like language, may not be described as contained within an order of moments, we might say that Buddhists are enjoined to go beyond the present twice-over: in some genres, like the narrative *avadāna* or stories of past lives, some protagonists (and implicitly, readers) are enjoined to recall in memory not only what they have forgotten of their past but their forgetting of it.[53] They are also enjoined to attend beyond the actual. They must see not only how their forgotten life has gone, but, like Dharmaruci, also reflect "on what would have been the continuous flow of [one's] life in the future, constant, uninterrupted cycle of rebirths."[54] Doing so is integral to the kind of ethical self-fashioning enacted by some Buddhist genres.

## BUDDHIST PRACTICAL PRESENTISM

There is also an ethical ideal one may recover for presentism. But one must do so with care. Rocky Todd's injunction—"Be Today! Be!"—offers scope for confusing two kinds of imperatives: Are we dealing with a norm enjoining a specific action (to do *thus and so*) or a proverbial one enjoining an overarching attitude but no specific action?

Curiously, the best example of an explicit and specific practice like attending to the present derives not from Buddhism but from the *Yogasūtra* III.52: "If one practices focused and unifying attention (*samyama*) on the [present] moment and its sequence ... one attains knowledge."[55] Attention to the present can unify the stream of thought and result in a state identified by the text with felicity. Here, commentators ally the practice with ontological presentism.[56] But focus on the present moment need not entail ontological presentism. In the case of the above practice from the *Yogasūtra*, the practitioner is said to move into an ultimate state that is not itself best described in episodic or temporal terms at all. Instead, it is a variety of eternalism, a non-temporally specified reality which subtends temporally describable processes.

Attention to the present can be more indirect and less programmatic, provided that we speak of attending to phenomena exemplifying presentness and not to metaphysically individuated present moments. The nun Paṭācāra, for example, contrasts attention to something like the dynamic present—exemplified by focusing on the flow of water from a height—with everyday busyness structured by practical rationality: doing $x$ for the sake of $y$.[57] To focus on the present can be to remove oneself and one's site of attention (the water) from the sphere of reasons and tasks. Paṭācāra does not use the water to bathe; instead, spontaneously, for no apparent reason, she attends to it. Freeing oneself from busyness allows the world to disclose itself in new ways, the poem lyrically suggests, changing what comes into view and how. Yet, however salutary, Paṭācāra's focus on the present is a prelude for a very different mode of being present, nirvana, which is described here only as freedom of mind and not as attention confined to the present.

To see why this matters, we must forego specific practices and look, instead, for practical presentism in Buddhist norms concerning overarching attitudes. At least here, the *Buddhist Bible* might not be on such tenuous ground: "[the radiant humans who shine like gods] do not grieve for the past; they do not long for the future; they live in the present," says the Buddha in the *Araññasutta*.[58] One might use "live in" to translate the verb "*yāpenti*," but it is better to be more literal: "they are content with," or "they *live on* the present." It's a recommendation to adopt with respect to time the kind of abstention ascetics exhibit with most necessities. One ought not to overindulge on what one does not, strictly, need.

The nonliteral rendering—couched without the overtones of the delightful verb "*yāpenti*" and asking us only to "live in the present"—gives us an all-too-general version of the norm, overly thin and suffering from its share of problems. First, such a norm would not be uniquely Buddhist: other examples can be found in ancient India.[59] Something this widespread, moreover, resonating across otherwise very different cultures, times, and philosophical orientations, might just be uninteresting, its precise valence lying somewhere between its being a truism and being vacuous.

Yet the Buddhist norm, unlike the overly thin one, is not entirely vacuous: it has a function beyond lexical humor. It reinforces an overarching ascetic culture, extending to time and inner virtues—manifested in patterns of attention—norms that were developed to regulate outer behaviors. Buddhist texts also offer arguments to complement such an extension: "One ought not seek to go over the past, nor anticipate in yearning the future (*atītaṃ nānvāgameyya nappaṭikaṅkhe anāgataṃ*)."[60] Why? Because, as the text goes on to argue, the present unlike the past ("which has already been left behind") and the future ("which is not yet to hand") is a unique sphere with respect to practical agency. It is available to us to make changes in. And we ought to try to make changes when we can, given the imminent possibility of death.[61] The idea is that some temporal modes of attention are self-defeating in the following way: they appear to involve the exercise of agency only to take us away from the sphere of practical efficacy altogether.

But Buddhists of the early period cannot believe (a) that attention to anything but the present is always infelicitous and (b) that having the present as one's object of attention is sufficient to make one's state of mind felicitous. Buddhist texts, including the *Bhaddekaratta sutta* from which I derived the argument earlier, do not endorse (b). One *can* cultivate infelicitous attitudes to present phenomena. As we saw earlier, "the present" and "attention to the present" are not empirical but normatively contested notions. The *Bhaddekarattasutta* distinguishes being "drawn away into present phenomena (*paccupanesu dhammesu saṃhīrati*)" and discerning (*vipas-*) the present.[62] The former is passive, the latter active and normatively stipulated. Given certain doctrinally mandated affective and cognitive skills, one no longer identifies with what is available in the present as one's own.[63]

If the present may also capture and hold hostage (*saṃhīra-*) attention in an infelicitous way, this weakens the asymmetry between past and future on the one hand and the present on the other. More pertinently, seeking to locate oneself in the present may run afoul of the deeper insight in early Buddhism that all modes of locating oneself in time might be suspect: "Give up what's in front (or, the future); give up what's behind (the past); give up the middle (the present) . . . with mind freed in every respect you will not return again to birth and old age."[64] The demanding conception of mental freedom does not privilege the present and requires freeing oneself from the order of temporal positioning entirely.

It also can't be that (a) attention to anything other than the present is always infelicitous. In Buddhist scholasticism, lack of shame for what one has done wrong, typically ranging over distant past actions as well touching on what has just been done, can be as infelicitous as being distracted from the present.[65] Such presentism won't do justice to the descriptions under which Buddhist donative rituals came to be understood over time. To give "for the sake of x and y," say for one's mother and father, can be to think of them as they were and as they might yet be. It is also to think of one's own future states.[66] In fact, presentism doesn't do justice to Buddhist commitments to the consequentialness of action more generally—to disregard past and future comes uncomfortably close to the kind of moral nihilism indicted as the paradigmatically wrong view in early Buddhism.[67]

It has been argued that some Buddhist historiographical genres (e.g., the Pāli and Sinhala *vaṃsa*-s) are sophisticated narrative experiments with temporal attention, attempting to generate in present readers a cognitive and affective dependency on events in the past,[68] thereby extending the causal efficacy the Buddha enjoyed in the past into the unfolding present, extending it into the future.[69] (Some genres, like narrative in story and law, support this more than others.[70]) There is certainly a link between such trans-temporal modes of attention and Buddhist modes of devotionalism, a particularly insightful explication of which we owe to Gyōnen's explanation of the Pure Land concept of *nen*, or intimate mind. According to this explanation, the thought of someone engaged in devotional practice in the present enacts the thought animating a Buddha's vow in the past to undertake arduous practice on behalf of sentient beings, including the practitioner. In practice, this unifies a practitioner's faith and the Buddha's wisdom, and, as Gyōnen writes, "[this condition of transtemporal nonduality] continues moment by moment."[71] From the perspective of thirteenth-century Japan, at least, it can seem as if it is deeply felt varieties of trans-temporal attention that constitute the most salient heritage of Buddhism.[72]

## IN SEARCH OF TIME PAST

Presentism threatens to attenuate the object by only considering the thinly defined present. Buddhist presentism, without the resources of substance metaphysics, can also attenuate the subject—the subject who can exemplify experiential presence is potentially pulled out of sociality and language,[73] producing someone entirely unlike one of the first Buddhist women, Ambapāli, who in *Therīgāthā* gave us a new role for memory.[74]

Her poem performs a variety of ways of self-knowing aimed at confirming the truth of the Buddha's teaching. It proceeds along three dimensions. First, she presents an anatomy of her bodily being, presenting herself as an inventory of parts—hair, head, eyebrows, eyes, and so on—attended to from her head to her feet. Second, each part is presented temporally: comparing what it was like at some previous time to what it is like now. Take, for example, the first verse: "The hairs on my head were once curly, / black, like the color of bees, / now because of old age / they are like jute."[75] And each verse ends by saying that this kind of variance is not at variance with what the Buddha taught. This hides a suggestion: since the Buddha taught the truth of variance, or change, the poem is arguing in effect that it takes time for the meaning and the truth of the Buddha's teaching to come into view. This is because the ultimate referent of his thought involves time.

Comprehension of the structure of truth requires a complex awareness. It seeks out not simply objects, but signs picked out from within an aesthetic frame of sensibility. Ambapāli does not only compare the body then and now; she compares, in effect, *perspectives* on the body. These perspectives are available at only some stages of life and from within a particular temporally appropriate cultural sensibility. She is offering a meta-comparison by comparing comparative frames.[76]

Ambapāli is not a creature of presence. She is neither passive nor confined to the present through sensation.[77] Time for Ambapāli is a set of interlocking epistemic standpoints. From the frame of the past and the culture of youth, the mood of the poem is nostalgic; interpreted again from the standpoint of the "now" of the poem—old age—the mood is freedom from such a temporally restricted (and implicitly presentist) sensibility. The temporal standpoints are not to be abandoned as one moves through time. They are to be recollected. There are two senses of recollection: (1) recalling the past in the sense of retrieving it and (2) being continuously mindful of how things look from the recovered frames. The past on such a mode of attention is a modality through which the meaning of the present can be revaluated.

There are also more direct ways in which the past can, so to speak, be present. The *Lotus Sūtra* invites us to think of the past existing in the present in something like a geological layer, which can be made explicit.[78] In a long-celebrated scene, a memorial emerges from the ground. The Buddha of our time enters into it and takes a seat alongside a Buddha of the past whose memorial it is. Just as some Buddhists argue that two objects cannot co-occupy a single space, so too some Buddhists think that more than one Buddha cannot occupy the same epoch. Not so the *Lotus*, with its vision of the coincidence and equality of times.

This is more radical than Ambapāli's meditation. Memorials typically house relics. And a relic need not be a sign. The relic might be the thing itself, present, even as the *Lotus* imagines the Buddha of the past to be present, out of sight.[79] Whereas Ambapāli's recovery of the past was hermeneutic, the *Lotus* suggests a visionary (and not a narrative) perspective on time.[80] Freud asked us to consider a psychical entity, Rome, with all its convoluted and fabulous history present and co-occupying a single layer.[81] The *Lotus* is asking of us a similar vision of sacred history. It is just that it is not a psychical space alone, but reality, which is being described. It need not be the past alone which is present.

Visionary quest narratives such as the *Gaṇḍavyūha* delight in characters coming into transformative visions of reality as past, present, and future, arrayed "as if they were contemporaneous realms in [variously imagined built] space,"[82] as if time were best captured in architectural and not chronological forms. Such scenes resonate with an apparent commonplace of early medieval South Asian narrative art. Buddhist narrative techniques favor depicting narrative progression involving some *x* by showing two or more tokens of *x* from different times in one place. With an eye on the plot of the story depicted, one can suggest that a "historical eye" would have seen different episodes. If one stays with the image, however, one can foreground the following historically situated possibility: the experience of a four-dimensional background which attention to nonvisual narrative can obscure.[83]

## VARIETIES OF BUDDHIST FOUR-DIMENSIONALISM

The Buddhist four-dimensionalist believes that their view on time flows out of what they make of our way of being in the world: we open out in thought to past and future, and not only in first-personal memory and anticipation.[84] We are stitched together by connections between what we do and the lasting changes induced in us at later times.[85] Thinking of our being persons, then, from inside and from sideways on, requires thinking of the existence of past and future.

Why? The core argument reconstructed for this view in Vasubandhu's *Treasury of Metaphysics* (hereafter, AKB) involves considering truth-makers and the grounds of intentional content. The Buddha spoke truly of past events and future consequences. Truth involves a real relation between utterances and truth-making entities. Real relations require their *relata* to exist. Thus, things past and future must exist.[86] More generally, "thinking of," intentionality or the directedness of thought, consists in a real relation between a present event (thinking) and whatever serves as its content. Past and future can serve as content and so exist.[87]

The response to the latter argument is to deny that intentionality requires real relations. The response to the former, along with denying truth-makers and strict correspondence as necessary for understanding truth,[88] runs as follows.[89] The four-dimensionalist's argument, Vasubandhu argues, treats the use of "exists" in certain sentences (e.g., "What was done exists.") as if it were a full-fledged verb, which is to treat it, in effect, as a tense-indifferent quantifier. As a result, one could say, for example, "There exists the lamp's having been on."[90]

Vasubandhu thinks this will saddle the four-dimensionalist with a possible inconsistency. This is because he treats existence as irreducibly tensed, and so treats tense as involving, in effect, irreducible sentence operators (e.g., WAS (Ø) or WILL (Ø)). Thus, to Vasubandhu, the aforementioned thought really expresses something like this: THERE NOW IS WAS (a lamp). Vasubandhu resolves the tension by arguing that, in natural language, "exists" does not always function as a verb (with quantificational force). It can function as what Sanskrit grammarians know as a tenseless particle with emphatic force.[91] Adding this to thinking with tense as a kind of sentential operator allows Vasubandhu to treat "There exists the lamp's having been on" as meaning "It is a fact that there was a lamp on," or simply: "WAS (there is a lamp)."

The questions are intricate and not merely verbal. The high-relief issue, again, concerns our picture of ourselves, our conceptions of truth and meaning, and our paradigmatic conception of existence. Is this conception tensed or not?[92] Even four-dimensionalists do not agree on some of these issues. In fact, it turns out that there is no one model of Buddhist four-dimensionalism. There are four, according to Vasubandhu's summary of the views of philosophers working from 50 C.E. to 200 C.E.[93]

With Dharmatrāta, one might think of a thing as a bundle of properties. To speak of change is to pick out some items in the bundle, which are different, while picking out others as the invariant frame. Temporal positions are like properties that can be gained or lost while we keep invariant the concrete particular (*dravya*) we are tracking, or the frame we use to track it. Perhaps a gesture toward thinking of temporal parts and "perdurance," this is unfairly assimilated by Vasubandhu to thinking of substantive change and "endurance."

With Ghoṣaka, one might think modally. He asks us to consider that a lustful person attracted to some particular woman could have been attracted to any number of other women. Ghoṣaka thinks of "being attracted to" as a two-place and real relation, given some one item $x$ and a field of possible items, which exist, but not all of which enter into a real relation with $x$. What does change, including temporal change—for "being at a time" is thought of as such a two-place relation—involve? Under some relevant relational description of $x$, change involves varying which items stand in real relation with $x$ and which others serve as possible candidates for such a relation.

With Vasumitra, we might think of how position confers value, as, to use their example, when a "|" in the tens' position represents a different value than in the hundreds' position.[94] Here too there is appeal to a preexisting structure of reality with respect to which change is deemed to have occurred. But Vasumitra's positions, unlike Ghoṣaka's relations, are actual and not merely possible.

The fourth position, that of Buddhadeva, is perhaps the earliest to note the distinction between talk of time in terms of what is present, past, and future, and talk of events in terms of being before and after. McTaggart would later enshrine these as the A-series and B-series, respectively.[95] Buddhadeva, in effect, was a B-theorist *avant la lettre*.[96] Moreover, he believed in the priority of the B-series: A-properties like "being past" should be analyzed in terms of their dependence on before and after (*pūrvāparama*).

Seeing things this way gives us relations, which can coexist, just as a woman can be mother and daughter at the same time. Vasubandhu thought such a view makes time effectively disappear.[97] For him, capturing the idea of change and thus of time requires some concept of progression and the mutual exclusivity of pastness, presentness, and futurity. Can relations of mutual ordering alone deliver that? Vasubandhu suggests that, to presentists, Vasumitra's structural realism of intrinsic direction and preexisting positions makes the best sense.

## REALITY, ETERNALITY, AND THE ONTOLOGICAL DISTINCTION

Buddhist four-dimensionalists believe the following: given a manifold of distinct types of phenomena, there do exist past, present, and future tokens of these types. But there are also Buddhist non-presentists who do not believe that reality is captured by a manifold of enumerable types. They believe in an ontological distinction between, on the one hand, concrete particulars and, on the other hand, something worth calling their reality. On this view, reality is nothing like a concrete particular or a set of concrete particulars. It is more like *the nature* of what is analyzed according to denumerable types of things. Reality so understood is not obviously captured by concepts of temporal existence like past, present, or future.

My appeal to an ontological distinction is based on Sthiramati's analysis of the philosophical grammar for a family of words for "what there really is" in his commentary to verse 25abc of Vasubandhu's *Thirty Verses*, which concludes that reality (*tathatā*) is so-called because of its always being thus (*tathābhāva*) or being an abstract state of affairs governing more than one type of particular, which means being invariant to change.[98] But there are other routes to the tenselessness of reality. The *Lotus Sūtra*, for example, believes that the state of being a Buddha is like nothing that can be expressed in an intrinsically temporal narrative order,[99] which conviction is emphasized again at the end of the *Vimalakīrtinirdeśasūtra*, when Vimalakīrti says of the Buddha: "I see him as not born of the past, not passing on into the future, and not abiding in the present. Why? Because this is the essence of reality."[100]

In a different genre, the Buddhist philosopher Nāgārjuna's arguments can be read as designed to induce in their readers a variety of attentional shift from time to timelessness. On such a reading, one can analyze his arguments as follows. Beginning with an ostensibly temporal context involving a dynamic process, an attempt at describing such a context metaphysically can yield an atemporal or tenseless context, one constituted by semantic entailments between concepts appealed to in the individuation of the apparently concrete phenomenon with which one began.[101] Nāgārjuna would have us understand that it is this tenseless context to which the Buddha was directing us, though the interpretation of what this, in turn, might mean has long been disputed.

Buddhist texts suggest two reasons why such eternalism can be overlooked. According to the *Lotus Sūtra*, our sense of temporality as impermanence suffuses our lives and our modes of valuation.[102] We orient ourselves in practical action by some variety of presentism, with the effect that eternalism is difficult to find intelligible or valuable. Second, it is easy to conflate empirical description with meta-conceptual descriptions tasked with underscoring modality, particularly given that Sanskrit employs temporal words in both capacities. Consider, for example, Vasubandhu's recognition that one can use "always" to indicate the necessity involved in identity, as when one speaks of some $x$'s always having the nature of $x$ and no other.[103]

The Buddha of the *Laṅkāvatārasūtra* says that "because the foolish naïve are attached to momentariness . . . they do away with even the unconditioned, committed to their view of utter destruction."[104] It is partly a certain impulse to presentism that has ruined them. The Buddha's own vision of reality, instead, is found in a later striking image: "Reality forever abides, and keeps its order, *like the roads* of an ancient city."[105] The text goes on to adduce an analogy to a person finding a lost city in the forest and discovering that its infrastructure is still sound. There are two points made here. The first is that, just like a lost city, reality pre-exists its discovery. That point is not new. In the *Nāgarasutta* of the Pāli canon,[106] the Buddha likens finding the path he has discovered to finding an ancient path to a city of old where the infrastructure, given suitable repairs, might still prove habitable. What's new in the *Laṅkavatārasūtra*'s use of the image is the emphasis on the structural features of the city, its network of roads. The world is a conjunction of structure and events, but reality—what really matters on this view—is order or structure without the kind of directionality which our lives or our search for knowledge and meaning impose on it. If Buddhadeva anticipated McTaggart's B series of time, the *Laṅkāvatārasūtra* anticipates McTaggart's recognition of the possibility of a non-temporal C-series exemplifying relations of order without directionality.[107] In attuning ourselves to such a non-directional order, the *Laṅkāvatāra* argues, lies freedom.

## CONCLUSION

Regrettably, one still comes across statements like the following: "Buddhists typically do not pay much attention to the passage of time."[108] The supposed reason for this is that Buddhists are preoccupied with a timeless felicity and aspirations of escape from physical time altogether. More common than this breathtakingly reductive generalization is a tacit appeal to the following disjunction: either Buddhists must subscribe to some variety of presentism or be judged to have sought only escape from time altogether.[109] In closing with Buddhist eternalism, I do not mean to contribute to oscillation between these options. My goal was to unseat the more troubling idea, which is this: presentism serves as the only source for meaningful conceptions of and attitudes toward time. Buddhist presentism, four-dimensionalism, and eternalism are complex responses to temporality, with none of them *obviously* involving an avoidance of time. At least, I hope our all-too-brief review of what I have called attentional landscapes of time in Indian Buddhist antiquity shows us the poverty of any armchair convictions on these issues.

Much more remains to be done. Some interlocutors in a Buddhist monastic code are depicted as believing that it is just not appropriate to go about one's life day to day not knowing one's place in time. The Buddha interceded. One must know, he said, "not only the date but the position of the sun and the stars and the moment [or, period of the day (*yud* in Tibetan, likely for Sanskrit *muhūrta*)] as well."[110] I take that to suggest that it will not do to divorce entirely the intelligibility of these attentional landscapes of time from the textures provided by everyday timekeeping. But that must be left for another time.

## NOTES

1. On the need to be precise here, see Natalie Fisk Quli's review of Ann Gleig's *American Dharma: Buddhism beyond Modernity* (New Haven: Yale University Press, 2019), in the *Journal of Global Buddhism* 20 (2019), 141.

2. Though not even at the beginning of white American enthusiasm for Buddhism would such generalization have been safe. Thus, even Jack Kerouac, not

the most informed or reliable student of Buddhist texts, saw fit to criticize what he had learnt of Zen for its valorization of conceptions of moments (or episodes of awakening) and, if I understand him aright, for privileging a certain conception of time (as episodic and consisting in sequentially present moments). He thought it occluded what he discerned of Mahāyāna commitments to "eternalism." See Kerouac, *Some of the Dharma* (New York: Viking, 1997), 301.

3. Quoted in Gudo Wafu Nishijima and Chodo Cross, *Shōbōgenzō: The True Dharma-Eye Treasury: Volume I*, BDK English Tripiṭaka Series (Moraga, CA: BDK America, 2007), 317.

4. One can find both attitudes in the phrase "immediacy of one's present-moment experience" used in Fronsdal, *The Buddha before Buddhism: Wisdom from the Early Teachings* (Boulder: Shambhala, 2016), 44. Nyanaponika Thera justifies his now infamous conception of "bare attention"—attention "concerned only with the *present*"—largely on pragmatic and therapeutic grounds, though the implication seems to be that past and future, unlike the present, do not fully exist; they are not "in the Here and Now." Nyanaponika Thera, *The Heart of Buddhist Meditation: A Handbook of Mental Training Based on The Buddha's Way of Mindfulness* (London: Rider and Company, 1973), 40. The failure to make the distinction between practical and ontological accents in Buddhist texts mars the otherwise superb work of Paul Mus, "La notion de temps reversible dans la mythologie bouddhique," *Annuaires de l'École pratique des hautes études* 47 (1937), 5–38, particularly 8–11.

5. I must confess to deliberately being vague. There is no standard periodization of South Asian history that is transparent and helpful, as has been argued in Christian Wedemeyer's *Making Sense of Tantric Buddhism: History, Semiology, and Transgression in the Indian Traditions* (New York: Columbia University Press, 2013), 60–65. I here mean by "antiquity" what students of Buddhist archaeology mean by "the early historic period" as seen from a slightly later period. On this, see Matthew Milligan, "The Development and Representation of Ritual in Early Indian Buddhist Donative Epigraphy," *Pacific World*, no. 15 (2003), 171. For the most part, I'll be citing works from 200 B.C.E. to 500 C.E.

6. See Jonardon Ganeri, "A Return to the Self: Indians and Greeks on Life as Art and Philosophical Therapy," *Royal Institute of Philosophy Supplement* 66 (2010), 119–135.

7. Jacques Derrida, "Violence and Metaphysics: an Essay on the Thought of Emmanuel Levinas," in *Writing and Difference*, tr. Alan Bass (Chicago: University of Chicago Press, 1978), 132.

8. See also Christoph Hoerl, "Experience and Time: Transparency and Presence," *Ergo* 5, no. 5 (2018), 127–151.

9. See, e.g., J. J. Valberg, "The Temporal Present," *Philosophy* 88, no. 3 (July 2013), 369–386.

10. My formulation of presentism is derived from a Buddhist debate on the semantics of existence, discussed further. Interestingly enough, an analogous debate also prefigures some contemporary approaches to what is called "existence presentism." See: Jonathan Tallant, "Defining Existence Presentism," *Erkenntnis* 79, no. 3 (2014), 479–501; Dean W. Zimmerman, "Persistence and Presentism,"

*Philosophical Papers* 25, no. 2 (1996), 115–126; Trenton Merricks, *Truth and Ontology* (Oxford: Oxford University Press, 2007), 123; and Ned Markosian, "A Defense of Presentism," *Oxford Studies in Metaphysics* 1, no. 3 (2004), 47–82. In what follows, I'll keep an eye on contemporary debates but take my bearings from Buddhist materials.

11. This formulation is derived from Zimmerman, "Persistence and Presentism," 213. Theodore Sider, "Four Dimensionalism," *Philosophical Review* 106 (1997), 197–231, treats four-dimensionalism as a thesis endorsing temporal parts. I will keep these issues separate, treating the former as concerned with *what* exists while committing to no further structure; the thesis of temporal parts, however, concerns *how* things exist. Even Buddhist presentists (like the Sautrāntika) might agree that things do not endure and should be spoken of as effectively having temporal parts, though these temporal parts do not have the ontological status the Buddhist four-dimensionalist wishes to grant them.

12. For speaking of *dharmāḥ* as tropes, see Jonardon Ganeri, *Philosophy in Classical India: Introduction and Analysis* (London and New York: Routledge, 2001), 99–103; Charles Goodman, "The *Treasury of Metaphysics* and the Physical World," *Philosophical Quarterly* 54, no. 216 (2004), 389–401.

13. Y. Karunadasa, *The Theravāda Abhidhamma: Inquiry into the Nature of Conditioned Reality* (Sommerville: Wisdom Press, 2019), 273–275; Steven Collins, *Nirvana and Other Buddhist Felicities: Utopias of the Pali Imaginaire* (Cambridge: Cambridge University Press, 1998), 143. This is not necessarily to say that *the meaning* of all the ways in which we talk about time reduce to one sort of thing, much less that the meaningfulness of all the ways in which one might conceptualize time may be reduced to facts about tropes. In the Theravāda tradition at least, the doctrine of a "plurality of times" (*samaya-nānatta*) seems to suggest that there *are various concepts* of time at play in convention, based on the various kinds of phenomena one seeks to bring under a description. Consider, to use one distinction articulated by Theravāda philosophers, the difference between concepts of temporal location, such as past, present, and future, and concepts of time involved in ordering of human life, ranging from daily routines to repetitive phenomena like seasons. The thesis of plurality of times seems to suggest that not all of these concepts need be commensurable. See Karunadasa, *Theravāda Abhidhamma*, 274, and Christoph Emmerich, "How Many Times? Monism or Pluralism in Early Jaina Temporal Description," in *Jaina Philosophy and Religion*, ed. Piotr Balcerowicz (Delhi: Motilal Banarsidass, 2002), 69–88.

14. Like Karunadasa (among others), one might wish to speak of the occurrence itself as an event. Dharmas, particularly when analyzed as sequences, are more event-like than substances, as recognized by Vasubandhu explicitly. On this, see Sonam Kachru, "Minds and Worlds: a Philosophical Commentary on the Twenty Verses of Vasubandhu," PhD Dissertation (University of Chicago, 2015), 79–80. But note that, unlike Sanskrit and English conceptions of an event, sequences possess internal causal structure. For later metaphysical accounts, see Itsuki Hayashi, "A Buddhist Theory of Persistence: Śāntarakṣita and Kamalaśīla on Rebirth," *Journal of Indian Philosophy* 47 (2019), 981–982.

15. Gelong Lodrö Sangpo, *Abhidharmakośabhāṣya, The Treasury of the Abhidharma and its (Auto) Commentary*, Vols. 1–4, tr. Louis de la Vallée Poussin (Delhi: Motilal Banarsidass, 2012), 1.587–591. See also Kachru, "Minds and Worlds," 110–112.

16. Karunadasa, *Theravāda Abhidhamma*, 275–276.

17. See: Holly Andersen, "The Development of the 'Specious Present' and James' Views on Temporal Experience," in *Subjective Time: the Philosophy, Psychology, and Neuroscience of Temporality*, eds. Dan Lloyd and Valtteri Arstila, (Cambridge MA: MIT Press, 2014), 25–42; Andersen and Rick Grush, "A Brief History of Time Consciousness: Historical Precursors to James and Husserl," *Journal of the History of Philosophy* 47, no. 2 (2009), 227–307.

18. Monima Chadha, "Time-Series of Epehemeral Impressions: the Abhidharma-Buddhist View of Conscious Experience," *Phenomenology and the Cognitive Sciences* 14, no. 3 (2014), 543–560.

19. Jonathan Silk, *Materials toward the Study of Vasubandhu's Viṃśikā I* (Cambridge MA: Harvard University Press, 2016), 217–219.

20. Th. Stcherbatsky, *Buddhist Logic*, Vol. 2 (London: Dover, 1962), 312; Helmut Krasser, Dharmottara's Theory of Knowledge in his *Laghuprāmānyaparīksa*," *Journal of Indian Philosophy* 23 (1995), 267.

21. Kachru, "Minds and Worlds," 416; Prahlad Pradhan, *Abhidharmakośabhāṣya of Vasubandhu* (Patna: K.P. Jayaswal Research Institute, 1975), 416.

22. Alexander von Rosspat, *The Buddhist Doctrine of Momentariness: a Survey of the Origins and Early Phase of this Doctrine up to Vasubandhu* (Stuttgart: Franz Steiner, 1995), 90–91. See also Davey Tomlinson's contribution in this volume.

23. K. L. Dhammajoti, *Abhidharma Doctrines and Controversies on Perception* (Hong Kong: Centre of Buddhist Studies, 2007), 136–141.

24. Vasubandhu, *Treasury of Metaphysics*, 5.25cd. See the translation by Leo Pruden, *Abhidharmakośabhasyam of Vasubandhu*, Vols. 1–4 (Berkeley: Asian Humanities Press, 1988–1990), 3.808. See also the *Questions of Milinda*, tr. T.W. Rhys Davids (Oxford: Clarendon, 1890), 2.2.9, 77–78. Finally, see Karunadasa, *Theravāda Abhidhamma*, 350.

25. Collins, "Remarks on the 'Visuddhimagga' and on its Treatment of the Memory of Former Dwelling(s) (pubbenivāsānussatiñāṇa)," *Journal of Indian Philosophy* 37, no. 5 (2009), 513.

26. Vasubandhu, *Abhidharmakośabhasyam*, 3.812.

27. Vasubandhu, *Abhidharmakośabhasyam*, 1.209–211.

28. Vasubandhu, *Abhidharmakośabhasyam*, 1.209–211.

29. Augustine, *Confessions*, tr. Henry Chadwick (Oxford: Oxford University Press, 1991), 11.23.30, 238. Chadwick here renders *distentio* as "extension." See also Sean Hannan, *Reading Augustine: On Time, Change, History, and Conversion* (London: Bloomsbury, 2020), 9–17.

30. Karunadasa, *Theravāda Abhidhamma*, 350.

31. cf. Cameron 2015, 7.

32. I am indebted to the blog "Fake Buddha Quotes" for this. See Bodhipaksa, "Do Not Dwell in the Past, Do Not Dream of the Future, Concentrate the Mind on the Present Moment," *Fake Buddha Quotes*, December 18, 2009:

https://fakebuddhaquotes.com/do-not-dwell-in-the-past-do-not-dream-of-the-future/.

33. G. K. Chesterton, *Heretics* (London: Lane and Co., 1905), 107.

34. See P. G. Wodehouse's 1925 *Carry On, Jeeves* (London: Arrow Books, 2008), ch. 5, as well as Edward Fitzgerald's translation of the *Rubaiyat of Omar Khayyam* (New York: Dodge, 1896), 26. My thanks to Jane Mikkelson for the references to Chesterton and Fitzgerald and for alerting me to the heady presentist brew that neo-Stoicism and Orientalism (among others) had served to ferment at the end of the century.

35. Vasubandhu, *Abhidharmakośabhaṣyam*, 1.84.

36. On Augustine and stoicism, see Sarah Byers, *Perception, Sensibility, and Moral Motivation in Augustine: a Stoic-Platonic Synthesis* (Cambridge: Cambridge University Press, 2013), as well as Hannan, *On Time, Change, History, and Conversion*, 78–82.

37. Zachary Irving, "Mind-wandering is Unguided Attention: Accounting for the Purposeful Wanderer," *Philosophical Studies* 173 (2016), 547–571.

38. Joshua A. Bergamin, "Being in the Flow: Expert Coping as Beyond Both Thought and Automaticity," *Phenomenology and the Cognitive Sciences* 16 (2016), 403–424.

39. Robert Nozick, *The Examined Life: Philosophical Meditations* (New York: Simon and Schuster, 1989), 61.

40. For texts and commentary, see Collins, *Nirvana and Other Buddhist Felicities*, 145–146.

41. Fronsdal, *Buddha before Buddhism*, 44.

42. This paragraph draws on: Georges Dreyfus, "Is Mindfulness Present-Centered and Non-Judgmental? A Discussion of the Cognitive Dimensions of Mindfulness," *Contemporary Buddhism* 12, no. 1 (2011), 41–54; Robert H. Sharf, "Mindfulness and Mindlessness in Early Chan," *Philosophy East and West* 64, no. 4 (2014), 933–964; and Sharf, "Is Mindfulness Buddhist? (And Why It Matters)," *Transcultural Psychiatry* 52, no. 4 (2015), 470–484.

43. Vasubandhu, *Abhidharmakośabhasyam*, 1.251–252; Pradhan, *Abhidharmakośabhāṣya*, 80–81.

44. David G. Stern, *Wittgenstein on Mind and Language* (New York: Oxford University Press, 1995), 136–138.

45. Vasubandhu, *Abhidharmakośabhāṣyam*, 1.252; Pradhan, *Abhidharmakośabhāṣyaṃ*, 81.

46. See Karunadasa, *Theravāda Abhidhamma*, 274–275, for some Buddhist views on the atemporality of concepts as abstractions.

47. Paul L. Swanson, *T'ien-T'ai Chih-I's Mo-Ho Chih-Kuan: Clear Serenity, Quiet Insight*, Vols. 1–3 (Honolulu: University of Hawai'i Press, 2018), 3.1618–1630.

48. Swanson, *T'ien-T'ai Chih-I's Mo-Ho Chih-Kuan*, 3.1619–1620.

49. Swanson, *T'ien-T'ai Chih-I's Mo-Ho Chih-Kuan*, 3.1621.

50. Daniel M. Stuart, "Becoming Animal: Karma and the Animal Realm Envisioned Through an Early Yogācāra Lens," *Religions* 10, no. 6 (2019), 363–378.

51. Swanson, *T'ien-T'ai Chih-I's Mo-Ho Chih-Kuan*, 3.1620: 905a27.

52. The analogy to actualism may actually have given presentism its name. See: Robert Merrihew Adams, "Time and Thisness," *Midwest Studies in Philosophy* 11 (1986), 321; Sider, "Presentism and Ontological Commitment," *Journal of Philosophy* 96 (1999), 325–347.

53. Sara McClintock, "Ethical Reading and the Ethics of Forgetting and Remembering," in *A Mirror Is for Reflection: Understanding Buddhist Ethics*, ed. Jake H. Davis (New York: Oxford University Press, 2017), 185–202.

54. Andy Rotman, *Divine Stories: Divyavadana*, Part 2 (Boston: Wisdom, 2017), 18.

55. Edwin F. Bryant, *The Yogasūtras of Patañjali* (New York: Farrar, Straus, and Giroux, 2009), 397.

56. Bryant, *Yogasūtras*, 398–399.

57. *Therigatha: Poems of the First Buddhist Women*, tr. Charles Hallisey (Cambridge MA: Harvard University Press, 2015), 67.

58. *Saṃyutta Nikāya* 1.10; Pāli Text Society S.i.4. The sentiment is repeated in other popular genres offering prudential wisdom, as in the story of Temiya in the *Mūgapakkha Jātaka*. See Sara Shaw, *The Jātakas: Birth Stories of the Bodhisattva* (Oxford: Penguin, 2006), 212. I am indebted to Sara McClintock for the reference.

59. See, for example, *Udyoga Parvan* 5.43.21, in Pratap Chandra Roy, *Mahabharata* (Calcutta: Bharata, 1886), 3.144: "O Bhārata, he that is liberated from the five senses, mind, the past and the future is happy." It must, however, be said that proverbial wisdom in Sanskrit is not uniform where the epistemic weight of possible temporal locations for one's attention are concerned. The ancient lexicologist Yāska argues that both the future and the present are similarly unknowable, treating, in effect, only what has happened as knowable. See *Nirukta* 1.6 in Lakshman Sarup, *The Nighantu and the Nirukta* (Lahore: University of Panjab, 1927), 9. But a proverb has it that it is the present which we know, with both past and future typically epistemically inaccessible and known only to yogis. On this, see Ludwig Sternbach, *Mahāsubhāṣitasaṃgraha* (Hoshiarpur: Vishveshvaranand Vedic Research Institute, 1974), 1.107, verse 628. See also Sternbach, 1.91, verse 533, for an interesting variation on the truism about engaging with the present; one might consult a proverbial saying, which argues as follows: the result of both past and future being epistemically and pragmatically inaccessible is the fact that, though the present is neither new nor worth immersing oneself in, the present—now *seemingly* unprecedented and unique—appears erroneously as intrinsically worth engaging to rich and poor alike. The genre of proverbs relating to time, attention, and knowledge deserves far more study.

60. *Bhaddekarattasutta*, Majjhima Nikāya 131, Pali Text Society M.iii.187.

61. See also verse 851 as cited in Fronsdal, *Buddha Before Buddhism*, 84

62. Fronsdal, *Buddha before Buddhism*, 9.

63. For more, see Ñanananda, *Ideal Solitude: an Exposition of the Bhadekaratta Sutta* (Kandy, Sri Lanka: Buddhist Publication Society, 1973), 188.

64. On verse 348 of the *Dhammapada*, see K. R. Norman, *The Word of the Doctrine* (Oxford: Pali Text Society, 2000), 50.

65. Akira Hirikawa, *A History of Indian Buddhism: From Śakyamuni to Early Mahāyāna* (Honolulu: University of Hawai'i Press, 1990), 155–156.

66. Milligan, "Development and Representation," 178.

67. In Ñanamoli Thera's translation of a passage from the *Saleyyaka Sutta* (Majjhima Nikāya: Pali Text Society M.i.285): "Or he has wrong view, distorted vision, thus: 'There is nothing given, nothing offered, nothing sacrificed, no fruit and ripening of good and bad [actions], no this world, no other world [typically referring to one's future states], no mother, no father.'" See "Saleyyaka Sutta: the Brahmans of Sala," in *Access to Insight* (Kandy: Buddhist Publication Society, 2013): http://www.accesstoinsight.org/tipitaka/mn/mn.041.nymo.html.

68. Kristin Scheible, *Reading the Mahāvaṃsa: The Literary Aims of a Theravāda Buddhist History* (New York: Columbia University Press, 2016), 7.

69. Stephen Berkwitz, *Buddhist History in the Vernacular: the Power of the Past in Late Medieval Sri Lanka* (Leiden: Brill, 2004), 31.

70. See: Maria Heim, *Voice of the Buddha: Buddhaghosa on the Immeasurable Words* (New York: Oxford University Press, 2018), 184–185; Donald S. Lopez, Jr., *The Lotus Sūtra: A Biography* (Princeton: Princeton University Press, 2016), 74–75.

71. See Pruden's review of Mark L. Blum, *The Origins and Development of Pure Land Buddhism: a Study and Translation of Gyōnen's Jōdo Hōmon Genrushō*, in *Japanese Journal of Religious* Studies 30, nos. 1–2 (2003), 165.

72. Dirck Vorenkamp, "B-Series Temporal Order in Dōgen's Theory of Time," *Philosophy East and West* 45, no. 3 (1995), 387–408.

73. Sharf, "Is Mindfulness Buddhist?" 476.

74. Hallisey, *Therīgāthā*, 129–141, verses 252–270.

75. Hallisey, *Therīgāthā*, 129, verses 252.

76. Yigal Bronner, "This Is No Lotus, It Is a Face: Poetics as Grammar in Dandin's Investigation of the Simile," in *The Poetics of Grammar and the Metaphysics of Sound and Sign*, eds. S. La Porta and David Shulman (Leiden, Brill: 2007), 89–108.

77. Cf. Gilles Deleuze, *Proust and Signs: the Complete Text*, tr. Richard Howard (Minneapolis: University of Minnesota Press, 2000), 4. Unlike Proust's involuntary memory, Ambapali's is effortful.

78. Donald S. Lopez, Jr., and Jacqueline Stone, *Two Buddhas Seated Side by Side: a Guide to the Lotus Sūtra* (Princeton: Princeton University Press, 2019), 142–143.

79. Sharf, "On the Allure of Buddhist Relics," *Representations* 66 (1999), 4. Though, against the supposition of real presence, the Pāli *Questions of Milinda* offers three ways of explaining the possibility of miracles at sites where relics of the Buddha, but not the Buddha, are present. T. W. Rhys Davids, *Questions of Milinda*, 35: 174–176.

80. Francisca Cho, *Seeing Like the Buddha: Enlightenment Through Film* (Albany: SUNY Press, 2012), 22.

81. Sigmund Freud, *Civilization and Its Discontents*, tr. James Strachey (New York: Norton, 1962), 17.

82. David L. McMahan, *Empty Vision: Metaphor and Visionary Imagery in Mahāyāna Buddhism* (London: Routledge, 2002), 140.

83. Monika Zin, "The Techniques of Narrative Representation in Old India," in *Image-Narration-Context: Visual Narration in Cultures and Societies of the Old World*, eds. Elisabeth Wagner-Durand, Barbara Fath, and Alexander Heinemann (Heidelberg: Propylaeum, 2019), 141–142.

84. Readers will no doubt be put in mind of Augustine's "threefold" of present experience: memory, awareness, and expectation or awaiting in *Conf.* 11.20.26. Augustine's contemporary, Vasubandhu, may have been the first in South Asian letters to analyze the concept of a person as entailing a similarly interconnected set of retrospective, prospective, and present modes of awareness. On this, see Jonardon Ganeri, "Buddhist No Self: An Analysis and Critique," in Irina Kuznetsowa, Jonardon Ganeri, and Chakravarthi Ram-Prasad, eds., *Hindu and Buddhist Ideas in Dialogue* (London and New York: Routledge, 2012), 63–77.

85. Cf. Pruden, *Abhidharmakośabhasyam of Vasubandhu*, Vol. III, 807.

86. AKB 5.25a in Pruden, *Abhidharmakośabhasyam of Vasubandhu*, Vol. III, 806. Intriguingly, the truth-making argument, which Vasubandhu reconstructs for the four-dimensionalist, is also an argument Augustine develops against presentism.

87. AKB 5.25b and 5.25c in Pruden, *Abhidharmakośabhasyam of Vasubandhu*, Vol. III, 807; Cox 1988.

88. Vasubandhu, *Abhidharmakośabhasyam*, 1.283–285.

89. Vasubandhu, *Abhidharmakośabhasyam*, 3.813.

90. In what follows, I summarize the arguments in Vasubandhu, *Abhidharmakośabhasyam*, 3.813–814. My reconstruction is indebted to Sider, "Presentism and Ontological Commitment." For a different presentation of the philosophical issues involved, see Jonathan Gold, *Paving the Great Way: Vasubandhu's Unifying Buddhist Philosophy* (New York: Columbia University Press, 2015), 22–59.

91. George Cardona, "A Note on *Asti*," in *Consciousness Manifest: Studies in Jaina Art and Iconography and Allied Subjects in Honour of Dr. U.P. Shah*, ed. R.T. Vyas (Vadodara: Abhinav, 1995), 138.

92. Vasubandhu, *Abhidharmakośabhasyam*, 3.810-811.

93. See Paul M. Williams, "Buddhadeva and Temporality," *Journal of Indian Philosophy* 4, no. 3 (1977), 279–294, alongside Bart Dessein, "The Existence of Factors in the Three Time Periods: Sarvāstivāda and Madhyamaka Buddhist Interpretations of Difference in Mode, Difference in Characteristic Marks, Difference in State, and Mutual Difference," *Acta Orientalia* 60, no. 3 (2007), 331–350. I follow Vasubandhu, *Abhidharmakośabhasyam*, 3.808–810, 5.25d.

94. For the exact analogy to the counting technology used, see Dominik Wujastyk, "Some Problematic Yoga Sūtras and Their Buddhist Background," in *Yoga in Transformation: Historical and Contemporary Perspectives*, eds. Karl Baier, Philipp A. Mass, and Karin Preisendanz (Göttingen: V and R, 2018), 41, note 71.

95. J. E. M. McTaggart, "The Unreality of Time," *Mind* 17, no. 68 (1908), 457–474.

96. Williams, "Buddhadeva and Temporality," 281–283.

97. Vasubandhu, *Abhidharmakośabhasyam*, 3.810.

98. Harmut Buescher, *Sthiramati's Triṃśikāvijñaptibhāṣya: Critical Editions of the Sanskrit Text and Its Tibetan Translation* (Vienna: Österreichische Akademie

der Wissenschaften, 2007), 130. See also Klaus Dieter Mathes, *Unterschiedung der Gegebenheiten von ihrem Wahren Wesen* (Swistal-Odendorf: Indica et Tibetica Verlag, 1996).

99. *Scripture of the Lotus Blossom of the Fine Dharma*, tr. Leon Hurvitz (New York: Columbia University Press, 2009), 220, 223.

100. Robert F. Thurman, *The Holy Teaching of Vimalakīrti: A Mahāyāna Scripture* (Philadelphia: University of Pennsylvania Press, 1976), 91.

101. Claus Oetke, "Remarks on the Interpretation of Nāgārjuna's Philosophy," *Journal of Indian Philosophy* 19, no. 3 (1991), 320–321.

102. *Scripture of the Lotus Blossom*, 221.

103. Gold, *Paving the Great Way*, 38.

104. *Laṅkāvatārasūtra* 86; see D.T. Suzuki, *The Lankavatara Sutra: A Mahayana Text* (London: Routldge, 1932), 236.

105. *Laṅkāvatārasūtra* 61; see Suzuki, *Lankavatara Sutra*, 124; my emphasis.

106. *Saṃyutta Nikāya* 12:65; Pāli Text Society S 2: 104.

107. McTaggart, "Unreality of Time," 462.

108. William M. Johnston and Christopher Kleinhenz, *Encyclopedia of Monasticism*, Vols. 1–2 (London: Routldge, 2015), 1293.

109. This is the dilemma implied by Martin Hägglund in "Why Mortality Makes Us Free," *The New York Times* (March 11, 2019).

110. Gregory Schopen, *Buddhist Monks and Business Matters: Still More Papers on Monastic Buddhism in India* (Honolulu: University of Hawai'i Press, 2004), 271.

*Chapter 16*

# Breaking the Stream of Consciousness
## *Momentariness and the Eternal Present*
Davey K. Tomlinson

In Book 11 of the *Confessions*, Augustine sets out for us an impossible aspiration. "But if only their minds could be seized and held steady," he laments, "they would be still for a while and, for that short moment, they would glimpse the splendor of eternity which is forever still."[1] There is an absolute contrast between our temporal condition and this "splendor of eternity." "Eternity is 'forever still' in contrast to things that are 'never still,'" Paul Ricoeur writes, "This stillness lies in the fact that 'in eternity nothing moves into the past: all is present. Time, on the other hand, is never all present at once.'"[2] It is the absolute contrast between creator and created, between God and His creatures. While our "time-bound minds" are ever and constitutively coming apart in time, "nevertheless, we can, as far as Augustine is concerned, aspire to having images of eternity in time."[3] These images, however, will be felt as a *lack*, a heightening of the contrast between our creaturely condition and our creator's perfection. Our minds cannot be seized and held steady; if we glimpse the splendor of eternity, it is only through a representation in time. However enlightening this glimpse may be, it does not yield for us God's experience of eternity.

Despite the dour sound of the first truth the Buddha taught in his first discourse—that everything is suffering—Buddhist philosophy is an optimistic and revolutionary enterprise. We can see this clearly by juxtaposing this sentiment of Augustine's with Buddhist reflections on time and timelessness, or, to borrow Augustine's phrase, a present where "all is present." The possibility of our experience of this radical presentism[4] is one of many expressions of the fundamental difference between Augustine's theology and Mahāyāna buddhology: whatever we may learn about God and our nature as opposed to God's, Augustine does not aim to tell us how we may *become* God. But the Buddha was just a man. Reflections on the nature and experience of buddhahood thus bear directly on our human condition, precisely insofar as each of us can, axiomatically in the Mahāyāna Buddhist tradition, become a buddha.[5] The philosopher, then, must make sense of the following three problems: how it is we are not already buddhas now; how our epistemic apparatus can be both mired in ignorance and yet capable of leading us to enlightenment; and what buddhahood is such that it is a possible attainment for us.

What I would like to show here is that, for a certain tradition of Indian Buddhist philosopher, while it may be a phenomenological given that we experience ourselves in time (perhaps even, we'll see, torn apart by our experience of time's passage), we can and should aim not to do so. Not only is the experience of ourselves as persisting selves a problem; more fundamentally, our experience of any temporal duration at all is at the root of our suffering in the world. Many Indian Buddhists subscribe to the doctrine of momentariness (*kṣaṇikavāda*), according to which any entity passes away as soon as it arises, giving rise to another entity, generally of very similar kind, in a continuum (*santāna*) of what are really discrete momentary entities. An entity's existence is, as Stcherbatsky memorably put it, a "staccato movement, momentary flashes of a stream of energy."[6] Because these arisings and passings away flash by with such speed, and because these discrete entities are most often exceedingly similar to one another, we cannot discern these entities with our ordinary perception; rather, we mistakenly conceive of them as a single temporally extended entity.

The defender of this doctrine aims to establish a number of related claims: first, it is possible to establish inferentially that any existent thing must instantaneously and spontaneously pass away, despite the fact that this is not perceived; second, we can explain our mistaken experience of temporally extended entities—which seems such an obvious phenomenological given—despite the fact that nothing perdures; third, despite its counterintuitiveness, we can come to directly experience this instantaneous passing away of all phenomena; and finally, this experience is liberative. In my discussion of these claims here, I will refer to works in the tradition of the great sixth- or seventh-century Indian Buddhist philosopher Dharmakīrti, particularly as his tradition was developed by the early eleventh-century authors Jñānaśrīmitra and his student, Ratnakīrti. Not all Buddhists held the views discussed here,[7] though they were taken as mainstream by many non-Buddhist philosophers in India during the so-called golden age of Indian philosophy (roughly the fifth through twelfth centuries CE). For this reason, I'll refer to Jñānaśrīmitra and Ratnakīrti by name, or use such formulations as "Dharmakīrti's text tradition" or "Dharmakīrtian," rather than the overly general "Buddhist." Where I use "Buddhist" to refer to the tradition generally, I do so advisedly.

## PROVING THE INSTANTANEOUS PASSING AWAY OF ALL PHENOMENA

Philosophers in Dharmakīrti's text tradition held there to be only two means of knowledge (*pramāṇa*): perception (*pratyakṣa*), which is direct and immediate, and inference (*anumāna*), which is conceptually mediated. Recognizing that its perceptual givenness is not only denied by common sense but was also a non-starter for competing non-Buddhist philosophers, the Dharmakīrtian aims to prove momentariness inferentially in the first place. One such proof of momentariness (the so-called *sattvānumāna*) hinges on causal efficacy (*arthakriyākāritva*) as the criterion of existence (*sattva*). For a thing to exist, it must produce some effect: whether we are considering one physical object interacting with another, an object's effect on the senses, or one cognition's effect on another, for something to exist is for it to have some causal efficacy. One way to frame the problem, then, is to ask whether a non-momentary thing can bring about an effect. If it cannot, it does not exist given this criterion.

And indeed a non-momentary thing cannot bring about an effect, the Dharmakīrtian argues. Were something to perdure across even two moments, $t_1$ and $t_2$, then this single perduring thing would possess contradictory properties at these different moments: at $t_1$, when it has not yet produced its effect, it is *not* an agent of an action; at $t_2$, in the moment it produces its effect, it *is* an agent. Since being an agent and being a non-agent are contradictory properties, we must in fact be dealing with two different things: at $t_1$, a non-agent; at $t_2$, an agent. If a seed is said to produce a sprout at $t_2$, we must in fact have two different moments of a seed-continuum at $t_1$ and $t_2$. At $t_1$, the seed is not an agent of sprout-production; at $t_2$, we have a very similar but discrete seed that is an agent. Now, this cannot mean that at $t_1$, the seed is not an agent *at all*, for to exist is to have some causal efficacy, to produce some effect. What we have, then, is one moment of a seed-continuum producing the next, until we come to that moment of the seed-continuum that produces a sprout.

One might respond to this line of argument by saying that the seed perdures, unchanging moment to moment, but the auxiliary conditions around it change—it is placed in soil, watered, and exposed to sunlight—and it is this change in the surrounding conditions that lets the seed produce the sprout. This, the Dharmakīrtian argues, makes no sense: if the seed remains unchanging throughout this whole process, it must really be the changes in soil, water, and sunlight—not the seed itself—that produce the sprout.[8] But this is absurd: we see that seedless soil, no matter how it is watered and exposed to the sun, will not produce sprouts. It is right, then, to call the seed the cause of the sprout; however, we must understand it as the momentary flux of a seed-continuum, each moment causing the next, rather than a perduring entity.

Another proof of momentariness (the so-called *vināśitvānumāna*) hinges instead on destruction (*vināśa*)—or, more generally, change. We know that pots are destroyed when hit with hammers. So what, then, is the nature of a pot? Is it to remain unchanging across time? This cannot be, because we see that it is destroyed: if it perdured by nature, the pot would not cease to exist even when struck with a hammer. Since the pot ceases, its nature must be not to perdure, and so *even upon the very moment of its production*, its nature must be not to perdure. As the twelfth-century author Mokṣākaragupta puts the point, "If it perishes, how can you say that it is produced by its causes so as to be imperishable?"[9] Rather, if all things must pass, they must do so immediately upon their arising insofar as it is their nature not to perdure more than a moment.

As a corollary to this, we should conclude things perish spontaneously or without an external cause. If it is a thing's nature to perish immediately upon arising, the pot is destroyed at each moment in the pot-continuum. One may reasonably ask, though, what the hammer does when we strike the pot: if the pot is destroyed by its own nature in every moment, why is the pot-continuum itself finally destroyed when the hammer hits it? The Dharmakīrtian argues that the hammer does not bring about the absence of the pot. Unlike certain realist traditions of Indian philosophy, the Dharmakīrtian denies the reality of absences. Given the definition of existence as causal efficacy, this makes good sense: absences don't *do* anything, and when we analyze supposed instances of absences acting in the world, we find that really some other entity is acting. As Tom Tillemans puts it, "while petrol may cause your car to run, it is not strictly speaking the absence of petrol that causes it to sputter and stop, as that absence doesn't really exist. It is rather the presence of something like the petrol-less air in your tank that is causally efficacious."[10] What we find when we analyze absences is really the apprehension of some other thing: petrol-less air rather than the absence of petrol, or potsherds on the ground where the pot used to be. The hammer-continuum, then, brings about a potsherd-continuum, in cooperation with the final moment of the pot-continuum.

From this brief presentation of these two proofs, the details of which become very complicated,[11] we can glean something essential about the Dharmakīrtian theory of momentariness. The issue at stake is not the presence of the point-like present. In Buddhist thought throughout its history, there are certainly discussions of just how long a moment (*kṣaṇa*) is: Is it a finger-snap? A sixty-fourth of a finger-snap? A billionth of a finger-snap?[12] But what is at stake in these proofs is not the measure of the present; rather, it is the passing away that is inherent in anything capable of acting or capable of change, and so anything that can be said to exist. While Indian authors often refer to "momentariness" (*kṣaṇikatva*), or even refer to Buddhism as

"The Theory of Moments" (*kṣaṇikavāda*),[13] Jñānaśrīmitra's and Ratnakīrti's treatises proving momentariness refer rather to *kṣaṇabhaṅga* in their titles: it is the *bhaṅga*, the "destruction," "decay," "cutting off," or "passing away" that happens at every instant, that is really at stake. *Kṣaṇa* in the compound *kṣaṇa-bhaṅga* functions almost adverbially: "at once," "immediately," "instantaneously." The measure of a moment is unimportant. What is essential is decay. To this extent, then, these authors stress part of the deep grammar of Buddhism: impermanence. Our suffering in the world is due to our expectation that things will last coupled with their inevitable failure to do so. This point is brought here to its extreme: not only will my life and the lives of my loved ones inevitably come to an end; my existence and the existence of everything around me are constantly perishing. Existence is a continuum of little deaths.

## CONSCIOUSNESS IN A FLEETING WORLD

All of this talk of a continuum of discrete entities and their instantaneous passing away will likely strike the reader as deeply counterintuitive. What about that great metaphor for our inner conscious life, the *stream*? As William James so influentially put it, consciousness "does not appear to itself chopped up in bits. Such words as 'chain' or 'train' do not describe it fitly as it presents itself in the first instance. It is nothing jointed: it flows. A 'river' or a 'stream' are the metaphors by which it is most naturally described."[14] The metaphor of the stream here is meant to capture not just the *flow* of consciousness, but something of the *porousness* of its present: "chain" or "train" fail to describe it because these images presume discrete boundaries between their respective links or cars. Rather, when we consider how consciousness presents itself, we find there is no discrete boundary between its past, present, and future.

Augustine develops this point elegantly in his image of the recitation of a psalm in Book 11 of the *Confessions*. As Augustine recites the psalm, he says,

> The scope of the action (*actionis*) I am performing is divided (*distenditur*) between the two faculties of memory and expectation, the one looking back to the part which I have already recited, the other looking forward to the part which I have still to recite. But my faculty of attention (*attentio*) is present all the while, and through it passes (*traicitur*) what was the future in the process of becoming the past.[15]

The *distentio* of the mind into its faculties of expectation, attention, and memory allows for the present existence of future and past things as one expects the words to come and recalls the words just spoken, in what Ricoeur characterizes as "an extended and dialectical present which itself is . . . neither the past, nor the future, nor the pointlike present, nor even the passing of the present."[16] Augustine generalizes this experience of the *distentio* from the recitation of a psalm to a person's whole life: the human mind generally is divided into these three faculties, constantly torn asunder by this experience of time's flow.

Isn't the thesis that everything is momentary, or that all phenomena instantaneously and spontaneously pass away, incompatible with James's or Augustine's apt characterization of our inner conscious life? Is the stream of consciousness even possible in a momentary world? One might quite reasonably object that it is not—and so, because momentariness so spectacularly fails to explain our lived experience, the Dharmakīrtian view must be rejected. If, as Alexander von Rospatt puts it in his important study of the doctrine, "the world (including the sentient beings inhabiting it) is at every moment distinct from the world in the previous or next moment,"[17] then at a given moment, I have no access to past or future moments: these are discrete and have either already flashed out of existence or have not yet been produced. Even granting the Dharmakīrtian view that the stream is an illusion we project onto what is really a staccato continuum of distinct momentary entities, how can we make this projection if, at a given moment, past and future moments do not exist? How do we take as our object of projection something nonexistent?

This line of questioning cuts to the heart of the first proof of momentariness we discussed earlier. How, philosophers in the Nyāya tradition (that is, Naiyāyikas) asked, are we supposed to experience causality given the thesis that everything—cognition included—is momentary? Existence, the Dharmakīrtian claims, is defined by causal efficacy. But if there is only the experience of the present fleeting moment, which passes away in the production of the next, there is no experiencer to witness both cause and effect and thus to establish a connection between them. One moment of cognition experiences the seed; another distinct moment experiences the sprout. How can a subsequent moment of cognition—distinct yet again from the first two—tie these two together and make sense of the seed's causal efficacy? Each of these moments of cognition should be as different from the other as my present cognition is from yours. And it would be absurd, of course, to claim that I could establish a causal relation based on your cognition of the seed and my cognition of the sprout. The Naiyāyika takes this as proof of the view that a perduring (indeed, eternal [*nitya*]) self (*ātman*) exists: this self witnesses each moment of consciousness, and so is able to tie them together to form a unity.[18]

This presumes, however, that the Dharmakīrtian takes a given moment of cognition to be nothing over and above the cognition of its peculiar content. That is, it presumes that in one discrete moment, there arises seed-cognition, in the next sprout-cognition. But cognition is not such a simple unity: it always arises bearing in itself some awareness (*vitti*) of the past. Of course, the past seed-cognition no longer exists after its instantaneous passing away.[19] Still, our cognition of the sprout arises perfumed by the previous moment of cognition's apprehension of the seed. The present cognition is infused with memory. As Mookerjee puts the point, "The cognitions are certainly self-contained and discrete, but by virtue of the causal relationship the subsequent cognition comes into being instinct with the memory-impression of the former cognition as its legacy."[20] Further, the Naiyāyika's supposition that only a perduring self would be capable of uniting past and present cognitions is superfluous. For, whether or not we presume some permanent substratum, "If a single perception is not endowed with the awareness of the preceding and the following [moments], how can the sequence be known when there exist two perceptions?"[21] That is, if the Naiyāyika supposes it is the self that unites past and present cognitions, he thus postulates a single cognition—here belonging to the eternal self—that contains within itself awareness of both the past and present cognitions. The Buddhist accomplishes the same thing without the metaphysical baggage of an eternal self by saying the present moment of cognition, conditioned and perfumed by the past, contains within itself some awareness of the past, on the basis of which it can lead to the inferential ascertainment of a causal relationship between the seed and sprout.[22]

The present is not only perfumed by the past. Because memory is present in a given moment of cognition, cognition contains within itself the capacity to incite activity toward the attainment of some desirable result. It contains within itself a capacity for expectation. An opponent might reasonably object that desire would be impossible if each moment of consciousness were truly discrete. Indeed, the Naiyāyika argues that the mere fact that we desire shows there is a perduring substratum to our fleeting experiences. The present moment of desire is grounded on a synthesis of the past experience of some pleasurable object and the present expectation that such pleasure will be found again. If there were just a continuity of discrete entities with no perduring substratum, it would be as if the past experience belonged to you, while the present experience belonged to me (for again, the Naiyāyika contends, two discrete moments of cognition should be as discrete as two cognitions in two different people): there would be no synthesis of the two, and so no way to make sense of my present desire.[23] However, Jñānaśrīmitra would respond, we have seen that the present moment of cognition is of content perfumed by past discrete moments in a causal continuum. This being so, the present cognition, stretching to incorporate (*ātanvatī*) the memory of results attained in the past, throws us into or instigates (*ākṣipati*) some purposeful activity (*pravṛtti*), activity that reasonably anticipates some particular result.[24] It does this without reliance upon some further synthetic cognition, for, as Jñānaśrīmitra puts it, the mind, struck by the perfumings of its past, "contains within itself the capacity to yield conceptualization that throws us into purposeful activity."[25] The present moment of cognition, then, is very much not a simple unity, absorbed wholly in its intentional content; rather, it is perfumed by memories, which are ineluctably tied to desires and expectations that impel us to act.

Jñānaśrīmitra here continues the Dharmakīrtian—or indeed Buddhist—project of making sense of the phenomenology of our everyday experience in spite of the counterintuitive view of selflessness and impermanence. Yet Buddhist philosophy generally is fundamentally *revisionary* rather than *descriptive*: while Buddhist metaphysicians do strive to make sense of our ordinary experience, given that a perduring self does not exist, ordinary experience is at the root of our suffering, and so if it remains intact, unaffected by the work of philosophy, philosophy has failed. Jñānaśrīmitra here, then, attests to the widespread experience of something like Augustine's threefold present. As the mind in the instant of its passage is "divided between time gone by and time to come . . . torn this way and that by the havoc of change,"[26] so too Jñānaśrīmitra aims to show how a present cognition is at once perfumed by the past and anticipatory of what is to come, despite the fact of its instantaneous and spontaneous perishing. That Jñānaśrīmitra can account for our experience of ourselves as continuous in this way, however, does not mean he aims to stop his inquiry there.

## SEEING THE INSTANTANEOUS PASSING AWAY OF ALL PHENOMENA

The experience of consciousness as a stream, flowing together due to the triple forces of expectation, attention, and memory, may seem a widespread phenomenon, given the analogies I've drawn here between Augustine, Jñānaśrīmitra, and James. But what if it is not the only way we might experience consciousness? Despite the apparent givenness of ourselves as perduring entities, the Dharmakīrtian argues that we may not only *infer* but may also come to *experience* the instantaneous passing away of all phenomena: kṣaṇabhaṅga is not only something we can ascertain conceptually; it is something we can train ourselves to see.

To an extent, the Dharmakīrtian tradition here builds on earlier Buddhist considerations of the perception of momentariness. In the early literature discussed by von Rospatt,[27] for instance, introspection alone leads to this perception: just by analyzing phenomena carefully, the practitioner comes to see their constant rise and fall. This experience is of particular soteriological significance. As von Rospatt puts it, "It is taught that only because of this vision disgust (*nirvid*) and the subsequent liberation from desire (*virāga*) leading to final emancipation (*vimukti*) are possible."[28] In a similar vein (though without the same soteriological commitments), Galen Strawson has recently proposed that, in his case at least, the stream metaphor is inapt. "Thought has very little natural continuity or experiential flow—if mine is anything to go by," he writes, "It keeps slipping from mere consciousness into self-consciousness and out again. It is always shooting off, shorting out, spurting and stalling. . . . It's as if consciousness is constantly restarting. It keeps banging out of nothingness. It's a series of comings-to."[29] Strawson suggests that the image of listening to music (or, were he so inclined, reciting a psalm) is not in fact generalizable to all of conscious life, as James or Augustine would have it, but is rather a special case. When so engaged by something ordered and continuous, "thought or experience may be felt to take on the ordered continuity of the phenomenon that occupies it."[30] But when left to its own devices, consciousness leaps from thought to thought with little obvious rhyme or reason, without any experience of flow. Strawson concedes this may be "a rash generalization" from his own case; still, not unlike von Rospatt's early Buddhists, he suggests that "careful mental self-examination may reveal the same to everyone."[31]

The Dharmakīrtian view of the experience of the instantaneous passing away of all phenomena is not quite so optimistic about our capacities for self-examination. Rather than simply looking inward and discovering momentariness, the experience is cultivated on the basis of firm inferential certainty. The Dharmakīrtian holds that a special type of immediate cognition is attainable in meditative cultivation: yogic perception (*yogipratyakṣa*), or the immediate cognition of a highly advanced practitioner of meditation, a yogin. Yet this yogic perception is fundamentally rational. The Dharmakīrtian holds that practitioners are able to transform truths come to inferentially, and so *conceptually*, into vivid, *nonconceptual* cognitions through sustained, repeated cultivation. The momentariness (*kṣaṇikatva*) of all conditioned things—a conceptually constructed, generic mental object—is ascertained on the basis of the arguments outlined earlier. Repeated, sincere, uninterrupted reflection is then brought to bear on it. Finally, after a long time, the instantaneous passing away of all phenomena becomes manifest to the practitioner.[32]

The possibility of this transformation of the conceptual into the nonconceptual is a topic of much dispute in first-millennium Indian philosophy, as are debates concerning its mechanics for the Dharmakīrtian, given the doctrine of momentariness.[33] Our concern here, however, will be the end of this path rather than the path itself. What is the yogin's experience of time like when the instantaneous passing away of all phenomena—the conceptual certainty that "all conditioned things are momentary" (*kṣaṇikāḥ sarvasaṃskārā iti*)—is made vividly manifest at the culmination of his meditation?[34]

Through this direct experience of the momentariness of all things, the yogin obtains *omniscience* (*sarvajña*), and his experience of time is fundamentally transformed.[35] This omniscience is supposed to include knowledge of past and future things, and so the Naiyāyika raises a sensible objection: "How can the past and future be cognitive objects? For what is non-existent has no phenomenal feature (*ākāra*) whatsoever."[36] The Naiyāyika assumes with Ratnakīrti that past and future entities do not exist. How then could they present representations to consciousness? Ratnakīrti responds first by considering just what omniscience is. Drawing on an old distinction, he notes that the yogin's omniscience regarding everything *useful* (*upayuktasarvajña*) is possible even if the past and future are not known; for simply through the direct realization of momentariness, the yogin reaches the cessation of suffering. Further, he can teach this realization to others, leading them from cyclic existence as well. Nothing besides this can truly be said to be useful (soteriologically, at least), and so we can call the yogin omniscient in this restricted sense.[37]

But, Ratnakīrti continues, total omniscience (*sarvasarvajña*)—including knowledge of past and future entities—need not be abandoned out of hand due to this objection. To understand how, we may turn to the innovative commentator on Dharmakīrti, Prajñākaragupta (ca. 750–810),[38] to whose work Jñānaśrīmitra and Ratnakīrti often show deference. Shinya Moriyama has recently shown how Prajñākaragupta makes sense of the direct manifestation of the whole universe to the omniscient yogin. As Moriyama puts it,

> Prajñākaragupta presupposes the Buddhist doctrinal view of dependent origination. According to this view, the whole universe has arisen due to the relation between causes and effects. Thus, through continuous meditation on these various kinds of causal relations, one becomes an omniscient being who knows the whole universe.[39]

This presents a problem, however, for it seems here as if the yogin is extrapolating from (an admittedly impressive) knowledge of just the present moment of the causal nexus, making inferences regarding past and future entities. Because this knowledge is inferential, and because inference and perception are different means of knowledge with different kinds of objects, past and future entities are not here vividly manifest to one who should, we imagine, perceive them immediately (*sākṣātdarṣṭṛ*).

Prajñākaragupta counters, however, with a rather startling claim, given his Dharmakīrtian pedigree: this inference regarding all aspects of all phenomena (*sarvākārānumāna*) is nothing other than an immediate perceptual acquaintance with all phenomena! To show this, Prajñākaragupta redefines perception as we, Buddhists, and Naiyāyikas commonly understand it. We might think some connection to a sense-faculty is necessary to make perception

perception (indeed, the Sanskrit *pratyakṣa* literally means "before the eyes," making perception sound fundamentally linked to our sensory apparatus). But not so. Perception is rather simply the immediate true awareness of a thing (*sākṣātsadbhūtapadārthavedana*). Whether its cause is sensory or mental is unimportant.[40] Repeated inferences regarding all aspects of all entities, then, gradually become sharper and sharper in the process of developing the yogic perception of the certainty, "All conditioned phenomena are momentary," until an immediate true awareness of all past, present, and future phenomena is manifest, caused by the former inferential cognition. "Due to practice repeated to the highest degree," Prajñākaragupta writes, "the yogin is immediately aware of the object of this [inference regarding all aspects of all entities], just as people are immediately aware of fire from smoke."[41] Using here the classic example of something *inferred*, Prajñākaragupta says (again surprisingly) that people come to *immediately* cognize fire they cannot see when they see smoke off in the distance, without the need to make an inference to this effect, given the frequency with which they'd made that inference in the past. So too, the yogin: as the repeated practice (*abhyāsa*) of this inference regarding all phenomena is brought to completion (*atyanta*), all phenomena are immediately manifest.

But if past and future entities are immediately manifest, in what sense are they past or future? They are past or future only to us—not to the yogin. "What is the meaning of the statement, '[The yogin] sees past and future entities'?" Prajñākaragupta clarifies: "He sees what is not being seen by other [ordinary people]; insofar as that is being seen, it is simply present (*vartamānam eva*)."[42] Jñānaśrīmitra echoes this point, and Ratnakīrti silently cites him, both writing, "If, then, there is the direct manifestation of the nature of past and future entities, they should be simply present (*vartamānataiva*)."[43] In the experience of total omniscience, past and future entities are simply present. Indeed, it is a mistake to think of them as differentiable into "past" or "future" in the first place. Something's being past or future (*atītāditva*) relies on ordinary ways of seeing. As Eli Franco glosses the idea in Prajñākaragupta, "only after coming out of his meditation session," and so no longer directly facing the manifest reality of all things, does the yogin "determine entities as past or future."[44] Or as Jñānaśrīmitra puts it:

> Upon arising from the completion of contemplation, through mere reflection (*saṃcityaiva*) there is the determination (*adhyavasāya*) of temporal difference in order to cognize the forms of things as temporally distinct. As it is said [in Śāntarakṣita's *Tattvasaṃgraha*, 3628]: "Whatever he wishes to understand he knows without fail—such is his power, for he has shaken off all immoral conduct."[45]

The accomplished yogin, then, no longer experiences time's passage when in meditation, directly experiencing all aspects of all things. Only afterward, returning to our conventional world out of his compassion for the sake of helping us see the liberative truth he has realized, does he engage in the kind of differentiation that makes temporal succession possible.[46]

## CONSCIOUSNESS AND THE ETERNAL PRESENT

The vivid manifestation of omniscience, grounded on the yogic perception of momentariness, breaks the yogin's experience of temporal extension and flow. All phenomena, regardless of their being determined as belonging to the past or future upon arising from meditation, are experienced as being presently manifest while directly facing the nature of reality. I will suggest here, in closing, that this is precisely the aim of the yogic perception of the instantaneous passing away of all phenomena, at least in Jñānaśrīmitra's view. As we noted earlier, we should stress the notion of "passing away," "decay," or "perishing," *bhaṅga*, in the compound *kṣaṇa-bhaṅga*. We should stress this all the more, it seems to me, because the proof that all things pass away instantaneously is meant to be cultivated and, gradually, to be cognized in such a way that it truly breaks (*bhaṅga*) our experience of temporality as such. We are brought by this contemplation, when it is finally perfected, to an experience of the presence of consciousness alone that is not divided by the constructions of past and future, earlier and later. We are brought—in a way that would seem impossible for Augustine—to a state outside time's passage, a present that is, as Augustine put it earlier, "forever still."

To abide in that state that is forever still, where there is no activity, is to be immersed in cognition's true nature: self-awareness (*svasaṃvedana*). The Dharmakīrtian account of self-awareness is notoriously complex.[47] Self-awareness is likened to the light or luminosity (*prakāśa*) of consciousness, which shines to make things manifest; it is that which makes cognition possible, that which differentiates a conscious state from an insentient one; it is free from the dualities of cause and effect (*hetuphala*), earlier and later (*pūrvāpara*), and object and subject (*grāhyagrāhaka*). Jñānaśrīmitra tells us:

> When one accepts that there is cognition of other things (*anātmasaṃvitti*), causal relationships and temporal sequence are suitable for the sake of conventional behavior (*vyavahāra*). But when absorbed in the awareness of its own nature (*svarūpasaṃvitti*), where is there the possibility of temporal sequence (*pūrvāparabhāva*), which is established through difference?[48]

The determination of one thing as occurring earlier and another as occurring later is possible only given the cognition of the difference between the two. But, Jñānaśrīmitra thinks, when "immersed in self-awareness" (*svasaṃvedanamagna*) or "directly facing the nature of reality" (*tattvarūpāmukhīkaraṇa*), there is no cognition of difference, and so there can be no experience of temporal sequence.[49]

This immersion in self-awareness is precisely what the yogin comes to experience when he realizes all aspects of all things as being simply present. To experience the past and future as present is no longer to experience them as objects colored by the phenomenal hues of memory or anticipation: to avail ourselves of the restrictive meaning of the Sanskrit particle *eva*, they are *only* present (*vartamānam eva*). As past and future are not differentiated, so too the perfumings of memory and anticipatory impulses are no longer experienced. Self-awareness is not thrown into transactional behaviors and purposeful activities. There is no stretching (*ātanvatī*) of cognition to incorporate memory and anticipation. "When considering consciousness alone," Jñānaśrīmitra tells us, "all activities stop."[50]

We are thus ultimately not time-bound, as Augustine might have thought. Cognition comes to a state here, immersed in its own nature, where it is no longer torn apart, where there is no *distentio*. This attainment is grounded on inferential certainty regarding the instantaneous passing away of all phenomena. As we cultivate this certainty, we come to experience all aspects of all phenomena as simply, only, and really (*eva*) present (*vartamāna*). This attainment of omniscience comes to break our experience of temporality in a fundamental way, rendering the past, present, and future undifferentiable as we sink down into simply the presence of self-awareness. With this, the stream of consciousness no longer has any traction: without memory and anticipation making its flow possible, its flow comes to a halt.

Augustine's reflection on time in the *Confessions* is surely not meant to leave us unaffected. The realization of the temporal nature of the human soul, and its radical opposition to God's eternity, may well, we imagine, reorient a person's life. Yet as he reaches the end of his reflections, Augustine's hopefulness can be only eschatological. He remains divided, torn asunder by time, until he can be "cast and set firm" in the mold of God's truth:

> But now *my years are but sighs*. You, O Lord, are my only solace. You, my Father, are eternal. But I am divided between time gone by and time to come, and its course is a mystery to me. My thoughts, the intimate life of my soul, are torn this way and that in the havoc of change. And so it will be until I am purified and melted by the fire of your love and fused into one with you.[51]

The Dharmakīrtian's optimism gives us a different picture wherein, we might say, there is no need for hope. The nature of cognition itself is always already "forever still," the pure presence of self-awareness devoid of temporal divisions. With the help of the doctrine of the instantaneous passing away of all phenomena, we just have to reason our way there.

## NOTES

1. Here and throughout, I refer to the R. S. Pine-Coffin translation of Augustine's *Confessions* (New York: Penguin, 1961). My thanks to Sean Hannan for our many conversations about time in Augustine and the Buddhist world, as well as to the other editors for inviting this contribution. My thanks, too, to Joy Brennan, Sonam Kachru, and James Wetzel for taking the time to read a near-final draft.

2. Paul Ricoeur, *Time and Narrative*, Vol. 1, tr. Kathleen McLaughlin and David Pellauer (Chicago: University of Chicago Press, 1984), 25, referring to *Confessions*, 11.13.

3. James Wetzel, *Augustine and the Limits of Virtue* (Cambridge: Cambridge University Press, 1992), 25.

4. As I hope will become clear over the course of this chapter, the experience of this radical presentism, and the omniscience (*sarvajña*) it implies for the authors who will be our focus further, is rather far removed from both the contemporary discourse of mindfulness and mindfulness as conceived in classical *Abhidharma* sources. On this issue in contemporary Buddhist studies, see in particular Georges Dreyfus, "Is Mindfulness Present-centred and Non-judgmental? A Discussion of the Cognitive Dimensions of Mindfulness," *Contemporary Buddhism* 12 (2011), 41–54, and John Dunne, "Toward an Understanding of Non-dual Mindfulness," *Contemporary Buddhism* 12 (2011), 71–88. For a lucid critique of present-centered views of mindfulness, bringing together Augustine and Buddhist sources, see Sean Hannan, *On Time, Change, History, and Conversion* (London: Bloomsbury, 2020), 71–89.

5. See Joy Brennan's contribution to this volume for another account of this issue in the Mahāyāna.

6. Th. Stcherbatsky, *Buddhist Logic* (London: Dover, 1962), 19. For an introduction to the doctrine of momentariness and arguments in support of it, see Stcherbatsky, *Buddhist Logic*, 79–118, and Satkari Mookerjee, *The Buddhist Philosophy of Universal Flux: An Exposition of the Philosophy of Critical Realism as Expounded by the School of Dignāga* (Calcutta: University of Calcutta Press, 1935), 1–86. For a discussion of the origins of the doctrine, see Alexander von Rospatt, *The Buddhist Doctrine of Momentariness: A Survey of the Origins and Early Phase of this Doctrine up to Vasubandhu* (Stuttgart: Franz Steiner, 1995). For an insightful exploration of the Theravāda account of momentariness and continuity, which we'll have opportunity to return to further, see Steven Collins, *Selfless Persons: Imagery and Thought in Theravāda Buddhism* (Cambridge: Cambridge University Press, 1982), 199–261.

7. See Sonam Kachru's contribution to this volume for Buddhist views quite opposed to those I discuss.

8. See Tom Tillemans, "Dharmakīrti," in the *Stanford Encyclopedia of Philosophy*, ed. Edward N. Zalta (https://plato.stanford.edu/archives/spr2017/entries/dharmakiirti/), 1.3. Tillemans offers a helpful analogy: "If an epidemiologist, for example, found that certain factors had been constant for quite some time before the outbreak of an infectious disease and remained unchanged at the time of the outbreak, he would tend to discount them as being responsible for the epidemic. And if he found that some new

powerful factors immediately preceded the outbreak, he most likely would pin the causality on them rather than on what had remained constant all along."

9. Yūichi Kajiyama, *An Introduction to Buddhist Philosophy: An Annotated Translation of the Tarkabhāṣā of Mokṣākaragupta* (Vienna: Arbeitskreis für Tibetische und Buddhistische Studien, 1998), 87.

10. Tillemans, "Dharmakīrti," note 16.

11. These details need not detain us here, though some of the objections raised by Naiyāyika philosophers, and the Buddhist responses to these objections, will concern us further. For sustained discussion of the intricacies of these proofs, see (in addition to Stcherbatsky, Mookerjee, von Rospatt, and Tillemans): John Dunne, *Foundations of Dharmakīrti's Philosophy* (Boston: Wisdom, 2004), 91–98; Jeson Woo's dissertation, *The Kṣaṇabhaṅgasiddhi-Anvayātmikā: An Eleventh-Century Buddhist Work on Existence and Causal Theory* (Philadelphia: University of Pennsylvania, 1999); and Joel Feldman and Stephen Phillips, *Ratnakīrti's Proof of Momentariness by Positive Correlation (Kṣaṇabhaṅgasiddhi-Anvayātmikā): Transliteration, Translation, and Philosophic Commentary* (New York: American Institute of Buddhist Studies, 2012). The *vināśitvānumāna* in particular deserves further study. While it is sometimes said to have fallen out of favor in later Buddhist traditions, which is then taken as evidence of its unsatisfying nature, it is presented as the paradigmatic proof of momentariness in Mokṣākaragupta's twelfth-century textbook, the *Tarkabhāṣā*. More to the point, it is considered at great length in Jñānaśrīmitra's eleventh-century *Kṣaṇabhaṅgādhyāya*. This section of the work, entitled "The Chapter on Causeless Destruction" (*ahetukavināśādhikāra*), is some fifty-two pages of closely printed Sanskrit prose in its modern edition and remains largely untouched in contemporary scholarship. Further, it is refuted at length in the Udayana's great *Ātmatattvaviveka*, a Naiyāyika response largely to Jñānaśrīmitra. Jñānaśrīmitra and Udayana, two of the preeminent philosophers of their day, are not ones to spend such time on an argument that is obviously bad or uninteresting. Future study will have to uncover the details of this dispute, though I hope to suggest here some reasons for thinking the *vināśitvānumāna* should remain of deep importance for these late Indian Buddhists.

12. See Collins, *Selfless Persons*, 234.

13. See Collins, *Selfless Persons*, 234.

14. William James, *The Principles of Psychology* (New York: Holt, 1890), cited in Collins, *Selfless Persons*, 255.

15. Augustine, *Confessions*, 28.38, cited in Ricoeur, *Time and Narrative*, 20.

16. Ricoeur, *Time and Narrative*, 11.

17. von Rospatt, *Buddhist Doctrine of Momentariness*, 1.

18. For this line of argument, see Mookerjee, *Buddhist Philosophy of Universal Flux*, 66, as well as Matthew Dasti and Stephen Phillips, *The Nyāya-Sūtra: Selections with Early Commentaries* (Indianapolis: Hackett Publishing Company, 2017), 74–94. For a discussion of this objection together with a line of Buddhist response, see Matthew Kapstein, *Reason's Traces: Identity and Interpretation in Indian and Tibetan Buddhist Thought* (Boston: Wisdom, 2001), 113–133, 347–392.

19. That this view was contested by some Buddhists who held that the past and future did exist is evidenced by Sonam Kachru's contribution to this volume.

20. Mookerjee, *Buddhist Philosophy of Universal Flux*, 67.

21. Woo, *Kṣaṇabhaṅgasiddhi-Anvayātmikā*, 183 (modified slightly); Sanskrit text at 69: *yadi nāmaikam adhyakṣaṃ na pūrvāparavittimat, adhyakṣadvayasadbhāve prākparāvedanaṃ katham.* Compare Mookerjee, *Buddhist Philosophy of Universal Flux*, 67–68. Ratnakīrti here tells us this verse comes from Prajñākaragupta's *Bhāṣyālaṃkāra* on Dharmakīrti's *Pramāṇavārttika*, which we'll have opportunity to refer to further, though Woo was (and I am) unable to find it there.

22. The details of the inferential ascertainment of causality in Ratnakīrti and Jñānaśrīmitra are complex and need not detain us here. What is important for us is that the present cognition is capable of making this inference insofar as it contains within itself memory-traces of past cognitions. For translations of and commentaries on Ratnakīrti's concise discussion of this in his *Kṣaṇabhaṅgasiddhiḥ Anvayātmikā*, see Woo, *Kṣaṇabhaṅgasiddhi-Anvayātmikā*, 180–183, and Feldman and Phillips, *Ratnakīrti's Proof of Momentariness*, 81–83. For Jñānaśrīmitra's view of the determination of causal relationships, see Kajiyama's "*Trikapañcakacintā*: Development of the Buddhist Theory on the Determination of Causality," in *Studies in Buddhist Philosophy (Selected Papers)*, ed. Katsumi Mimaki et al. (Kyoto: Rinsen Book Company, 2005), 475–490.

23. See, for instance, Vātsyāyana's formulation of this argument in the *Nyāyasūtrabhāṣya*: "The self, having previously acquired pleasure through contact with an object of a certain type, desires to possess an object of that very type whenever it sees it. It is [evidence for the existence] of the self that this desire-to-possess occurs, because a single seer synthesizes (*pratisaṃdhā-*) the seeing. For even with respect to a determinate object, that [synthesis] cannot be based solely upon discrete mental events (*buddhibheda*), e.g., [the discrete mental events associated with] different bodies." This passage is translated in Kapstein, *Reason's Traces*, 147, 378. I have inserted "evidence for the existence" for Kapstein's "the mark" (*liṅga*). Again, compare Dasti and Phillips, *Nyāya-Sūtra*, 74–94.

24. This is a paraphrase of Jñānaśrīmitra's point, developed over the course of the second chapter of the *Sākārasiddhiśāstra*, and summarized in an elegant verse in *Jñānaśrīmitranibandhāvali (Buddhist Philosophical Works of Jñānaśrīmitra)*, ed. Anantalal Thakur (Patna: Kashi Prasad Jayaswal Research Institute, 1959), 395: *sarvā nirviṣayaiva kalpanamatir vyāvṛttibhedānugasvākārotkalitā tu vīkṣitaphalasmṛtyādim ātanvatī, lokasyākṣipati pravṛttim anapekṣyaivānyad adhyakṣavad vastvāropa itīrito 'rciṣi jalāropo janānām iva.* "All conceptual cognition really has no object. Nevertheless, inasmuch as it has sprung up with its proper appearance that conforms to a particular exclusion, stretching to incorporate (*ātanvatī*) such things as the memory of a result perceived in the past, conceptual cognition instigates (*ākṣipati*) purposeful activity on the part of ordinary people without requiring anything else at all, in this respect being like perceptual cognition. It is said to be the superimposition of an entity, just like the superimposition of water onto rays of light on the part of ordinary people [when they experience a mirage]." Thakur's edition reads *jalānām*, against the manuscript's *janānām*: see the manuscript of Jñānaśrīmitra's work, preserved in the collection of Göttingen with the shelf-mark Xc 14/25.

25. Thakur, *Jñānaśrīmitranibandhāvali*, 403.13–14.

26. Augustine, *Confessions*, 11.29, 279.
27. See chapter II.E of von Rospatt, *Buddhist Doctrine of Momentariness*, entitled "The Experience of Momentariness," 196–218.
28. von Rospatt, *Buddhist Doctrine of Momentariness*, 198.
29. Galen Strawson, *Things That Bother Me: Death, Freedom, the Self, Etc.* (New York: New York Review of Books, 2018), 36–39.
30. Strawson, *Things That Bother Me*, 37.
31. Strawson, *Things That Bother Me*, 39.
32. On yogic perception, see Steven Goodman's dissertation *A Buddhist Proof for Omniscience: The "Sarvajñasiddhi" of Ratnakīrti* (Temple University, 1989); John Dunne, "Realizing the unreal: Dharmakīrti's theory of yogic perception," *Journal of Indian Philosophy* 34 (2006), 497–519; the essays in *Yogic Perception, Meditation and Altered States of Consciousness*, ed. Eli Franco, in collaboration with Dagmar Eigner (Vienna: Verlag der Österreichische Akademie der Wissenschaften, 2009); and finally, three works by Jeson Woo: "Gradual and Sudden Enlightenment: The Attainment of *yogipratyakṣa* in the Later Indian Yogācāra School," *Journal of Indian Philosophy* 37 (2009), 179–188; "Buddhist Theory of Momentariness and Yogipratyakṣa," *Indo-Iranian Journal* 55 (2012), 1–13; and "On the Yogic Path to Enlightenment in the Later Yogācāra," *Journal of Indian Philosophy* 42 (2014), 499–509. See Parimal Patil, *Against a Hindu God: Buddhist Philosophy of Religion in India* (New York: Columbia University Press, 2009), 328–329, note 33, for Ratnakīrti's initial presentation of the inference for yogic perception's possibility: "Every mental element that is accompanied by repeated reflection that is sincere, uninterrupted, and continues for a long period of time is capable of becoming manifest, like the mental image of a young woman to her lover. And these mental images, whose objects are the four noble truths, are mental elements that are accompanied by repeated reflection." For the Sanskrit, see Anantalal Thakur, *Ratnakīrtinibandhāvaliḥ (Buddhist Nyāya Works of Ratnakīrti)*, Second Revised Edition (Patna: Kashi Prasad Jayaswal Research Institute, 1975), 1.18–21. Note that, as Patil argues (330–332), we may understand "selflessness" and "momentariness" by "the four noble truths" in Ratnakīrti's system.
33. We can say that, generally, it is the Mīmāṃsā tradition that objects to the *possibility* of yogic perception, while the Nyāya tradition, which accepts yogic perception, argues that it is not possible *for the Buddhist who is committed to momentariness*. For our considerations here, Buddhist responses to Nyāya will be of particular importance. For a consideration of the Mīmāṃsā critique of yogic perception and Buddhist responses to this line of critique, see in particular Larry McCrea's "'Just Like Us, Just Like Now': The Tactical Implications of the Mīmāṃsā Rejection of Yogic Perception," 55–70, and John Taber's "Yoga and our Epistemic Predicament," 71–92, both in Franco, *Yogic Perception*.
34. See, for instance, Thakur, *Ratnakīrtinibandhāvaliḥ*, 31.13–17; Goodman, *Buddhist Proof for Omniscience*, 272.
35. In addition to the introduction in Goodman's *Buddhist Proof for Omniscience*, see Sara McClintock, *Omniscience and the Rhetoric of Reason: Śāntarakṣita and Kamalaśīla on Rationality, Argumentation and Religious Authority* (Boston:

Wisdom, 2010), for a fascinating study of omniscience in Buddhist philosophy. My understanding is largely indebted to her work, although, as we'll see, Jñānaśrīmitra and Ratnakīrti nuance their account of omniscience differently from her principal subjects, Śāntarakṣita and Kamalaśīla.

36. Thakur, *Ratnakīrtinibandhāvaliḥ*, 21.22–23; Goodman, *Buddhist Proof for Omniscience*, 239.

37. Thakur, *Ratnakīrtinibandhāvaliḥ*, 21.23–26; Goodman, *Buddhist Proof for Omniscience*, 239.

38. The proposed dates are those of Motoi Ono, cited in Shinya Moriyama, *Omniscience and Religious Authority: A Study of Prajñākaragupta's Pramāṇavārttikālaṅkārabhāṣya ad Pramāṇavārttika II.8–10 and 29–33* (Leipzig: LIT Verlag, 2014), 2.

39. Moriyama, *Omniscience and Religious Authority*, 69.

40. See Moriyama, *Omniscience and Religious Authority*, 69–71.

41. *Pramāṇavārtikabhāshyam or Vārtikālaṅkāraḥ of Prajñākaragupta (Being a Commentary on Dharmakīrti's Pramāṇavārtikam)*, ed. Rāhula Sāṅkṛtyāyana (Patna: Kashi Prasad Jayaswal Research Institute, 1953), 114.23; Moriyama, *Omniscience and Religious Authority*, 73 (translation modified).

42. Sāṅkṛtyāyana, *Pramāṇavārtikabhāshyam*, 113.7–8; Franco, "Perception of Yogis: Some Epistemological and Metaphysical Considerations," in *Religion and Logic in Buddhist Philosophical Analysis, Proceedings of the 4th International Dharmakīrti Conference, Vienna, August 23–27, 2005*, ed. H. Krasser et al. (Vienna: Verlag der Österreichische Akademie der Wissenschaften, 2011), 81–98, here 96.

43. Thakur, *Jñānaśrīmitranibandhāvali*, 331.15–16; Thakur, *Ratnakīrtinibandhāvaliḥ*, 22.4; Goodman, *Buddhist Proof for Omniscience*, 240.

44. Franco, "Perception of Yogis," 96.

45. Thakur, *Jñānaśrīmitranibandhāvali*, 331.23–26: "In order to cognize the forms of things as temporally distinct," or more literally, "as partaking of temporal difference," *kālabhedabhāgivasturūpapratitaye*. As is common practice, Jñānaśrīmitra only cites the first quarter rather than the whole of verse 3628 of the *Tattvasaṃgraha*. Thakur already notes the reference in his footnote. I give the whole verse in my translation. See Ganganatha Jha, *The Tattvasaṅgraha of Śāntarakṣita, with the Commentary of Kamalaśīla* (Baroda: Baroda Oriental Institute, 1937–39).

46. The question of how things look to the yogin who thus determines past and future only upon arising from meditation is an important question that, unfortunately, takes us beyond the scope of our current discussion. Suffice it to say, Jñānaśrīmitra and Ratnakīrti explore the problem, unpacking the yogin's knowledge of things as constituted by resemblance alone, and not by both resemblance and a causal relation, as in the case of our knowledge. It is like, they suggest, a true dream (*satyasvapnavad*) brought on by the power of a deity (*devatādhipatyāt*). For Jñānaśrīmitra, see Thakur, *Jñānaśrīmitranibandhāvali*, 330.24–331.8. For Ratnakīrti, see Thakur, *Ratnakīrtinibandhāvaliḥ*, 21.31–33, and Goodman, *Buddhist Proof for Omniscience*, 239–245, esp. 240.

47. There is a large literature on *svasaṃvedana*, self-awareness, or reflexive awareness, in the tradition of Dignāga and Dharmakīrti. One would do

well to start with the classic account in Mookerjee, *Buddhist Philosophy of Universal Flux*, 319–336; Paul Williams, *The Reflexive Nature of Awareness. A Tibetan Madhyamaka Defense* (Richmond: Curzon Press, 1998); Dan Arnold, "Is Svasaṃvitti Transcendental? A Tentative Reconstruction Following Śāntarakṣita," *Asian Philosophy* 15 (2005), 77–111; and the articles collected in the special issue of the *Journal of Indian Philosophy* 38, no. 3 (June 2010): "Buddhist Theories of Self-awareness (*svasaṃvedana*): Reception and Critique," particularly those of Birgit Kellner, Shinya Moriyama, and Dan Arnold.

48. Thakur, *Jñānaśrīmitranibandhāvali*, 412.18–21. I have replaced Jñānaśrīmitra's "all this," *samastam etat*, with the implied "causal relationships and temporal sequence," *hetuphalabhāva* and *pūrvāparabhāva*, as per the foregoing objection to which this verse is the beginning of a lengthy response. My understanding of Jñānaśrīmitra here is influenced by the remainder of his discussion. See chapters 4 and 5 of my dissertation, *Buddhahood and Philosophy of Mind: Ratnākaraśānti, Jñānaśrīmitra, and the Debate over Mental Content (Ākāra)* (University of Chicago, 2019).

49. For these characterizations, see, respectively, Thakur, *Jñānaśrīmitranibandhāvali*, 416.16–18, and Tomlinson, *Buddhahood and Philosophy of Mind*, 249; Thakur, *Jñānaśrīmitranibandhāvali*, 439.24–27, and Tomlinson, *Buddhahood and Philosophy of Mind*, 343.

50. Thakur, *Jñānaśrīmitranibandhāvali*, 439.24–25: *vinmātracintāyāṃ punaḥ sarvavyāpāroparamaḥ*. The implications of this radical presentism for Jñānaśrīmitra's buddhology are complex and take us beyond the scope of this chapter. I have begun to unpack them in Chapter 5 of *Buddhahood and Philosophy of Mind*, where I discuss the wondrous (*āścārya*) character of buddhahood, marked by Buddha's manifestation in the world despite this view of his immersion in self-awareness. For a general discussion of this basic buddhological problem—how does Buddha, whose realization seems to transcend the world of time and action, nevertheless compassionately manifest in the world to lead us from suffering?—see Paul Griffiths, *On Being Buddha: The Classical Doctrine of Buddhahood* (Albany: SUNY Press, 1994).

51. Augustine, *Confessions*, 11.29, 278–279.

*Chapter 17*

# Out of the Abyss

## On Pedagogical Relationality and Time in the Confessions *and the* Lotus Sutra

Joy Brennan

I approach the topic of time in the work of Augustine as, first, a longtime student and lover of the Buddhist tradition, both its rich intellectual legacy and its living practice. I am also, not equally in commitment or measure but equally in a certain sort of intellectual ardor, a student and lover of Augustine's *Confessions*. From the perspective of Buddhist thought, the first striking thing about the *Confessions* is that it accomplishes something similar to what was accomplished by the *Abhidharma* textual tradition of Buddhist reflection (roughly equivalent to something like the systematic theology of the Christian tradition). It rewrites human life in accordance with a vision of ultimate reality and invites its readers into the process of reordering themselves so that they may live anew, bringing their own lives along in the wake of the intellectual accord established between our frail finite selves and, as the Buddhist tradition has it, things as they are.

But unlike *Abhidharma* texts—which are, it must be said, not much fun to read until one is well along in that process of reordering, and even then the texts require the supplements of the intellect and the imagination to become compelling—the invitation of the *Confessions* into this reordering is both sweetened and darkened by its full embrace of the eroticism of life, omnipresent in the text not in spite of but because of the author's struggle to, and apparent success in, reordering one's own desires away from the bodily and toward God. Sex and the body's desires or capacities for pleasure appear almost nowhere in the *Abhidharma*. And when they do, it is clinical. Indeed, this might be thought to be true of whole swaths of the Buddhist textual tradition.[1] Where in this tradition is the desire and pursuit of bodily pleasure, even pleasurable pain? And, more pointedly for present purposes, where is eros, that cycle of anticipation and fulfillment that seems to mix the desire for pleasure with a desire for truth and eternity?

I want here to place side-by-side two scenes, one from the *Confessions* and one from a Buddhist text in which I think we do find a form of eros, in which human desire is directed, much like Augustine's bodily desires are ultimately redirected, toward something vast and encompassing, expressing a kind of ultimacy that represents the highest ideals of the tradition. The text I will look at, the *Lotus Sutra*, is part of the broad and far-ranging corpus of Mahayana sutra (scriptural) literature.[2] Unlike *Abhidharma* texts, these sutras purport to be the words of the Buddha, and they are not always or primarily concerned with comprehensive systematicity. But they do both envision a life reordered and encourage that reordering in readers, and like the *Confessions*, they often do so through narrative.

From the perspective of anyone well versed in the textual heritage of Buddhist East Asia, the *Lotus Sutra* is a go-to text for reflections on the Buddhist tradition's relationship to the problems of temporality. In particular, it uses the framework of *vow* to exemplify a kind of relationship into which finite beings—limited in both time and space—have the capacity and responsibility to enter in order to attain salvation from suffering for oneself and all other beings. I'd like to situate this vow as parallel to the form that desire for God seems to take in Augustine's *Confessions*, where bodily desire reordered becomes desire for God, itself a kind of gateway to the eternal. Beyond this, I am interested in a scene from the *Lotus Sutra* that forms an illuminating parallel to a passage from the *Confessions*, one to which I've long been drawn. These scenes, placed side by side, show how vow and desire work in these respective texts, as well as how each is a particular response to a problem associated with time.

The sameness of the two scenes lies in their shared sense that humans are in an essentially pedagogical relationship with perfection itself, where perfection is understood primarily in terms of eternity and secondarily in terms of the knowledge of that eternality. In the *Lotus Sutra*, this pedagogical relationship is mutually occurring among all beings: ordinary beings, those on the Buddhist path, bodhisattvas, and even buddhas. Any ostensible hierarchy among beings based on wisdom—like the difference between an ordinary person and a Buddha—is flattened in light of this pedagogical mutuality. In the *Confessions*, this relationship occurs between the mortal and the creator, but here the hierarchy is strengthened rather than weakened by an increase in understanding, though the strengthening of the hierarchy, of the sense of difference between a mortal and God, seems for Augustine to increase the mortal's commitment to their relationship with God, precisely by unifying our desires in the direction of this being. And in each case, temporality itself is the medium for the fulfillment of this perfection or for the pursuit of that fulfillment. For the *Lotus Sutra*, the capacity to undertake a vow that requires an eternal enactment is itself a personalization, or personal cultivation, of perfection. For the *Confessions*, it is time as the shadow of eternity, time within which desire enacts the stretching toward the eternal, that forms the vehicle for perfection. Finally, in both cases, the body remains central to the project of salvation insofar as it is transformed into a site of pedagogical relationality.

I will begin with the scene from the *Confessions*, as it is likely to be more familiar to readers of this volume. The passage in which I take interest arrives in Book VIII, whose conversion narrative ends the drama of Augustine's personal struggle and initiates a new mode of expression in the text, wherein the author writes with the serenity and confidence of the reordered. Just prior to the conversion, and forming a key step in the sequence leading up to it, is another scene, one which leaves us with an odd double-feeling. The reader might pass it by quickly as yet another instance of what (on the first many passes through the text) strikes one as a kind of repeated self-flagellation Augustine metes out to himself in punishment for his continued pursuit of his own sexual fulfillment. But the reader might also get stuck here, as I have done many times, coming back again and again to scrutinize the scene for something it seems to intimate but does not want to divulge. Here is Augustine narrating the episode, from Sarah Ruden's translation:

> This was the story Ponticianus told us. But while he was speaking, you, Master, twisted me back to myself,[3] catching me from behind, where I'd take up position in my unwillingness to pay any attention to what I was. You stood me firmly in front of my own face, so that I could see how ugly I was, how deformed and dirty, blotched with rashes and sores. I saw, and I shuddered with disgust, but I had nowhere to make off to. If I so much as tried to turn my gaze away from myself, there Ponticianus was, telling that story of his, and you again confronted me with myself and forced me to look, so that I would find my sin and hate it. I knew it, but I tried to pretend I didn't; I tried to squelch any awareness of it, and to forget.[4]

There are many striking things about this scene. It is vivid, not least because we the readers are invited to see what Augustine sees. It is dramatic, because the whole sweep of the author's telling of his own life story up to this point seems to be captured by and expressed in the look of the body that he is now made to behold. And it contains a kind of puzzle: How can one take up position behind one's own self? How can one, having done so, ever be brought right again? That the latter puzzle is resolved by the hand of God does not mitigate the first problem. We can still ask: What could possibly have brought this situation about? And what is it *like* to hide behind oneself? But another striking thing about this scene—and this is what I want to examine here—is that it envisions a human refusal to reckon honestly with both temporality and the prospect of eternity.

This point is illuminated through comparison to the parallel scene from the *Lotus Sutra*, and the comparison itself is rooted in two shared features of the two scenes. First, both scenes show the protagonist from each text doubled and encountering his double. Second, both scenes activate the literary figure of *mise en abyme*, or placing into the abyss, one by employing it and the other by intimating but ultimately refusing its use. This intimation and refusal functions, in the *Confessions*' scene, as an invitation and rejection of the opportunity for Augustine's character-double to narrate his own life, where narration requires memory of the past, awareness of the present, and anticipation of some future. That this double lacks the capacity to narrate, that he is *only* desiring body, heightens our sense that the body is for Augustine both intrinsically temporal (insofar as it is subject to time), and yet has the capacity to act in ways that induce it into atemporality, which I here understand as an opposition not just to temporality, but also to eternity. In particular, narrator-Augustine ties character-Augustine to the body's sexuality, and the weakness of the will that is symptomatic of it. Insofar as the sexual life of the body happens in time but ignores that time is, by its nature, the medium for the fulfillment of the desire for eternity, the person then does not and seemingly cannot participate in the act of reaching toward eternity, an act that serves as the true calling of temporal creatures. This reaching is desire reoriented, and properly oriented, toward God. So for Augustine, at least the Augustine of the *Confessions*, to pursue desire's fulfillment through the vehicle of the sexually desirous body is to refuse, among other things, both the reality of the experience of temporality and the invitation to eternity. On this view, the opacity of the sexually desirous body blocks not only the light of the world but also the light of the intellect as that which is illuminated by memory, awareness, and anticipation. But our scene's placement will show that the intellect is illuminated by the erotically desirous body—the body joined with other bodies in a community oriented toward God.

The *Lotus Sutra*'s use of *mise en abyme* functions to show that the Buddhist vow to continue the work of salvation is both a response to and resolution of a paradox of time, in particular the paradox of undertaking the task of the salvation of all beings when those beings are endless both in space and throughout time. This vow itself transforms human desire for impermanent objects of the world—including for worldly sorts of relationships—into the desire for liberation for all. Our scene shows that the very undertaking of the vow is its own fulfillment, and that moreover this undertaking must be enacted with and through one's spatial and temporal finitude, here exemplified and instantiated by the body. Let us first look to the *Lotus Sutra*, and later return to the scene of Augustine and his double in *Confessions* 8.

The best context within which to approach the *Lotus Sutra*'s scene of doubling and *mise en abyme* is the text's many innovations vis-à-vis the Buddhist tradition. A Buddhist sutra is always a record of some teaching moment of the Buddha. It is a story with setting, plot, and characters, where the message and meaning is what the Buddha taught to those present. In non-Mahayana sutras, commonly taken to represent the teachings of the early Buddhist tradition, a given sutra's setting and characters appear mundane, without challenge to worldly conventions about scene, character, and dialogue. The Buddha appears to be just a man. The sutra locates him at a specific, historically attested place. The interlocutors—maybe his students, maybe adherents of other schools of practice, and maybe just curious people—approach with questions or to debate. The Buddha engages. His audience and we, the readers, learn from his discourse. Mahayana sutras, on the other hand, play with narrative setting, the notion of a Buddha, and even the notion of what the Buddha's teachings should be like. First appearing nearly half a millennium after the death of the historical figured called the Buddha, these texts explode the scene: the setting is grand, cosmic even, dripping in jewels, arrayed with garlands, extending infinitely in all directions. In a palace, on a mountaintop, under a jeweled canopy of infinite expanse, the audience throngs, bringing together humans, gods and other mythical beings common to South Asian literature and iconography. No longer is the Buddha just a man, at least as we normally understand a man to be. Instead, he is godlike, with the marks of a great man, among them a tuft of hair between his eyes and a light shining forth from his forehead illuminating all realms. He can even proliferate in space or send emanations into the infinite cosmic realms. Sometimes, all of these emanations join in to hear the preaching.

The *Lotus Sutra* begins with just such a quintessentially Mahayanic explosion of the conventions of time and space, as well as of literary expectations about a Buddhist sutra. The opening finds the Buddha at one of his frequented spots, Vulture's Peak in Rajagrha. But there the text's use of the conventions of early sutra literature ends. Here, the Buddha's audience is vast: 12,000 monks, a chief nun and her 6,000 followers, 80,000 bodhisattvas, and a thronging multitude drawn from the Indic pantheon of gods and other mythical beings. The Buddha first preaches another short sutra called the *Sutra on Immeasurable Meanings*, which acts as a preface to the *Lotus Sutra* by reminding the reader that all teachings, even these absolutely true dharma teachings, are without fixed meaning. He then silently emits a ray of white light from between his eyebrows. The ray illuminates the infinite realms of the cosmos, each containing its own Buddha as dharma teacher, at which moment flowers rain from the sky and fragrant breezes delight the assembly. The text explains this magical occurrence through a dialogue between the Bodhisattva Maitreya, whom any reader familiar with the Buddhist tradition will recognize as the figure marked as the "future Buddha," and another bodhisattva, known for his great wisdom, named Mañjuśri. Why is this ray of light emanating from the Buddha's forehead, Maitreya asks? The bodhisattva Mañjuśri tells us that it is, in short, because now the Buddha will preach the dharma, or the Buddhist teachings. Through these many contraventions of the conventions of Buddhist scriptures, the *Lotus Sutra* announces a new figuration of the concepts of space and buddhas: space is infinite but fully available to a Buddha, and buddhas are infinite but fully present to hear, preach, and understand the dharma.

Then in chapter 11 of the *Lotus Sutra*, we encounter something else entirely new. Not only is the space of the sutra's setting cosmicized and the concept of a Buddha multiplied seemingly to infinity, but time does something new, too. Here the text narrates and then fulfills the vow of a past Buddha to be always present in attendance when the *Lotus Sutra* itself is preached. This figure, named Many Jewels, lived as the Buddha—the being who not only realized how to end suffering for himself, but brought these saving teachings to the beings of his time—many eons in the past. When his lifetime as the Buddha came to an end and he was nearing entrance into extinction (nirvana), or in conventional terms as he neared death, he vowed that he would appear to hear and praise the teachings of the *Lotus Sutra* whenever and wherever it is preached. In fulfillment of this vow, chapter 11 of the text sees Many Jewels' stupa emerge suddenly from the ground in front of Shakyamuni Buddha (the historical founder of Buddhism and also the Buddha of the present eon), who is preaching the sutra, as well as in front of the entire cosmic audience in attendance. All assembled hear a voice emerge from the stupa extolling Shakyamuni for preaching the *Lotus Sutra*. A bodhisattva in the assembly asks about the stupa and the voice, and Shakyamuni relays Many Jewels' vow. Then, in response to the assembly's desire to see Many Jewels' body, Shakyamuni opens the stupa's door. The assembly sees Many Jewels in his full living form, his body perfectly unimpaired by his apparent death many eons ago. He is seated on a lion throne (a common symbol of the majesty a Buddha possesses in virtue of his knowledge of the truth of the dharma) as he listens to and praises the *Lotus Sutra* while Shakyamuni preaches it. Once Many Jewels has made room on his throne so that Shakyamuni may take a seat next to him, the latter rises up into the air and sits aside Many Jewels. At the scene's climax, the entire assembly desires to float in the air to see the two buddhas together as they continue to listen to the sutra. In response, Shakyamuni lifts them up with his supernatural powers and holds them suspended in the air as they gaze at the two buddhas, and continue to listen to and appreciate the teachings of the *Lotus Sutra*, which itself has seventeen more chapters after this scene.

For the reader who understands the structure and parameters of contemporary Buddhist schemas of time, the central scene of this text is startling for many reasons. In the earliest forms of Buddhism and for many later forms too, there was only one buddha in a given eon, and the common trope of past, present, and future buddhas expresses this teaching. The three buddhas are all known to us by name, for the Buddhist literature accounts for the biography of the past Buddha Dipamkara, the present Buddha Shakyamuni, and the Buddha of the next eon, called the future Buddha, none other than the Maitreya of the *Lotus Sutra's* opening scene. And these three are just specified relative to our (the living's) place in the present, since there is in fact an infinite number of buddhas stretching into the past and another infinite set stretching into the future.

In this way, the tradition takes in the scope of the cycle of life, death, and rebirth—which occurs endlessly throughout cosmic time, itself understood to be an infinitely recurring cycle of the rise and fall of eons—and indicates to us, through the naming of the three buddhas, that it has us covered, so to speak, at all times.

So a past Buddha is supposed to be just that: past, or rather passed on, having died just like any mortal dies. But here, a Buddha from the distant past, Many Jewels, turns out not to have died at all, or at least to have the miraculous ability to revive whenever he needs to fulfill his vow by appearing to listen to the *Lotus Sutra*. Corresponding to this refiguration of a Buddha is the transformation of the notion of the stupa. These monuments, common to the South Asian landscape and transformed into pagodas in East Asia, are supposed to hold the relics of a buddha or other important Buddhist figure. And, of course, they should rest on the ground. But here the stupa is buried beneath the ground, its subliminal perdurance emblematizing the patience, persistence, and ever-presentness of the vow of the buddha within. More startlingly, it contains the living figure of the Buddha himself, transforming the notion of nirvana from that of extinction (after which we cannot say whether a buddha "is" or "is not," though certainly he has ceased living as an embodied creature) to a nirvana in which the Buddha continues to have not only a life but also a mission in accord with his Buddhahood.

While these changes alter our conceptions of both Buddhist time and of the nature of a Buddha, perhaps most puzzling is Many Jewels' vow. In non-Mahayana Buddhism, just as there is only one Buddha per eon, there is also in any given eon only one bodhisattva, a being who is working on becoming the Buddha for the next eon. This being becomes "the bodhisattva" of an eon by vowing to become the Buddha in a future lifetime. So he is different from all of the others listening to and learning from the Buddha of his age. While they simply hope to save themselves from suffering, he vows to become the next Buddha, the one in the next eon who will preach and teach so as to help release all beings from suffering.

But here we learn that Many Jewels, during his life as the Buddha, took yet another vow: the vow to always appear at any place and time where the *Lotus Sutra* is being preached. This is a perplexing thing to do: Why should a buddha, already enacting his vow to save all beings, take on another vow? And this particular vow is even more perplexing to the reader of the *Lotus Sutra*, who quickly learns that the text at least appears to be without any central teaching. There is no chapter or section in the sutra where the reader feels she has arrived at the central teaching. Rather, though punctuated with references to itself as the supreme one true teaching, the text seems to simply meander through these frequent instances of self-reference, predictions of future Buddhahood for members of the Buddha's audience, stories about past and present buddhas and disciples, and a number of parables. Here is Brook Ziporyn, echoing the eighteenth-century Japanese Zen Master Hakuin in describing a common reaction to the *Lotus Sutra*:

> What's all this about being the "King of the Sūtras"? This is just a bunch of muddled parables and tall tales! There's the declaration that the Buddhas appear in the world for one purpose only, but, then, what *is* that purpose? Something about the knowledge and experience of a Buddha, but it never tells us what *that* is . . . . It has been called, with some justice and considerable wit, a long prologue without a book: talking again and again about a teaching called "The *Lotus Sūtra*" and how amazing it is, and then—we never get the teaching, so it seems.[5]

Given all of this, what was the Buddha Many Jewels affirming when he vowed to show up for all preachings of this apparently empty teaching? If we can't figure out what this text is about, why is Many Jewels so committed to it that he waits patiently in his underground mausoleum for it to be preached? And what does it mean in the text when he does show up, in such grand fashion, in a scene that climaxes with two buddhas sitting next to each other on a shared throne, facing their audience, whose suspension in the air gazing back at the two buddhas seems to transmute into a suspension of and in the present moment, lending the whole scene a time-freezing effect?

I approach an answer to this by first taking note of the central literary technique employed in this scene, *mise en abyme* or placing into the abyss. André Gide coined this figure in reference to heraldic icons, and it is commonly applied to both images and narratives.[6] In its narrative form it offers, or at least intimates the offering of, a replication of the whole narrative in one of its parts. Using reflection as a metaphor, we might say that narrative *mise en abyme* occurs when a part of the narrative reflects the whole narrative, such that the reflected whole also contains the reflecting part, which, in turn, again contains the reflected whole, and so on. When this occurs, the reflective process intimates its own infinitude. This is the "abyss" of the figure's name.[7]

I here focus on a particular way of thinking about *mise en abyme* offered by Mieke Bal as an interpretation of Gide's particular interest in coining the term. Gide introduced the term in a journal entry, writing:

> In a work of art, I rather like to find transposed, on the scale of the characters, the very subject of that work. Nothing throws a clearer light upon it or more surely establishes the proportions of the whole.[8]

Bal notices that the term "subject" may refer to either the thematic content or the narrating subject of the work, next observing that Gide's primary interest is "the power of the narrating subject, a power that appears to accumulate when the subject doubles itself."[9] From this, Bal draws out an interpretation of Gide that Moshe Ron describes in the following fashion. For Bal, a narrative that includes such a doubled narrating subject would count as employing *mise en abyme* when two conditions are met:

(1) the presence of at least two narratorial instances, marked by a clear-cut diegetic downshift from one to the other; and (2) a relation of homology between the relation of the higher narrator to this narrative and the character-narrator's to his.[10]

There are problems with using these two requirements to formulate a definition of *mise en abyme* that is both adequate and properly delimitative.[11] But it is useful here because these conditions are precisely those that interest me in the two scenes here compared.

The *Lotus Sutra*'s doubling of the buddhas through the application and enactment of the concept of vow is a relatively a straightforward instance of *mise en abyme*. Shakyamuni Buddha is at least ostensibly the higher narrator, for he is the central subject, preaching the text, while the past Buddha Many Jewels is the character-narrator, standing in a seemingly subordinated relationship to Shakyamuni, while yet having his own relationship to the text. The "abyss" of the figure is intimated when Many Jewels appears to listen to Shakyamuni preach the text, of which the scene of Many Jewels emerging from his stupa to listen appreciatively is a narrative component. Many Jewels therefore hears a narration of his own vow and his own appearance within the story, and the Many Jewels referenced in that narrative will also hear *his* own story told, and so forth into the abyss of infinite replications through infinite time, as the figure's name would have it.

Now we might reflect that ostensibly, or at least by name, these are not the same Buddha, and thus the subject is not in fact duplicated. But I think the point of the text is that we should understand the two buddhas as the same subject, given that both stand in the same relationship to the meaning conveyed by the narrated text itself. That is, as buddhas, both have complete and perfect understanding of the text, which is exemplified when Shakyamuni preaches it and Many Jewels fulfills his vow to hear, appreciate, and praise it.

To understand Bal's second condition for *mise en abyme*, we need to understand the text's use of the concept of vow, and vow's relationship to time. It is after all Many Jewels' vow to appear and hear the *Lotus Sutra* whenever it is preached that sets the scene into motion. This vow is an odd one in the context of Buddhist, and especially Mahayana Buddhist, understandings of vow. As such it is best approached in the context of another much more common Mahayana vow, which is the vow that the bodhisattva later to become the Buddha Many Jewels would have taken: the vow to become a Buddha so that he might save all beings. This itself is the basic bodhisattva vow. And, it turns out, this vow aims at an impossible goal. In the Buddhist cosmos, beings are infinite, not only in space, but also in time, while a Buddha is just a mortal. Moreover, even the eon in which he is the Buddha will eventually end, along with the dharma teachings that he preached. His eon will be replaced by the next eon, *ad infinitum*, and he will be replaced by the next Buddha, and so forth into the infinite expanse of future time. So with this bodhisattva vow, a mortal, limited, finite being, living within a limited and finite world-system, undertakes the impossible: saving all beings, everywhere, for all time.

That the bodhisattva's vows capture this paradox is well expressed by the formulation of four bodhisattva vows outlined by a latter Chinese Buddhist thinker whose thinking was shaped through and through by the *Lotus Sutra*, which formed the basis of the new Buddhist school that he developed. Tiantai Zhiyi lived in the sixth century and was the first Chinese Buddhist to formulate what may be called an indigenous Chinese school of Buddhism. The four bodhisattva vows as Zhiyi formulated them are these:

Beings are numberless, I vow to save them
Delusions are inexhaustible, I vow to end them
Dharma gates are boundless, I vow to study them
The Buddha's way is unsurpassable, I vow to attain it.[12]

Each vow expresses a supreme and life-orienting commitment to an impossibility, and the impossibility is a direct result of the boundlessness of both space and time. These vows express a set of paradoxes that are spatial (numberless beings), temporal (inexhaustible delusions), and conceptual (boundless dharma gates or teachings).

Many Jewels' particular vow here in the *Lotus Sutra* serves as a resolution to the paradoxes of the bodhisattva vows. When Many Jewels appears to hear the sutra preached, his vow is not enacted through his striving toward an unreachable final act. Instead, it is perfectly fulfilled just in and by his acts of appearing, hearing, and praising. This is apparent in the way the text signals Many Jewels' status: he is not *just* a past Buddha. Instead, he is given the highest seat—a lion throne—while Shakyamuni preaching the text sits cross-legged on the ground. And eventually, when Many Jewels invites Shakyamuni to sit next to him, the two are envisioned as complete equals, and indeed as one being, where a being here is specified not as a person with a life history, but as a complete circuit of preaching, hearing, and knowing the dharma, all motivated and circumscribed by the concept of vow.

Thus, the doubling of the Buddha subject that characterizes the scene only at first appears to be a "diegetical downshift" as Bal terms it. Many Jewels appears and seems narratively subordinate to Shakyamuni, just another member of the audience, though an important and highly regarded one. But when the two form a circuit of preaching and hearing in mutual understanding, they become equals in their perfect understanding and expression of the dharma, for this circuit is necessary for the dharma to be understood and upheld, and for the wisdom it expresses to be realized. This equality is of course signified by the image of the two buddhas seated side by side, and with this equality, the frame of how to understand buddhas themselves shifts from a temporal one to a relational one.

As for Bal's second condition, the homology between each Buddha's respective relationship to the narrative itself is expressed in the text's portrayal of the very nature of Buddhahood as a commitment to pedagogical relationality. I draw this phrase from Eve Kosofsky Sedgwick, who in a wonderfully perceptive essay on pedagogy in Buddhism writes that the bodhisattva is "a being whose commitment to pedagogical relationality approaches the horizon of eternity."[13] Sedgwick here captures both the sense of the bodhisattva vows as commitments to an end goal, as well as the sense of the impossibility of ever achieving that goal.

From the position of a student of the buddha(s), I am compelled by this phrase, by how beautifully it captures the aspirations of the bodhisattva. But as a reader of the *Lotus Sutra*, I think Sedgwick errs in leaving the relationship one of means and ends, and one that travels along the course of time, even if time itself is thrown into question by the horizon of eternity. We see Sedgwick move toward an abandonment of a means/ends understanding of vow when she summarizes that statement about a bodhisattva as saying that in "Mahayana scriptures, scenes of teaching and learning are universally desired ends as much as they are instrumental means."[14] Transforming pedagogical relationality from means to ends, Sedgwick reframes it as the goal. Still, if it is an end, some means would seem to be necessary to achieve it. But in the *Lotus Sutra*, there are no such means. Instead, the very point of the text seems to be that we are all already in this relationship, but we just don't know it. This is how I read the text's teaching that all beings will become buddhas, situated alongside the text's portrayal of a buddha as a figure who participates in the circuit of hearing, preaching, and praising this very teaching, which is to say the teaching that all will become buddhas just through these acts of hearing, preaching, and praising.

To depict such a moment of hearing, preaching, and praising among buddhas—which is to say among the two named buddhas, their audience, and we the readers—is then to portray eternity, or the absence of any possible means/end relations mediated by temporal succession. This is the text's sense of perfection itself, and the buddhas already know this perfectly, though our lack of knowledge about it does not thereby make us less perfect, for as the students to their teachers, we are equally necessary for the fulfillment of this pedagogical relationality in its eternal expression.

Whereas the *Lotus Sutra*'s doubling of the buddhas through the application and enactment of the concept of vow is a relatively straightforward instance of *mise en abyme*, the doubling of Augustines refuses to accommodate itself to this literary figure, to strong effect. That Augustine's double appears on the scene invites the reader to think this doubled figure will have his own relationship to the narrative of Augustine's life, just as the Buddha Many Jewels has his own relationship to the narrative of the sutra as preached by Shakyamuni Buddha. What motivates Bal's interpretation of Gide's use of the term "subject," which she takes to refer to the narrating subject rather than simply to the thematic content (the latter being the more obvious interpretation), is that she sees in Gide's work a guiding interest in the narrating subject's relationship to his own narrative. On this reading, when a narrating subject narrates in his own double, we can expect that double to stand in his own relationship to the story or even to another story, but one in which he too figures as narrator. And indeed, I always half expect to hear character-Augustine tell me something, or account for himself in some way, which I think explains my own continual return to and searching attention toward the scene. But instead he appears as just a body, and a diseased one at that. He doesn't speak. He doesn't even seem to look back at narrator-Augustine, who is forced to gaze at him, and does so with shame, disgust, and despair. He is given no internal life. He is body as loathsome object. This body is so mute and insensate that, while Augustine is forced to behold it, it appears to be left without the capacity to peer back. It is narratable only as a scene is narratable. It is a *topos* more than a person.

The sense that this scene calls out for an instance of *mise en abyme* is heightened by its occurrence amid a memorial chain of other figures recounting their own relationships to various narratives. Augustine's doubling here, while effected by the hand of God, is prompted by Ponticianus's account of his own conversion, an account prompted when Ponticianus sees a biblical text (the Epistles of Paul) on the table before him while he sits visiting Augustine. In this narrative, Ponticianus tells of hearing others give an account from the *Life of Antony*, after which he was "amazed and set on fire," "filled with holy love and sobering shame." And if Augustine's doubting comes in the midst of Ponticianus' conversion narrative, it quickly gives way to Augustine's own conversion in the garden at Milan. Again, this conversion is prompted by hearing a biblical text. Again, that text is from the letters of Paul (Romans). And this conversion scene ends Book VIII, allowing Book IX to announce a transition beyond the (at least somewhat straightforwardly) autobiographical account of the first eight books of the *Confessions*, whose narrative significantly climaxes with the conversion account, as though the details of personal or private life were most significant only up to that point. After this turning point in Book IX, we are then met with a series of reflections on memory and time, primarily mediated through interpretations of Genesis, which animate Books X through XIII of the *Confessions*.

The appearance of character-Augustine occurs amid this narrative chain. Others' memories of conversion stretch back in time on one side. The narrative of Augustine's own remembered and recounted conversion stretches forward on the other. Along the way, each subject of conversion stands in a relationship of transformation to another subject's conversion narrative. These figures are all in a pedagogical relationship to each other, where the pedagogical force is derived from and effected through God's agency, but the human relationships are necessary as the medium of that agency. So why doesn't character-Augustine take up his place in the center of this chain?

To this chain of memories and relationships, Augustine's character-double forms a kind of blockage, his body preventing the soul from learning from the experiences of others and from using the medium of time for the purpose of salvation by adopting its own place in this chain, or its own relationship to others' narratives and to his own story. We can then read the mute, bodily Augustine as Augustine the person's own refusal to reckon with time, for it is a refusal to stand in a relationship to one's own narrative, where that narrative is itself authored by God. This refusal is then a refusal of the pedagogical relationship with perfection, or eternity, that is a human's purpose and task.

It is character-Augustine not just as body but also as sexually desirous body that refuses to reckon with the fact or experience of being temporally mediated. Throughout Books I–VIII, we find a smattering of references to sex as a waste of time. Here of course we can understand that time has been wasted because it has not been used in fitting or maximally beneficial ways. On this read, time is a tool for the pursuit of goals. But more pointedly, I think we should take Augustine to mean that time has been wasted in the sense of laid waste to. The use of desire to pursue sexual fulfillment with and in the body destroys the possibility that time offers, which is the desirous stretching toward that which is outside of time, the eternity of God. Here time is not a tool that helps bring us to our goals. It is rather the medium through which we stand in relationship to eternity, and in relationship to others who also turn toward eternity by standing within time in this same way. To allow oneself to be narrated by God, as Ponticianus does, as his friends do when they read the *Life of Antony*, as Antony himself did, and as Augustine eventually does in the garden at Milan, is to situate oneself within a resolution of time's paradoxes. When character-Augustine blocks this possibility, he refuses the scene's offer of *mise en abyme*, or its offer that Augustine enter into the chain of subjects who stand in relationship to each other and to God through their shared desire and mutual encouragement. The fact of the doubled subject, and the narrator's ensuing confrontation with himself, functions not as a fulfillment through the medium of pedagogical relationality, but as the exemplification of that relationality refused. And this relationality refused becomes eternity denied.

The *Lotus Sutra*'s use of *mise en abyme* in the scene where its narrator is doubled helps us to see more clearly the significance of the refusal to follow through with it in *Confessions* 8. In taking up the challenge of the intimated abyss, the *Lotus Sutra* shows us that relationships of teaching and learning are eternal. In failing to take up this challenge, the *Confessions* shows us that to deny these relationships is to deny eternity.

But this failure, in turn, helps us see more clearly the significance of its success in the *Lotus Sutra*. In particular, the parallel draws out a perhaps unexpected—from the position of many strands of Buddhist thought anyways—understanding of how bodies function within the pedagogical relationships portrayed in the sutra.

From the contemporary American cultural context, the *Lotus Sutra* might seem like a decidedly unsexy text. Its tales are strange; some are even morbid or gruesome. And while replete with descriptions of beauty and majesty, these never center on or dwell with the kinds of physical beauty that make people sexually attractive. In fact, I don't want to suggest that sex itself is present in any way, since I just don't think it is. But I do want to say that eros is here, where by eros I mean relationships that take place in and through bodily presence and that create a pulsing circuit of anticipation (parallel to arousal) and fulfillment (parallel to climax) that both binds two or more people together and is experienced as timeless.

We have seen that the frame for thinking about differences between buddhas in the *Lotus Sutra* is not the tri-partite temporal division of past, present, and future buddhas. The text shatters that conceit with the appearance of Many Jewels himself. Instead, the differences between the two buddhas in the text are spatial and bodily, where the necessary function of bodies is to serve as the condition that makes possible a pedagogical relationality whose very occurrence is the fulfillment of vow. When Many Jewels appears, he appears in a perfect bodily form, ensconced inside his perfectly preserved stupa. When the audience asks to see him, they don't just ask to see Many Jewels; they ask to see his body. When his stupa is opened, he uses his eyes to behold the scene, his ears to hear Shakyamuni's preaching, and his voice to audibly appreciate and praise it. He offers Shakyamuni a seat right next to him on his lion throne, a physical symbol of the majesty of the dharma. And there the two sit, side-by-side. The physicality of the scene, including its setting, the stupa and throne, and the two buddhas' uses of their bodies, demarcates not just the setting of the vow, but the possibility of its fulfillment. Through this scene, these two buddhas show their audience how vow is fulfilled. The audience then wants to participate in this relationship of teaching and learning, signified by their desire to be lifted into the air to gaze at the two buddhas seated side-by-side. We the readers, in turn, observe first the pedagogical relationality of the buddhas, then the pedagogical relationality between these two buddhas and their audience, and finally find ourselves drawn into the scene, for as we watch the audience watch the buddhas, we become participants in this many-layered form of relational teaching, wherein just to listen and learn is to fulfill a vow itself.

While in the *Lotus Sutra*, the scene of a doubled subject functions to intimate eternity just through its employment of *mise en abyme*, the *Confessions* intimates the abyss by doubling the subject, only to quickly refuse the intimation in a way that suggests that the body's matter requires the notion of eternity just so it might exemplify its own nature by refusing it. The body is the central image in both scenes, but used very differently, accompanied as it is by different conceptions of the relationship of experiences in time to eternity itself and of the body to both. Many Jewels' body functions as a medium for the infinitude of the eternal truth of the dharma, itself manifested just in the mutuality of beings joining together to form a circuit that expresses understanding of this truth. Augustine's doubled body functions to block narration, and through that, to block the experience of time, the invitation to eternity, and the relationships that foster them.

But in some sense, the scene from the *Lotus Sutra* also refuses something central to the conceit of *mise en abyme*. Our scene in *Confessions* 8 refuses the invitation to eternity and the pedagogical relationships that foster the desire for it. If this is a refusal of an abyss, it is yet abysmal, witnessed by Augustine's account of the diseased specter of this body and his shame in seeing it. In reverse fashion, the *Lotus Sutra* accepts the narrative abyss through its use of *mise en abyme*, but refuses to make of it an abysmal descent. Not only does the image of abyss suggest a falling, while the image of Many Jewels' stupa is quite the opposite—a tower both emerging and rising—but the fixity of the scene seems to refuse precisely something like Augustine's distinction between time and eternity that makes a temporal abyss possible. The two buddhas seated together on the throne in the tower; the audience suspended in the air and, one senses, in time, looking at the buddhas; the intimation of mutual gazing, as we imagine the two buddhas looking back at the audience; all of this forms a scene of not longing, but climax, not hope, but fulfillment. Here, the seeming intimation of infinity (not eternity, but rather a sequence of moments that extends indefinitely) through the use of *mise en abyme* is broken by the fact that this scene is a fulfillment not just of vow but of realization itself. On this reading, what is abysmal is the background condition that sets the stage for the bodhisattva's vow: the facts that beings are numberless and delusions are inexhaustible. Against this backdrop, time becomes the medium for understandings of truths that are eternal. And in understanding these truths, the participants in this scene of teaching and learning find themselves outside of time, suspended not just in the air, but in the eternity expressed in their mutual commitment to each other's salvation, itself nothing other than this mutual commitment. Where Augustine's character-double refuses the abyss and denies looking toward eternity, the buddhas and their audience accept the abyss and, in doing so, paradoxically find themselves already in eternity.

## NOTES

1. I don't want to overstate this point, since there are other swaths of the Buddhist tradition, notably the Vajrayāna, in which the body's desires are central to the tradition's understating of, and modes of practice that deal with, the problematic condition of sentient beings and its resolution.

2. There are a number of reliable English translations of the *Lotus Sutra*. I use that of Bunnō Katō, Yoshirō Tamura, and Kōjirō Miyasaka, *The Threefold Lotus Sutra* (Tokyo: Kosei, 1992), for it includes translations of two other short sutras that often accompany the *Lotus Sutra*, one of which is the *Sutra of Innumerable Meanings*, which I reference further. Another reliable English language translation is Burton Watson's *The Lotus Sutra* (New York: Columbia University Press, 1993).

3. Ruden seems to have straightforwardly made a mistake in translation, rendering "retorquebas me ad me ipsum" as "you turned me back to yourself" rather than "you turned me back to myself." I have corrected the final word of this clause's translation on the basis of James J. O'Donnell, ed., *Augustine Confessions*, vol. 1: Introduction and Text (Oxford: Oxford University Press, 1992), 95.

4. *Confessions* 8.16, tr. Sarah Ruden (New York: Modern Library, 2017), 222–223.

5. Brook Ziporyn, *Emptiness and Omnipresence: An Essential Introduction to Tiantai Buddhism* (Bloomington: Indiana University Press, 2016), 70.

6. I find imagistic uses of *mise en abyme* to convey its central technique quite easily. Think of the old Quaker Oats poster advertisement. It shows an image of a

man holding a box of Quaker Oats, on which is affixed a label that itself shows this same image of this man holding this box of oats, and so forth, at least as far as the eye can see. In general, imagistic uses of this figure rely on spatial intimations of infinity, while its narrative uses rely on temporal ones.

7. A student of Buddhist philosophy and history cannot help but note that this notion of reflection as visual example of and vehicle for understanding narrative uses of *mise en abyme* brings to mind the seventh-century Chinese Buddhist monk Fazang's creation of a hall of mirrors with a Buddha figure at the center to illustrate the teaching of interdependence. See the Internet Encyclopedia of Philosophy's entry on Fazang for a description: https://www.iep.utm.edu/fazang/

8. Quoted in Mieke Bal, "Mise en abyme et iconicité," *Littérature* 29 (1978), 116–128, here 117.

9. Ibid., 117.

10. Moshe Ron, "The Restricted Abyss: Nine Problems in the Theory of *Mise En Abyme*," *Poetics Today* 8, no. 2 (1987), 417–438, here 419.

11. Ron is positively disposed toward Bal's interpretation, yet his own essay focuses on the many technical and conceptual problems that arise when trying to fix a definition of *mise en abyme*.

12. For an introduction to the bodhisattva vows as formulated by Zhiyi, see David W. Chappell, "Searching for a Mahāyāna Social Ethic," *Journal of Religious Ethics* 24, no. 2 (1996), 351–375, 352.

13. Eve Kosofsky Sedgwick, "Pedagogy of Buddhism," in *Touching Feeling: Affect, Pedagogy, Performativity* (Durham: Duke University Press, 2003), 161.

14. Ibid., 161.

# Bibliography

Adams, Marilyn McCord. "Universals in the Early Fourteenth Century." In *The Cambridge History of Later Medieval Philosophy*. Edited by Norman Kretzmann, Anthony Kenny, and Jan Pinborg. Cambridge: Cambridge University Press, 1982. 411–439.

———. *William Ockham*. South Bend: Notre Dame, 1987.

Adams, Robert Merrihew. "Time and Thisness." *Midwest Studies in Philosophy* 11 (1986): 315–329.

Adamson, Peter. "Galen and al-Rāzī on Time." In *Medieval Arabic Thought: Essays in Honour of Fritz Zimmermann*. Edited by Rotraud Hansberger, Muhammad Afifi al-Akiti, and Charles Burnett. London and Turin: Warburg Institute and Nino Aragno Editore, 2012. 1–14.

Alaimo, Stacy, and Susan Hekman, eds. *Material Feminisms*. Bloomington: Indiana University Press, 2008.

Alexander of Aphrodisias. "On Time. Translated and Annotated, with an Introduction, by Robert W. Sharples." *Phronesis* 27, no. 1 (1982): 58–81.

Alexander of Lycopolis. *Of the Manichaeans*. Translated by J B. H. Hawkins. In *Ante-Nicene Fathers*. Edited by P. Schaff. Vol. 6. Peabody, MA: Hendrickson Publishers, 2004. 241–252.

Anderson, Holly. "The Development of the 'Specious Present' and James' Views on Temporal Experience." In *Subjective Time: The Philosophy, Psychology, and Neuroscience of Temporality*. Edited by Dan Lloyd and Valtteri Arstila. Massachusetts: MIT Press, 2014. 25–42.

Anderson, Holly, and Rick Grush. "A Brief History of Time Consciousness: Historical Precursors to James and Husserl." *Journal of the History of Philosophy* 47, no. 2 (2009): 227–307.

Annas, Julia. "Aristotle, Number and Time." *Philosophical Quarterly* 25 (1975): 97–113.

Aristotle. *De Interpretatione*. LCL 321. Translated by Harold Cook. Cambridge, MA: Harvard UP, 1938.

———. *Metaphysics*. LCL 287. Translated by Hugh Tredennick. Cambridge, MA: Harvard UP, 1933.

———. *Metaphysics*. Translated by William David Ross. In *Aristotle: The Complete Works of Aristotle*. Edited by Jonathan Barnes. Vol. 2. Princeton: Princeton University Press, 1995.

———. *Physics*. Vol. 1: Books 1–4.LCL 228. Translated by P.H. Wicksteed and F.M. Cornford. Cambridge, MA: Harvard University Press, 1957.

Armstrong, A.H. "Gnosis and Greek Philosophy." In *Gnosis: Festschrift für Hans Jonas*. Edited by U. Bianchi, M. Krause, J. Robinson, and G. Widengren. Göttingen: Vandenhoeck and Ruprecht, 1978. 87–124.

Arnold, Dan. "Is *Svasaṃvitti* Transcendental? A Tentative Reconstruction Following Śāntarakṣita." *Asian Philosophy* 15 (2005): 77–111.

Arthos, John. "'A Limit that Resides in the Word': Hermeneutic Appropriations of Augustine." In *Augustine for the Philosophers: The Rhetor of Hippo, the Confessions, and the Continentals*. Edited by Calvin L. Troup. Waco, TX: Baylor University Press, 2014. 93–106.

———. "The Fullness of Understanding? The Career of the Inner Word in Gadamer Scholarship." *Philosophy Today* 55, no. 2 (June 2011): 166–83.

Artigas, Mariano, Rafael A. Martinez, and Thomas F. Glick, eds. *Negotiating Darwin: The Vatican Confronts Evolution, 1877–1902*. Baltimore: The Johns Hopkins University Press, 2006.

Augustine of Hippo. *Concerning the City of God against the Pagans*. Translated by Henry Bettenson. London: Penguin, 2003.

———. *Confessiones*. PL 32. Edited by J. P. Migne. http://www.augustinus.it/latino/confessioni/index2.htm.

———. *Confessions*. Translated by R.S. Pine-Coffin. London: Penguin, 1961.

———. *Confessions*. Translated by William Watt. Cambridge, MA: Harvard University Press, 1992.

———. *Confessions*. Translated by F. J. Sheed. Indianapolis: Hackett, 1993.

———. *Confessions*. Translated by Henry Chadwick. Oxford: Oxford University Press, 1998.

———. *Confessions*. Translated by Vernon J. Bourke. Washington, D.C.: Catholic University of America Press, 2008.

———. *Confessions*. Translated by Maria Boulding, OSB. 2nd edition. New York: New City Press, 2012.

———. *Confessions: Books 1–8*. LCL 26. Edited and translated by Carolyn J.-B. Hammond. Cambridge, MA: Harvard University Press, 2014.

———. *Confessions: Books 9–13*. LCL 27. Edited and translated by Carolyn J.-B. Hammond. Cambridge, MA: Harvard University Press, 2016.

———. *Confessionum libri XIII*. Edited by L. Verheijen, O.S.A. Corpus Christianorum Series Latina 27. Turnhout: Brepols, 1981.

———. "*Confissões*, livro XI." Translated with an introduction and notes by Cristiane Negreiros Abbud Ayoub and Moacyr Novaes. In *Antologia de textos filosóficos*, edited by Jairo Marçal (Curitiba: SEED, 2009). 18–55. http://www.diaadia.pr.gov.br/deb/.

———. *De 83 Diversis Quaestionibus*. PL 40. Edited by J.P. Migne. http://www.augustinus.it/latino/ottantatre_questioni/index2.htm.

———. *De Genesi ad Litteram Libri Duodecim*. Edited by I. Zycha. Corpus Scriptorum Ecclesiasticorum Latinorum 28. Vienna: Tempsky, 1894. 1–456.

———. *De Genesi contra Manichaeos*. Edited by Dorothy Weber. CSEL 91. Vienna: Verlag der Österreichischen Akademieder Wissenschaften, 1998.

———. *City of God*. Translated by Henry Bettenson. London: Penguin Books, 2003.

———. *City of God against the Pagans*. Translated by Robert W. Dyson. Cambridge: Cambridge University Press, 1998.

———. *De Civitate Dei*. 2016. http://www.thelatinlibrary.com/august.html.

———. *De Diversis Quaestionibus ad Simplicianum*. PL 40. Edited by J.P. Migne. http://www.augustinus.it/latino/questioni_simpliciano/index2.htm.

———. *De Genesi ad Litteram*. *Corpus Augustinianum Gissense*. Edited by Cornelius Mayer. Charlottesville VA: 2000. https://www.augustinus.de/projekte-des-zaf/corpus-aug-gissense/cag-online/cag-online-english.

———. *De Trinitate libri XV*. Edited by W. Mountain. Corpus Christianorum Series Latina, 50–50A. Turnhout: Brepols, 1968.

———. *Enchiridion on Faith, Hope and Love*. Translated by Thomas S. Hibbs. Washington, DC: Regnery, 1996.

———. *Homilies on the Gospel of John*. Translated by Edmund Hill, O.P. Edited with an introduction and notes by Alan Fitzgerald, O.S.A. Hyde Park, NY: New City Press, 2009.

———. *Les Confessions*. Livres VIII–XIV. Translated by Eugène Tréhorel and Guilhem Bouissou. Edited by M. Skutella. Introduction and notes by Aimé Solignac. BA 14. Paris: Études Augustiniennes, 1996.

———. *Letters 100–155*. Translated by Roland Teske. Edited by Boniface Ramsey. Hyde Park, NY: New City Press, 2003.

———. *Literal Meaning of Genesis*. Vol 1. Translated and edited by John Hammond Taylor, S.J. New York: Newman, 1982.

———. *On Genesis*. Translated by Edmund Hill, O. P. Edited by John E. Rotelle O. S. A. Hyde Park, NY: New City Press, 2002.

———. *On Rebuke and Grace*. Translated by Roland J. Teske, S.J. Hyde Park, NY: New City Press, 1997.

———. *On the Magnitude of the Soul*. Translated by Roland J. Teske, S.J. Hyde Park, NY: New City Press, 1997.

———. *Opera Omnia*. Edited by J.-P. Migne. PL 35, 38, 39, 44. Paris: 1841–1846.

———. *Sermones Moriniani ex collectione Guelferbytana*. *Corpus Augustinianum Gissense*. Edited by Cornelius Mayer. Charlottesville VA: 2000. https://www.augustinus.de/projekte-des-zaf/corpus-aug-gissense/cag-online/cag-online-english.

———. *Sermones selecti duodeviginti*. Edited by D. C. Lambot, O.S.B. Stromata Patristica et Mediaevalia 1. Brussels: Spectrum, 1950.

———. *Sermones de Vetere Testamento, id est Sermones I-L*. Edited by C. Lambot, O.S.B. Corpus Christianorum Series Latina 41. Turnhout: Brepols, 1961.

———. *Sermons (230–272B) on the Liturgical Seasons*. Translated by Edmund Hill, O.P. Edited by John E. Rotelle, O.S.A. New Rochelle, NY: New City Press, 1993.

———. *Sermons (341–400) on Various Subjects*. Translated by Edmund Hill, O.P. Edited by John E. Rotelle, O.S.A. New Rochelle, NY: New City Press, 1995.

———. *The Trinity*. 2nd edition. Translated by Edmund Hill. Edited by John E. Rotelle. New York: New City Press, 1991.

Avicenna. *The Metaphysics of The Healing*. Edited, translated, and annotated, with an introduction, by Michael E. Marmura. Provo: Brigham Young University Press, 2005.

———. *The Physics of The Healing*. Edited, translated, and annotated, with an introduction by Jon McGinnis. Provo: Brigham Young University Press, 2009.

Bal, Mieke. "Mise en abyme et iconicité." *Littérature* 29 (1978): 116–128.

Bartky, Sandra Lee. "Toward a Phenomenology of Feminist Consciousness." *Social Theory and Practice* 3, no. 4 (1975): 425–439.

Bauckham, Richard, ed. *God Will Be All in All: the Eschatology of Jürgen Moltmann*. Edinburgh: T&T Clark, 1999.

Bavaud, G. "Un thème augustinien: Le mystère de l'Incarnation, à la lumière de la distinction entre le verbe intérieur et le verbe proféré." *Revue Augustinienne* 9, no. 1 (1963): 95–101.

BeDuhn, Jason David. *The Manichaean Body: In Discipline and Ritual*. Baltimore: The Johns Hopkins University Press, 2000.

———. "The Manichaean Jesus." In *Alternative Christs*. Edited by Olav Hammer. Cambridge: Cambridge University Press, 2009. 51–70.

———. *Augustine's Manichaean Dilemma, I: Conversion and Apostasy, 373–388 C.E*. Philadelphia: University of Pennsylvania Press, 2010.

Beer, C. S. de. "MUTHOS, LOGOS, NOUS: In Pursuit of the Ultimate in Human Thought." *Phronimon* 7, no. 1 (2006): 55–68.

Begbie, Jeremy S. *Theology, Music, and Time*. Cambridge: Cambridge University Press, 2000.

Beierwaltes, Werner. "Augustins Interpretation von *Sapientia* 11, 21." *Revue d'Études Augustiniennes et Patristiques* 15, no. 1 (1969): 51–61.

Bergamin, Joshua A. "Being in the Flow: Expert Coping as Beyond Both Thought and Automaticity." *Phenomenology and the Cognitive Sciences* 16 (2017): 403–424.

Berger, Karol. *Bach's Cycle, Mozart's Arrow: Essays on the Origins of Musical Modernity*. Berkeley: University of California Press, 2007.

Berkwitz, Stephen. *Buddhist History in the Vernacular: The Power of the Past in Late Medieval Sri Lanka*. Leiden: Brill, 2004.

Blumenthal, H. J. "Soul, World-Soul and Individual Soul in Plotinus." In *Le Néoplatonisme: colloque de Royaumont, 9–13 juin 1969*. Paris: Colloques internationaux du CNRS, 1971. 55–63.

Bochet, Isabelle. "Interprétation Scriptuaire et comprehension de soi: du *De doctrina christiana* aux *Confessions* de Saint Augustin." In *Comprendre et interpréter: le paradigme herméneutique de la raison*. Edited by Jean Greisch. Paris: Beauchesne, 1993. 21–50.

Bodhipaksa. "Do Not Dwell in the Past, Do Not Dream of the Future, Concentrate the Mind on the Present Moment." *Fake Buddha Quotes* (December 18, 2009): https://fakebuddhaquotes.com/do-not-dwell-in-the-past-do-not-dream-of-the-future/.
Boehner, Philotheus, O.F.M. "A Medieval Theory of Supposition." *Franciscan Studies* 18, no. 3–4 (September–December 1958): 240–89.
Boethius. *De Consolatione Philosophiae*. Edited by H.F. Stewart. Cambridge, MA: Harvard University Press, 1918.
Bonaventure. *Epistola de tribus quaestionibus*. In *Opera Omnia*, Vol. 8. Edited by the Fathers of the College of Saint Bonaventure. Florence: Quaracchi, 1898.
——. *In IV Libros Sententiarum*. In *Opera Omnia*, Vols. 1–4. Edited by the Fathers of the College of Saint Bonaventure. Florence: Quaracchi, 1885–1889.
Bouwsma, O. K. "The Mystery of Time (or, the Man Who Did Not Know What Time Is)." *Journal of Philosophy* 51, no. 12 (1954): 341–63.
Bowin, John. "Aristotle on the Order and Direction of Time." *Apeiron* 42, no. 1 (2009): 33–62.
Bronner, Yigal. "This is No Lotus, It Is A Face: Poetics as Grammar in Daṇḍin's Investigation of the Simile." In *The Poetics of Grammar and the Metaphysics of Sound and Sign*. Edited by Sergio La Porta and David Shulman. Leiden: Brill, 2007. 89–108.
Brown, Peter. *Augustine of Hippo: A Biography*. Berkeley, CA: University of California Press, 2000.
——. *The Body and Society*. New York: Columbia University Press, 1988.
——. *The World of Late Antiquity: AD 150–750*. New York: Norton, 1989.
Bryant, Edwin F. *The Yogasūtras of Patañjali*. New York: North Point Press; Farrar, Straus and Giroux, 2009.
Buescher, Harmut. *Sthiramati's Triṃśikāvijñaptibhāṣya, Critical Editions of the Sanskrit Text and its Tibetan Translation*. Vienna: Österreichische Akademie der Wissenschaften, 2007.
Burns, J. Patout. "Marital Fidelity as a *remedium concupiscentiae*." *Augustinian Studies* 44, no. 1 (2013): 1–35.
Burrus, Virginia. "Fleeing the Uxorious Kingdom: Augustine's Queer Theology of Marriage." *Journal of Early Christian Studies* 19, no. 1 (2011): 1–20.
——. *The Sex Lives of Saints: An Erotics of Ancient Hagiography*. Philadelphia: University of Pennsylvania Press, 2004.
Burrus, Virginia, Mark D. Jordan, and Karmen MacKendrick, eds. *Seducing Augustine: Bodies, Desires, Confessions*. New York: Fordham University Press, 2010.
Byers, Sarah. *Perception, Sensibility, and Moral Motivation in Augustine: a Stoic-Platonic Synthesis*. Cambridge: Cambridge University Press, 2013.
Callahan, John. "Basil of Caesarea: a New Source for St. Augustine's Theory of Time." *Harvard Studies in Classical Philology* 63 (1958): 437–454.
Caluori, Damian. *Plotinus on the Soul*. Cambridge: Cambridge University Press, 2015.
Cardona, George. "A Note on *Asti*." In *Consciousness Manifest: Studies in Jaina Art and Iconography and Allied Subjects in Honour of Dr. U. P. Shah*. Edited by R. T. Vyas. Vadodara, University of Baroda: Abhinav, 1995. 137–141.

Carter, Jason. "St. Augustine on Time, Time Numbers, and Enduring Objects." *Vivarium* 49, no. 4 (2011): 301–323.

Cavadini, John C. "Feeling Right: Augustine on the Passions and Sexual Desire." *Augustinian Studies* 36, no. 1 (2005): 195–217.

———. "Time and Ascent in *Confessiones* XI." In *Augustine*: Presbyter Factus Sum. Edited by Joseph T. Lienhard, S. J. Earl, C. Muller, S.J., and Roland J. Teske, S.J. New York: Peter Lang, 1994. 171–185.

Chadha, Monima. "Time-Series of Ephemeral Impressions: The Abhidharma-Buddhist View of Conscious Experience." *Phenomenology and the Cognitive Sciences* 14, no. 3 (2014): 543–560.

Chappell, David. W. "Searching for a Mahāyāna Social Ethic." *Journal of Religious Ethics* 24, no. 2 (1996): 351–375.

Chesterton, G. K. *Heretics*. London: John Lane and Co., 1905.

Cho, Francisca. *Seeing Like the Buddha: Enlightenment Through Film*. Albany: State University of New York Press, 2017.

Chrétien, Jean-Louis. *La Joie Spacieuse: essai sur la dilatation*. Lonrai: Les Éditions de Minuit, 2007.

Ciammetti, Daniela. *Necessità e Contingenza in Gregorio Da Rimini*. Pisa: ETS, 2011.

Cilleruelo, Lope. "'Deum uidere' en San Augustín." *Salmanticensis* 12 (1965): 3–31.

Clark, Elizabeth A. "Adam's Only Companion: Augustine and the Early Christian Debate on Marriage." *Recherches augustiniennes* 22 (1986): 139–162.

———. "Theory and Practice in Late Ancient Asceticism: Jerome, Chrysostom, and Augustine." *Journal of Feminist Studies in Religion* 5, no. 2 (1989): 25–46.

Clemmons, Thomas. "The Common, History, and the Whole: Guiding Themes in *De uera religione*." *Augustinianum* 58 (2018): 125–154.

———. "On the Two Wills: Augustine against Agonism toward Peace." In *Agustin de Hipona como Doctor Pacis*. Vol. 2. Edited by A. Dupont, E. Eguiarte Bendimez, and C. A. Villabona Vargas. Bogota: Editorial Uniagustiniana, 2019. 269–288.

———. "*De Genesi aduersus Manichaeos*: Augustine's Anthropology and the Fall of the Soul." *Augustinian Studies* 51, no. 1 (2020): 47–78.

Cline, Erin M. "Augustine's Change of Aspect." *Heythrop Journal* 46 (2005): 135–148.

Collier, Trent. "Time and Self: Religious Awakening in Dōgen and Shinran." *Eastern Buddhist* 32, no. 1 (2000): 56–84.

Collingwood, R. G. *The Principles of Art*. Oxford: Clarendon, 1967 [1938].

Collins, Steven. *Nirvana and Other Buddhist Felicities: Utopias of the Pali Imaginaire*. Cambridge: Cambridge University Press, 1998.

———. "Remarks on the *Visuddhimagga* and on its Treatment of the Memory of Former Dwelling(s) (*pubbenivāsānussatiñāṇa*)." *Journal of Indian Philosophy* 37, no. 5 (2009): 499–532.

———. *Selfless Persons: Imagery and Thought in Theravāda Buddhism*. Cambridge: Cambridge University Press, 1982.

Coole, Diana H., and Samantha Frost. *New Materialisms: Ontology, Agency, and Politics*. Durham: Duke University Press, 2010.

Coope, Ursula. *Time for Aristotle.* New York: Oxford University Press, 2005.
Courcelle, Pierre. *Recherches sur les Confessions de saint Augustin.* Paris: E. de Boccard, 1968.
Courtenay, William J. "Antiqui and Moderni in Late Medieval Thought." *Journal of the History of Ideas* 48, no. 1 (1987): 3–10.
———. *Capacity and Volition: A History of the Distinction of Absolute and Ordained Power.* Bergamo: Lubrina, 1990.
———. "John of Mirecourt and Gregory of Rimini on Whether God Can Undo the Past: Bradwardine and Buckingham." *Recherches de théologie ancienne et médiévale* 40, no. Janvier-Décembre (1973): 147–74.
———. "John of Mirecourt and Gregory of Rimini on Whether God Can Undo the Past: Bradwardine and Buckingham." In *Covenant and Causality in Medieval Thought: Studies in Philosophy, Theology and Economic Practice.* London: Variorum Reprints, 1984. 147–74a.
———. "Late Medieval Nominalism Revisited: 1972–1982." *Journal of the History of Ideas* 44, no. 1 (1983): 159–64.
Cox, Collett. "On the Possibility of Non-Existent Objects of Consciousness: Sarvāstivādin and Dārṣṭāntika Theories." *Journal of the International Association of Buddhist Studies* 11, no. 1 (1998): 31–89.
Coyle, John Kevin. "Characteristics of Manichaeism in Roman Africa." In *New Light on Manichaeism: Papers from the Sixth International Congress on Manichaeism.* Edited by J. BeDuhn. Leiden: Brill, 2009. 101–114.
Craig, William Lane. *Divine Foreknowledge and the Problem of Future Contingents.* Leiden: Brill, 1988.
Cross, Richard. *The Physics of John Duns Scotus.* Oxford: Clarendon, 1998.
———. "Scotus on Timelessness and Eternity." *Faith and Philosophy* 14, no. 1 (1997): 3–25.
Cushman, Robert E. "Greek and Christian Views of Time." *Journal of Religion* 33, no. 4 (1953): 254–65.
Dasti, Matthew, and Stephen Phillips, eds. *The Nyāya-Sūtra: Selections with Early Commentaries.* Indianapolis: Hackett, 2017.
Dauphinais, Michael, Barry David, and Matthew Levering, eds. *Aquinas the Augustinian.* Washington, DC: CUA Press, 2007.
Davies, Brian, and Eleonore Stump, eds. *The Oxford Handbook of Aquinas.* Oxford: Oxford University Press, 2012.
Decret, François. *Aspects du Manichéisme dans l'Afrique Romaine: Les controverses de Fortunatus, Faustus, et Felix avec saint Augustin.* Paris: Études Augustiniennes, 1970.
DelCogliano, Mark. "Basil of Caesarea Versus Eunomius of Cyzicus on the Nature of Time: a Patristic Reception of the Critique of Plato." *Vigiliae Christianae* 68, no. 5 (2014): 498–532.
Deleuze, Gilles. *Proust and Signs: The Complete Text.* Translated by Richard Howard. Minneapolis: University of Minnesota Press, 2000.
Derrida, Jacques. *Writing and Difference.* Translated by Allan Bass. Chicago: University of Chicago Press, 1978.

Dessein, Bart. "The Existence of Factors in the Three Time Periods: Sarvāstivāda and Madhyamaka Buddhist Interpretations of Difference in Mode, Difference in Characteristic Marks, Difference in State, and Mutual Difference." *Acta Orientalia* 60, no. 3 (2007): 331–50.

Deutscher, Penelope. "The Evanescence of Masculinity: Deferral in Saint Augustine's *Confessions* and Some Thoughts on Its Bearing on the Sex/Gender Debate." In *Feminist Interpretations of Augustine*. Edited by Judith Chelius Stark. University Park, PA: Pennsylvania State University Press, 2007. 281–300.

Dhammajoti, K. L. *Abhidharma Doctrines and Controversies on Perception.* Hong Kong: Centre of Buddhist Studies, University of Hong Kong, 2007.

Dolnikowski, Edith Wilks. *Thomas Bradwardine: A View of Time and a Vision of Eternity in Fourteenth-Century Thought.* Leiden: Brill, 1995.

Doody, John, Kim Paffenroth, and Adam Goldstein, eds. *Augustine and Science.* Lanham, MD: Rowman & Littlefield, 2012.

Doss, S. R. "Copernicus Revisited: Time Versus 'Time' Versus Time." *Philosophy and Phenomenological Research* 31, no. 2 (1970): 193–211.

Dreyfus, Georges. "Is Mindfulness Present-centred and Non-judgmental? A Discussion of the Cognitive Dimensions of Mindfulness." *Contemporary Buddhism* 12 (2011): 41–54.

Dunne, John. *Foundations of Dharmakīrti's Philosophy.* Boston: Wisdom, 2004.

———. "Realizing the Unreal: Dharmakīrti's Theory of Yogic Perception." *Journal of Indian Philosophy* 34 (2006): 497–519.

———. "Toward an Understanding of Non-dual Mindfulness." *Contemporary Buddhism* 12 (2011): 71–88.

Eberhard, Philippe. "Gadamer and Theology." *International Journal of Systematic Theology* 9, no. 3 (2007): 283–300.

Emmerich, Christoph. "How Many Times? Monism or Pluralism in Early Jaina Temporal Description." In *Essays in Jaina Philosophy and Religion*. Edited by Piotr Balcerowicz. Delhi: Motilal Banarsidass, 2002. 69–88.

Fausto-Sterling, Anne. "The Bare Bones of Sex: Part 1—Sex and Gender." *Signs* 30, no. 2 (2005): 1491–527.

Feldman, Joel, and Stephen Phillips, eds. *Ratnakīrti's Proof of Momentariness by Positive Correlation (Kṣaṇabhaṅgasiddhi-Anvayātmikā): Transliteration, Translation, and Philosophic Commentary.* New York: American Institute of Buddhist Studies, 2012.

Ferri, Riccardo. *Gesù e la verità: Agostino e Tommaso interpreti del Vangelo di Giovanni.* Collana di teología 59. Rome: Città Nuova, 2007.

Findlay, J. N. "Time: A Treatment of Some Puzzles." *Australasian Journal of Philosophy* 19, no. 3 (1941): 216–235.

Fiorentino, Francesco. *Gregorio Da Rimini: Contingenza, Futuro e Scienza nel Pensiero Tardo-Medievale.* Roma: Antonianum, 2004.

Fitzgerald, Edward. *The Rubaiyat of Omar Khayyam.* New York: Dodge, 1896.

Flasch, Kurt. *Was ist Zeit? Augustinus von Hippo. Das XI. Buch der Confessiones. Historisch-Philosophische Studie.* Frankfurt am Main: Klostermann, 1993.

Foucault, Michel. *The History of Sexuality: Volume I: An Introduction.* Translated by Robert Hurley. New York: Pantheon, 1978.

Franco, Eli, ed. "Perception of Yogis: Some Epistemological and Metaphysical Considerations." In *Religion and Logic in Buddhist Philosophical Analysis, Proceedings of the 4th International Dharmakīrti Conference, Vienna, August 23–27, 2005*. Edited by H. Krasser et al. Vienna: Verlag der Österreichische Akademie der Wissenschaften, 2011. 81–98.

———. *Yogic Perception, Meditation and Altered States of Consciousness*. In collaboration with Dagmar Eigner. Vienna: Verlag der Österreichische Akademie der Wissenschaften, 2009.

Freud, Sigmund. *Civilization and Its Discontents*. Translated by James Strachey. New York: Norton, 1962.

Fronsdal, Gil. *The Buddha Before Buddhism: Wisdom from the Early Teachings*. Boulder: Shambhala, 2016.

Frost, Gloria. "Thomas Bradwardine on God and the Foundations of Modality." *British Journal for the History of Philosophy* 21, no. 2 (Mar/Apr 2012): 368–80.

Frost, Samantha. "The Implications of the New Materialisms for Feminist Epistemology." In *Feminist Epistemology and Philosophy of Science: Power in Knowledge*. Edited by H. E. Grasswick. Dordrecht: Springer, 2011.

Gadamer, Hans-Georg. *Gesammelte Werke*. 10 Volumes. Tübingen: Mohr Siebeck, 1986–1995.

———. *Truth and Method*. Translated by Joel Weinsheimer and Donald G. Marshall. 2nd revised edition. London: Bloomsbury, 2013.

Gale, Richard M. "Some Metaphysical Statements About Time." *Journal of Philosophy* 60 (1941): 225–37.

Galen. *Compendium Timaei Platonis alioquorumque dialogorum synopsis quae extant fragmenta*. Edited, with an introduction, by Paul Kraus and Richard Walzer. London: Warburg Institute, 1951.

Gallagher, Kenneth T. "Wittgenstein, Augustine, and Language." *New Scholasticism* 56 (1982): 462–470.

Ganeri, Jonardon. "A Return to the Self: Indians and Greeks on Life as Art and Philosophical Therapy." *Royal Institute of Philosophy Supplement* 66 (2010): 119–135.

———. "Buddhist No Self: An Analysis and Critique." In *Hindu and Buddhist Ideas in Dialogue*. Edited by Irina Kuznetsova, Jonardon Ganeri and Chakravarthi Ram-Prasad. London and New York: Routledge, 2012. 63–77.

———. *Philosophy in Classical India: Introduction and Analysis*. London and New York: Routledge, 2001.

Gardner, Iain. "The Docetic Jesus." In *Coptic Theological Papyri II*. Edited by Iain Gardner. Vienna: Hollinek, 1988. 57–85.

———. *The Kephalaia of the Teacher*. Leiden: Brill, 1995.

Gaskin, Richard. "Peter of Ailly and Other Fourteenth-Century Thinkers on Divine Power and the Necessity of the Past." *Archiv für Geschichte der Philosophie* 73, no. 3 (2009): 273–91.

Genest, Jean-François. "Le *De futuris contingentibus* de Thomas Bradwardine." *Recherches Augustiniennes* 14 (1979): 249–336.

Geoffrey Chaucer. *The Canterbury Tales: Fifteen Tales and the General Prologue.* Edited by V.A. Kolve and Glending Olson. 2nd edition. New York: Norton, 2005.

Gibb, John, and William Montgomery. *The Confessions of Augustine.* New York and London: Garland, 1980.

Gilbert, N.W. "Ockham, Wyclif, and the 'Via Moderna.'" In *Antiqui Und Moderni: Traditionsbewusstsein Und Fortschrittsbewusstsein Im Späten Mittelalter.* Edited by Albert Zimmermann. Berlin: de Gruyter, 1974. 85–125.

Gioia, Luigi. *The Theological Epistemology of Augustine's De Trinitate.* Oxford: Oxford University Press, 2008.

Gold, Jonathan. *Paving the Great Way: Vasubandhu's Unifying Buddhist Philosophy.* New York: Columbia University Press, 2015.

Goodman, Charles. "The *Treasury of Metaphysics* and the Physical World." *Philosophical Quarterly* 54, no. 216 (2004): 389–401.

Goodman, Steven. *A Buddhist Proof for Omniscience: The "Sarvajñasiddhi" of Ratnakīrti.* Dissertation. Philadelphia: Temple University, 1989.

Gregory of Rimini. *Gregorii Ariminensis, Oesa, Lectura Super Primum Et Secundum Sententiarum.* Vol. 3. Edited by Adolf Damasus Trapp, Manuel Santos-Noya, Venicio Marcolino, Walter Simon and Wolfgang Urban. Berlin: de Gruyter, 1984.

Griffiths, Paul J. *Decreation: The Last Things of All Creatures.* Waco, TX: Baylor University Press, 2015.

———. *On Being Buddha: The Classical Doctrine of Buddhahood.* Albany: SUNY Press, 1994.

Grondin, Jean. "Gadamer und Augustin." In *Der Sinn für Hermeneutik.* Darmstadt: Wissenschaftliche Buchgesellschaft, 1994. 24–39.

———. "La thèse de l'herméneutique sur l'être." *Revue de Métaphysique et de Morale* 4 (October 2006): 469–481.

———. *The Philosophy of Gadamer.* Translated by Kathryn Plant. Continental European Philosophy. Chesham, UK: Acumen, 2003.

Grosse, Patricia L. "Love and the Patriarch: Augustine and (Pregnant) Women." *Hypatia: A Journal of Feminist Philosophy* 32, no. 1 (2017): 119–134.

Grosz, Elizabeth. *Becoming Undone: Darwinian Reflections on Life, Politics, and Art.* Durham: Duke University Press, 2011.

———. *The Incorporeal: Ontology, Ethics, and the Limits of Materialism.* New York: Columbia University Press, 2017.

———. "The Nature of Sexual Difference: Irigaray and Darwin." *Angelaki* 17, no. 2 (2012): 69–93.

———. *The Nick of Time: Politics, Evolution, and the Untimely.* Durham: Duke University Press, 2004.

———. *Time Travels: Feminism, Nature, and Power.* Durham: Duke University Press, 2005.

Gundersdorf von Jess, Wilma. "Divine Eternity in the Doctrine of St. Augustine." *Augustinian Studies* 6 (1975): 75–96.

Gurtler, Gary. "Plotinus and the Alienation of the Soul." In *The Perennial Tradition of Neoplatonism.* Edited by John J. Cleary. Leuven: Leuven University, 1997. 221–234.

Gurtner, Daniel M., Grant Macaskill, and Jonathan T. Pennington, eds. *In the Fullness of Time: Essays on Christology, Creation, and Eschatology in Honor of Richard Bauckham*. Grand Rapids: Eerdmans, 2016.
Hägglund, Martin. "Why Mortality Makes Us Free." *The New York Times*. March 11, 2019. https://www.nytimes.com/2019/03/11/opinion/why-mortality-makes-us-free.html.
Hallisey, Charles, trans. *Therigatha: Poems of the First Buddhist Women*. Murty Classical Library of India. Cambridge, MA: Harvard University Press, 2015.
Haloun. G and W.B. Henning. "The Compendium of the Doctrines and Styles of the Teaching of Mani, the Buddha of Light." *Asia Major* 3, no. 2 (1952): 184–212.
Halverson, James L. *Peter Aureol on Predestination: A Challenge to Late Medieval Thought*. Studies in the History of Christian Thought. Leiden: Brill, 1998.
Hammond, Carolyn J.-B. *Augustine Confessions*. Vol. 1: Books 1–8. Loeb Classical Library 26. Cambridge, MA: Harvard University Press, 2014.
Hannan, Sean. *On Time, Change, History, and Conversion*. London: Bloomsbury, 2020.
Harrison, Carol. *Beauty and Revelation in the Thought of St. Augustine*. Oxford Theological Monographs. Oxford: Clarendon, 1992.
———. *On Music, Sense, Affect and Voice*. Kindle Version. London: T&T Clark, 2019.
———. *The Art of Listening in the Early Church*. Oxford: Oxford University Press, 2013.
Hayashi, Itsuki. "A Buddhist Theory of Persistance: Śāntarakṣita and Kamalaśīla on Rebirth." *Journal of Indian Philosophy* 47 (2019): 979–1001.
Heim, Maria. *Voice of the Buddha: Buddhaghosa on the Immeasurable Words*. New York: Oxford University Press, 2018.
Hekman, Susan. "Feminist New Materialism and Process Theology: Beginning the Dialogue." *Feminist Theology* 25, no. 2 (2017): 198–207.
Henry, Paul. *Plotin et L'Occident*. Louvain: Spicilegium Sacrum Lovaniense, 1934.
Hirakawa, Akira. *A History of Indian Buddhism: From Śakyamuni to Early Mahāyāna*. Translated and Edited by Paul Groner. Hawaii: University of Hawaii Press, 1990.
Hoenen, M. J. F. M. *Marsilius of Inghen: Divine Knowledge in Late Medieval Thought*. Leiden: Brill, 1992.
Hoerl, Christoph. 2018. "Experience and Time: Transparency and Presence." *Ergo* 5, no. 5 (2018): 127–151.
Hogarth Rossiter, Sarah. "Foreknowledge, Free Will, and the Divine Power Distinction in Thomas Bradwardine's *De futuris contingentibus*." Dissertation. Western University, 2017. https://ir.lib.uwo.ca/etd/4432.
Hunter, David G. "Augustine and the Making of Marriage in Roman North Africa." *Journal of Early Christian Studies* 11, no. 1 (2003): 63–85.
———. "Augustinian Pessimism? A New Look at Augustine's Teaching On Sex, Marriage and Celibacy." *Augustinian Studies* 25 (1994): 153–177.
Hurvitz, Leon, trans. *Scripture of the Lotus Blossom of the Fine Dharma*. Revised Edition. New York: Columbia University Press, 2009.

Irving, Zachary. "Mind-wandering is Unguided Attention: Accounting for the Purposeful Wanderer." *Philosophical Studies* 173 (2016): 547–571.
Jha, Ganganatha. *The Tattvasaṅgraha of Śāntarakṣita, with the Commentary of Kamalaśīla*. Baroda: Baroda Oriental Institute, 1937–9.
Johnston, William M., and Christopher Kleinhenz. *Encyclopedia of Monasticism: Volumes 1 and 2*. London and New York: Routledge, 2015.
Jordan, Robert. "Time and Contingency in St. Augustine." *Review of Metaphysics* 8 (1955): 394–417.
Kachru, Sonam. "Minds and Worlds: A Philosophical Commentary on the Twenty Verses of Vasubandhu." Dissertation. University of Chicago, 2015.
Kaiser, Hermann-Josef. *Augustinus: Zeit und Memoria*. Bonn: H. Bouvier, 1969.
Kajiyama, Yūichi. *An Introduction to Buddhist Philosophy: An Annotated Translation of the Tarkabhāṣā of Mokṣākaragupta, Reprint with Corrections in the Authors Hand*. Vienna: Arbeitskreis für Tibetische und Buddhistische Studien, Universität Wien, 1998.
———. *Studies in Buddhist Philosophy (Selected Papers)*. Edited by Katsumi Mimaki et al. Kyoto: Rinsen Book Company, 2005.
Kaluza, Zenon. *Les Querelles Doctrinales à Paris: Nominalistes et Realistes aux Confins du XIV$^e$ Et Du XV$^e$ Siècles*. Bergamo: Lubrina, 1988.
Kapstein, Matthew. *Reason's Traces: Identity and Interpretation in Indian and Tibetan Buddhist Thought*. Boston: Wisdom, 2001.
Karunadasa, Y. *The Theravāda Abhidhamma: Inquiry into the Nature of Conditioned Reality*. Sommerville: Wisdom, 2019.
Katō, Bunnō, Yoshirō Tamura, and Kōjirō Miyasaka, trans. *The Threefold Lotus Sutra*. Tokyo: Kosei Publishing Company, 1992.
Kato, Takeshi. "La voix chez Origéne et saint Augustin." *Augustiniana* 40, no.1/4 (1990): 245–258.
Keller, Catherine. *The Face of the Deep: A Theology of Becoming*. London: Routledge, 2003.
Keller, Catherine, and Mary-Jane Rubenstein, eds. *Entangled Worlds: Religion, Science, and New Materialisms*. New York: Fordham University Press, 2018.
Keller, Simon. "Presentism and Truth-making." In *Oxford Studies in Metaphysics, Vol. 1*. Edited by Dean Zimmerman. New York: Oxford University Press, 2004. 83–104.
Kemp, Kenneth W. "Science, Theology, and Monogenesis." *American Catholic Philosophical Quarterly* 85 (2011): 217–36.
Kerouac, Jack. *Some of the Dharma*. New York: Viking, 1997.
Kirwan, Christopher. *Augustine*. London and New York: Routledge, 1989.
Knuuttila, Simo. "Time and Creation in Augustine." In *The Cambridge Companion to Augustine*. Edited by Eleonore Stump and Norman Kretzmann. Cambridge: Cambridge University Press, 2001. 103–115.
Krasser, Helmut. "Dharmottara's Theory of Knowledge in his *Laghuprāmānyaparīksa*." *Journal of Indian Philosophy* 23 (1995): 247–271.
Ku, John Baptist. "Interpreting Genesis 1 with St. Thomas Aquinas." http://www.thomisticevolution.org/disputed-questions/interpreting-genesis-1-with-st-thomas-aquinas/#rf7-207.

Lammer, Andreas. *The Elements of Avicenna's Physics: Greek Sources and Arabic Innovations.* Berlin and Boston: De Gruyter, 2018.
Langlois, Luc. "L'universalité du *verbum interius.*" *Philosophiques* 22, no. 1 (1995): 137–157.
Lawrence, Fred. *"Ontology* of *and* as *Horizon:* Gadamer's Rehabilitation of the Metaphysics of Light." *Revista Portuguesa di Filosofia* 56, no. 3/4 (July 2000): 389–420.
Le Poidevin, Robin, and Murray MacBeath, eds. *The Philosophy of Time.* Oxford: Oxford University Press, 1993.
Lee, Gregory W. *Today When You Hear His Voice: Scripture, the Covenants, and the People of God.* Grand Rapids, MI: Eerdmans, 2016.
Leff, Gordon. *Bradwardine and the Pelagians: A Study of His De Causa Dei and Its Opponents.* New York: Cambridge University Press, 1957.
Leftow, Brian. *Time and Eternity.* Ithaca, NY: Cornell University Press, 1991.
Levison, Arnold B. "Events and Time's Flow." *Mind* 96 (1987): 341–353.
Lieu, Samuel. *Manichaeism in the Later Roman Empire and Medieval China.* Manchester: Manchester University, 1985.
Llanes, María Guadalupe. "Gadamer y la igualdad sustancial de pensamiento y lenguaje en San Agustín." *Studia Gilsoniana* 2 (2013): 145–159.
Loewe, Can L. "Gregory of Rimini on the Intension and Remission of Corporeal Forms." *Recherches de théologie et philosophie médiévales* 81, no. 2 (2014): 273–330.
Lopez, Donald S., Jr. *The Lotus Sūtra: A Biography.* Princeton and Oxford: Princeton University Press, 2016.
Lopez, Donald S., Jr., and Jacqueline Stone. *Two Buddhas Seated Side by Side: A Guide to the Lotus Sūtra.* New Jersey: Princeton University Press, 2019.
Lössl, Joseph. "The One (*unum*) – A Guiding Concept in *De uera religione*: An Outline of the Text and the History of Its Interpretation." *Revue des Études Augustiniennes* 40 (1994): 79–103.
———. "Augustine on 'The True Religion': Reflections on Manichaeism in *De vera religione.*" In *Augustine and Manichaean Christianity: Selected Papers from the First South African Conference on Augustine of Hippo, University of Pretoria, 24–26 April 2012.* Edited by J. van Oort. Leiden: Brill, 2013. 137–154.
Magno, Joseph A. "Ockham's Extreme Nominalism." *Thomist: A Speculative Quarterly* 43 (July 1979): 414–49.
Majumdar, Deepa. *Plotinus on the Appearance of Time and the World of Sense: A Pantomime.* Burlington, VT: Ashgate, 2007.
Mammì, Lorenzo. *A fugitiva: ensaios sobre música.* 1$^{st}$ edition. São Paulo: Companhia das Letras, 2017.
———. "Canticum Novum: música sem palavras e palavras sem som no pensamento de Santo Agostinho." *Estudos Avançados* 14, no. 38 (2000): 347–366.
———. *Santo Agostinho, o tempo e a música.* Dissertation. University of São Paulo, 1993.
Markosian, Ned. "A Defense of Presentism." *Oxford Studies in Metaphysics* 1, no. 3 (2004): 47–82.

Marrou, Henri-Irénée. *L'Ambivalence du temps de l'histoire chez saint Augustin*. Paris: Vrin, 1950.
Marusic, Berislav. "Wittgenstein on Time." *Synthesis Philosophica* 16 (2001): 97–101.
Marshall, Bruce D. "Absorbing the World: Christianity and the Universe of Truths." In *Theology and Dialogue: Essays in Conversation with George Lindbeck*. Edited by Bruce D. Marshall. Notre Dame, IN: University of Notre Dame Press, 1990.
Mathes, Klaus Dieter. *Unterschiedung der Gegebenheiten von ihrem Wahren Wesen*. Swistal-Odendorf: Indica et Tibetica Verlag, 1996.
Matter, E. Ann. "*De cura feminarum:* Augustine the Bishop, North African Women, and the Development of a Theology of Female Nature." *Augustinian Studies* 36, no. 1 (2005): 87–98. Also in *Feminist Interpretations of Augustine*. University Park, PA: Pennsylvania State University Press, 2007. 203–214.
———. "Women." In *Augustine through the Ages: An Encyclopedia*. Edited by Allan Fitzgerald and John C. Cavadini. Grand Rapids, MI.: W.B. Eerdmans, 1999. 887–892.
McClintock, Sara. "Ethical Reading and the Ethics of Forgetting and Remembering." In *A Mirror is for Reflection: Understanding Buddhist Ethics*. Edited by Jake H. Davis. New York: Oxford University Press, 2017. 185–202.
———. *Omniscience and the Rhetoric of Reason: Śāntarakṣita and Kamalaśīla on Rationality, Argumentation and Religious Authority*. Boston: Wisdom, 2010.
McDuffie, Felecia. "Augustine's Rhetoric of the Feminine in the *Confessions*: Woman as Mother, Woman as Other." In *Feminist Interpretations of Augustine*. Edited by Judith Chelius Stark. University Park: Pennsylvania State University Press, 2007.
McEvoy, James. "St. Augustine's Account of Time and Wittgenstein's Criticisms." *Review of Metaphysics* 37, no. 3 (1984): 547–577.
McGinnis, Jon. *Time and Time Again. A Study of Aristotle and Ibn Sīnā's Temporal Theories*. Dissertation. Philadelphia: University of Pennsylvania, 1999.
———. *Avicenna*. New York: Oxford University Press, 2010.
———. "Ibn Sīnā on the Now." *American Catholic Philosophical Quarterly* 73, no. 1 (1999): 73–106.
———. "Review of Aristotle on Time: A Study of the Physics by Tony Roark." *Philosophy in Review* 32, no. 6 (2012): 518–520.
McKeough, Michael J. *The Meaning of the Rationes Seminales in St. Augustine*. Dissertation. Washington, DC: Catholic University of America, 1926.
McMahan, David L. *Empty Vision: Metaphor and Visionary Imagery in Mahāyāna Buddhism*. London: Routledge, 2002.
McMullin, Ernan. "Darwin and the Other Christian Tradition." *Zygon* 46, no. 2 (2011): 291–316.
McTaggart, James. "The Unreality of Time." *Mind* 17, no. 68 (Oct. 1908): 457–474.
Merricks, Trenton. *Truth and Ontology*. Oxford: Oxford University Press, 2007.
Merwe, Dirk G. van der, and P. Y. Albalaa. "The Metaphor of Light Embedded in the Johannine Prologue, Part 1: The Light Before the Incarnation." *In die Skriflig/In Luce Verbi* 47, no. 1 (2013): 1–10.

Miles, Margaret R. *Carnal Knowing: Female Nakedness and Religious Meaning in the Christian West.* New York: Wipf & Stock, 1989.

———. *Desire and Delight: A New Reading of Augustine's Confessions.* Eugene, OR: Wipf & Stock, 2006.

———. "From Rape to Resurrection: Sin, Sexual Difference, and Politics." In *Augustine's City of God: A Critical Guide.* Edited by James Wetzel. New York: Cambridge University Press, 2012. 75–92.

———. "Not Nameless but Unnamed: The Woman Torn from Augustine's Side." In *Feminist Interpretations of Augustine.* Edited by Judith Chelius Stark. University Park, PA: Pennsylvania State University Press (2007). 167–188.

———. "Sex and the City (of God): Is Sex Forfeited or Fulfilled in Augustine's Resurrection of Body?" *Journal of the American Academy of Religion* 73, no. 2 (2005): 307–327.

———. "Vision: The Eye of the Body and the Eye of the Mind in Saint Augustine's *De trinitate* and *Confessions.*" *Journal of Religion* 63, no. 2 (1983): 125–142.

Miller, Julie B. "To Remember Self, to Remember God: Augustine on Sexuality, Relationality, and the Trinity." In *Feminist Interpretations of Augustine.* Edited by Judith Chelius Stark. University Park, PA: Pennsylvania State University Press, 2007. 243–279.

Milligan, Matthew. "The Development and Representation of Ritual in Early Indian Buddhist Donative Epigraphy." *Pacific World.* 15 (2013): 171–186.

Mookerjee, Satkari. *The Buddhist Philosophy of Universal Flux: An Exposition of the Philosophy of Critical Realism as Expounded by the School of Dignāga.* Calcutta: University of Calcutta Press, 1935.

Morgan, Edward. *The Incarnation of the Word: The Theology of Language of Augustine of Hippo.* London: Clark, 2010.

Moriyama, Shinya. *Omniscience and Religious Authority: A Study of Prajñākaragupta's Pramāṇavārttikālaṅkārabhāṣya ad Pramāṇavārttika II.8–10 and 29–33.* Leipzig: LIT Verlag, 2014.

Muñiz, Vicente. *Introducción a la filosofía del lenguaje. Problemas ontológicos.* Barcelona: Anthropos, 1989.

Mus, Paul. "La notion de temps reversible dans la mythologie bouddhique." *Annuaires de l'École pratique des hautes études* 47 (1937): 5–38.

Ñānananda (Bhikkhu). *Ideal Solitude: An Exposition of the Bhadekaratta Sutta.* The Wheel 188. Kandy: Sri Lanka, 1973.

Nightingale, Andrea. *Once Out of Nature: Augustine on Time and Body.* Chicago: University of Chicago Press, 2011.

Nishijima, Gudo Wafu, and Chodo Cross. *Shōbōgenzō: The True Dharma-Eye Treasury: Volume I.* BDK English Tripiṭaka Series. Moraga, California: BDK America, 2007.

Noonan, Harold W. "Presentism and Actualism." *Philosophia* 47, no. 2 (2019): 489–497.

Normore, Calvin. "Descartes's Possibilities." In *René Descartes: Critical Assessments.* Vol. 3. Edited by Georges J.D. Moyal. New York: Routledge, 1991. 68–83.

Novaes, Moacyr. *A razão em exercício, estudos sobre a filosofia de Agostinho*. São Paulo: Discurso, 2007.
Nozick, Robert. *The Examined Life: Philosophical Meditations*. New York: Simon and Schuster, 1989.
Nyanaponika Thera. *The Heart of Buddhist Meditation: A Handbook of Mental Training Based on The Buddha's Way of Mindfulness*. London: Rider and Company, 1973.
Oakley, Francis. "The Absolute and Ordained Power of God in Sixteenth- and Seventeenth-Century Theology." *Journal of the History of Ideas* 59, no. 3 (1998): 437–461.
Oberman, Heiko A. *Archbishop Thomas Bradwardine: A Fourteenth-Century Augustinian*. Utrecht: Kemink & Zoon, 1958.
———. "Some Notes on the Theology of Nominalism: With Attention to Its Relation to the Renaissance." *Harvard Theological Review* 53, no. 1 (1960): 47–76.
O'Connell, Robert J., S.J. *Art and Christian Intelligence in St. Augustine*. Cambridge, MA: Harvard University Press, 1978.
———. "*Ennead* VI 4–5 in the Works of Saint Augustine." *Revue des Études Augustiniennes* 9 (1963): 1–39.
———. *St. Augustine's Early Theory of Man, A.D. 386–391*. Cambridge, MA: Belknap, 1968.
———. "The *De Genesi contra Manichaeos* and the Origin of the Soul." *Revue des Études Augustiniennes* 39 (1993): 129–141.
O'Daly, Gerard. "Augustine on the Measurement of Time: Some Comparisons with Aristotelian and Stoics Texts." In *Neoplatonism and Early Christian Thought: Essays in Honour of A.H. Armstrong*. Edited by H. J. Blumenthal and R. A. Markus. London: Variorum, 1981. 171–179.
———. *Augustine's Philosophy of Mind*. Berkeley, CA: University of California Press, 1987.
———. "Time as *Distentio* and St. Augustine's Exegesis of Philippians 3, 12–14." *Revue des Études Augustiniennes* 23 (1977): 265–271.
O'Donnell, James J. *Augustine's Confessions: A Text and Commentary*. New York: Oxford University Press, 1992.
O'Donnell, James J., and Anne Mahoney, eds. *The Confessions of Augustine: an Electronic Edition*. 1992: http://www.stoa.org/hippo/
Oetke, Claus. "Remarks on the Interpretation of Nāgārjuna's Philosophy." *Journal of Indian Philosophy* 19, no. 3 (1991): 315–323.
Oliva, Mirela. *Das innere Verbum in Gadamers Hermeneutik*, Hermeneutische Untersuchungen zur Theologie 53. Tübingen: Mohr Siebeck, 2009.
Pasnau, Robert. *Metaphysical Themes, 1274–1671*. New York: Oxford University Press, 2011.
———. "On Existing All at Once." In *God, Eternity, and Time*. Edited by Christian Tapp and Edmund Runggaldier. Burlington, VT: Ashgate, 2011.
Patil, Parimal. *Against a Hindu God: Buddhist Philosophy of Religion in India*. New York: Columbia University Press, 2009.

Pegueroles, Juan. *El Pensamiento filosófico de San Agustín*. Barcelona: Editorial Labor, 1972.
Pelikan, Jaroslav. *The Mystery of Continuity: Time and History, Memory and Eternity in the Thought of Saint Augustine*. Charlottesville: University Press of Virginia, 1986.
Plantinga, Alvin. "On Ockham's Way Out." *Faith and Philosophy: Journal of the Society of Christian Philosophers* 3 (July 1986): 235–269.
Power, Kim. *Veiled Desire: Augustine's Writing on Women*. London: Darton, Longman, & Todd, 1995.
Pradhan, Prahlad. *Abhidharmakośabhāṣya of Vasubandhu*. Patna: K. P. Jayaswal Research Institute, 1975.
Pranger, M.B. "Time and Narrative in Augustine's *Confessions*." *Journal of Religion* 81, no. 3 (2001): 377–393.
Pruden, Leo M., trans. *Abhidharmakośabhasyam of Vasubandhu*. Translated from the French version of Louis de la Vallée Poussin. Volumes I–IV. Berkeley, CA: Asian Humanities Press, 1988–1990.
Pruden, Leo M. "Review of Mark L. Blum, *The Origins and Development of Pure Land Buddhism: A Study and Translation of Gyōnen's Jōdo Hōmon Genrushō*." *Japanese Journal of Religious Studies* 30, no. 1–2 (2003): 162–165.
Putnam, Hilary. "Time and Physical Geometry." *Journal of Philosophy* 64, no. 8 (Apr. 1967), 240–247.
Quinn, John M. "The Concept of Time in St. Augustine." *Studies in Philosophy and the History of Philosophy* 4 (1969): 75–127.
Quli, Natalie Fisk. "Review of Ann Gleig, *American Dharma: Buddhism Beyond Modernity*." *Journal of Global Buddhism* 20 (2019): 139–142.
Rau, Catherine. "Theories of Time in Ancient Philosophy." *Philosophical Review* 62, no. 4 (1953): 514–525.
Ravasi, Gianfranco. "'Cantate a Dio con arte': il teologico e il musicale nella Bibbia." In *La Musica e la Bibbi: Atti del Convegno Internazionalle di Studi promosso da Biblia e dall'Accademia Musicale Chigiana. Siena 24–26 agosto 1990*. Edited by Pasquale Troia. Rome: Garamond, 1992. 65–110.
Ravicz, Marilyn Ekdahl. "St. Augustine: Time and Eternity." *The Thomist* 22, no. 4 (1959): 542–554.
Read, Stephen. "The Liar Paradox from John Buridan back to Thomas Bradwardine." *Vivarium* 40, no. 2 (Spring 2002): 189–218.
———. "Bradwardine's Revenge." In *Revenge of the Liar: New Essays on the Paradox*. Edited by J. C. Beall. Oxford: Oxford University Press, 2007. 250–261.
Ricoeur, Paul. *Time and Narrative*. Vol. 1. Translated by Kathleen McLaughlin and David Pellauer. Chicago: University of Chicago Press, 1984.
Riel, Gerd van. "Augustine's Exegesis of 'Heaven and Earth' in *Conf.* XII: Finding Truth amidst Philosophers, Heretics and Exegetes." *Quaestio* 7 (2007): 191–228.
Ripanti, Graziano. "L'allegoria o l''intellectus figuratus' nel *De doctrina christiana* di Agostino." *Revue des Études Augustiniennes* 18, no. 3–4 (1972), 219–232.
Rist, John. *Augustine: Ancient Thought Baptized*. Cambridge: Cambridge University Press, 1994.

Rivington, J., and Rivington, J.G.F., eds. *The British Magazine and Monthly Register of Religious and Ecclesiastical Information, Parochial History, and Documents Respecting the State of the Poor, Progress of Education, etc.* London: J. Petheram, 1840.

Roark, Tony. *Aristotle on Time: A Study of the Physics.* Cambridge: Cambridge University Press, 2011.

Rogers, Katherine. "St. Augustine on Time and Eternity." *American Catholic Philosophical Quarterly* 70, no. 2 (1996): 207–223.

Romele, Alberto. "The Ineffectiveness of Hermeneutics: Another Augustine's [sic] Legacy in Gadamer." *International Journal of Philosophy and Theology* 75, no. 5 (2014): 422–439.

Ron, Moshe. "The Restricted Abyss: Nine Problems in the Theory of *Mise En Abyme*." *Poetics Today* 8, no. 2 (1987): 417–438.

Rothschild, Norman Harry. "Fazang." *Internet Encyclopedia of Philosophy.* Accessed May 15, 2020: https://www.iep.utm.edu/fazang/.

Rothstein, Eric. "Augustine and the 'Poetic Composition' of *Philosophical Investigations*." *Clio* 35, no. 1 (2005): 1–27.

Rotman, Andy. *Divine Stories: Divyavadana.* Part 2. Boston: Wisdom, 2017.

Roy, Pratap Chandra. *Mahabharata.* Calcutta: Bharata Press, 1886.

Ruden, Sarah, trans. *Confessions.* New York: Modern Library, 2017.

Ruether, Rosemary Radford. "Augustine: Sexuality, Gender, and Women." In *Feminist Interpretations of Augustine.* Edited by Judith Chelius Stark. University Park, PA: Pennsylvania State University Press, 2007. 47–67.

Russell, Bertrand. *A History of Western Philosophy.* New York: Simon and Schuster, 1945.

———. *Human Knowledge: Its Scope and Limits.* New York: Simon and Schuster, 1948.

———. "Saleyyaka Sutta: the Brahmans of Sala." MN 41. Translated by Ñanamoli Thera. *Access to Insight (BCBS Edition).* Kandy: Buddhist Publication Society, 2013. http://www.accesstoinsight.org/tipitaka/mn/mn.041.nymo.html

Sangpo, Gelong Lodrö. *Abhidharmakośabhāṣya, The Treasury of the Abhidharma and its (Auto) Commentary, Volumes I–IV.* Delhi: Motilal Banarsidass, 2012.

Sāṅkṛtyāyana, Rāhula, ed. *Pramāṇavārtikabhāshyam or Vārtikālaṅkāraḥ of Prajñākaragupta (Being a Commentary on Dharmakīrti's Pramāṇavārtikam).* Patna: Kashi Prasad Jayaswal Research Institute, 1953.

Saracino, Michele. "Moving Beyond the 'One True Story.'" In *Frontiers in Catholic Feminist Theology: Shoulder to Shoulder.* Edited by Susan Abraham and Elena Procario-Foley. Minneapolis: Fortress Press, 2009.

Sarup, Lakshman. *The Nighaṇṭu and the Nirukta.* Lahore: University of Panjab, 1927.

Schabel, Christopher. "Redating Pierre D'ailly's Early Writings and Revisiting His Position on the Necessity of the Past and the Future." In *Pierre D'ailly: Un Esprit Universel À L'aube Du XV<sup>e</sup> Siècle.* Edited by Jean-Patrice Boudet, Monica Brînzei, Fabrice Delivré, Hélène Millet, Jacques Verger and Michel Zink. Paris: Inscriptions et Belles-Lettres, 2019.

———. *Theology at Paris, 1316–1345: Peter Auriol and the Problem of Divine Foreknowledge and Future Contingents*. Burlington, VT: Ashgate, 2001.
Scheible, Kristin. *Reading The Mahāvaṃsa: The Literary Aims of a Theravāda Buddhist History*. New York: Columbia University Press, 2016.
Schopen, Gregory. *Buddhist Monks and Business Matters: Still More Papers on Monastic Buddhism in India*. Honolulu: University of Hawai'i Press, 2004.
Scotus, John Duns. *Lectura*. Vol. 16. Città del Vaticano: Typis Polyglottis Vaticanis, 1960.
Sedgwick, Eve Kosofsky. *Touching Feeling: Affect, Pedagogy, Performativity*. Durham: Duke University Press, 2003.
Shanzer, Danuta. "*Avulsa a Latere Meo*: Augustine's Spare Rib: *Confessions* 6.15.25." *Journal of Roman Studies* 92 (2002): 157–176.
Sharf, Robert H. "Is Mindfulness Buddhist? (And Why It Matters)." *Transcultural Psychiatry* 52, no. 4 (2015): 470–484.
———. "Mindfulness and Mindlessness in Early Chan." *Philosophy East and West* 64. No. 4 (2014): 933–964.
———. "On The Allure of Buddhist Relics." *Representations* 66 (1999): 75–99.
Shaw, Sara. *The Jātakas: Birth Stories of the Bodhisattva*. Oxford: Penguin, 2006.
Shields, Philip R. *Logic and Sin in the Writings of Ludwig Wittgenstein*. Chicago: University of Chicago Press, 1993.
Sider, Theodore. "Four Dimensionalism." *Philosophical Review* 106 (1997): 197–231.
Sider, Theodore. "Presentism and Ontological Commitment." *Journal of Philosophy* 96 (1999): 325–347.
Silk, Jonathan. *Materials Towards the Study of Vasubandhu's Viṃśikā (I)*. Cambridge, MA: Harvard University Press, 2016.
Simplicius. *In Aristotelis Physicorum libros quattuor priores commentaria*. Edited by Hermann Diels. Berlin: Verlag Georg Reimer, 1882.
Skow, Bradford. "Relativity and the Moving Spotlight." *Journal of Philosophy* 106 (2009): 666–678.
Slattery, John P. *Faith and Science at Notre Dame: John Zahm, Evolution, and the Catholic Church*. Notre Dame, IN: University of Notre Dame Press, 2019.
Slotemaker, John T. "Reading Augustine in the Fourteenth Century: Gregory of Rimini and Pierre D'Ailly on the *Imago Trinitatis*." In *Studia Patristica: Papers Presented at the Sixteenth International Conference on Patristic Studies Held in Oxford 2011*. Edited by Markus Vinzent. Leuven: Peeters Publishing, 2013. 345–57.
Smith, Andrew. "Eternity and Time." In *The Cambridge Companion to Plotinus*. Edited by Lloyd Gerson. Cambridge: Cambridge University Press, 1996. 196–216.
———. "Soul and Time in Plotinus." In *Psyche – Seele – Anima: Festschrift für Karin Alt*. Edited by J. Holzhausen. Stuttgart: B.G. Teubner, 1998. 335–344.
Solignac, Aimé. "Notes Complémentaires à Livre VII." In vol. 13 of *Oeuvres de Saint Augustin: Les Confessions Livres I–VII*. Paris: Brouwer, 1962.
Sorabji, Richard. *Time, Creation, and the Continuum: Theories in Antiquity and the Early Middle Ages*. Ithaca: Cornell University Press, 1983.

Soskice, Janet. "Aquinas and Augustine on Creation and God as 'Eternal Being.'" *New Blackfriars* 95, no. 1056 (2014): 190–207.
Stambaugh, Joan. "Time, Finitude, and Finality." *Philosophy East and West* 24, no. 2 (1974): 129–135.
Stark, Judith Chelius. "Augustine on Women: In God's Image, But Less So." In *Feminist Interpretations of Augustine*. Edited by Judith Chelius Stark. University Park, PA: Pennsylvania State University Press, 2007. 215–241.
———. "Introduction." In *Feminist Interpretations of Augustine*. Edited by Judith Chelius Stark. University Park, PA: Pennsylvania State University Press, 2007. 1–45.
Stcherbatsky, Th. *Buddhist Logic*. London: Constable and Company, 1962.
Stern, David G. *Wittgenstein on Mind and Language*. New York and Oxford: Oxford University Press, 1995.
Sternbach, Ludwig. *Mahāsubhāṣitasaṁgraha: Volume 1*. Hoshiarpur: Vishveshvaranand Vedic Research Institute, 1974.
Strange, Steven K. "Plotinus on the Nature of Eternity and Time." In *Aristotle in Late Antiquity*. Ed. L. Schrenk. Washington, DC: Catholic University of America, 1994. 22–53.
Strawson, Galen. *Things That Bother Me: Death, Freedom, the Self, Etc.* New York: New York Review of Books, 2018.
Stuart, Daniel M. "Becoming Animal: Karma and the Animal Realm Envisioned Through an Early *Yogācāra* Lens." *Religions* 10, no. 6 (2019): 363–378.
Studer, Basil. *Zur Theophanie-Exegese Augustins. Untersuchung zu einem Ambrosius-Zitat in der Schrift* De uidendo Deo *(Ep. 147)*. Studia Anselmiana 59. Rome: Herder, 1971.
Stump, Eleonore, and Norman Kretzmann. "Eternity." *Journal of Philosophy*, 78, no. 8 (1981): 429–458.
Suarez, Francisco. *De Scientia Dei Contingentium Futurorum Absolutorum*. In *Opera Omnia*. Vol. 11. Edited by Carolo Berton. Paris: Vivès, 1858.
Suter, Ronald. "Augustine on Time with Some Criticisms from Wittgenstein." *Revue internationale de philosophie* 16, no. 61/62 (1957): 378–394.
Suzuki, D. T. *The Lankavatara Sutra: A Mahayana Text*. London: Routledge, 1932.
Swanson, Paul L. *T'ien-T'ai Chih-I's Mo-Ho Chih-Kuan: Clear Serenity, Quiet Insight*. Translation and Commentary. Volume 3. Honolulu: University of Hawai'i Press, 2018.
Tachau, Katherine H. *Vision and Certitude in the Age of Ockham: Optics, Epistemology, and the Foundations of Semantics, 1250–1345*. Leiden: Brill, 1988.
Tallant, Jonathan. "Defining Existence Presentism." *Erkenntnis*, 79, no. 3 (2014): 479–501.
Teske, Roland J., S.J. *Paradoxes of Time in St. Augustine*. Milwaukee: Marquette University Press, 1996.
———. "The World-Soul and Time in St. Augustine." *Augustinian Studies* 14 (1983): 75–92.
———. *To Know God and the Soul: Essays on the Thought of Saint Augustine*. Washington, DC: Catholic University of America Press, 2008.
———. "'*Vocans Temporales, Faciens Aeternos*:' St. Augustine on Liberation from Time." *Traditio* 41 (1985): 29–47.

Thakur, Anantalal, ed. *Jñānaśrīmitranibandhāvali (Buddhist Philosophical Works of Jñānaśrīmitra)*. Patna: Kashi Prasad Jayaswal Research Institute, 1959.

———, ed. *Ratnakīrtinibandhāvaliḥ (Buddhist Nyāya Works of Ratnakīrti)*. Second Revised Edition. Patna: Kashi Prasad Jayaswal Research Institute, 1975.

Theobald, Michael. *Im Anfang war das Wort: Textlinguistische Studie zum Johannesprolog*, Stuttgarter Bibelstudien 106. Stuttgart: Katholisches Bibelwerk, 1983.

Thomas Aquinas. *De potentia*. Translated by the Fathers of the English Dominican Province. London: Burns, Oates, and Washbourne, 1932–34.

———. *Expositio libri Perihermeneias*. Textum Leoninum Taurini, 1955. https://www.corpusthomisticum.org/cpe.html.

———. *In IV libros Physicorum*. Textum Leoninum Taurini, 1954. https://www.corpusthomisticum.org/cpy011.html.

———. *Quaestiones Disputatae de Veritate*. Textum Leoninum Taurini, 1970. https://www.corpusthomisticum.org/qdv01.html.

———. *Summa contra Gentiles*. Textum Leoninum Taurini, 1961. https://www.corpusthomisticum.org/scg1001.html.

———. *Summa Theologiae*. Textum Leoninum Romae, 1888. https://www.corpusthomisticum.org/sth0000.html.

———. *Summa Theologiae*. Translated by the Fathers of the English Dominican Province. London: Burns, Oates, and Washbourne, 1920.

Thomas Bradwardine. *De causa Dei contra Pelagium et de virtute causarum*. Edited by Henry Seville. London: 1618. Reprinted in Frankfurt: Minerva, 1964.

———. *De futuris contingentibus (On Future Contingents)*. In "Le *De futuris contingentibus* de Thomas Bradwardine." Edited by Jean-François Genest. *Recherches Augustiniennes* 14 (1979): 249–336.

Thompson, Caleb. "Wittgenstein, Augustine and the Fantasy of Ascent." *Philosophical Investigations* 25, no. 2 (2002): 153–171.

Thurman, Robert F. *The Holy Teaching of Vimalakīrti: A Mahāyāna Scripture*. Philadelphia: University of Pennsylvania Press, 1976.

Tillemans, Tom. "Dharmakīrti." *The Stanford Encyclopedia of Philosophy*. Edited by Edward N. Zalta. 2016. https://plato.stanford.edu/archives/spr2017/entries/dharmakiirti/.

Tomlinson, David. *Buddhahood and Philosophy of Mind: Ratnākaraśānti, Jñānaśrīmitra, and the Debate over Mental Content (Ākāra)*. Dissertation. Chicago: University of Chicago, 2019.

Torchia, N. Joseph, O.P. "'*Pondus meum amor meus*': The Weight-Metaphor in St. Augustine's Early Philosophy." *Augustinian Studies* 21 (1990): 163–176.

———. *Plotinus, Tolma, and the Descent of Being: An Exposition and Analysis*. New York: Peter Lang, 1993.

Trapp, Damasus. "Augustinian Theology of the 14th Century: Notes on Editions, Marginalia, Opinions and Book-Lore." *Augustiniana* 6 (1956): 146–274.

Truesdell, Clifford. *Essays in the History of Mechanics*. New York: Springer, 1968.

Tzamalikos, P. "Origen: The Source of Augustine's Theory of Time." *Filosofia* 17 (1987): 396–418.

Valberg, J. J. "The Temporal Present." *Philosophy* 88, no. 3 (July 2013): 369–386.

Van Dusen, David. *The Space of Time: A Sensualist Interpretation of Time in Confessions X–XII*. Leiden: Brill, 2014.

Van Fleteren, Frederick. "Authority and Reason, Faith and Understanding in the Thought of St. Augustine." *Augustinian Studies* 4 (1973): 33–71.

———. "Augustine's '*De vera religione*': A New Approach." *Augustinianum* 16 (1976): 475–497.

Vessey, David. "Gadamer, Augustine, Aquinas, and Hermeneutic Universality." *Philosophy Today* 55, no. 2 (May 2011): 158–165.

von Rospatt, Alexander. *The Buddhist Doctrine of Momentariness: A Survey of the Origins and Early Phase of this Doctrine up to Vasubandhu*. Stuttgart: Franz Steiner, 1995.

Vorenkamp, Dirck. "B-Series Temporal Order in Dōgen's Theory of Time." *Philosophy East and West* 45, no. 3 (1995): 387–408.

Walpole, Arthur Sumner. *Early Latin Hymns: With Introduction and Notes*. Cambridge: Cambridge University Press, 1922.

Watson, Burton, trans. *The Lotus Sutra*. New York: Columbia University Press, 1993.

Watson, Gerard. "St. Augustine and the Inner Word: The Philosophical Background." *The Irish Theological Quarterly* 54 (1988): 81–92.

Webb, Melanie. "On Lucretia Who Slew Herself: Rape and Consolation in Augustine's *De ciuitate dei*." *Augustinian Studies* 44, no. 1 (2013): 37–58.

Wedemeyer, Christian K. *Making Sense of Tantric Buddhism: History, Semiology, and Transgression in the Indian Traditions*. New York: Columbia University Press, 2013.

Westphal, Jonathan, and Carl Levenson, eds. *Time*. Indianapolis: Hackett, 1993.

Wetzel, James. *Augustine and the Limits of Virtue*. Cambridge: Cambridge University Press, 1992.

———. "The Original Sin: Sex and Christian Ethics." In *A Companion to Augustine*. Edited by Mark Vessey. Oxford: Wiley-Blackwell, 2012. 199–208.

———. "Time after Augustine." *Religious Studies* 31, no. 3 (1995): 341–357.

Whitrow, G. J. *The Natural Philosophy of Time*. New York and Evanston: Haper Torchbooks, 1961.

Wikshåland, Ståle. "*Tempus Fugit*: Voice, Intentionality, and Formal Invention in Augustine and Monteverdi." *Journal of Aesthetics and Art Criticism* 66, No. 2 (2008): 129–148.

William (of) Ockham. *Predestination, God's Foreknowledge, and Future Contingents*. 2nd edition. Translated and edited by Marilyn McCord Adams and Norman Kretzmann. Indianapolis: Hackett, 1983.

———. *Opera philosophica et theologica*. Edited by Gedeon Gál *et al.*, in 17 volumes. St. Bonaventure, N.Y.: The Franciscan Institute, 1967–88.

Williams, Paul. "Buddhadeva and Temporality." *Journal of Indian Philosophy* 4, no. 3–4 (1977): 279–294.

———. *The Reflexive Nature of Awareness. A Tibetan Madhyamaka Defense*. Richmond: Curzon, 1998.

Williams, Rowan. *On Augustine*. London: Bloomsbury Continuum, 2016.

Winden, J. C. M. van. "Frühchristliche Bibelexegese. 'Der Anfang.'" In Archè: *A Collection of Patristic Studies by J. C. M. Van Winden*. Edited by J. Den Boeft and D. T. Runia, Supplements to Vigiliae Christianae 41. Leiden: Brill, 1997. 3–48.
Wittgenstein, Ludwig. *Philosophical Investigations*. New York: MacMillan, 1953.
———. *The Blue and Brown Books*. New York: Harper & Row, 1958.
Wodehouse, P. G. *Carry On, Jeeves*. Reprint. London: Arrow Books, 2008.
Woo, Jeson. *The Kṣaṇabhaṅgasiddhi-Anvayātmikā: An Eleventh-Century Buddhist Work on Existence and Causal Theory*. Dissertation. Philadelphia: University of Pennsylvania, 1999.
———. "Gradual and Sudden Enlightenment: The Attainment of *Yogipratyakṣa* in the Later Indian Yogācāra School." *Journal of Indian Philosophy* 37 (2009): 179–188.
———. "Buddhist Theory of Momentariness and *Yogipratyakṣa*." *Indo-Iranian Journal* 55 (2012): 1–13.
———. "On the Yogic Path to Enlightenment in the Later Yogācāra." *Journal of Indian Philosophy* 42 (2014): 499–509.
Wujastyk, Dominik. "Some Problematic Yoga Sūtras and Their Buddhist Background." In *Yoga in Transformation: Historical and Contemporary Perspectives*. Edited by Karl Baier, Philipp A. Mass, and Karin Preisendanz. Göttingen: V and R, 2018. 21–48.
Wyclif, John. *De Ente Predicamentali*. Edited by Rudolf Beer. London: Trubner & Co., 1891.
Yourgrau, Palle. *The Disappearance of Time: Kurt Gödel and the Idealistic Tradition in Philosophy*. New York: Cambridge University Press, 1991.
———. *A World Without Time: The Forgotten Legacy of Gödel and Einstein*. New York: Basic Books, 2005.
Zagzebski, Linda. "Foreknowledge and Free Will." *Stanford Encyclopedia of Philosophy* (Summer 2017 Edition). Edited by Edward N. Zalta: https://plato.stanford.edu/archives/sum2017/entries/free-will-foreknowledge/.
Zahm, J. A. *Evolution and Dogma*. Chicago: McBride, 1896.
Zimmerman, Dean W. "Persistence and Presentism." *Philosophical Papers* 25, no. 2 (1996): 115–126.
———. "The Privileged Present: Defending an "A-Theory" of Time." In *Contemporary Debates in Metaphysics*. Edited by Theodore Sider, John Hawthorne, and Dean W. Zimmerman. Oxford: Blackwell, 2007. 211–225.
Zimmermann, Jens. "Confusion of Horizons: Gadamer and the Christian Logos." *Journal of Beliefs and Values* 22, no. 1 (April 2001): 87–98.
———. *Recovering Theological Hermeneutics: An Incarnational-Trinitarian Theory of Interpretation*. Grand Rapids, MI: Baker, 2004.
Zin, Monika. "The Techniques of Narrative Representation in Old India." In *Image-Narration-Context: Visual Narration in Cultures and Societies of the Old World*. Edited by Elisabeth Wagner-Durand, Barbara Fath, Alexander Heinemann. Heidelberg: Propylaeum, 2019. 137–157.
Ziporyn, Brook A. *Emptiness and Omnipresence: An Essential Introduction to Tiantai Buddhism* Bloomington: Indiana University Press, 2016.

# Index

*Abhidharma*, 284n4, 291–92
absence, 45–46, 48–52, 180, 183, 274
Adam and Eve, 114–17, 147
Adams, Marilyn McCord, 215–16, 224n22
Albert the Great, 237
Alexander of Aphrodisias, 162–63, 174nn6–7
Ambapāli, 257–58
Ambrose, 15, 27, 63, 79, 81–83, 87n17, 92
angels, 15, 114, 124n31, 134, 139n17, 184
Anselm of Canterbury, 198, 212, 215, 233, 236
Antichrist, 197, 232
anticipation, 9, 21–22, 24, 29–30, 35n30, 85, 137, 192, 204n14, 253, 255, 258, 277–78, 283, 292, 294, 304
Aristotle, xii, 35n24, 35n30, 109, 115, 162–64, 169, 174n4, 174n10, 175n11, 175nn17–18, 177n40, 185, 187, 193–95, 204n14, 204n16, 205n24, 206n35, 208n65, 213–14, 216, 234
Arthos, John, 90, 98
attention, x, 27, 35n30, 39, 42, 63, 65, 71n66, 77–78, 81–84, 85n2, 245–47,
249–52, 254–58, 261–62, 263n4, 267n59, 275, 278, 293, 302
Auriol, Peter, 229
Avicenna, xii, 161–73, 174n4, 174n10, 175nn16–19, 176n24, 177n43
awareness, x, xiii, 34n12, 42, 44, 46, 73, 143, 247, 250, 257, 269n84, 277, 281–83, 288n47, 289n50, 293–94

Bach, Johann Sebastian, vii
Bal, Mieke, 299–302
Bartky, Sandra, 134
Basil of Caesarea, 92, 163, 180, 182–84, 187
Bavaud, Georges, 93
Berger, Karol, vii
Bochet, Isabelle, 92
bodhisattva, 295–97, 300–301, 307n12
Boethius, 194, 205n30, 206n33, 214–15, 222, 224
Bonaventure, 191, 237
Bradwardine, Thomas, xii–xiii, 208n67, 209–15, 218–22, 224n23, 239n16
Buddha, 254, 256–58, 260–62, 268n79, 271–72, 289n50, 292, 295–302, 304–6, 307n7
Buddhadeva, 260, 262
Burrus, Virginia, 129, 136–37

*caelum caeli*, 3, 101n33
Callahan, John F., 163
Calvin, John, 211, 222
Calvinism, 209
Carter, Jason, 163
Cartesianism, 99, 212, 224n16
causality, 201–2, 276, 286n22
celestial bodies, 5–7, 9, 25–26, 77–79, 161–65, 168, 170, 184, 262
Chaucer, Geoffrey, 222, 225n39
Chesterton, G. K., 250, 266n34
Cilleruelo, Lope, 98
Clark, Elizabeth, 148
compatibilism, 205n28, 229, 240n20
*concupiscentia*, 128, 132–34, 137, 138n2, 139n7
consciousness, x, 21, 28–29, 37, 42–43, 46, 192, 275–79, 282–83
contemplation, 9, 13, 22, 120–21, 147, 281–82
*contuitus*, 76–77
Courcelle, Pierre, 59
Courtenay, William, 235, 241n28
Craig, William Lane, 195, 205n28
creation, ix, xii, 12–13, 15, 20n98, 28, 39, 57, 59, 61–62, 66, 68, 89, 91–94, 109, 111–16, 122, 131, 133–34, 145, 148–49, 151, 153, 163, 171, 173, 179–80, 183–88, 192–93, 197–98, 213

D'Ailly, Pierre, 240n20, 241n26
Darwin, Charles, 143–45, 188n3
death, 20n98, 47, 50, 84, 116–17, 120, 136, 146, 161, 172, 210, 222, 224n23, 225n29, 228, 251, 255, 275, 295–97
DelCogliano, Mark, 163
demiurge, 162
Derrida, Jacques, 142, 246
desire, 6, 31, 46, 48–49, 51–52, 75, 78–79, 84–85, 111, 128, 132, 134–37, 143, 145–47, 190n26, 277–79, 291–94, 296, 301, 303–5
determinism, 149, 229

*Deus creator omnium* (hymn), xi, 10, 26, 35n28, 63, 79, 81–84
Dharmakīrti, 272–74, 276, 278–80, 282–83, 288n47
Dharmaruci, 253
Dharmatrāta, 259
Dharmottara, 247
*distentio animi*, x, 3, 26, 43–46, 50–52, 71n66, 77–79, 123n9, 175n15, 176n24, 192–93, 204n7, 249, 265n29, 275–76, 283
Dolnikowski, Edith Wilks, 209–10, 212
dreams, 249, 253, 288n46
Duns Scotus, 191, 195–98, 203, 216, 224n23, 225n33

Eberhard, Philippe, 91, 96
ecclesiology, 119, 129, 188, 210–11
Eihei Dōgen, 245
emotion, 38, 136–37
empiricism, 39
Epicureanism, 204n16
eros, 46, 51, 292, 304
eschatology, xi, xiii, 109–10, 128, 133–37, 146, 283
eternalism, 191, 194–202, 203n3, 246, 254, 261–62, 263n2
eternity, viii–ix, xii, xiv, 3–16, 21–23, 28, 34n7, 35n28, 46–48, 52n2, 58, 62, 64, 74–76, 79–81, 83–85, 85n2, 89, 91–93, 97–99, 109–10, 112–14, 120–21, 123n6, 132, 136–37, 139n17, 161, 164–65, 170–71, 190n26, 191–203, 205n28, 207n60, 213–14, 217, 219, 224n16, 229–30, 232, 271, 276–77, 282–83, 292–94, 301–6
evil, 11, 14, 112, 115, 117, 124n30, 128, 132, 231, 235
evolution, xii, 142–45, 149–55, 179, 185, 187–88
exegesis, ix, xi–xii, 11–12, 79, 92, 112, 148, 187
expectation, x, 8, 10, 15–16, 21, 24, 27, 42, 50, 63, 76–77, 80–81, 84, 249, 269n84, 275, 277–78

# Index

Fausto-Sterling, Anne, xi, 142
Fazang, 307n7
feminism, 127–28, 133–35, 141–46, 149, 152, 154
Filastrius, 92
Findlay, J. N., 30
foreknowledge, 194, 196, 205nn28–29, 206n35, 214–15, 217–22, 224nn19–20, 229, 240n20, 241n25
Foucault, Michel, 142, 155n5
Franco, Eli, 281
free will, 33n2, 205n28, 206n35, 212, 214, 222, 226n39, 240n20
Freud, Sigmund, 46, 258
Frost, Gloria, 212
future contingents, xii–xiii, 195–96, 198–99, 205n28, 206n35, 211–12, 217–21, 229, 233, 241n25

Gadamer, Hans-Georg, ix, xi, 89–91, 93–99
Galen, 162, 174nn7–8, 175n17
gender, xi, 127, 130–31, 133–35, 141, 143, 145–46, 148–50
Genesis, ix–xii, 11–12, 75, 83, 92, 112, 116, 163, 179, 182–84, 186, 303
Genest, Jean-François, 210
Ghoṣaka, 259
Gide, André, 298–99, 302
Gioia, Luigi, 148
grace, xii, 116, 211–12
Gregory of Rimini, ix, xiii, 227–38, 240n20, 241nn25–26
Grondin, Jean, 90–91, 93, 95–97, 99
Grosz, Elizabeth, ix, xi, 143–45, 149, 151–52, 154
Gyōnen, 256

Hadot, Pierre, 245
Hakuin, 298
Hammond, Carolyn J.-B., 58
Heidegger, Martin, 90, 94
Hekman, Susan, 152–53
Henry of Harclay, 216, 224n23
hermeneutics, viii, xi, 11–12, 81, 90–91, 97, 99, 180, 183, 185, 187–88, 258

Hermogenes, 92
humility, 182

idealism, 24, 39
*imago Dei*, 95
immutability, xii, 59, 109, 113, 123n6, 204n18, 217–18, 220–21
impermanence, 76, 78, 84–85, 248, 261, 275, 278, 294
incarnation, xi, 6, 9–10, 13–15, 20n98, 21, 59, 89, 92–93, 96, 99, 139n18, 151, 153, 155
infinity, xiv, 22, 121, 144, 153, 155, 167–68, 171, 192, 199, 219, 295–97, 299–300, 305–6, 307n6
*intentio*, x, 3, 8, 10, 15, 31, 43, 51, 71n62, 73, 110, 258–59, 278

James, William, 275–76, 278–79
Jesus Christ, 10, 119, 136, 146, 156n34, 215
Jñānaśrīmitra, xiii, 272, 275, 277–78, 280–83, 285n11, 286n22, 286n24, 288nn45–46, 289n50
John of Mirecourt, 233–34, 241n26
Joshua, x, 77–79, 83
*jubilus* (war chant), x, 79, 82–84

Kaluza, Zenon, 235
Kant, Immanuel, 28, 38
Keller, Catherine, 152–53
Khayyam, Omar, 250
Knox, John, 211, 222
Ku, John Baptist, 179

Leff, Gordon, 222
Leftow, Brian, 191
lived experience, 96, 127, 276
Llanes, María Guadalupe, 90–91
*Lotus Sutra*, xiv, 257–58, 261, 291–306

Mahāyāna, 263n2, 271–72, 292, 295, 297, 300–301
Maitreya, 295–97
Mammì, Lorenzo, 82, 87n18

Manichaeism, ix–xi, 3–7, 10–15, 65, 114
Mañjuśri, 296
Many Jewels, 296–302, 304–5
Marrou, Henri–Irénée, 110
Mary Magdalene, 146, 156n34
*materia informis*, 64–66, 71n73
materialism, xi, 5, 141–43, 145, 148–55
McTaggart, J. M. E., xii, 191, 203n3, 260, 262
measurement, 9, 24–27, 32, 35n24, 35n28, 41–44, 51, 53n18, 63–64, 71n66, 76–77, 79–80, 83, 85, 113, 115, 148, 161–63, 169–71, 174n4, 192–93, 196, 199, 204n7, 213, 236, 274–75
Memling, Hans, 215
memory, x, 8, 10, 15–16, 21, 24, 27, 35n30, 41–42, 45, 48–51, 63, 76–77, 80–83, 85n2, 94, 98, 137, 149, 157n34, 192, 204n14, 214, 222, 234, 247–49, 253, 257–58, 269n84, 275, 277–78, 283, 286n22, 286n24, 294, 302–3
metaphysics, 25, 28–29, 32, 37, 90, 151–52, 191, 200, 206n35, 216, 235, 246–48, 250, 254, 256, 261, 277–78
Miles, Margaret, 127, 129, 135–37
mindfulness, xiii, 263n4, 284n4
miracles, 185, 268n79
*mise en abyme*, xiv, 294–95, 298–300, 302, 304–6, 307n7
Mokṣākaragupta, 274, 285n11
momentariness, xiii, 23, 27, 30, 42, 76, 111–12, 115, 121, 153, 192, 198, 207n60, 217, 245, 247–50, 252–54, 256, 261–62, 263n2, 263n4, 271–82, 284n6, 285n11, 287n33, 298, 302, 306
Mookerjee, Satkari, 277
Moriyama, Shinya, 280
Moses, 181–82
motion. *See* movement
movement, 8–9, 12, 14–15, 22–27, 31–32, 78–79, 84, 109, 111–15, 118–20, 136, 148, 151, 154, 161–73, 174n10, 185, 192, 213
Mozart, Wolfgang Amadeus, vii
music, vii, x, 3, 9, 26, 35n28, 67, 69n32, 70n57, 79, 82, 279
mutability, 12, 20n98, 22, 57–68, 79, 85, 89, 109–11, 113–15, 117–18, 148, 220–21
mysticism, 38, 40, 45, 58–59

Nāgārjuna, 261
Naiyāyika, 276–77, 280, 285n11
Neoplatonism, xi, 15, 123n6, 221
New Feminist Materialism, xi, 141–43, 145, 148–55
Nigidius Figulus, 163
nirvana, 246, 254, 296–97
nominalism, xiii, 216, 224n22, 228, 234–35, 237
Normore, Calvin, 212

Oberman, Heiko, 210, 212, 222, 228, 234–35
objectivity, ix–x, 3, 15, 22, 37, 44, 76, 115, 127, 199
Oliva, Mirela, 90, 93–96, 98
ontology, viii, 24, 91, 109–11, 115, 117–18, 120–22, 143–44, 161, 164, 169–70, 195–97, 200, 202, 245–46, 249, 254, 260, 263n4, 264n11

Panaccio, Claude, 94
Pasnau, Robert, 198, 200–201
past contingents, xiii, 227–30, 233
Paṭācāra, 254
Paul (Apostle), 20n106, 70n50, 116, 119, 303
Pegueroles, Juan, 192
Pelagianism, xiii, 210–12, 222, 235
perception, 9, 24, 39, 53n19, 59, 63, 68, 69n29, 71n60, 73, 77, 109–12, 117, 192, 247, 253, 272–73, 277–82, 287nn32–33
Peter Lombard, 211, 228, 230

phenomenology, 111, 134, 214, 230, 248, 252, 272, 278
Plantinga, Alvin, 215, 224
Plato, 35n24, 35n30, 46, 98, 162–64, 167
Platonism, viii, 5–6, 13, 18n42, 53n19, 57–60, 65, 72n77, 98, 205n21, 216
Plotinus, 3–8, 10–11, 15, 17n21, 58, 65, 109, 112, 123n6
poetry, 9, 26, 35n28, 99, 249, 254, 257
Power, Kim, 134–35, 145, 147
Prajñākaragupta, xiii, 280–81, 286n21
predestination, 217, 238n3
presence, xiii, 15–16, 42, 73, 75–76, 80, 84, 93, 110, 121–22, 151, 153, 155, 192, 200, 213, 246, 250–53, 256–57, 274, 282–83, 304
presentism, xiii, 191, 193–95, 197–203, 208n67, 245–51, 253–54, 256–57, 260–62, 263n10, 264n11, 266n34, 269n86, 271, 284n4, 289n50
Prior, A. N., x, 25
prophecy, 5, 12–14, 24
Proust, Marcel, 21, 268n77
providence, 5–6, 9, 13, 20n106, 131, 151, 205n24, 206n33, 219

*rationes seminales*, 148, 179, 183, 186
Ratnakīrti, xiii, 272, 275, 280–81, 286n22, 288n46
Ravasi, Gianfranco, 79
reformation, xiii, 209, 211, 222, 237
*regio dissimilitudinis*, 110
resurrection, xi, 8–9, 12, 16, 20n98, 109–12, 115–16, 118–22, 123n6, 128, 130–38, 156n33, 215
Reuther, Rosemary Radford, 135
Ricoeur, Paul, 271, 275
Rist, John M., 112, 147
Romele, Alberto, 94
Ron, Moshe, 299, 307n11
Russell, Bertrand, 38–41, 43–44

sabbath, 110, 120
Samiddhi, 250–51
Śāntarakṣita, 281
*sapientia*, 147
Saracino, Michele, 149
Sarvāstivāda, 246
Satan, 124n31
*scientia*, 147
Sedgwick, Eve Kosofsky, 301
sexuality, xi, 98, 128–29, 131–37, 143–50, 250–51, 293–94, 303–4
Shakyamuni, 296–97, 299–302, 305
Simplicius, 162, 175n17
sin, x, 4, 12, 14, 38, 41, 48–51, 53, 110–12, 115–18, 129, 145–46, 148, 154–55, 231, 293
Solignac, Aimé, 110, 117
song, x, 62–67, 81–83, 85
soteriology, 57, 70n53, 278–80
Stcherbatsky, Th., 272
Sthiramati, 260
Stoicism, xiii, 100n10, 148, 250, 266n34
Strawson, Galen, 279
Suarez, Francisco, 191, 195, 197–200, 203, 207n60
Suter, Ronald, 28

teleology, 35n30, 227
temporal experience, vii–viii, x, xiv, 12, 21–22, 27–29, 33n2, 35n28, 35n30, 37, 39, 44–45, 47, 51, 58–59, 73–74, 76–77, 79–82, 84–85, 85n2, 110–12, 118, 120–22, 213–14, 247–53, 258, 263n4, 269n84, 271–72, 276–83, 284n4, 294, 303–5
tense, 22–23, 25, 191, 232, 248, 259, 261
terminism, 228, 234, 241n28
Tertullian, 92
Teske, Roland, 78–79, 122n2, 123n6, 124n16, 176n24
theodicy, 124n30
Thomas Aquinas, ix, xii, 90, 97, 179–88, 189n8, 194–96, 198, 215–16
threefold present, 24, 42–44, 77
Tillemans, Tom, 274, 284n8

timelessness, ix, xii, 7, 22, 43, 45, 47–48, 51–52, 75, 85n2, 89, 92–93, 171, 213–14, 224n16, 261–62, 271, 304
Trapp, Damasus, 228, 234–36
Trinity, 13, 20n98, 90, 94, 147, 238n3

Ufford, John de, 211

van Dusen, David, 71n66, 192–93, 203nn4–5, 204n7
van Riel, Gerd, 92
van Winden, J. C. M., 92
Vasubandhu, 247–48, 250–52, 259–60, 264n14, 269n84
Vasumitra, 260
Vessey, David, 95
Vimalakīrti, 261
Von Rospatt, Alexander, 276, 278–79

Webb, Melanie, 129–30, 138n7
William of Ockham, 209–11, 215–21, 224nn22–23, 225n29, 234–35, 242n37
Williams, Rowan, 141, 148, 151, 153
Wittgenstein, Ludwig, x, 22, 28, 30–32, 33n2, 38–41, 50–52, 53n8, 53n18, 252
Wodehouse, P. G., 249
world soul, 3–4, 15, 17n17, 176n24
Wyclif, John, ix, xii, 191, 195, 199–203, 207n65, 222

Zen, 263n2, 298
Zhiyi, 300
Zimmermann, Jens, 89–90, 105n140
Ziporyn, Brook, 298

# About the Editors and Contributors

**John Doody** is senior visiting professor at Arizona State University. He is a member of the School for Civic and Economic Thought and Leadership.

**Kim Paffenroth** is professor of religious studies and the director of the Honors Program at Iona College. He has written extensively on Augustine, the Bible, and on the interface between Christian belief and popular culture. In the last category, he produced *Gospel of the Living Dead: George Romero's Visions of Hell on Earth* (2006), which won the Bram Stoker Award and led Dr. Paffenroth to write several popular zombie novels. His newest work on Augustine, *On King Lear, The Confessions, and Human Experience and Nature*, is due out in 2021 from Bloomsbury.

**Sean Hannan** is an assistant professor in the Humanities Department at MacEwan University in Edmonton, Alberta, Canada. His first book, *On Time, Change, History, and Conversion*, was published by Bloomsbury in 2020. With W. Ezekiel Goggin, he is currently coauthoring *Mysticism and Materialism in the Wake of German Idealism* (under contract with Routledge).

**Thomas Clemmons** is assistant professor of Latin Patristics and Church History at the Catholic University of America. He has received an MA from Vanderbilt University, an MA in Classics and Early Christian Studies from the University of Notre Dame, and a PhD from Notre Dame in the History of Christianity. His research and publications focus on Jerome, Ambrose, Augustine (especially his early writings and his reception), Manichaeism, and Christianity in North Africa.

**Alexander R. Eodice** is professor of philosophy and chair of the Philosophy Department at Iona College, where he has also served as director of Honors and, from 2001 to 2008, as dean of the School of Arts and Science. In 2009, he was a visiting scholar at Blackfriars Hall, Oxford University, where he delivered a featured lecture on legal obligation and coercion. He is the author of *Action and Character: An Introduction to Moral Philosophy* (2016) and coeditor (with John Doody and Kim Paffenroth) of *Augustine and Wittgenstein* (2018); his past publications include papers on law and morality, moral innocence, and the idea of certainty.

**James Wetzel** is professor of philosophy, Augustinian Endowed Chair, and director of the Augustinian Institute at Villanova University. He is the author of *Augustine and the Limits of Virtue* (Cambridge University Press, 1992), *Augustine: A Guide for the Perplexed* (2010), and *Parting Knowledge: Essays after Augustine* (2015).

**Makiko Sato** is a research fellow at Tokyo Gakugei University and a former professor at the University of Toyama in Japan. Her research has focused on how theological anthropology was formed and deepened in Late Antiquity by biblical exegesis.

**Cristiane Negreiros Abbud Ayoub** is a professor at the Federal University of ABC in Santo André, São Paulo, Brazil. Her research situates Augustine within the wider world of Latin-language philosophy in late antiquity, with a special focus on his relationship to Aristotle and his treatment of the topic of *confessio*.

**Matthew W. Knotts** received his PhD from KU (Katholieke Universiteit) Leuven, where he was a fellow of the Flanders Research Foundation. He is the author of *On Creation, Science, Disenchantment, and the Contours of Being and Knowing* (2020).

**Paul Ulishney** is a DPhil student in history and Stavros Niarchos Scholar at the University of Oxford. He holds a BA in biblical studies, as well as two master's degrees—one in patristic theology, and another in late antique and byzantine studies. His doctorate is generously funded by the Stavros Niarchos Foundation through the Oxford Centre for Byzantine Research.

**Patricia Grosse** is an independent scholar living in the Upper Peninsula of Michigan in the United States. Her research interests include Ancient Greek and Roman philosophy (especially the thought of Augustine of Hippo) and the philosophy of love and sex. Her current book project, *Moving St.*

*Monnica's Bones*, explores the philosophical and theological impact of the materiality of Monnica on her son, Augustine.

**Megan Loumagne Ulishney** received her DPhil in theology from the University of Oxford. She now works as a postdoctoral research fellow in the department of Theology and Religious Studies at the University of Nottingham, and her current research is funded by the John Templeton Foundation as part of the "God and the Book of Nature" project. Her project explores theories of sexual selection, the extended evolutionary synthesis, and their relevant points of connection with theologies of nature.

**Celia Hatherly** is an assistant professor of philosophy in the Humanities Department at MacEwan University in Edmonton, Alberta, Canada. Her research focuses on Avicenna's metaphysics and its influence on Latin medieval philosophy. Her work has been published in *History of Philosophy Quarterly*.

**Daniel W. Houck** serves as senior pastor of Calvary Hill Baptist Church in Fairfax, Virginia, and adjunct professor of theology at the John Leland Center for Theological Studies. An Ecclesial Fellow at the Center for Pastor Theologians, he retrieves insights from the Christian tradition to address contemporary issues in theology and science. His first book, *Aquinas, Original Sin, and the Challenge of Evolution*, was published by Cambridge University Press in 2020. He can be reached on Twitter @DanielWHouck.

**Brendan Case** is the associate director for research in the Human Flourishing Program at Harvard University and author of *The Accountable Animal: Justice, Justification, and Judgment* (2021). His research interests include systematic and historical theology, contemporary philosophy of mind and language, and the intersection of theology with the social and behavioral sciences.

**Sarah Hogarth Rossiter** is an instructor in the Department of Philosophy and Humanities at Douglas College in the Lower Mainland of British Columbia. Her doctoral dissertation, completed at the University of Western Ontario, concerns free will and divine foreknowledge in Thomas Bradwardine's *De futuris contingentibus*.

**Matthew Vanderpoel** is a teaching fellow in the Divinity School and the College at the University of Chicago. Their research and teaching center on the intellectual and literary history of Christianity in the late medieval and early modern periods and attend to the scholastic tradition, the question of human constitution, and hermeneutics. Their current book project reconsiders nominalist philosophy as fueling a vibrant, pastorally engaged literary renewal among theologians at the University of Paris in the later Middle Ages.

**Sonam Kachru** is an assistant professor in the Department of Religious Studies at the University of Virginia, where his teaching and writing has centered on the history of Buddhist philosophy in ancient South Asia. His first book, *Other Lives: Mind and World in Indian Buddhism*, is forthcoming with Columbia University Press.

**Davey K. Tomlinson** is an assistant professor of philosophy at Villanova University. His research is focused on Indian and Tibetan Buddhist philosophy of mind and philosophy of religion.

**Joy Brennan** teaches Buddhism and East Asian religions at Kenyon College. She reads and writes mainly about the Yogacara and Zen schools of Buddhist thought.

www.ingramcontent.com/pod-product-compliance
Lightning Source LLC
Chambersburg PA
CBHW021340300426
44114CB00012B/1025